D1190592

TO SALAMAUA

Following his acclaimed book *The Battle for Wau*, Phillip Bradley turns his attention to the Salamaua campaign – the first of the New Guinea offensives by the Australian Army in the Second World War.

Opening with the pivotal air and sea battle of the Bismarck Sea, this important title recounts the fierce land campaign fought for the ridges that guarded the Japanese base at Salamaua. From Mount Tambu to Old Vickers and across the Francisco River, the Australians and their American allies fought a desperate struggle to keep the Imperial Japanese Army diverted from the strategic prize of Lae.

To Salamaua covers the entire campaign in one volume for the first time. From the strategic background of the campaign and the heated command conflicts, to the mud and blood of the front lines, this is the extraordinary story.

Phillip Bradley is the author of two previous books in the Australian Army History series, *On Shaggy Ridge* and *The Battle for Wau*. He writes for *After the Battle* and *Wartime* magazines.

OTHER TITLES IN THE AUSTRALIAN ARMY HISTORY SERIES

Series editor
David Horner

Jean Bou *Light Horse: A History of Australia's Mounted Arm*
Phillip Bradley *The Battle for Wau: New Guinea's Frontline 1942–1943*
Mark Johnston *The Proud 6th: An Illustrated History of the 6th Australian Division 1939–1946*
Garth Pratten *Australian Battalion Commanders in the Second World War*

TO SALAMAUA

PHILLIP BRADLEY

CAMBRIDGE
UNIVERSITY PRESS

CAMBRIDGE UNIVERSITY PRESS
Cambridge, New York, Melbourne, Madrid, Cape Town, Singapore, São Paulo, Delhi, Dubai, Tokyo

Cambridge University Press
477 Williamstown Road, Port Melbourne, VIC 3207, Australia

Published in the United States of America by Cambridge University Press, New York

www.cambridge.org
Information on this title: www.cambridge.org/9780521763905

First published 2010

Designed by Rob Cowpe Design
Typeset by Aptara Corp.
Printed in China by Printplus

A catalogue record for this publication is available from the British Library

National Library of Australia Cataloguing in Publication data
    Bradley, Phillip 1955–
    To Salamaua / Phillip Bradley.
    9780521763905 (hbk.)
    Australian Army history series.
    Includes index.
    Bibliography.
    Australia. Army.
    Campaigns – New Guinea – Salamaua.
    World War, 1939–1945 – Campaigns – New Guinea.
    United States – Armed Forces.
    940.54265471

ISBN 978-0-521-76390-5 Hardback

CONTENTS

FOREWORD

The six-month military campaign conducted in Papua between July 1942 and January 1943 by the Australian army, with help from the United States, saw some of the famous battles of Australian military history. These included the fighting retreat on the Kokoda Trail, the defence at Isurava, the battle at Milne Bay, the counter-offensive over the Kokoda Trail culminating in the victory at Oivi-Gorari and the gruelling battles at Buna, Gona and Sanananda.

Then, seven months later, the Australian army began a series of spectacular military operations in New Guinea. On 4 September 1943 the 9th Australian Division landed from the sea near the town of Lae. Next day the 7th Division began to arrive by air at the captured airstrip at Nadzab, and together the divisions closed in on Lae. Less than a month later the 9th Division carried out another amphibious landing, at Finschhafen, and the battles there ended with the seizure of the Japanese mountain stronghold at Sattelberg. Meanwhile, with the assistance of daring work by Australian commandos and American transport aircraft, the 7th Division advanced up the Markham and into the Ramu Valley. This thrust finished with the successful capture of Shaggy Ridge early in 1944. The campaign was an outstanding orchestration of the land, sea and air forces of two countries.

Yet between these two campaigns, both geographically and chronologically, the Australian army fought another gruelling campaign that deserves to be better known. The campaign really began with the Japanese landing at Salamaua on 8 March 1942. Australian commandos harassed the enemy until January 1943, when the Japanese tried to seize the inland town of Wau. In a heroic defensive battle, brilliantly described by Phillip Bradley in his book *The Battle for Wau*, Australian infantry, commanded by Brigadier Murray Moten, held off the Japanese and started a counter-offensive.

The 3rd Australian Division under Major General Stanley Savige took over the campaign in April 1943, and for almost six months his infantry pursued a grim war through a jungle-covered tangle of mountains, ridges and valleys. Unknown to the soldiers and their commanders, their task was not to recapture Salamaua, but to draw the Japanese on to themselves like a magnet, thus ensuring that the troops who landed at Lae would have an easier fight.

It was a complex campaign. Savige never had a full-strength division as it could not have been supplied in this geographically isolated area. When American troops were brought in to ease his supply difficulties by securing the coast, they created command problems. It was difficult to provide artillery support, aircraft found it hard to locate the enemy in the maze of jungle-covered ridges, and supplies needed to be brought forward by native carriers. Eventually, after the success of the Lae landing, the troops captured Salamaua, but Savige and many of the men who had earned the victory had been relieved by fresher commanders and soldiers who had come in towards the end.

The story of the campaign needs to be told. Here the Australian army refined its techniques of jungle warfare and kept the pressure on the Japanese while other forces prepared for the major offensive later in the year. But the campaign presents problems for the historian. It lacks the spectacular large-scale battles of other campaigns, and instead consists of countless patrols, ambushes and battalion-level attacks on remote mountain tops. It is difficult to reach the area, and the terrain is also daunting for any historian who wants to research the battlefield.

In his third book on the fighting in New Guinea, Phillip Bradley has met the challenge of this most difficult of campaigns. He has trekked into the mountains to gain great insight into the problems faced by the soldiers, and to understand the tactical aspects of the key battles. He has researched both Australian and Japanese records. He has also interviewed a large number of the participants, to give the reader a first-hand account of what it was like to fight this war of close-quarter battles. And he has put it all together to give us a compelling story of one of the Australian army's more important Second World War campaigns. The result, this book, *To Salamaua*, is a wonderful tribute to the unpretentious but brave and determined men who helped win the war, and another major contribution to Australian military history.

David Horner
Professor of Australian Defence History
Australian National University
October 2009

ILLUSTRATIONS

PHOTOGRAPHS

MAPS

ACKNOWLEDGEMENTS

My thanks to the Iwal people who welcomed me to their beautiful land. Specifically, to Stephen, Steven, Beno, Gado and the other villagers of Komiatum. To Rudolph, Kesip, Phillip and Ananias at Salamaua. To Ian Priestley for his hospitality and assistance in Lae, and to John Douglas and Frank Taylor for the same in Port Moresby.

To those veterans of the Salamaua campaign who preceded me and who helped me in the writing of this book. All are noted in the bibliography. Previous outstanding work by David Hay, Syd Trigellis-Smith, Ron Garland, Russell Mathews, Stan Benson and Hargis Westerfield in contacting veterans for their unit histories was also of great benefit. David Dexter's volume of the official history also provided an excellent framework. His extensive records and those of Gavin Long provided exceptional background material.

To the Australian Army for the support of this series of books and for recognising the necessity for the extensive research required. In the light of recent operations, the relevance of studying military operations in such testing terrain as New Guinea is clear. To David Horner for his unwavering support and for his enlightened foreword. To Roger Lee, Andrew Richardson and the staff of the Army History Unit who helped facilitate the project, including providing the maps and many of the photographs used. Keith Mitchell's work on the maps was outstanding as was the work of Rohan Bola, a Papua New Guinean cartographer, eager to build his skills. To Mark Johnston for his research grant support and to Sava Pinney for permission to use her father's original diary transcripts.

To Leslie Grimes for access to her father's USAAF photo archive and to Geoff Watson for his photos.

To the staff of the Australian War Memorial research centre for their help and patience with my requests and for instigating the unit war diary digitisation project, a wonderful research resource. To Steven Bullard for his *Senshi Sosho*, *Maru* magazine and other translations. To the National Archives of Australia for its work on the digitisation of RAAF and service personnel records.

Finally to the staff of Cambridge University Press for their support and for the professional polish of the final production.

Phillip Bradley
Lennox Head
September 2009

Abbreviations

2IC	second-in-command
AA	anti-aircraft
ADS	Advanced Dressing Station
AIF	Australian Imperial Force
ANGAU	Australian New Guinea Administrative Unit
App	appendices
ASV	Air-to-Surface Vessel
ATIS	Allied Translator and Interpreter Section
Aust	Australian
AWM	Australian War Memorial
BAR	Browning Automatic Rifle
Bde	Brigade
Bdr	Bombardier
BG	Bombardment Group
Bn	Battalion
Brig	Brigadier
BS	Bomb Squadron
C in C	Commander-in-Chief
Capt	Captain
Cdr	Commander
Ck	creek
CO	Commanding Officer
Col	Colonel
Coy	Company
Cpl	Corporal
DCM	Distinguished Conduct Medal
Div	Division
Docs	documents
DSC	Distinguished Service Cross
DSO	Distinguished Service Order

EBSR	Engineer Boat and Shore Regiment
EY rifle	extra yoke rifle (with grenade discharger)
FDL	Forward Defensive Line
Flt Lt	Flight Lieutenant
FOO	forward observation officer
FUP	forming-up point
Gen	General
GHQ	General Headquarters
Gnr	Gunner
GOC	General Officer Commanding
Gp	Group
GPS	Global Positioning System
HE	High Explosive
How	Howitzer
HQ	Headquarters
IJAF	Imperial Japanese Armed Forces
Ind Coy	Independent Company
Inf	Infantry
Intel	Intelligence
IO	Intelligence Officer
IR	Interrogation Report
LAD	Light Aid Detachment
L of C	line of communication
L-Cpl	Lance-Corporal
L-Sgt	Lance-Sergeant
LMG	light machine-gun
Lt	Lieutenant
Lt-Col	Lieutenant-Colonel
Maj	Major
MC	Military Cross
MG	machine-gun
MIA	missing in action
MID	Mentioned in Dispatches
Mk	mark
MLC	Motorised Landing Craft
MM	Military Medal
MMG	medium machine-gun
MP	military police
MV	Motor Vessel
NAA	National Archives of Australia

NCO	non-commissioned officer
NGF	New Guinea Force
NGVR	New Guinea Volunteer Rifles
No.	number
OC	Officer Commanding
OP	observation post
Ops	Operations
OR	other rank
PIB	Papuan Infantry Battalion
Pl	Platoon
POW	prisoner of war
Pte	Private
Ptn	Platoon
Pubs	publications
RAAF	Royal Australian Air Force
RAE	Royal Australian Engineers
RAF	Royal Air Force
RAP	Regimental Aid Post
Regt	Regiment
RMO	Regimental Medical Officer
RSM	Regimental Sergeant Major
Sgt	Sergeant
SL	Start Line
SLNSW	State Library of New South Wales
SNLP	Special Naval Landing Party
Sqn	Squadron
SS	Steam Ship
SWPA	South-West Pacific Area
TCG	Troop Carrier Group
TF	Task Force
TSMG	Thompson submachine-gun
US	United States
USAAF	United States Army Air Forces
USS	United States Ship
WD	War Diary
WWI	World War I
WWII	World War II

INTRODUCTION

The Salamaua campaign began as the Kokoda campaign ended and ended as the Markham–Ramu Valley campaign began. In scale, it was the largest commitment by the Australian army in New Guinea up to that time and during a period when the war against Japan was still in the balance. In the end it was a diversion, a feint for the subsequent operation to seize Lae, a magnet to draw the Japanese away from the main game. Yet it involved some of the most intense and drawn-out fighting of the entire war, undertaken on a battlefield of the devil's choosing.

From the northern crest of Mount Tambu there is a view to die for, and many men did. Below are the ridges marching down to the Francisco River, much like the gnarled fingers of a claw, a claw that held three armies in its grasp for much of 1943. If not for the deep green canopy it could be the broken terrain of Gallipoli, your eyrie as Chunuk Bair. Beyond the ridge and the river, the shimmering blue sea of the Huon Gulf beckons like the Dardanelles. Like the craggy ranges above Anzac Cove, it is as absurd a place to fight a battle as you could find.

The battles here are little known and seldom mentioned; the dead and those who endured deserve better. This story is theirs.

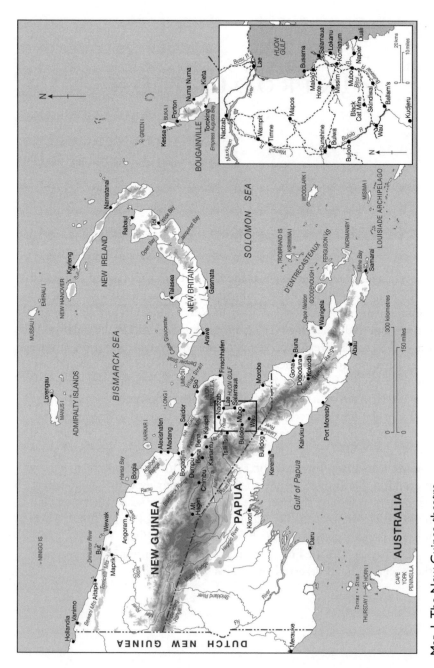

Map 1 The New Guinea theatre

CHAPTER 1

DEATH IN THE BISMARCK SEA

The glassy blue surface of the Bismarck Sea shimmered beneath a cloudless sky, the morning mist gone 'as though wiped away' by the sun. Major-General Kane Yoshihara, the Chief of Staff of the Japanese Eighteenth Army, was aboard the destroyer *Tokitsukaze*, part of a fifteen-vessel convoy afloat on the Bismarck Sea, headed for Lae. Although *Tokitsukaze* translated as 'favourable wind', the weather would do the Japanese convoy no favours on this morning. Yoshihara was below deck discussing debarkation procedures with the troops when disaster struck from the sky. The destroyer then stopped dead in the water, 'as though the ship had struck a rock'. By the time he reached the deck, a bewildered Yoshihara could see that only half the convoy vessels were left afloat and, like the *Tokitsukaze*, smoke billowed skywards from most of them, signifying their fate.[1]

By the end of February 1943 World War II was at a turning point. In the European theatre the German army on the eastern front had been decisively defeated at Stalingrad and was in retreat, desperately trying to hold back the Soviet tide. In North Africa it was a similar story for the German army as the British and American armies approached Tunisia. In the Atlantic Ocean the crucial battle for control of the convoy routes over the marauding U-boats was approaching its climax while in the skies above Western Europe Allied air power was remorselessly gaining the upper hand.

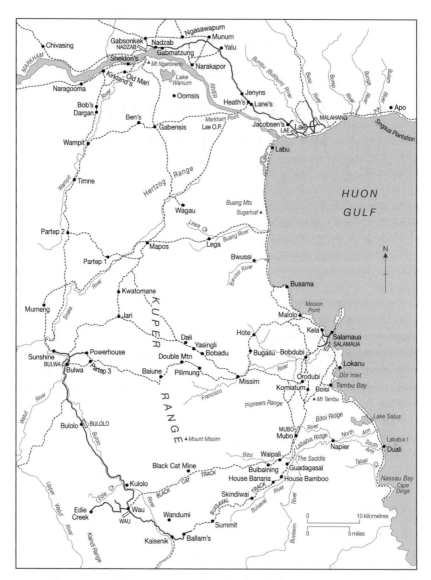

Map 2 The Lae–Salamaua–Wau area

In the Central Pacific, the US Navy, having crippled the Imperial Japanese Navy at Midway in June 1942, was gathering strength to move its considerable might closer to Japan. Meanwhile, US Navy submarine operations increasingly strangled the Japanese supply lines both to and from Japan. In the South-West Pacific the Japanese armed forces had been defeated at Guadalcanal and in Papua.

In New Guinea the Japanese had established a new defence perimeter north of the Owen Stanley Range. A bold advance by a Japanese army detachment to the outskirts of Wau in January 1943 had caught the Australian command off guard and had been defeated only at the eleventh hour. Emboldened by that near success, the Japanese command was not only determined to hold the Lae–Salamaua area but would again try to capture Wau and drive the Australians from that area.

On the Allied side, the way the Salamaua campaign was fought was decided by higher command decisions in early 1943. At the end of January 1943, the Allied Combined Chiefs of Staff met at Casablanca to consider the priorities for 1943. The first priority was to win the Battle for the Atlantic, second was assistance to Russia, third was the capture of Sicily in the Mediterranean theatre, fourth was the build-up of forces in the United Kingdom and fifth concerned the operations in the Pacific and Far East theatre.[2]

Thus the Pacific theatre was a lower priority for the Allied commanders at this time. This was the result of the 'beat Germany first' strategy, which limited the war in the Pacific to maintaining the initiative against Japan. Much to his chagrin, the commander of the South-West Pacific area, General Douglas MacArthur, had an even lower priority, with most of the American resources in the Pacific theatre being allocated to Admiral Chester Nimitz's Central Pacific area, including almost all naval forces. Without further significant reinforcements and denied access to the major US Navy forces, MacArthur was facing an extended hiatus while his air and ground forces recovered from the exceptionally heavy fighting of the Papuan campaign.

General MacArthur's tasks for 1943 began with the capture of Lae, followed by the capture of bases on the Huon Peninsula, including Finschhafen, and finally the capture of Madang on the northern coast of New Guinea. Operations in New Britain and Bougainville were also proposed with the objective of capturing Kavieng and Rabaul. With his reliance on land-based air power, MacArthur's operations would be aimed at obtaining a string of suitable air bases ever closer to Rabaul and the Philippines. Coordinated with MacArthur's operations, Admiral Nimitz's naval forces would capture New Georgia and re-establish control over the Solomon Islands.

In January 1943 a bold incursion by two Japanese battalions behind the Australian lines had reached the outskirts of Wau. After flying in desperately needed reinforcements, the Australians had managed to hold

Wau and its vital airfield before driving the Japanese force back down the Jap Track towards Mubo.[3] By late February Japanese troops still held the vital high ground around Waipali and Guadagasal, a prerequisite for any renewed operations against Wau. However, what was the most significant action of the Salamaua campaign would take place at sea.

While the Australians made their plans and deployments to attack the Japanese at Mubo and thus threaten Salamaua, the Japanese Eighth Area Army commander in Rabaul, Lieutenant-General Hitoshi Imamura, made reciprocal plans to reinforce the Japanese presence in front of Salamaua. Considerable reinforcements from the 51st Division had gathered in Rabaul, the division having been carried in eight transports from Korea in mid-November 1942. Sailing from Whampoa via Hong Kong and Palau, the convoy had arrived in Rabaul in December 1942.[4] Following the successful transport of most of the division's 102nd Regiment from Rabaul to Lae in January, it was proposed that another convoy be sent from Rabaul at the end of February 1943. The aim of the operation was to 'strengthen the strategic position in the Lae–Salamaua sector and prepare for further operations'.[5]

Included in the convoy were 172 men from the 51st Division HQ, 2205 men from Lieutenant-Colonel Torahei Endo's 115th Infantry Regiment, 374 men of the 14th Field Artillery Regiment and 481 men from Lieutenant-Colonel Hiroshi Hondo's 51st Engineer Regiment. There would also be 152 men from the 3rd Field Hospital, 346 men from the 21st Independent Brigade and 262 men from the 50th Anti-Aircraft Battalion in the convoy. Another thousand men were earmarked for unloading the ships.[6]

A total of 6616 men from army units were to be carried by the convoy as well as some naval troops and the ship crews. Table 1.1, based on a movement order issued one week before the convoy sailed, shows the major units to be carried.

The force would be carried in a convoy of eight vessels and would leave Rabaul for Lae on 28 February. Lessons had been learned from the previous convoy that had followed the southern coast of New Britain, and this time the convoy would follow a route along the northern coast. This would put more distance between the convoy and the Allied reconnaissance aircraft until the convoy reached Vitiaz and Dampier Straits.

The eight transport vessels in the convoy were:

- *Nojima*, a naval collier of 8251 tons that carried naval supplies as well as some Special Naval Landing Party troops not included in the loading table.

Table 1.1: Units allocated to the Lae convoy

Unit	Transports	Destroyers
18th Army headquarters	83 men	94 men
21st Independent Brigade	346 men	
50th Anti-Aircraft battalion	362 men	
18th Army signals	70 men	
15th Independent Engineer Regiment	50 men	
8th Shipping Engineer Regiment	570 men	184 men
3rd Debarkation Unit	370 men	
51st Division headquarters	172 men	103 men
115th Infantry Regiment	2205 men	400 men
14th Field Artillery Regiment	374 men	50 men
51st Engineer Regiment	481 men	54 men
51st Division signals	78 men	73 men
3rd Field Hospital	152 men	
Miscellaneous	50 men	
Water purifying unit	25 men	
Nada Unit	270 men	
Total:	5658 men	958 men

Source: ATIS enemy publications, AWM 55, 5/1, EP-05.

- *Kyokusei Maru*, a 5493-ton vessel, carried 1203 personnel. On board were four large Motorised Landing Craft (MLC), ten smaller collapsible boats, eight rowing boats and 500 sealed supply drums. Three anti-aircraft guns and six field guns were also carried.[7]
- *Oigawa Maru*, a 6493-ton coal-burner built in 1941, carrying 1324 personnel. Also carried were eight large Daihatsu MLCs, six of them on the forward deck and 300 sealed supply drums. Three anti-aircraft guns and six field guns were carried as well as 150 to 200 50-litre gasoline drums.[8]
- *Teiyo Maru*, a 6869-ton vessel, carried 1923 personnel. In August 1942 the ship had sailed unescorted from Yokohama to Rabaul. Six large Daihatsu MLCs and 500 sealed supply drums were on board. Two anti-aircraft guns were carried, one forward and one aft, as well as one field gun and two pom-pom guns.[9]
- *Shinai Maru*, a 3793-ton vessel, carried 1052 personnel. Two or three MLCs were carried on board and, for defence, two anti-aircraft guns were positioned fore and aft as well as two pom-pom guns.[10]

- *Aiyo Maru*, a 2746-ton vessel, carried 252 personnel along with five large MLCs, fuel and ammunition. For defence the ship had two anti-aircraft guns, one field gun and two pom-pom guns.[11]
- *Taimei Maru*, a 2883-ton vessel, carried 200 personnel as well as at least eleven large MLCs and 200 sealed supply drums. The bulkheads between holds 1 and 2 and between holds 3 and 4 had been removed, making two long holds that were more readily accessible. The ship was defended by two 75mm field guns, one heavy machine-gun forward and aft and two single 25mm pom-pom guns amidships on the bridge. In early January the *Taimei Maru* had taken twelve large and twelve small MLCs from Rabaul to Wewak, and in early February the ship had made a similar delivery to the Shortland Islands.[12]
- *Kembu Maru*, a 900-ton vessel, commonly known as a sea truck, was less than six months old and carried a crew of thirty. It had arrived in Rabaul from Truk on 19 February and would carry a small number of personnel from the 221st Airfield Battalion not included in the loading table. The ship mainly carried gasoline, which was stored in 300 drums in the two holds. While in Rabaul two 12mm guns were installed on the bridge with 600 rounds for each. The guns were operated by fifteen men under Probationary Officer Kinjiro Oku.[13]

Although most of the transports could travel at ten knots, the *Shinai Maru* was only capable of eight and a half knots, so the convoy was limited to that speed. The troopships would travel in two centre rows with a screen of destroyers on either side. The eight escorting destroyers were *Shirayuki*, *Tokitsukaze*, *Arashio*, *Yukikaze*, *Asashio*, *Uranami*, *Shikinami* and *Asagumo*. These destroyers carried 958 personnel as well as 1650 crewmen. Admiral Masatomi Kimura, commander of the 3rd Destroyer Flotilla and the convoy, travelled on *Shirayuki*. The Eighteenth Army commander, General Hatazo Adachi, travelled on *Tokitsukaze*, and the 51st Division commander, Lieutenant-General Hidemitsu Nakano, travelled on board *Yukikaze*.[14]

The convoy was scheduled to reach Lae by 1630 on 3 March, although this was later adjusted to 2300. Upon arrival at Lae the ships would anchor 600 metres apart along the shoreline from just west of the airfield to the mouth of the Busu River, around 500 metres offshore. It was also planned to establish smoke screens over the anchorage, which would be operated from collapsible boats by three squads from the 'Smoke Group' of the 8th Shipping Engineer Regiment. Floating smoke candles would be used to mask both the unloading vessels and the shore storage areas if any air attacks occurred. An escort of forty naval and six army aircraft would provide aerial protection over the convoy from 0500 to 1800 on each day.[15]

On 19 February 1943 Allied intelligence reports had warned that further troop movements to Lae could be expected but also stated that submarines were being used to bring supplies to Lae and that an alternative supply line was being set up via Madang and Wewak. The report concluded, 'It is likely therefore, that the enemy has found surface convoys into Lae too costly for normal running.' However, the same report observed that there were fifteen warships and fifty-one transport vessels in Rabaul harbour on 14 February, far in excess of normal supply and maintenance needs. Further reconnaissance on 22 February showed the large concentration of ships still present, and Allied intelligence raised the possibility of another convoy to Lae, observing, 'It is possible that an effort will be made again.'[16]

Although aerial reconnaissance hinted at such a convoy, Allied intelligence was working with an ace up its sleeve, ULTRA decrypts from the Japanese naval signals. When war broke out with Japan, a foundation of crypto-analysts was already in place, and Japanese naval message decrypts had already proved decisive during the Coral Sea and Midway naval actions. On 19 February Lieutenant Rudolph J. Fabian's Fleet Radio Unit in Melbourne had handed MacArthur Japanese naval decrypts that indicated there would be a convoy to Lae in early March. It had taken eight days to decipher the critical message, but it gave MacArthur vital lead time to organise an appropriate response. Further decrypts pinpointed the date for the arrival in Lae on or around 5 March.[17]

General Sir Thomas Blamey, commander of Allied land forces in the South-West Pacific Area, realised the impact such a convoy could have on his ground forces in New Guinea. In a letter to New Guinea Force headquarters, Blamey observed that radio intercepts from 23 and 25 February indicated that the departure of a major convoy from Rabaul to Lae was imminent. It was estimated that ten to twenty destroyers would be involved as well as six large merchant ships and an aerial escort of 120 to 150 fighter planes. Blamey wrote, 'Every effort will be made by our own air force to deal with the enemy as he approaches.'[18]

The commander of the Allied Air Forces, comprising the Fifth United States Army Air Force (United States Army Air Force, Fifth) and the Royal Australian Air Force (RAAF), was Lieutenant-General George C. Kenney, who reported directly to MacArthur in Brisbane. The 5th USAAF had been activated in September 1942, although many of its component units had been operating since early 1942 with the Advanced Echelon headquarters based in Port Moresby under the command of Brigadier-General Ennis Whitehead. Whitehead was responsible for the operation of V Fighter Command and V Bomber Command. Air Service Command, later renamed Troop Carrier Command, was based in Brisbane, although the 374th Troop Carrier Group was under the operational control of Whitehead in Port Moresby.[19]

Brigadier-General Paul Wurtsmith's V Fighter Command comprised three fighter groups, the 8th, 35th and 49th, each of three squadrons, all based at Port Moresby. Although Wurtsmith's command had 330 fighter aircraft available, only about eighty of them were P-38 Lightnings, the most capable Allied fighter at that time. The 8th Fighter Group, which had been based at Milne Bay where malaria was rampant, was withdrawn to Australia in February 1943.[20]

At the start of February 1943 Brigadier-General Howard Ramey's V Bomber Command comprised two heavy-bomber groups, each of four squadrons. The 43rd Bombardment Group was equipped with B-17 Flying Fortresses, and the 90th Bombardment Group flew the B-24 Liberator. Of the eight heavy-bomber squadrons, five were based on airfields at Port Moresby. The 43rd Bombardment Group had fifty-five B-17s on strength, about twenty of which were undergoing overhaul and only half the remainder were available for operations at any time. Most of these operations were regular reconnaissance flights, leaving only fourteen aircraft available for strike missions. The 90th Bombardment Group had the same problems with the sixty B-24 Liberators it had on establishment, having no more than fifteen aircraft available for strike missions at any one time.[21]

General Kenney had two medium-bomber groups available at this time, the 22nd and the 38th. The 22nd Bombardment Group was equipped with four squadrons of B-26 Marauders and had been in action since April 1942, losing thirty aircraft in that time and receiving only eight replacement aircraft. In January 1943 the entire group, now down to twenty-eight worn-out aircraft, had been withdrawn to Australia to be rebuilt. The 38th Bombardment Group comprised four squadrons of B-25 Mitchells, but two of them had never reached Australia, having being diverted to the South Pacific area. The two other squadrons, the 71st and 405th, were based at Port Moresby, although their twenty-seven aircraft only represented 73 per cent of their authorised strength of thirty-seven aircraft.[22]

The 3rd Bombardment Group, nicknamed the Grim Reapers, was Kenney's only light-bomber group, made up of the 8th, 13th, 89th and

90th Bomb Squadrons. The four squadrons had originally been equipped with Douglas Dauntless dive bombers but, after a disastrous raid on Buna in August 1942, when six out of seven aircraft were shot down, the unit was withdrawn from combat. Two squadrons, the 8th and 89th, were re-equipped with Douglas A-20 Bostons and the other two, the 13th and 90th, with North American B-25 Mitchells. It was very much a case of make-do for Kenney with regard to what type and what quantity of aircraft he could obtain, given the priority the European theatre had on aircraft. At this time Kenney was not even receiving sufficient aircraft to cover the attrition of his air force, which was exacerbated by the difficult climate. By February 1943 the two Boston squadrons had been combined as one and the two Mitchell squadrons were still in training.[23]

The A-20 Bostons used by the 3rd Bombardment Group had arrived in Australia with four .30-calibre machine-guns and not enough range to fly across the Owen Stanley Range from Port Moresby and back. With Kenney's approval, the 3rd Bombardment Group matèriel officer, Major Paul 'Pappy' Gunn, set about making significant modifications to the aircraft before they left Australia for New Guinea. The original machine-guns were replaced by four .50-calibre guns and two 450-gallon long-range fuel tanks were fitted to the bomb bay. Kenney was very keen on the 'attack aviation' concept using low-level strafing and bombing methods.

Gunn next turned his attention to the B-25 Mitchells, which now equipped two of the Grim Reaper squadrons. The lower turret and the tail gun were removed, and four .50 calibre machine-guns were installed in the nose and another four in forward-firing chin blisters. With the top turret also firing its guns forward, the plane boasted extraordinary strafing firepower yet could still carry six 100-pound bombs and sixty small 23-pound fragmentation bombs. The small bombs were fitted with parachutes so that they could be used for low-level bombing of airfields without damaging the aircraft that dropped them.[24]

Kenney had been privy to the Japanese naval decrypts, and the mission to destroy the Japanese convoy had been given the highest priority.[25] The Allied air forces, aware of their failure to coordinate their attacks on the January convoy to Lae, had been training for the next opportunity, and the 3rd Bombardment Group would have the key role in any attack. The 13th and 90th Bomb Squadrons, the latter under the command of Major Ed Larner, were originally trained to carry out bombardier assisted missions from altitude, but the modified B-25 C1 Mitchells they were now using were designed for masthead bombing attacks without a bombardier.

The new planes dispensed with two of the five original crew members, the bombardier and the navigator.

Training was carried out using the shipwreck SS *Pruth* as the target. The *Pruth* was a British cargo vessel that had run aground on Nateara Reef while trying to enter the Basilisk Passage to Port Moresby during a storm on 30 December 1923. During training, the planes would gather over Cape Hood, a similar distance from the anticipated target area to what Cape Ward Hunt would be. Cape Ward Hunt, between Buna and Morobe on the northern coast, would be the forming-up point for the anticipated attack on the Lae convoy. Apart from skip-bombing, the B-25s also practised direct bombing by aligning a reference point in the nose of the aircraft with the target. During training it was found that by directly targeting the sides of the ship in this way the results were better than skip-bombing into it. The B-25s would attack in pairs, approaching from 500 feet down to masthead height, strafing the ship from end to end before bombing. The Bostons from the 8th and 89th Bomb Squadron, as well as the RAAF No. 30 Squadron Beaufighters, also practised on the wreck. On 5 February one of the 90th Bomb Squadron Mitchells, Second Lieutenant Fred Schierloh's plane, was lost when it collided with the *Pruth*'s mast, one of four aircraft lost during training over the wreck. Peter Hemery, the ABC correspondent, accompanied a training mission and later wrote: 'The water looked horribly close. Then we levelled off and there was the wreck dead ahead, and rushing at us.'[26] The training honed vital skills, as Kenney later noted after watching Ed Larner's Mitchells. 'They didn't miss. It was pretty shooting and pretty skip-bombing . . . we really had something, I was sure.'[27]

Group Captain William 'Bull' Garing was the commander of RAAF No. 9 Group, responsible for all operational Australian air units in New Guinea. No. 9 Group came under the operational control of Allied Air Force Headquarters. Kenney thought highly of Garing, later saying he was 'active, intelligent, knew the theatre and had ideas about how to fight the Japs'.[28] Garing had noted the poor Allied attempts to prevent a number of Rabaul convoys reaching the New Guinea mainland and was determined to put in place a suitable plan for the next convoy to try. Garing persuaded Whitehead that a properly rehearsed plan integrating all available aircraft was needed for the operation.

Garing's plan was for the planes to gather over Cape Ward Hunt at 0930 and then be over the convoy at 1000 in quick succession, totally overwhelming the enemy escorting aircraft and the anti-aircraft defences. As soon as it was determined that the convoy was heading through

Vitiaz or Dampier Straits towards Lae, it would come within range of the USAAF medium bombers. Part of Garing's plan fell back on his experience with the navy, where he had spent seven years with the RAAF seaplane squadron. He knew that if the ship commanders and senior officers could be killed, then the ships would be much easier targets for the follow-up bombers. He directed the RAAF Beaufighters to strafe the ships' bridges.[29]

At least two rehearsals were carried out, but the first one failed to impress. Garing had persuaded Whitehead of the need for training but 'the first rehearsal was dreadful, they were all over the God damn time scale . . . Whitehead tore a most unholy strip off them for their navigation and their timing.' The flight commanders participated in the second rehearsal and 'that turned out to be damn good'.[30]

After the supplies had been loaded, the Japanese personnel boarded the ships on 28 February, and the sixteen-vessel convoy departed Rabaul for Lae at around 0200 on the morning of 1 March.[31]

Allied air reconnaissance had been hampered by stormy weather between 27 February and 1 March, but a report from two 321st Bomb Squadron B-24 Liberators, patrolling the north and south coasts of New Britain, noted that the weather was clearing on 1 March. A third Liberator was sent to join them and, at 1500 on 1 March, this aircraft made the first convoy sighting, reporting fourteen vessels escorted by Zero fighters around 70 kilometres north-west of Ubili, heading west. A bomber strike by two squadrons of B-17s was organised but then cancelled at 1620. Meanwhile, the Japanese destroyer *Shirayuki* had intercepted an Allied message saying that the convoy had been spotted. At 2030 an abandon ship drill was carried out on the *Teiyo Maru* then, at 2200, flares were dropped nearby, confirming the Japanese fears that the convoy had been discovered. One of the soldiers on board noted in his diary, 'The moon has already dropped below the horizon and we sailed on with uneasiness in the darkness.'[32]

On the morning of 2 March the weather was cloudy with occasional showers. Six RAAF No. 22 Squadron A-20 Bostons, led by Wing-Commander Keith Hampshire, also took off at 0520 and bombed and strafed Lae airfield to prevent it being used by the Japanese fighter escorts operating over the convoy.[33] Although the convoy was still too far away for a coordinated Allied attack, the heavy-bomber squadrons were sent out. They were escorted by P-38 Lightnings equipped with long-range

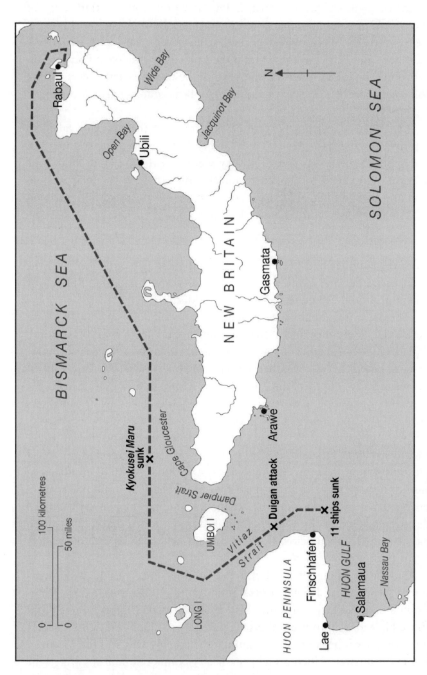

Map 3 Lae convoy: 1–3 March 1943

drop tanks. A Liberator from 320th Bomb Squadron located the convoy, and eight B-17s from the 63rd Bomb Squadron took off to attack it. Hindered by the cloud cover, the twelve escorting Lightnings missed the rendezvous, leaving the bombers vulnerable to the Japanese fighters. The B-17s found the convoy and reported eight merchant vessels with five destroyers and one light cruiser as escorts.

Three of the B-17s, led by Major Ed Scott, made the first attack at about 0945 and claimed five bomb hits on one of the transports. Two ships were claimed sunk, one 'breaking in half and sinking within two minutes'.[34] *Teiyo Maru* was hit aft by two bombs but was not badly damaged and continued at the same speed while other bombs landed astern of *Oigawa Maru*, causing no damage. The *Kyokusei Maru*, a thousand metres to the port side of *Teiyo Maru*, was not so fortunate. Soon after the first warning, it took direct hits on number 1 and 2 holds, a fire broke out and the stricken vessel drew away from the convoy. The transport commander ordered the ship to be abandoned at 1030 and it sunk at 1122. Some 850 troops, mainly from the III/115th Battalion (i.e. the 3rd Battalion of the 115th Regiment), along with two mountain guns were transferred to the destroyers *Asagumo* and *Yukikaze* before the ship sunk. The two destroyers then raced ahead of the convoy and landed the rescued troops, along with General Nakano, at Lae that night.[35] A second attack by eighteen B-17s was hampered by broken cloud and rain squalls and, despite claims from the airmen, no more ships were sunk. As the B-17s were bombing from a considerable height, and the bomb blasts on the ocean seemed to obliterate anything in the vicinity, such claims were not surprising.[36]

Troops on other vessels were ordered below when the alarm was sounded, donning life jackets and waiting. At 1700 another air raid warning sounded on the *Teiyo Maru* and more B-17s attacked through the rain squalls from the north, across the starboard bow. In all, forty-three 1000-pound bombs were dropped by the eleven B-17s in this attack and, although two hits were claimed, they were only near misses, two bombs landing within 20 metres on either side of the vessel's stern. Stretched out for 20 kilometres and zigzagging regularly, the convoy was unlikely to be stopped by high-level bombing.[37] Once again, the fighter escort for the B-17s did not arrive, but the numerous Japanese escorting fighters showed little aggressive intent, although one fighter was reported shot down by the bombers. Contrastingly, a soldier on *Oigawa Maru* wrote that he saw twenty Japanese fighters on the previous morning of 1 March, but none after that.[38]

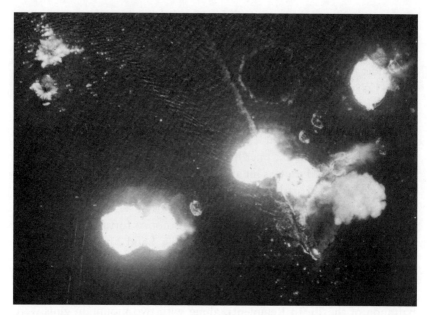

Photo 1 Bombs, probably from a B-17 Flying Fortress, exploding next to a convoy ship. (USAAF)

RAAF Catalina crews took over the shadowing of the convoy that night. A Catalina flying boat (A24–14) from No. 11 Squadron, piloted by Flight Lieutenant Terry Duigan with Squadron Leader Geoff Coventry aboard, had left Cairns just after midday on 2 March, initially searching for survivors from a missing Catalina. After topping up with fuel at Milne Bay, Duigan's Catalina was diverted to the convoy search area to determine whether it was heading west to Wewak or south through Dampier or Vitiaz Strait to Lae. Duigan had little difficulty identifying the convoy on his Air-to-Surface Vessel (ASV) radar equipment. The moonless night was dark and the ships were well separated and, despite dropping flares, Duigan was unable to get an accurate count. His estimate, partly based on observing the fluorescence from the ships' wake, was 'half a dozen substantial ships, with hints of more beyond the illumination'. Geoff Watson transmitted the vital radio message back to Port Moresby, giving the key information that the convoy was heading south through Vitiaz Strait towards Lae.[39]

Duigan's Catalina remained over the convoy for more than four hours, sending back updated reports and trying to disrupt the convoy with flares. That night two 250-pound anti-submarine bombs were dropped on

Photo 2 Terry Duigan (second from left) and the crew of Catalina A24-14 at Cairns just before takeoff on 2 March 1943. Geoff Coventry is at far right. (Watson)

separate ships, without result. This was followed by four 250-pound General Purpose bombs dropped from 1200 metres on what Duigan took to be an enemy cruiser but which was one of the escorting destroyers. He watched as 'the bursts came marching up the middle of the wake and the last one shaved the stern'. Unfortunately the navigator, Bob Burne, had entered the ship as 'stationary' in the bomb sight and, if he had allowed for its movement, the bombs may well have struck home. After a mission lasting 15 hours and 35 minutes, Duigan's aircraft returned to Cairns.[40]

Late on the afternoon of 2 March there was a briefing at 5th USAAF headquarters for the commanders of all units slated for the attack on the Lae convoy. Captain John Henebry from the 90th Bomb Squadron was there with his commander Major Ed Larner and noted that it was 'an unusual gathering. Never before had all squadrons been represented at a briefing at one time.' The briefing presented the latest information on the convoy, although the exact destination was not yet known. The twelve Mitchell strafers of Major Larner's 90th Bomb Squadron would soon be flying their first operational mission.[41]

At 0400 on 3 March eight Beauforts from RAAF No. 100 Squadron took off from Milne Bay, armed with torpedos. These Beauforts were the only torpedo-carrying aircraft available under Kenney's command. Only two of the Beauforts made it through a heavy weather front, and Pilot Officer Ken Waters made an unsuccessful run on a destroyer. The other Beaufort, piloted by Flying Officer Lou Hall, selected a transport, but the torpedo hung up and would not release, and Hall had to be satisfied with a strafing run.[42] However, the use of the Beaufort torpedo bombers had made the Japanese commanders aware of the torpedo danger. When the Beaufighters attacked later that morning the ships would tend to react as if in response to torpedos and turn beam on to the threat, exposing the length of the vessels to strafing. At 0510, four Boston bombers from RAAF No. 22 Squadron took off from Wards Drome at Port Moresby to hit Lae airfield at dawn as they had done the previous morning, trying to prevent any Japanese aircraft from using the strip.[43] This time they caught several planes on the ground, and they would now be unavailable to help protect the convoy.[44]

The day dawned clear over Port Moresby, and the sound of aircraft taking off reverberated from the surrounding ranges. The plan was for the attack force to rendezvous over Cape Ward Hunt at 0930, and they did so at 0925. The force included B-17 heavy bombers, Mitchell medium bombers, Boston light bombers, Beaufighter strafers and Lightning fighters. The planes gathered at staggered altitudes, the B-17s at 9000 feet, one squadron of Mitchells at 8000 feet with another below them, and thirteen Beaufighters at 6000 feet. Two more tiers of Mitchells gathered below the Beaufighters and a squadron of Bostons below them. Above all the attack aircraft, the Lightning fighters formed an umbrella. Sergeant Dave Beasley, the observer in Pilot Officer George Drury's Beaufighter, noted, 'The sky looked jammed full of planes.'[45]

The planes now adopted their correct formation, the B-17s leading off in echelon, levelling out at 7000 feet. In groups of three, the Mitchells set off behind the B-17s at the same speed, the first planes at 4000 feet and those behind them at successively lower altitudes. Squadron Leader Brian 'Black Jack' Walker's RAAF No. 30 Squadron Beaufighters descended smoothly to just 500 feet, each flight in line abreast. The low-level 90th Squadron Mitchells followed with the 89th Squadron Bostons behind them. Above them all, at 12,000 feet, were the Lightnings, weaving around to maintain the correct speed. Although he had been grounded by the medical officer, 'Black Jack' Walker flew his Beaufighter up with the Lightning escorts to watch over the battle.[46]

The thirteen B-17s bombed at 1022, from about 7500 feet, apparently hitting two vessels. One B-17, *Ka-Puhio-Wela*, which means 'double trouble' in Hawaiian, piloted by First Lieutenant Woodrow Moore, was hit during the bomb approach, and it attracted a group of about ten enemy fighters and was shot down. Lightnings from Major George Prentice's USAAF 38th Fighter Squadron then unwisely engaged in dogfighting the large pack of enemy Zeros.[47] Three of the Lightnings were shot down, but the attention of the escorting Zeros had been diverted from the main force, causing havoc at lower altitudes.

The Beaufighters came in just above the waves. With four 20mm Hispano cannon in the nose and six .303 Browning machine-guns in the wings, their menace was substantial. Expecting a torpedo attack, the ship captains misread the threat and turned their bows to the attackers, thus allowing the entire length of their vessels to be strafed. Each Beaufighter picked its own target. The RAAF planes had strict radio silence, but when the excitable Americans got over the convoy they had a lot to say. 'Oh baby, look at those boys down there. Let's go get 'em.' However, the American pilots got ahead of time so the bombs were falling around the Beaufighters as they went in.[48]

Flight Lieutenant Dick Roe was strafing at masthead height when a bomb from a Mitchell exploded on the deck of his target vessel, the debris denting his machine. Roe's observer, Flight Sergeant Peter Fisken, had missed the action; he was busy reloading the Hispano cannon with new 50-round magazines. Flight Lieutenant George Gibson had a similar experience when a bomb exploded amidships as he flew between the vessel's masts.[49] Flight Lieutenant Fred Cassidy was the observer in Sergeant Moss Morgan's Beaufighter and, as Morgan lined up on a transport, he was aware of something travelling at the same height alongside the plane. It was a 500-pound bomb, heading for the same transport after having been skipped off the water surface by one of the Mitchells.[50] Moss Morgan had just opened fire when the Mitchell passed in front of him, dropping two bombs. The first bomb hit the ship and 'the whole thing blew up right in front of me' while the second flew over the top. Morgan observed, 'It seemed a nasty experience to see a 500 lb bomb whistling past your ear.'[51]

Flying at only 10 metres above the waves, George Drury managed to line up three of the transports in a row and made his run on the first of them. He said, 'It was the start of five minutes of mayhem and pumping adrenaline.' He was attacking the ships from the side as he was moving too fast to allow him to get beam on. As Drury strafed his first target there was a tremendous vibration as his four cannon and six machine-guns opened fire, the recoil slowing the plane by around 25 knots. He watched as a Mitchell bomber came in at masthead height and landed a bomb on the stern of one of the ships, spreading flame and debris in all directions. As he pulled up for a run at the second freighter he realised that the terrific vibration from the guns had blown the globe in his gun sight out of alignment. However, with tracer bullets placed one in four, he was able to aim the tracers at the ship's waterline, then ease the nose up to fire at the bridge. He had to bank his plane at the end of his strafing run in order to go between the masts and could see fires starting as he passed overhead.[52]

Drury had pulled his plane up for the run on the third freighter when his observer, Dave Beasley, shouted, 'Bandit! Dive left.' So Drury headed off close to the waves where he knew, from previous contact at Rabaul, that the Beaufighter and Zero were essentially equal in speed. To make a harder target he jinked the aircraft about, walking the rudder from side to side. In the back, Dave Beasley watched as a Mitchell headed for one of the destroyers in a skip-bombing attack. The bomb made a direct hit, Dave later wrote that it 'blew the arse right off' the enemy warship.[53] This was probably the *Shirayuki*.

The Beaufighter of Flying Officer Bob Brazenor and Fred Anderson strafed a 7000-ton transport from stern to bow. Then, as he made an attack on a second vessel, Brazenor was jumped by a Zero; Anderson could see the enemy plane coming down at them from above, the gun ports smoking. He yelled out to warn Brazenor who, like Drury, stayed low and headed out of the battle, dragging the Zero with him.[54] In another Beaufighter, Sergeant Ron Downing and Danny Box were caught by anti-aircraft fire and the port engine and elevator were disabled. Downing received two shrapnel wounds to his shoulder while Box had bullet wounds but, despite this, Downing managed to crash-land the aircraft at the forward airstrip at Popondetta.[55] The Beaufighters were sturdy steeds.

Flight Lieutenant Ron 'Torchy' Uren's crew carried Damien Parer, the legendary Australian war photographer. Parer stood behind Uren, his legs braced across the entrance well with his movie camera balanced on Uren's head as Uren brought the plane around and began his strafing run. Parer later wrote, 'The first thunder of fire gives you a shock. It jars at your feet and you see the tracers lashing out ahead of you, and orange lights dance before your eyes on the grey structure of the ship.'[56] After

Photo 3 Photo taken by Damien Parer from 'Torchy' Uren's Beaufighter show-ing cannon shells impacting on a convoy vessel. Camera shake caused by gunfire has affected the photo. (AWM 127967)

Parer ran out of film and had to reload, Uren made a second pass for his benefit, thus producing some of the most amazing footage of the war. Corporal Louis Dusting saw Parer when he landed back at Port Moresby and observed how Parer 'came back literally frothing at the mouth with excitement. He had got about 5000 feet of the best material he had ever seen.'[57]

'Black Jack' Walker's Beaufighters had had a decisive effect on the course of the battle. In around 20 minutes their devastating strafing attacks had knocked out many of the anti-aircraft positions on the con-voy vessels. Those gun crews who survived were forced under cover by the strafing or overboard by the fires that had been started among the fuel drums stored on deck. Second, the Beaufighters had distracted those Japanese fighter escorts that had come down to low level and thus allowed the Mitchells and Bostons an easier passage to the targets. Third, the ships' bridges had been hit hard and any command and control that remained was now unable to respond to the approaching waves of low-level bombers.

As the Beaufighters went in, thirteen conventional Mitchells from the 13th and 71st Bomb Squadrons bombed from medium altitude before Major Ed Larner's twelve Mitchell strafers came in at low level. When they were about five kilometres from the convoy, the strafers, led by Larner flying *Spook II* descended to sea level. As his plane approached one of the destroyers, probably the *Shirayuki*, Larner told his men, 'I'm making a run on that lead cruiser. You guys pick out your own targets.' Larner went in broadside, strafing first and then crashing two delayed-action bombs into the side of the warship, one of which struck home. Larner's example inspired the other pilots as the low-level Mitchells made their bomb runs almost alongside the Beaufighters. Out of thirty-seven bombs dropped by Larner's squadron, seventeen were claimed as direct hits.[58] Twelve Bostons from the 89th Bomb Squadron then also came in at low level, dropping twenty bombs and claiming eleven hits. Emulating Larner's men, the 405th Bomb Squadron Mitchells dropped thirty-five 500-pound bombs from low level and claimed four direct hits.[59]

At 1003, *Shirayuki* was the first vessel hit after being strafed and bombed by waves of three planes at extremely low level. Most of those on the bridge were casualties, including Admiral Kimura, who was wounded in the arm. A bomb hit the aft turret, starting a fire and causing an explosion in the magazine. After the stern broke off and the ship flooded, *Shirayuki* sunk at 1135 and most of the crew transferred to the destroyer *Shikinami*. Private Tagayasu Kawachida, one of the anti-aircraft gunners on board the *Kembu Maru*, had watched the well-directed attack on one of the Japanese destroyers, probably the *Shirayuki* or *Arashio*. The first aircraft, probably a Beaufighter, attacked from the port side and strafed the ship with machine-gun fire. As the destroyer took evasive action, altering helm and zigzagging, a second aircraft attacked, planting bombs squarely in the centre of the ship. Kawachida's own vessel soon suffered the same fate.[60]

After the destroyer *Arashio* was hit it collided with the disabled and abandoned naval supply ship *Nojima*, which had been struck during the initial attacks. The stricken destroyer listed 30 degrees and was later abandoned. Masuda Reiji, who was working in the engine room, observed: 'Our bridge was hit by two 500-pound bombs. Nobody could have survived...Somehow those of us down in the engine room were spared.' The chief engineer and Reiji took over the ship, still able to make five or six knots. A second attack caused further damage, but

Photo 4 One of the convoy vessels, probably the *Kembu Maru*, burns furiously. (USAAF)

eight men continued to steer the 'ship of horrors'. Later that night the remaining seventeen *Arashio* crewmen were taken off by the *Yukikaze* and returned to Rabaul.[61] Another of the men on the *Arashio* was Chief Seaman Yasuo Yokoyama, who was picked up by the *Asashio*, which was itself sunk later that afternoon. Yokoyama subsequently landed at Buna in a lifeboat and was captured by US troops on 14 March.[62] Aboard the *Tokitsukaze*, hit by the low-level bombers at around 1010, the 18th Army headquarters staff hurriedly abandoned ship with the crew, transferring to the *Yukikaze*, which had returned from Lae after its earlier rescue mission.[63]

The *Kembu Maru* was attacked at 1010 when one or two bombs struck aft and set the ship on fire, no doubt due to the 200 fuel drums carried on board. The ship sunk within five minutes, one of the first to do so.[64] From higher altitude one of the American airmen watched as the low-flying Mitchells attacked the vessel. He noted: 'Now they turn their attention to a small cargo vessel, perhaps a 500-tonner. One hit is made right off. It is too easy. Another hit on the port side. She lumbers about in the foam and then catches fire. Four near misses help to put her completely out of action.'[65]

Like the other six transports, *Shinai Maru* was attacked within that first deadly 15 minutes, and a bomb dropped amidships, between number 3 hold and the bridge, set the vessel ablaze. All men were ordered overboard, but there were insufficient lifeboats available and many of those capsized in the rush. Lieutenant-Colonel Hiroshi Hondo, commander of the 51st Engineer Regiment, was mortally wounded and died after being lowered into a collapsible boat. The vessel sunk in about an hour.[66]

On the *Oigawa Maru*, Second Lieutenant Kiyoshi Nishio watched as 'a cloud of aircraft appeared'. The ship increased speed but was struck just aft of amidships by two bombs and immediately caught fire. The engine room had been hit and the ship stopped. With the boilers out of action, the steam gear was inoperable and the MLCs could not be launched, but some smaller boats were lowered. Most of the survivors had to swim or cling to wreckage while other men stayed on board. One group remained under cover until the first wave of planes had gone, then fought to keep the fire from the anti-aircraft ammunition. But 20 minutes after the attack, they also took to a boat and were around five kilometres away when the blazing vessel sunk soon after dusk. The heavy-artillery commander, Colonel Takahashi, was killed during the attack, as was Colonel Endo, the 115th Regiment commander. After the first air warning, the regimental standard was dismantled and packed inside a weighted rubber inner tube. When the ship was abandoned, the standard bearer was the first off with orders to throw the weighted tube overboard if his lifeboat was later attacked.[67] The colours were presumed lost but, carried by Lieutenant Ozaki from the shipping unit they were brought back to Rabaul and, on 31 May, delivered by submarine to the re-formed regiment in Lae.[68]

The *Taimei Maru* was hit five times, twice in number 2 hold, twice on the bridge and once in number 3 hold. The lifeboats were smashed, and the troops and crew jumped overboard. The ship was abandoned 20 minutes later, although it took a while longer to sink.[69] The *Aiyo Maru* had been hit aft, the boiler exploded and the vessel sunk three hours later. No boats were launched as the winches were out of order, and the men used bamboo poles and planks to stay afloat.[70]

At 0900 a reconnaissance plane had attacked *Teiyo Maru* from the starboard side and strafed the forward section of the vessel. The war diary of the II/115th Battalion reported the ship was 'sailing on with uneasiness'. When the swarm of Allied aircraft swept in from three directions, the transport fired every gun it had. Onboard, the helpless Japanese soldiers watched the Boston and Mitchell low-level bombers do their work, one later writing, 'They seemed to skim the water and climbed just before releasing bombs.' The vessel was hit by two 'aerial torpedos' on the port bow, the first hitting the top deck, the second stopping the engines, while extensive fires broke out fed by the fuel drums on deck. The ship soon began to list heavily, and at 1100 the transport commander gave the order to abandon ship. Each hold in turn was evacuated and, as it was not possible to launch MLCs or lifeboats, many men just jumped overboard. At 1130 the evacuation was complete and the ship lay abandoned, sinking around an hour and a half later.[71]

When the *Teiyo Maru* was hit, two destroyers raced to the scene. One of them, the *Uranami*, lowered all its boats to rescue those in the water, and about 300 men were rescued as the boats made a number of trips back and forth to the destroyer. One boat had made four trips but, as the boat returned from a fifth trip, bombing again commenced and the *Uranami* left the area and did not return.[72] By 1015 all seven transports had been hit and were sinking.[73]

Back at Port Moresby, as the second series of air attacks began, William Travis at 5th USAAF headquarters wrote in his diary, 'They're going out; bombing; returning; loading up again: and going back out. B-17s are taking off with three engines! A-20s: the crews are drawing straws and fighting to see who gets to go out next! B-25s are bombing from ten feet above sea level. B-24s – a bucket brigade.'[74]

At the RAAF No. 22 Squadron base at Durand five Bostons took off at 1325 with Squadron Leader Charles Learmonth coordinating the strike. The squadron found one of the Japanese destroyers, the *Asashio*, still afloat. Learmonth's Bostons attacked in pairs with a short delay between them to allow for any change in direction by the destroyer.[75] The 250-pound bombs had been fitted with five-second fuses to allow low-level skip bombing and, despite the heavy anti-aircraft barrage, two of them hit the *Asashio* amidships, one being dropped by Flying Officer Dick Hunt's plane. Four Zeros attacked Flying Officer Harry Craig's plane but he turned into them and, under his heavy fire, they broke away.[76] At 1530 *Asashio* sent out its final message, stating that it was under attack by thirty aircraft before the signal stopped.[77]

The four surviving destroyers, two of them damaged, withdrew up Vitiaz Strait and lined up alongside each other east of Long Island. There they were joined by the destroyer *Hatsuyuki*, which had come from Rabaul or Kavieng, and was able to refuel the destroyers. The wounded personnel were transhipped to the *Hatsuyuki* and the damaged *Uranami*, and these two destroyers then headed for Rabaul with 2700 survivors, arriving on the morning of 5 March. General Yoshihara, on one of the destroyers, later wrote, 'To say they were overcrowded was no figure of speech.' Three intact destroyers, with minimum crew, refuelled and headed back to the scene of the convoy battle to rescue survivors before heading to Kavieng at 2230.[78] Over the course of the battle the Japanese destroyers rescued 3800 survivors. Japanese submarines also contributed. Submarine I-17 rescued thirty-four survivors on 4 March before returning on 6 March with the I-26 to rescue more while submarine R-101 reached the area on 7 March and was able to recover forty-seven parched survivors from three lifeboats.[79]

On 4 March the Beaufighters were back over Lae, strafing the airfields. Four Zeros, in the process of refuelling, were set alight on Malahang strip. During the strafing runs, George Drury's plane was hit by ground fire, causing one engine to cut out on the way back to base. Drury did not quite make Dobodura and crash-landed on a kunai patch, later writing, 'The grim reaper nearly had another customer today.'[80]

There was another, less palatable mission for the Beaufighters. The pilots were ordered to strafe the survivors of the convoy attack as they clung to their overloaded lifeboats. In four separately recorded cases of strafing, more than a third of the fifty-seven men in the boats were killed. Four separate groups of survivors near Cape Ward Hunt were strafed by five Beaufighters on 5 March. The first group had around twenty-five survivors in each of four barges and a supply barge, and all were left sinking after the five aircraft went to work. The second group comprised fourteen rafts, each of twelve men, and four lifeboats with six men in each. A single Beaufighter found and strafed them. The third and fourth groups were of small barges, all of them apparently empty. The strafing of the survivors was unpopular work and against many of the accepted norms of warfare but, in that regard, it was in line with the way the war was increasingly being fought. However, it was not against the rules of war as the Japanese soldiers had not surrendered and, if they reached the shore north of Morobe, they would soon have taken their place in the front lines. It was soon apparent that the lifeboats would drift much further south and end up in Allied controlled territory.

Not all the killing was done from the air. On the night of 8 March an American PT boat off Wanigela intercepted an enemy boat containing fifty-one Japanese survivors from the convoy. Of these, forty-three were killed and only eight taken prisoner.[81] In the aftermath of the convoy sinking 352 Japanese troops were estimated to have been killed as a result of aircraft strafing and patrol boat attacks.[82]

Two men from the *Oigawa Maru* clung to a raft and drifted for ten days before being found by Australian troops, more dead than alive and unable to walk when taken ashore. Another survivor, Private Kanami Mayeda, claimed to have drifted on a raft for 20 days before being found by natives. All he had to sustain him were a tin of bully beef and a full water bottle, but they had lasted only five days. Fortunately he obtained drinking water from the frequent rain squalls.[83] Various boat-loads drifted for from four to 12 days, reaching the Trobriands and other island groups.[84]

Some boatloads of survivors landed on Goodenough Island. From 8 to 14 March Australian troops of the 47th Battalion, garrisoning Good-enough Island, recorded eight Japanese landings. Of 116 Japanese sur-vivors encountered, seventy-two were killed, another forty-two captured and two remained at large. Another nine men were found dead on a raft. Of those killed, thirty-four had been occupying Waibula village, which had been surrounded and attacked by an Australian patrol commanded by Lieutenant Colin Baker on 8 March.[85] On 9 March a patrol under Lieutenant Joe Pascoe killed a group of eight Japanese survivors, and 'the badges showed some of the Japanese dead were in the brass hat class and had some official looking boxes which they tried to take away into the bush'. The boxes were found to contain sealed tins full of documents, which were sent back to Brisbane for examination. A complete list of Japanese officers and their units was discovered, providing a very accu-rate picture of Japanese army deployments. Captain Aubrey McWatters later observed, 'We gradually learned the show had picked up the stud book and all the box and dice, etc.'[86]

On 4 March a commendation was sent to all air force units in New Guinea. MacArthur stated: 'It cannot fail to go down in history as one of the most complete and annihilating combats of all time. My pride and satisfaction in you is boundless.' Kenney added: 'Tell the whole gang that I am so proud of them I am about to blow a fuse.' Back in the United States, Robert A. Lovett, the Assistant Secretary for War, commented, 'It was a demonstration which will rank with the Battle of Britain from a defensive standpoint and with the Battle of Midway from the standpoint of technique.'[87]

On 7 March MacArthur issued a communiqué to the press in which he estimated that Japanese army casualties were 15,000, all of whom had perished. Letters on the subject then passed between MacArthur, the Australian prime minister, John Curtin, and the secretary of the War Cabinet, Frederick Shedden. On 16 March a new statement based on Australian analysis put Japanese personnel losses at 6000–7000, less than half MacArthur's figure, with 3000–4000 survivors. MacArthur's response was to declare that these new figures were 'glaringly wrong, I cannot fail to take exception to them.' MacArthur added that the revised figures 'did not include crews of the lost ships'. He also continued to insist that twenty-two vessels were involved in the convoy: twelve transports and ten destroyers.[88]

It is extraordinary, although a credit to the historians who wrote it, that in the US Official History nearly as many words were devoted to this controversy over MacArthur's inflated claims as were given to the description of the Bismarck Sea action itself. In 1943 the Army Air Force Historical Office in Washington studied all the relevant records from the Bismarck Sea action, including photo intelligence, and this 'offered conclusive proof of the presence of no more than sixteen ships in the original convoy'. It was also established that no other ships later joined the convoy. MacArthur's arrogant response was to suggest that 'some action might be taken against those responsible for calling the claim into question'.[89] Despite also having access to the facts, Kenney reinforced MacArthur's pretence in his 1949 book, *General Kenney Reports*, stating that eleven to fourteen merchant vessels and six escorting warships had been sunk. For good measure he repeated MacArthur's claim that up to 15,000 Japanese personnel had been lost.[90] Damien Parer later observed, 'The war's a phoney MacArthur made one. He's blown up a big balloon full of bullshit and someone will pick it up one day.'[91]

Post-war, it was established that 8740 personnel had been on board the ships, comprising 2130 crew and naval personnel and 6610 troops. Of these, 2890 men were lost, 2450 of them army and marine troops.[92] That the Japanese command took such a risk in reinforcing Lae spoke volumes for their appreciation of the critical strategic situation in New Guinea. It was summed up by Allied intelligence: 'It is more than evident that the enemy considers Lae–Salamaua as a key position both as his main outpost protecting Rabaul from the SW and also as a base from which further attacks can be made on our positions in New Guinea.'[93]

The Battle of the Bismarck Sea was a major victory for Allied air power, and MacArthur later described it as 'the decisive aerial engagement' in the South-West Pacific theatre of war.[94] The action had directly delayed the deployment of one Japanese infantry regiment and indirectly delayed at least three others reaching Lae. However, the fate of the Japanese at Lae and Salamaua would always hinge upon just when the Allied command could assemble the resources necessary to commence an operation against Lae. The effect of the loss of eight merchant ships also needs to be considered in the light of the US Navy's devastating impact on the ability of the Japanese merchant fleet to supply all the far-flung garrisons from Japan. In the same month of March 1943, US submarines sunk twenty-six merchant vessels; the loss of the four destroyers was perhaps more serious to the Japanese command.

The most direct consequence of the loss of the convoy was that the Japanese units defending Salamaua were denied considerable reinforcements, equipment and supplies, but this did not cause the Japanese to fall back from Mubo. The failure of the Australians immediately to contest the area allowed this. However, the opportunity for an even greater prize was also refused by the Australian command; the loss of the reinforcements and supplies had left Lae almost defenceless. Before the failed attempt to reinforce Lae, the Japanese Eighteenth Army command had noted that 'it did not believe its weak military strength could secure the Lae area'.[95] Perhaps MacArthur's 'most decisive aerial action' claim required a preface stating it 'could have been'.

General Blamey did acknowledge the benefit of the victory for his ground troops. He wrote, 'The brilliant action has inspired all land forces. It has considerably lightened [the] burden of the troops in New Guinea and danger area at Wau.' The acting New Guinea Force commander, Lieutenant-General Sir Iven Mackay, added what the air force's success meant to his command, noting that 'the whole New Guinea force admires their skill and thoroughness, for you have inflicted more casualties on the Japanese in three days than we could do in three months.'[96]

―――――――――

Lieutenant Masamichi Kitamoto watched a group of Japanese survivors of the Battle of the Bismarck Sea come ashore at Tuluvu at the western edge of New Britain.

> One group was made up of seriously injured men whose faces were
> covered black with oil. Their eyes were all glassy and deeply sunk
> into their faces. All were jittery and full of fear as if they were seeing
> a horrible dream. They were all worn out and their tired water

soaked bodies could be seen from beneath their torn and tattered uniforms. They were just a bunch of men with their fighting spirit completely lost. A pitiful scene of a vanquished and defeated army.[97]

One later wrote: 'Faces of fellows float before my eyes, how deeply I hate the Dampier.'[98]

CHAPTER | 2

OPPOSING FORCES

The cornerstone of the Australian army in New Guinea was the brigade, composed of three battalions as well as brigade headquarters and specialised artillery, engineering and medical units. The infantry battalions deployed to New Guinea in 1943 utilised the new tropical-scale establishment of thirty-three officers and 753 other ranks. The battalion comprised four rifle companies, each of five officers and 127 men, and a headquarters company of six platoons: signals, machine-gun, mortar, tank attack, pioneer and administration. A regimental aid post was attached to each battalion. Each rifle company comprised a headquarters of fifteen men and three rifle platoons of thirty-nine men, made up of a six-man headquarters and three eleven-man infantry sections.

Each infantry section had one Bren gun, which was operated by two men, a number 1, who fired the gun, and a number 2, who carried and reloaded the magazines for the gun. A section had one or two submachine-guns, and these were normally carried by the forward scouts. Thompson submachine-guns were used in the early part of the campaign but were replaced by the Australian-designed Owen gun as they became available. The rest of the section was equipped with the tried and sturdy Lee Enfield .303 rifle, and on occasion a sniper's or grenade-discharging extra yoke version was made available. First-line ammunition was fifty rounds for the rifle, five Bren magazines, six Owen gun magazines and two grenades. These figures were generally doubled during an attack.[1]

The main Australian force in the theatre at the start of the Salamaua campaign was Brigadier Murray Moten's 17th Brigade comprising the

2/5th, 2/6th and 2/7th Battalions. The authorised strength of these battalions, formed before the new jungle establishment, was thirty-five officers
and 870 men. Due to the arduous nature of the Wau campaign and the
ongoing wastage brought on by the New Guinea climate and terrain, all
three battalions were well under strength. On 4 March the three battalions were 299, 351 and 330 men under strength respectively, so they were
only at two-thirds or less of their authorised strength. Three weeks later
the battalions still had average deficiencies of 230 men.[2] These deficiencies were invariably first felt at the front-line section level, most of which
never had a full complement of eleven men throughout the campaign.

Each independent company consisted of three fifty-man platoons broken down into three sixteen-man sections, each commanded by a lieutenant. There were eighteen Bren guns on strength, and both the 2/3rd
and 2/5th Independent Companies also had Vickers machine-guns, operated by the transport section. Engineer, signals and medical sections were
also attached. The officers and men who served were all volunteers who
were keen to take part in the tough fighting that commando-type operations promised. Fit and well trained at the commando training centre
at Wilsons Promontory in Victoria, many of them shone in the harsh
environment of New Guinea, their enthusiasm, stamina and expertise to
the fore. Captain Bob Hancock from the 2/3rd wrote of the quality of
reinforcements his unit had received in early April: 'some excellent men,
in all branches of army work who have dropped stripes to be commandos.
The unit really is becoming a first class show.'[3] As of March 1943 three
independent companies were deployed in the Wau area: the 2/3rd, 2/5th
and 2/7th. The authorised strength was seventeen officers and 253 men
for the 2/3rd Independent Company and nineteen officers and 282 men
for the other two companies. All three companies were essentially at full
strength at this time.

While the Australians made their plans, the Japanese commanders struggled with the realities of military operations under the dark shadow of
Allied air superiority. Lieutenant-General Hatazo Adachi's Eighteenth
Army commanded those forces operating in New Guinea. A career soldier like his father, Adachi had commanded a combat division in China
before being appointed to the command of Eighteenth Army on 6 November 1942, the same day that his wife died. He did not attend her funeral
but headed south for Rabaul, leaving Japan forever. Although it involved
considerable risk, Adachi always wanted to be at the front with his men

and ultimately would take his own life to share the fate of most of them.[4] As of 1 March 1943 Adachi's Eighteenth Army comprised three infantry divisions, the 20th, 41st and 51st.

The 20th Division had left Korea in early January 1943 and arrived at Wewak and Hansa Bay at the end of January 1943. The unit was involved in road construction between Wewak and Madang, and that work would continue in the future. There were three regiments, the 78th, 79th and 80th. Colonel Matsujiro Matsumoto's 78th Regiment would be used to construct the road through the mountains behind Madang and, in late 1943, would defend the Finisterre Ranges against the Australian 7th Division. Colonel Kaneki Hayashida's 79th Regiment would be sent to Finschhafen where it would come up against the Australian 9th Division in late 1943. Colonel Sadahiko Miyake's 80th Regiment would be ordered to the Lae–Salamaua area later in the campaign, but only Major Otoichi Jinno's I/80th Battalion would reach Lae. The II/80th and III/80th had only reached the Finschhafen area when the Australian landings at Lae prevented them moving further. The commander of the 20th Division was Lieutenant-General Shigemasa Aoki, but he would die from disease in New Guinea and be superseded by Lieutenant-General Shigeru Katagiri.

The convoy carrying the 41st Division had left Tsingtao in northern China in early February 1943 and arrived at Wewak later that month. There were three regiments in the division, the 237th, 238th and 239th, and all were initially involved in airfield and other construction around Wewak. Colonel Tokazu Kashiwagi's 238th Regiment would be sent to Alexishafen and then by coastal barge to Finschhafen and to Lae by foot, two battalions arriving in late August 1943. Colonel Naro's 237th Regiment and the 239th Regiment remained at Wewak before moving to Madang in October 1943 in response to the Australian threat in the Ramu Valley. The division commander was Major-General Heisuke Abe, but he died of illness in New Guinea in June 1943 and Lieutenant-General Goro Mano took over command. According to a staff officer with the division, only 600 of the 20,000 men who served with the 41st Division in New Guinea returned to Japan at the end of the war.[5] Similar losses were suffered by the other two of Adachi's divisions.

As previously noted, the 51st Division had been carried in eight transports from Whampoa in Korea in mid-November 1942 and had sailed via Hong Kong and Palau, before arriving in Rabaul in December 1942.[6] The division's three regiments were the 102nd, 115th and 66th. Most of Colonel Kohei Maruoka's 102nd Regiment had been transported to Lae in early January and had then taken part in the Wau offensive. Colonel Endo's 115th Regiment had been substantially weakened during the Bismarck Sea action but was re-formed under Lieutenant-Colonel Takayoshi Matsui. Colonel Katsutoshi Araki's 66th Regiment began moving from Rabaul to Lae once new transport arrangements could be put into place in April.

The 51st Division commander was Lieutenant-General Hidemitsu Nakano. Commissioned in 1912, Nakano had been appointed to his 51st Division command in Manchuria in 1941. After an extraordinary crossing of the Saruwaged Range from the north coast, Second Lieutenant Masamichi Kitamoto reported to Nakano in Lae in early April 1943: 'He had a soft laughing face with a white beard. The kind eyes showed that he was a man of warm and sincere nature. The commander was sixty years old at that time. Although he was short, measuring only five foot and several inches, he was a brave soldier, a man of quick decision and action.' Nakano gave Kitamoto a bottle of sake, telling him, 'This is not much, but share it with your men.'[7]

Each Japanese infantry division consisted of three infantry regiments plus ancillary headquarters units. Each regiment contained three infantry battalions as well as specialised regimental headquarters, supply, signals, labour, artillery and anti-tank gun components. The latter two units were normally combined in New Guinea and, due to the transport and ammunition supply difficulties, only two or three of their guns were utilised. Each infantry battalion was made up of four infantry companies, one machine-gun company and a battalion gun platoon as well as a headquarters and supply unit. Authorised battalion strength was 1100 men. Each infantry company had a company headquarters and three rifle platoons, with a total of 181 men. A machine-gun company comprised a headquarters platoon, three machine-gun platoons and an ammunition platoon, 174 men in all.[8]

Rifle platoon strength was fifty-four men, made up of a lieutenant in command, a liaison NCO and four sections. There were three rifle sections and a grenade discharger section, each of one NCO and twelve men. Each rifle section was equipped with a light machine-gun, commonly known as a Nambu light machine-gun and served by three men: a firer, a loader and an ammunition carrier. Most Japanese riflemen were equipped with the Type 38 Meiji rifle, a modified German Mauser design developed in 1905. Japanese sections contained one designated sniper, who operated without a telescopic sight. Each rifleman carried 120 rounds and two Type 97 grenades. There were four grenade dischargers in that particular section, each served by three men. Each machine-gun platoon comprised four gun sections, each of one NCO and ten men equipped with one Type 92 heavy machine-gun. This was an air-cooled Hotchkiss design, commonly known as a Juki and which fired thirty 7.7 mm rounds from thirty-round metal strips. Two men carried the machine-gun, two carried the tripod, four carried ammunition and two had rifles. The section NCO carried tools for the weapon. Platoon strength was forty-six men, made up of a lieutenant in command, a liaison NCO and four eleven-man sections. The ammunition platoon was commanded by an NCO with three sections of seven men, twenty-two men in all.[9]

The establishment strength for the infantry regiments in New Guinea was never attained even before the units had left Rabaul. For example, in one of the 51st Division regiments that would later deploy to New Guinea, the machine-gun company was split into four 21-man platoons. These comprised only two sections, each with a machine-gun, carried and operated by four of the men. Another four men each carried a box of machine-gun ammunition, made up into twenty 30-round strips. One of the 102nd Regiment battalions that had fought at Wau was even weaker, with only three machine-gun platoons, each of two sections. Heavy mortars were also issued to the battalion gun platoon in lieu of some of the artillery pieces. In terms of officers, the front-line companies and platoons suffered severely in New Guinea and lieutenants generally ended up commanding companies and NCOs platoons.[10] Despite being severely under strength, the remnants of the 102nd Regiment had the main task of holding the Japanese positions in front of Salamaua from February to April 1943.

There were two Special Naval Landing Parties (*Rikusentai*) deployed during the Salamaua campaign, the 5th Sasebo SNLP and the 2nd Maizuru SNLP. Both these units had an authorised strength of 1069 men, similar to that of an infantry battalion, but with a different structure incorporating many of the arms usually found at regimental level in an army unit. Other SNLPs varied considerably in strength and weaponry, depending on their roles. Some of them were trained for parachute operations. The 2nd Maizuru SNLP was originally split into two companies, each of one officer, seven warrant officers and 292 men. Each company had a headquarters platoon of thirty-six men, four rifle platoons of fifty-one men and a heavy machine-gun platoon of fifty-six men. Each SNLP also had a heavy weapons unit with three gun platoons of fifty-one men and three howitzer platoons of forty-one men. There was also a separate headquarters platoon of forty-six men and dedicated supply, transport, medical, communications and engineer units attached.[11]

One company of the 5th Sasebo SNLP had landed with the South Seas Force at Buna in July 1942. The unit was later slated for the Milne Bay landing, but a major component of 353 men was marooned on Good-enough Island when air attacks sunk the unit's seven landing barges on 25 August 1942. Following the Australian landings on the same island in October 1942, the SNLP survivors were recovered by two barges and taken to nearby Fergusson Island on 24 October and thence, by the light cruiser *Tenryu*, to Rabaul two days later.[12] The re-formed 5th Sasebo SNLP arrived at Salamaua a month later and was built up to 700 men. The unit commander, Lieutenant Commander Torashige Tsuioka, was killed in a bombing raid at Salamaua on 29 June 1943 and was replaced by Captain Fukuo Ikeda.[13]

Brutally trained and specialising in independent operation, these naval units proved to be the sternest of opponents. Both prisoners from the 5th Sasebo SNLP who were taken during the Salamaua campaign asked to be killed upon capture.[14] The 2nd Maizuru SNLP had taken part in the invasions at Wake Island and Kavieng before the landing at Lae in March 1942. It had suffered 116 casualties during the fighting against the Australian commandos at Mubo in early January 1943.[15] There were also two Naval Garrison battalions deployed in Lae. On 14 April Allied intelligence estimated that there were 5200 to 5700 Japanese troops at Lae and Salamaua.[16]

Japanese equipment was not ideally suited to the type of warfare encountered in New Guinea. One prisoner, a sergeant who served throughout most of the Salamaua campaign, considered that the troops had the wrong training and equipment for the jungle conditions. The rifles and machine-guns were considered too heavy and more suited to fighting over flat terrain than in the close conditions of the jungle where action took place suddenly and rapid automatic fire was necessary. The lack of submachine-guns in the Japanese infantry sections was a noticeable deficiency in the close confines of the jungle. One Japanese prisoner wrote, 'These were very deadly and demoralising... men armed with rifles did not have much chance against them in close jungle fighting.'[17] Combining portability and automatic fire, the most effective Japanese weapons in the fighting around Salamaua were the Type 96 and Type 99 Nambu light machine-guns.

Whatever deficiencies there may have been in strength or equipment, the Japanese soldiers were of a high calibre, although their physical condition soon deteriorated in the harsh jungle conditions. On arrival in New Guinea the new troops proved to be tactically inept offensively, restrained by a lack of initiative and flexibility at lower levels of command. As Major-General Stan Savige, commander of the Australian 3rd Division, later observed, the Japanese soldier was 'ruled by his textbook'.[18] This inflexibility had already been shown at Wau and would later be demonstrated at Lababia Ridge. However, the Japanese proved to be excellent troops when called on to hold ground, and their ability to use the terrain and put up with the accompanying hardships was unmatched. Most of the Japanese positions were taken only over the dead bodies of the defenders, and very few Japanese prisoners were captured during the campaign. One prisoner insisted that 'it was better for his family to think him dead'. Another had been told at Salamaua that all POWs would be killed by the Australians, and each man had a hand grenade to take his own life. The prisoner did not wish to return to Japan and, if he did, he would have to kill himself as being a POW was worse than death.[19] This attitude was in line with the Imperial Rescript, an 1883 document from Emperor Meiji, which forged a link between ancient Japanese traditions and the modern military organisation. Each Japanese soldier carried a copy, and the text included the telling statement, 'Duty is weightier than a mountain while death is lighter than a feather.'[20] In January 1941 the revised Field Service Regulations also enjoined soldiers to avoid the humiliation of being taken prisoner.[21]

On 12 March 1943 a military conference was held in Washington to decide on the allocation of forces within the Pacific theatre. General MacArthur's chief of staff, Major-General Richard Sutherland, his operations officer, Brigadier-General Stephen Chamberlin, and his air commander, Kenney, represented MacArthur. Sutherland put forward the Elkton plan, which had been finalised by General MacArthur on 28 February 1943. This plan synthesised MacArthur's objectives for 1943 into a coordinated series of tasks. Task 1 was the successful completion of the Guadalcanal operation in the Solomon Islands. Task 2 involved further operations in the Solomon Islands as well as operations in New Guinea. Task 3 was the seizure and occupation of Rabaul. On 28 March a new directive was issued in line with task 2 of the Elkton plan. The US Joint Chiefs of Staff ordered MacArthur and Admiral William 'Bull' Halsey, the South Pacific Area naval commander, to establish airfields on Woodlark and Kiriwina, seize the Lae–Salamaua–Finschhafen–Madang area in New Guinea and occupy western New Britain. The Solomon Islands was to be seized as far as southern Bougainville.[22]

The Allied strategy in New Guinea limited Australian planning to these objectives and, with a year to achieve them, preparation and planning would be the bywords of these operations. Consolidating the forces necessary for the operations would certainly require some time. The severe losses suffered by the four Australian Imperial Force (AIF) brigades during the Kokoda campaign and the subsequent Papuan beachhead battles would need to be made good and the units involved brought back to combat readiness. As Lieutenant-General Edmund Herring observed, 'These AIF brigades must be our spearhead as training and battle experience in the Middle East had made them far the most efficient troops we had.'[23] The air assets necessary to achieve the objectives were also still well short of what had been anticipated. Until those units were in theatre and the bases necessary for their operation had been completed, no sustained offensive operations were considered possible.

This was unfortunate, as the loss of most of the Japanese 102nd Regiment at Wau and the 115th Regiment in the Bismarck Sea had given the Australian command a great opportunity, not just to advance on Salamaua but also to cross the Markham River, capture the excellent airfield sites at Nadzab and advance directly on Lae. Japanese combat strength at Lae and Salamaua was weak, and Allied intelligence knew this from captured documents that had been translated by 11 March. According to these captured documents, the Japanese had 2500 naval and 1000 army troops at Lae and another 1500 army and naval troops at Salamaua.[24] However, of these 5000 troops, at least half were from a non-combatant 7th Naval Base Unit, and all troops suffered from supply deficiencies, exacerbated by the loss of the convoy. In terms of front-line infantry, Japanese resources were very limited, with only a weakened infantry battalion and two weakened SNLP battalions available at Salamaua and two naval garrison battalions at Lae.

The Japanese command considered the defence of Salamaua to be integral to the defence of Lae. To defend Lae, 'enormous combat forces were required', and this was considered beyond the capability of the Eighteenth Army. To prevent attacks on Lae either from the sea or from the Markham Valley, the Japanese command depended on their air forces.[25] However, by March 1943 the Japanese air forces were clearly incapable of challenging Allied air superiority over the Lae area. This had been conclusively demonstrated following the Japanese inability to protect the Lae convoy and the loss of aviation fuel in the convoy, which would severely restrict any air operations from Lae. The situation had been acknowledged with work to develop forward airfields in the Wewak area now being underway. Both on the ground and in the air, the Japanese command did not have the strength to hold Lae in March 1943, and even six months later Nadzab was still undefended. As Captain Bill Dexter, whose company was based on the opposite side of the Markham River for a number of months, told Gavin Long, the Official Historian of Australia's World War II campaigns, 'You didn't have to be a general to realise this was the key to Lae.'[26]

The domination of the Allied air forces over Lae would only increase with the seizure of the Nadzab area, ideal for airfields. One reason that there was no move into the Markham Valley was the disruption caused by the battle for Wau and the fear of another attempt. However, the Japanese had incurred the greater losses at Wau, losing two infantry battalions, and the subsequent loss of the 115th Regiment had removed another threat for the foreseeable future. So, although the battle for Wau had been a clear-cut tactical victory for the Australians, strategically it was proving to have been of most benefit to the Japanese. The battle had sowed trepidation into the Australian command structure, and this was confirmed by the three roles given to the 3rd Division headquarters when it moved into the area at the end of April. The division was ordered to prevent Japanese moves into the Wau and Bulolo valleys, protect the airfields therein and prevent the Japanese forming a base south of the Markham River, all of which were defensive tasks.[27]

The reticence of the Australian command to undertake large-scale offensive operations in March, April or May was also due to critical supply limitations. Those limitations were outlined in a letter sent to Mackay by Whitehead on 9 March 1943. Whitehead set out a series of factors regarding the crucial air transport operation to Wau, an operation that fundamentally underpinned all Australian military action in the theatre. At that time two transport squadrons with a total of eighteen aircraft were available for transport operations from Port Moresby to Wau. However, in the two previous weeks weather conditions had restricted air movements to an average of only 14.1 loads per day. It was considered that the weather would deteriorate even further over the next six weeks, with the cloud building up earlier in the day, leading to rain showers across the intervening Owen Stanley Range after midday. This would allow only a four- to five-hour window for operations daily. Transport to Wau also had to be carried out in an escorted convoy formation to ensure fighter coverage, and this put further restrictions on when the transport aircraft could operate. Forward air-dropping at Guadagasal, Skindiwai and Ballam's would also not be possible at this time.[28]

Whitehead also had important supply considerations at Dobodura, the new airfield complex being constructed north of the Owen Stanley Range between Popondetta and Buna. It had initially been hoped that Dobodura could be supplied from the nearby port of Oro Bay, and a road was scheduled for completion by 15 March. But heavy rains had washed out the road bridges and the road would not be suitable for limited traffic until 1 April. In the interim, USAAF fighter and bomber units using the Dobodura strip needed to be entirely supplied by air transport. Steel Marsden matting for further airfield expansion was also required, and this supply operation would require at least two troop carrier squadrons and, at times, a third.[29]

Due to these considerations, Whitehead made a series of recommendations with which the Australians were in no position to argue. He advised that a reserve of food and ammunition be built up for those forces currently deployed in the Wau area and that no more troops be deployed there until such reserves were sufficient. He also stated that any troops moved forward of Ballam's would need to be supplied by native carriers and that any offensive action against Mubo or Salamaua would need to supplied from the sea. Whitehead noted that no more troop carrier aircraft could be expected in New Guinea in the near future and that transport aircraft might actually decrease as squadrons returned to Australia for parachute troop training.[30] Work had begun in January 1943 on an alternative land route to Wau via the Bulldog Road from the southern coast, but it would be August before that road would be ready for even limited usage.

Whitehead's sobering assessment essentially determined the Australian strategy for the coming months. New Guinea Force headquarters confirmed the view at a conference on 13 March, stating, 'On the whole the air supply position, rather than improving as we had hoped, will deteriorate in the next few weeks.' To the contrary, the flying weather improved, and from 9 to 15 March there were 178 flights to the Wau area, averaging twenty-five loads per day. Then, from 22 to 29 March, deliveries averaged thirty-three planeloads per day, generally two-thirds to Wau and one-third to Bulolo.[31] However, Whitehead's appraisal also reflected the opinions of MacArthur and Kenney, both of whom were concerned at the run-down condition of the 5th USAAF following the arduous Papuan and Wau campaigns.[32] Only General MacArthur could have changed the Allied strategy by instructing Blamey to assemble the ground troops and Kenney to provide the aircraft for an operation against Nadzab in April or May 1943. The opportunity to seize the undefended Nadzab area and then strike at the Japanese force at Lae while it was at its weakest was not taken, and thus the Salamaua campaign evolved.

Mackay's plan at this stage was made clear in a letter to Moten on 21 March: 'As soon as supplies permit of it, I should like to see a brigade of two bns looking after Bulolo and to the north.' Moten agreed that his main task was to ensure that Wau and the Bulolo Valley were never again threatened, but he told Mackay he did not have the force available to prevent a Japanese crossing of the Markham River. If this was to occur Moten planned to defend the Bulolo Valley at a bottleneck near Partep II. He had therefore moved the 2/6th Battalion to the Bulolo Valley, leaving the 2/5th Battalion and his independent companies to guard against another incursion from Mubo to Wau. Both the 2/6th and 2/5th had two companies forward with the other two retained close to the jeepheads at Sunshine and Ballam's respectively. The 2/7th Battalion was held in reserve at Wau, thus giving Moten considerable flexibility, with two-thirds of his strength uncommitted and able to respond promptly to any enemy move either from the Markham Valley or from Mubo. He had sufficient reserves in Wau in the shape of the 2/7th Battalion to concentrate a battalion rapidly at that point if required.[33]

Murray Moten was a burly man with a composed demeanour, but he had been casual, if not dismissive, in his command during the lead-up to the Japanese incursion to the very outskirts of Wau in late January. His brigade had ultimately won that critical battle but had clearly shown that the Japanese threat could not be underestimated. Moten had therefore deployed his brigade to cover such an eventuality while New Guinea Force command had decided to provide further reinforcements to allay the threat.

With plans to move a separate brigade into the Bulolo area, a divisional command would be set up that would be responsible both for the newly allocated 15th Brigade and for Moten's 17th Brigade. On 27 March a cadre of 3rd Division headquarters personnel was established at Wilde's house in Wau, although it would be nearly a month before the headquarters would be in a position to assume command. By then the headquarters would have moved down the valley to Bulolo.

The 3rd Division had been formed in Victoria and had been based in Queensland since 1942. The division normally consisted of the 4th, 10th and 15th Brigades, but the 10th Brigade had been disbanded in September 1942 when eight battalions were amalgamated into four. In early 1943

Photo 5 Brigadier Murray Moten. Painting by Geoffrey Mainwaring. (AWM ART26668)

the 4th Brigade had deployed to Milne Bay and the 15th Brigade to Port Moresby. Only the latter brigade would deploy to Wau.[34]

The 3rd Division commander was Major-General Stan Savige. He was fifty-two years old at the time of his appointment and had given admirable service in World War I, serving in the later stages at Gallipoli with the 24th Battalion AIF, where he was commissioned in the field. He was on the staff of Brigadier-General John Gellibrand's 6th Brigade headquarters on the Western Front and later served with distinction with Dunsterforce in modern day Iran. Post-war, Savige served with the militia forces and helped found Legacy in 1923. Savige was a good friend of Blamey and had given him support in 1936 when Blamey was forced to resign as the Victorian Police Commissioner.[35]

At the start of World War II, Stan Savige had joined the AIF and was given command of the 17th Brigade, which he led during the fighting at Bardia in January 1941. Savige's brigade took heavy casualties during that operation, and his command was criticised by the regular staff

Photo 6 Lieutenant-General Savige (left) with General Blamey (centre), as always, watching his back. Lieutenant-General Berryman is on the right. The photo was taken on Bougainville in March 1945, by which time Savige and Berryman had been promoted. (AWM 090025)

officers within the 6th Division. Savige went to Greece and then to Syria with the 17th Brigade before returning to Australia to take up a recruiting position. Soon after the outbreak of the Pacific War he was put in command of the 3rd Division but, partly as a result of his Bardia experience, he became increasingly suspicious of his Regular Army contemporaries and more defensive of his own performance. This would lead to considerable tension between Savige and his superiors, Lieutenant-General Edmund Herring, the New Guinea Force commander, and Major-General Frank Berryman, Deputy Chief of the General Staff, during the Salamaua campaign. According to Savige, Herring had originally chosen Brigadier George Wootten to command the 3rd Division in New Guinea, but Wootten had been given the 9th Division. Savige was required to pass a medical examination before taking up his command and later wryly observed, 'These incidents did not offer much prospect for happy campaigning in the future.'[36] He also later said that, 'Herring did his best to stop me coming to NG. Thereafter we used to say our enemies were 1) NGF [New Guinea Force] 2) terrain 3) weather 4) supplies 5) Japs.'[37] Savige's view perplexed Herring, who later wrote, 'He seems to have viewed with suspicion everything that emanated from Moresby.'[38]

Savige had arrived in New Guinea on 23 March, reporting to Mackay, who wanted to increase the strength of the Australian force in the Wau–Bulolo area to 6500 men. After a visit to Milne Bay, Savige flew into Wau on 2 April and, within 48 hours, he was on his way forward to the 2/5th Battalion front line at Mubo, 'where a lad loaned me his rifle to do a bit of sniping'. Savige had a special bond with this battalion, which had served under him throughout the Libyan, Greek and Syrian campaigns. Savige called them 'my favourite team'.[39]

The Official Historian said of Savige, 'He is loyal both to his seniors and juniors . . . he receives loyalty in return . . . not a brilliant mind – his staff invariably beat him badly at chequers, he has a gift of leadership, knowledge of men, great tact and much commonsense.'[40] Lieutenant-Colonel William Refshauge later called him 'the best man manager in the Australian army'.[41] Herring later praised Savige's trips to the front line, which 'helped the morale of all the men', and commented that 'the personal contacts with his Brigadiers must have been a real source of encouragement to them'.[42] Damien Parer met Savige later in the campaign and wrote: 'Saw General Savige & had a good yarn with him. He's a soldier and a gentleman.'[43] Stan Savige would require both qualities in spades during the campaign that lay ahead.

On 18 April Mackay had written to Kenney requesting extra transport flights to fly 1300 troops into the Wau area. This would almost double the number of daily flights from nineteen to thirty-six for six days. On 21 April Kenney made twenty-seven aircraft available for the task and, over just three days, fifty-six officers and 1218 other ranks and supplies were flown across the range from Port Moresby to Wau–Bulolo.[44] The units carried were the 3rd Division headquarters and the 24th Battalion, the first unit from the 15th Brigade. At the same time forward air-dropping was resumed, at Guadagasal.

On 23 April Mackay was replaced as the commander of New Guinea Force by the returning Herring. Mackay had known his appointment had only been a temporary one and had earlier told Blamey, 'I am very grateful to have had the opportunity of commanding here, if only for a short period.'[45] On the same day that Mackay left, Savige flew into Bulolo with his 3rd Division headquarters to assume responsibility for all forces in the Wau theatre. Kanga Force (the former designation of those units in the area) ceased to exist, although the tasks for 3rd Division remained similar. Key among them was the continued security of the Wau–Bulolo area and the development of that region as a base for further operations against Salamaua and Lae. At this stage there was still no move to take an offensive role either in front of Salamaua or into the Markham Valley.

On 29 April Savige completed an appreciation of his position and outlined the three roles for his division: (1) deny the enemy the use of the airfields at Wau, Bulolo, Bulwa and Zenag; (2) prevent the enemy from entering the Wau, Bulolo, Partep 2 areas from any direction; and (3) deny the enemy a secure base south of the Markham River in the northern area of the division's operations.[46] To perform these roles, the division was deployed to cover the three approaches to Wau, as Lieutenant-Colonel John Wilton, Savige's chief staff officer, had proposed following an extensive tour of the area.[47] Savige had recommended that unit staffs should walk the terrain over which their units were to fight and, if possible, adjacent sectors. This inspection of the ground was Wilton's first action on arrival, as it was Savige's.[48] Savige had immediately recognised three critical issues that would influence the campaign: understanding the terrain, looking after the troops and improving the lines of supply. He stressed the need to provide dry clothing for the troops and for staging camps to be constructed along the lines of communication. Savige set out the three areas of operations – Mubo, Missim and Markham – and requested that the jeep road to Ballam's be extended to the Summit and, if possible, beyond. In the Bulolo Valley, the jeep road was to be extended from Sunshine down to Partep 2.

Savige had developed an interesting relationship with Moten after Moten had taken over the command of 17th Brigade from Savige in Syria in December 1941. On that occasion Moten had arrived at the brigade headquarters only two or three hours before Savige was due to depart so there was no smooth transition. Most of the staff who had served with Savige's brigade headquarters were subsequently moved on by Moten, and one of the battalion commanders was removed. As Savige later wrote, his arrival at Wau disappointed Moten, who 'had no doubt been led to believe he would command a stronger Kanga Force'.[49] Moten's failure to prevent the earlier Japanese incursion to Wau might well have influenced the decision to bring in Savige despite Herring's later comment that Wau

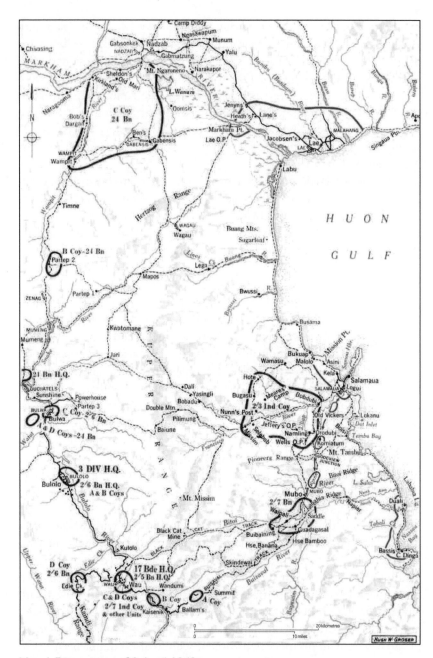

Map 4 Dispositions: 30 April 1943

was 'a very sticky assignment' for Moten 'and one out of which he came extremely well'.[50]

Both men were very different in their command styles; Savige being happiest when mixing with his men whereas Moten was more stand-offish, reflected in his decision to base his headquarters in Wau. Savige wanted Moten to move his headquarters forward and ultimately had to order him to do so. The clarification that 17th Brigade would now be responsible only for the Mubo area made this a sensible move. In short time the two men would develop an excellent working relationship, and Savige's later appreciation of the brigadier reflected his honest opinion that 'Moten was excellent'.[51]

The operations of the 3rd Division at Salamaua would be affected throughout the campaign by what would today be referred to as 'the elephant in the room', in this case the planned operation against Lae, Operation Postern. The combined amphibious–air operation to capture Lae would bypass Salamaua and thus consign that campaign to the status of a diversionary one. There can be few examples in military history of a campaign that went on as long as the Salamaua campaign where the overriding objective was not to be victorious but only to hold the main enemy forces in place. How was it possible to engender enthusiasm within the lower commands for such an operation? One way was not to tell them that the operation was a feint, and the best way to do that was to keep the commander in the dark. Savige was apparently unaware that the Salamaua campaign was just a feint until at least 15 June 1943, two months after he took command.

However, Savige would have known that some form of operation against Lae was planned, if only from his own subordinates. In January Blamey had told Moten of the Lae plan, before Moten had gone to Wau.[52] This is not surprising as General Herring, New Guinea Force commander at that time, had already drawn up plans to capture Lae in late 1942. He later told David Dexter that 'even previous Oct/Nov [1942] we had plans to push on quickly to Lae and even had ships with gear to go forward'.[53] It had been hoped that after the Japanese forces had been driven back from Kokoda to the Papuan beachheads, those positions would quickly fall and an advance on Salamaua and Lae could commence immediately.[54]

That had not been the case so the order to capture Lae was not issued until mid-May. On 6 May MacArthur's headquarters issued a plan covering a series of operations to be conducted in the South Pacific and

South-West Pacific areas that were intended to advance Allied air bases towards Rabaul. Once airfields were available in the Markham Valley and Huon Peninsula areas, air support could be provided for operations against western New Britain. On 16 May Herring and Blamey met in Brisbane to plan the capture of Lae and the Markham Valley with follow-up operations to capture Finschhafen and Madang. On the following day an order was issued from Brisbane headquarters for the capture of Lae: Operation Postern, scheduled for early August.[55]

Planning for Postern was obviously progressing by the start of June. After a meeting on 3 June with MacArthur's naval commander, Vice-Admiral Arthur Carpender, Berryman observed, 'On leaving, the Admiral asked me to tell Gen Herring he would do his very best to help Postern op.' After a meeting with Blamey on 8 June, Berryman also stated that if the aircraft could be secured, Nadzab should be seized as soon as possible. He wrote, 'If air situation permits we think we should get Eather's bde [25th Brigade] & a parachute Bn to take out N [Nadzab] & build up airfield & strength before bringing Wootten [9th Division] into action.' Indeed the astute Blamey had sent George Vasey to investigate the area as far back as October 1942.[56] Nadzab was an obvious target, undefended and of immense value, not only for the Lae operation but also for extending the range of Allied air power.

Savige stated that it was not until 20 May, when Herring visited, that his 3rd Division headquarters heard of the planned Postern operation. Herring confirms this, later observing, 'General Savige knew of plan when I visited him in May, well before Berryman went forward. I told him of Lae and Nadzab plans.' However, although Savige knew that a separate operation to take Lae was now planned, he was apparently not at this stage aware that Blamey's plan was to leave Salamaua untaken until Postern was launched. When David Dexter as official historian asked Savige whether Herring had told him at the summit conference on 15 June that Salamaua was not to fall until the Lae show started, Savige answered 'yes', so he might have known at that stage. On this point Herring disagreed with Savige, and he told Dexter as much, saying, 'My impression is that Savige did not know of it until Berryman's visit in August.' Adding to the confusion, Savige also wrote in his comments on the official history that he sent New Guinea Force headquarters a plan for the capture of Salamaua in mid-July and that he didn't know of the feint plan until 19 August, when Berryman told him. Up to that point Savige considered that Salamaua was 'always regarded as our ultimate goal'. The spiteful relationship between Herring and Savige made for poor communication both during and after the war and, although Savige was officially kept in the dark until at least 15 June, the role of the Salamaua campaign as a feint to cover the Lae operation had been decided earlier.[57]

The first mention of the role of Salamaua in masking plans for the capture of Lae came during the meeting Moten had with Blamey in Port Moresby before being sent to Wau in January 1943. Moten was shown some of the plans being drawn up by Major-General George Vasey for the Lae operation, which at that stage, before the battle for Wau, was projected to take place in June or July 1943. Apart from the role of defending the Bulolo Valley, Moten's Kanga Force was given the task of threatening Salamaua in order to draw Japanese forces from Lae. Herring later acknowledged that it was probably Blamey's idea, telling Dexter, 'I saw Blamey fishing at Mallacoota Inlet and the matter was then decided as well as to push on with Lae and Nadzab ideas.' This was in early February 1943 after Herring had left New Guinea.[58]

Further mention of Salamaua was made in an operation instruction issued by Berryman to Mackay on 19 February. The instruction stated: 'By actively threatening the approaches to Salamaua we should be able to conceal our intentions in regard to Lae.'[59] The operational orders for Savige's 3rd Division were set out in a meeting in Port Moresby on 25 May when the astute Wilton requested a definite objective that would clarify the ambiguous order to 'threaten Salamaua'. Perhaps perceiving that the 3rd Division role was a diversionary one, Wilton and Savige had already drawn up a suggested mission statement, that being 'to destroy the enemy forces in the Mubo area and ultimately to drive the enemy north of the Francisco River'. Salamaua town and airfield were north of the river.[60]

Although plans did not include direct land operations against the town of Salamaua, air operations were unrestricted.

Following the Bismarck Sea battle the 5th USAAF had maintained the pressure on the Japanese bases at Lae and Salamaua. RAAF No. 22 Squadron's A-20 Boston bombers, using the same tactics that had proved successful over the Bismarck Sea, carried out low-level attacks along the coastline. During March the Bostons flew seventy-two sorties over Salamaua, six of them on 18 March. On this day Flight Lieutenant Bill Newton was the pilot of Boston A28-3 with Flight Sergeant John Lyon as his navigator and Sergeant Basil Eastwood the rear gunner. During

Photo 7 Depiction of the action over Salamaua in which Flight Lieutenant Bill Newton was shot down. Painting by Roy Hodgkinson. (AWM ART21716)

a similar attack two days earlier Newton had suffered four hits from anti-aircraft fire but, despite damage to wings, engine and fuel tank, he had managed to return to the squadron's Ward's Drome base at Port Moresby.[61] However, on this morning he had not been so fortunate.

Two 2/3rd Independent Company observers, Bill Murray and Allan Oehlman, watched from a lookout west of Salamaua as a gaggle of A-20 Boston bombers crossed the Kuper Range behind them, then flew low over Missim heading for the coast. 'They passed over us very low, flattening the kunai grass as they passed over our ridge; they were RAAF and they were so low that we had a clear view of the pilots and gunners.' The Bostons hugged the trees as they powered down over the ridges to the coast at Salamaua, dropped their bombs on the airfield, then turned to strafe the adjacent buildings. Murray then watched one plane go down into the sea beyond the drome as it was hit by anti-aircraft fire from Salamaua.[62]

After bombing a building adjacent to an anti-aircraft battery, Newton had been hit and, as Murray had observed, he was forced to ditch his burning plane into the ocean off the Salamaua isthmus.[63] Other crew members circled their planes for around 30 minutes and watched as two of the crew members swam to the shore from the ditched aircraft. The two survivors were Newton and Lyon, Eastwood having been killed in the action. Both men were captured that day, then taken to Lae, where the Japanese captors said of Newton that 'he is a person of importance, possessing considerable rank and ability'. Newton and Lyon told their Japanese captors that a cannon shell had hit their fuel tank and the plane had crashed in flames. They told their interrogators that they were only attacking the store buildings, not Japanese personnel, and stressed that 'we are fighting to preserve the Australian mainland'. Newton's fate was not uncommon for captured Allied airmen. He was returned to Salamaua and beheaded by the callous Japanese on 29 March, his body recovered from a bomb crater at Kela Point after the fall of Salamaua. John Lyon suffered a similarly despicable fate when he was bayoneted adjacent to the Lae airfield.[64]

Bill Newton had been flying his 52nd operational mission when his plane was shot down. About 90 per cent of those missions had taken place under enemy anti-aircraft fire. For his outstanding devotion to duty, he was awarded his country's highest military honour, the Victoria Cross. It would be the only such award made during the entire Salamaua campaign.

CHAPTER 3

WARFE'S TIGERS

Despite Moten's major role at this stage being to protect Wau, a message relayed from New Guinea Force headquarters on 2 March contained a general instruction from Blamey to Mackay for more pressure to be applied to the Japanese positions in front of Salamaua. The message stated: 'I would be glad if you would give consideration to the question of inflicting a severe blow on the enemy in the Salamaua area with a view to seizing the opportunity should it present itself, since it may have far reaching results if successful.'[1]

A General Staff minute issued on 16 March reinforced Blamey's view: 'The C in C [Blamey] would undoubtedly like to see an advance towards Salamaua, and I believe that with caution, Moton [sic] may achieve something in accordance with the C in C's wish.'[2] Given that Moten's Kanga Force was the only Allied ground force in contact with the enemy in the entire South-West Pacific Area at that time, it is not surprising that higher commanders wanted to see some show of superiority over the Japanese. However, this directive would push the Australian army into the tangled web of terrain that guarded Salamaua. Although some limited attacks would be made in the Mubo area, Moten's 'severe blow' would come from another direction. He had decided to use Major George Warfe's 2/3rd Independent Company to make a wide flanking move into the west flank of the Japanese forces in front of Salamaua.

Warfe had originally served with the 2/6th Battalion in the Middle East and had then transferred to the independent companies, taking over command of the 2/3rd on 27 September 1942. Having flown into Wau

Photo 8 Major George Warfe. Warfe later noted how 'a small operation on my knee kept me fuming under a kunai hut while Ivor Hele drew my portrait'. (AWM ART22499)

on 31 January, at the height of the Japanese attack, Warfe's men found themselves on a steep learning curve in fighting the Japanese. But by the time Warfe had led his men across the Jap Track, on the heels of the Japanese units retreating from Wau, they had become very astute jungle fighters. Warfe was a man who attracted respect, from privates to generals. Lieutenant-Colonel George Smith had served in a platoon commanded by Warfe in the Middle East. Warfe, he wrote, 'would make your blood go cold at his superlative courage and cool savagery . . . gamest man I know of.' Captain Bob Hancock, who served as Warfe's second in command during the campaign, wrote: 'The CO is very good to work for – he leaves one full discretion – though it means a lot of work for a start.' Sandy Matheson echoed the thoughts of many in the ranks, referring to Warfe as 'a champion bloody soldier'.[3]

However, opinions of Warfe from his two immediate commanders were only grudgingly complimentary. Moten, who commanded Warfe at

Wau and in the early stages of the Salamaua campaign, described him as 'a very capable and inspiring leader whose great weakness was a complete disregard for the truth... [D]espite all this, one could not help liking the blighter.' Brigadier Heathcote 'Tack' Hammer, who would command Warfe for most the Salamaua campaign, added that he was 'inclined to exaggerate and treat things with a wave of the hand'. That said, Hammer had enough regard for Warfe to promote him to command one his front line battalions later in the campaign. Major-General Savige had no doubts about the man, noting, 'Warfe was ready and willing to fight the whole Jap force in those days. He was magnificent.'[4]

At the beginning of March the 2/3rd Independent Company was still engaged out along the Black Cat Track towards Waipali, sweeping out the remnants of the Japanese 102nd Regiment following the abortive attack on Wau. On 4 March Warfe received orders to move his company to Bulwa in the Bulolo Valley. Peter Pinney, who wrote a secret diary of his experiences with the 2/3rd Independent Company, was keener to keep going towards Mubo and Salamaua. 'For chrissakes', he wrote, 'we slogged our way up that rotten trail to get as far as this: we've paid our entrance fee, we're all here armed and provisioned and in pretty good nick, what the hell's the point of going back?'[5]

But back they went, and on 6 March two reconnaissance parties left Bulwa to reconnoitre a native track across to Pilimung and on to Missim.[6] Corporal Ken McLean, who had spent time in New Guinea before the war, led one seven-man patrol and travelled across and back in six days. On the map, the distance from Bulwa across to Missim was not a problem, but the terrain was another issue as the rarely used track crossed the formidable Kuper Range, which included the daunting Double Mountain. Of all the difficult tracks Warfe's men had faced, this one was the darkest nightmare.

Led by Warfe, A and C Platoons departed Bulwa for Missim on 9 March, following the track blazed by McLean's patrol. Every man who made the Double Mountain crossing never forgot it. Keith Myers thought, 'It was seven or eight false crests on Double Mountain, mud up to your knees, all the troops walking over it.'[7] Norm Bear said, 'Double Mountain was high up and there were two peaks. There was no jungle as it was too high. It was a rare atmosphere and cold. The depth of the humus was up to your knees in places. I can't believe how the original recon made a track, just with compass and instinct.'[8] Bill Murray later wrote, 'The climb to the top of Double Mountain seemed never ending with false crests every so often – we would think at last we're at the top, but then another steep climb would appear ahead . . . the top of the mountain was in almost continuous cloud and everything was very dark and gloomy.'[9] Brian Walpole observed, 'You had to use both hands to get up there and I can remember you would get up and then you slide back ten or twelve feet and . . . you'd almost feel like crying . . . Later I went up to Borneo . . . it was a piece of cake.'[10] Later that month a party of United States army personnel sent forward to Missim to observe the 2/3rd operations were 'compelled to give up owing to sheer physical exhaustion'.[11]

By 14 March two platoons had been established at Missim while B Platoon remained at Powerhouse outside Bulwa. Peter Pinney: 'Missim consists of some fifteen huts, eight of them taken over by the Company; indifferently made, leaky, but shelter . . . we're defended by three Vickers with 3000 rounds each, and the tracks are patrolled.'[12] Although Warfe now had two platoons at Missim, he had major supply problems as the tenuous track across Double Mountain broke down under heavy rains. The carriers arrived at Pilimung exhausted. Although air-dropping was tried at Pilimung on 23 and 24 March, it could deliver only a fraction of requirements.

The immediate task for Warfe's company was to establish a firm base at Missim and to set up an observation post overlooking Salamaua from the west. By 16 March Warfe had established a standing patrol at Bobadu and Bugasu and an observation post adjacent to Missim that overlooked Salamaua and the intervening Bobdubi Ridge from the west. On 18 March Warfe was ordered to prepare an ambush along Vial's Track to interdict any Japanese troops moving back from Observation Hill at Mubo, and Lieutenant Stan Jeffery's section was allocated the task. The original intention was for Warfe's company to operate against the main Japanese supply line between Lae and Salamaua, but this strategy had been changed given that the major tracks in the area were under enemy observation and the major villages were under enemy influence.[13]

Warfe returned to Powerhouse in the Bulolo Valley on 21 March for discussions about his company's role. With the addition of forty-six reinforcements on 24 March, the company was at near full strength, but due to the supply problem, it was decided that only one platoon was to remain at Missim, with only one section forward. Two sections of C Platoon returned to Powerhouse, with one section remaining at Bobadu.[14]

On 30 March Lieutenant Jeffery established an observation post eight kilometres east of Missim, overlooking the Komiatum Track. Meanwhile, on the morning of 31 March, an eleven-man patrol under Second

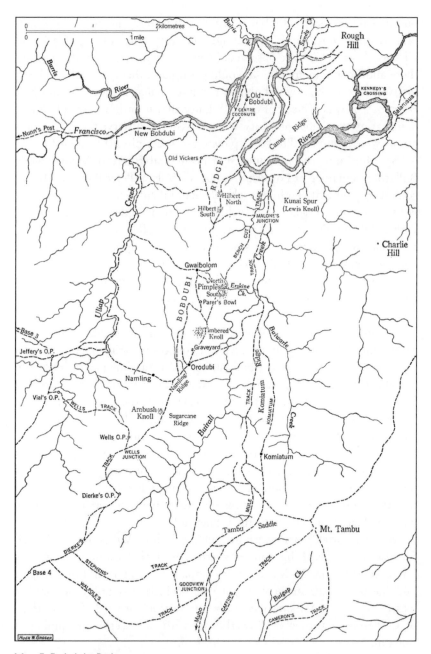

Map 5 Bobdubi Ridge area

Lieutenant Yamamoto had left Salamaua heading west. After spending the night on the northern bank of the Francisco River, six men under Yamamoto headed west towards Missim and by mid-morning had discovered Jeffery's observation post. Yamamoto's men cut the signal line back to Missim, then made a surprise attack from the rear. Although Yamamoto was killed during the attack, the Australians were forced to pull back, carrying one wounded man. The Japanese patrol left the post untouched and returned to Salamaua, arriving on the evening of 3 April. No doubt alarmed at the presence of Australian troops in this area, Japanese troops occupied the northern end of Bobdubi Ridge on 10 April.[15]

On 12 April Warfe's men had cut a track on to Bobdubi Ridge and were in a position to head in either direction along the top. Warfe indicated to Moten that he wanted to 'bash Bobdubi', but he was reminded that his primary objective was to link up with 2/5th Battalion patrols at the southern end of Bobdubi Ridge. Warfe was told that he could not attack Bobdubi but could attack enemy forces around Komiatum, but only when he had linked up with the 2/5th Battalion patrols.[16]

The track along Komiatum Ridge was a vital supply line for the Japanese forces at Mubo. With steep slopes on either side, the ridge was covered by kunai grass at the lower end, with no trees for cover. This meant that the track along the top of the ridge was easily observed from the air and from the adjacent heights of Bobdubi Ridge. Food and ammunition was sent to Mubo on the backs of Japanese troops and, to avoid aerial attacks during the day, ascents and descents of the ridge were carried out at dawn or dusk. The Japanese Eighteenth Army Chief of Staff, Major-General Kane Yoshihara, later wrote of the importance of the feature: 'As the loss of the strategic Komiatum Hill would as a result mean the loss of Salamaua, even though ten thousand difficulties should be encountered, it must be held come what might.'[17]

Warfe allocated Lieutenant Ken Stephens' 8 Section to make the first attack on Komiatum Ridge. On 14 April the unit left Vial's Junction on Bobdubi Ridge and descended through difficult country down the ridge, losing its bearings and ending up reaching the local village of Namling, on the same side of the valley as the patrol had started from. Stephens' section then returned to Vial's Junction chastened by the difficulties of navigating through the intricate terrain. The war diary noted, 'Disappointment was shown on our lads' faces after days of hard work cutting tracks through most difficult country to find no slaughter at the end of it.'[18]

Lieutenant John Winterflood's section was the next to try reaching Komiatum Ridge, guided across the Buirali Creek valley by three Namling locals, but unable to find a way up the other side. Lieutenant Stephens' section was now given a second go at it and, led by the local guide Salamon, this time got up on to Komiatum Ridge by blazing a track above the headwaters of the Buirali Creek valley that came to be known as Stephens' Track. Under instructions to attack and destroy all enemy parties using the track and then to move to Komiatum village, Stephens' section lay in ambush on the nights of 20 and 21 April. No enemy troops appeared on the first night, and on the second night a small party was allowed to pass through in anticipation of bigger fish to fry. Stephens' instincts were proved correct when, at 2047, a larger party approached from the direction of Salamaua. The forty men who were visible were spread over a hundred metres of the track, and more followed behind when the ambush was sprung.[19]

The twelve Australian commandos were lined up along one side of the track, and Ray Lennox opened fire with his Bren gun on the leading man at point-blank range. He later noted, 'My mates opened up immediately and the target melted in front of us.' Lennox rapidly fired off two thirty-round magazines while the other men chimed in with 400 rounds from their tommy guns and sixteen grenades. About twenty enemy naval troops were felled in the 15-second ambush with only an odd pistol shot being fired back by the shocked Japanese party. As Lennox observed, 'Their white uniforms made them better targets.' Having mounted the first major challenge to Japanese control of the Komiatum Track, and having suffered no casualties, the Australians withdrew down Stephens' Track and reached Wells OP at 0200 the next morning.[20]

Stephens' section had ambushed an enemy food transport unit in a thinly timbered area 500 metres south of the Komiatum food supply relay post. The Japanese report noted that the Australians were supposedly driven off by covering units and forty men from the supply point, with only one of the Japanese soldiers being killed and another wounded. Given the nature of the ambush, the losses were surely closer to the Australian claim of twenty Japanese killed. An officer and nine men were despatched from Captain Yoshio Arai's 3rd Machine-Gun Company in Salamaua to link up with twenty-four men from Lieutenant Toshio Gunji's 10 Company to find the route that the Australian patrol had used to reach Komiatum Ridge.[21]

On 28 April Lieutenant Alan Crawford's 5 Section moved along Stephens' Track to carry out a second ambush on the Komiatum Track.

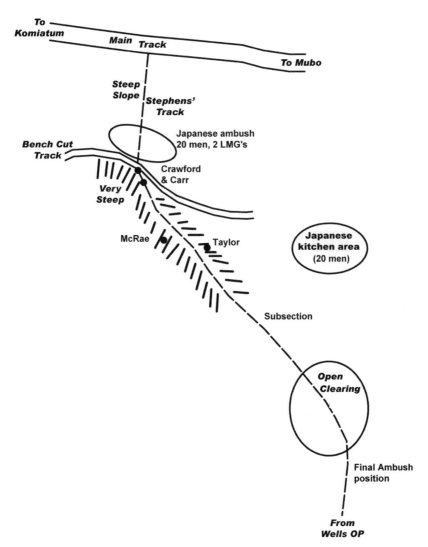

Map 6 Goodview Junction, 27 April 1943

Warfe's idea was simple: 'Crawford to move south along Stephens' Track and repeat Stephens' tea party in same area.' What Crawford did not know was that the Japanese had found Stephens' Track and, by 27 April, had deployed nineteen of Arai's machine-gunners and seventeen men from 5 Company to protect the Komiatum Track.[22]

Crawford moved his men to within 200 metres of the Bench Cut Track junction where there was a small clearing. Here he left four men under Corporal Bart Lamb on the western side of the clearing to act as a withdrawal ambush. As the four men from the second ambush party moved up, their leading scout, Fred Taylor, spotted a booby trap wire, yelled out, then dived over the side of the ridge as two enemy machine-gun positions opened fire. Behind him Joe Taylor was killed, and further back Corporal Keith McRae was shot in the leg as he jumped down the side of the cliff on the left. Crawford crawled along the track and went down the steep slope to find McRae around three metres below. McRae's shin had been shattered, and Crawford applied a field dressing. Above them six men from the Japanese party moved along the track.[23]

Hearing the gunfire, Corporal Lamb now decided to move his three men forward. He soon saw the six Japanese soldiers who had moved down the track. They were inspecting Joe Taylor's body when Lamb opened fire with his tommy gun, killing four of them. The other two went over the side of the track, not far from Crawford and McRae, and headed back to the machine-gun position. Crawford let them go, unwilling to betray his position. Up on the track Lamb's party, now joined by Sergeant John Carr, was threatened on the flank by around twenty Japanese troops at a kitchen area and withdrew further back down Stephens' Track.[24] Lamb's foray was later confirmed by Japanese accounts, which also noted that four men had been killed and four others wounded: 'As the enemy retreated, our men advanced carelessly without mopping up and received fierce fire and sustained casualties.'[25]

Meanwhile, Crawford made McRae comfortable behind a log and left him a tommy gun and rations as he went to get help. Crawford headed back but was apparently unable to get back up to the main track due to the cliff-like terrain. He then heard sustained fire and, thinking that Lamb's party was giving covering fire, apparently headed back to McRae's position, but McRae was no longer there. Crawford then returned by a roundabout route to Wells OP, arriving at 1700 and meeting up with the rest of his men. Lamb told him that the gunfire had not come from his party, but they had also heard it. It was from a tommy gun followed by an enemy light machine-gun, and they figured that it must have been from McRae. The assumption was that McRae had crawled forward and opened fire on the Japanese before the return fire killed him.[26]

Back at Wells OP, Crawford contacted Warfe by wireless to report on the action. Warfe did not agree that McRae must have been killed, and he immediately sent a reluctant Crawford back to confirm McRae's death, telling him to 'bring him out dead or alive'. Days later, as Crawford's patrol moved through the jungle, a familiar voice was heard to say, 'Don't take life so seriously. There are no Japs around for miles.' It was McRae, using his hands and backside to move along the track dragging his splinted leg behind him. It was 1800 on 1 May, some 80 hours since he had been left behind. Following the Australian incursions the Japanese supply schedule to Mubo was cut in half to once per week, both convoys being amalgamated.[27]

Meanwhile, on 23 April, Kanga Force was dissolved and all units in the Wau theatre, including the 2/3rd Independent Company, came under the direct command of Savige's 3rd Division. The previous day the first units of the 24th Battalion had flown into Bulolo to replace the 2/5th Independent Company and the 2/6th Battalion units that had been deployed at the Markham River end of the Bulolo Valley. For the 2/5th Independent Company it meant the end of 11 months in the area, an extraordinary deployment. With the help of the local New Guinea Volunteer Rifle unit this company had defended the approaches to Wau for eight months and also carried out raids at Lae and Salamaua. The men had well and truly done their bit.

The 24th Battalion, a militia unit, was one part of the former Kooyong Regiment from Melbourne and had been under the command of Lieutenant-Colonel Alexander Falconer since October 1940. It was the first battalion from 15th Brigade to be deployed, and by the end of April Captain George Chandler's C Company had taken over positions along the south bank of the Markham River, directly west of Lae. Captain Robert Cameron's B Company was positioned further back at Partep while A Company and D Company remained in reserve at Hidden Valley. Savige considered Falconer 'an able young man but rather temperamental and difficult' and had had discussions with him in Port Moresby about his demeanour. Falconer's demise finally came after Savige had watched the 24th Battalion strung out along the road from Wau to Bulolo, struggling under the weight of kit they were required to carry. Despite Savige then telling Falconer to adapt to local conditions, the troops were again overburdened the next day as they moved to Sunshine.[28] On 5 May Savige had Falconer replaced by the former 2/6th Battalion officer, Major George Smith, known among his fellow officers by his cartoon-inspired moniker 'Larry the Bat'.

Savige had clearly recognised that officers experienced in the punishing New Guinea conditions were required for battalion command. Smith was also left in no doubt regarding Savige's expectations, telling him, 'If you waste one man's life unnecessarily, I'll snarler you a bloody sight quicker than you can get back to your battalion.' Smith immediately adopted a harsh regime, visiting his widely scattered units across the most difficult country in New Guinea. The problems associated with operating in the area were well illustrated when, less than a month later, twenty-three men based down in the Wampit area were diagnosed with dengue fever.[29]

The 24th Battalion had a difficult role in the Salamaua campaign, patrolling the vast area south of the Markham River and west of Markham Point, the most malarial country in the theatre. Savige would give Smith 'the rounds of the kitchen' each week regarding the wastage of his strength by malaria. The berated Smith proceeded to make one of the most valuable contributions to the campaign, evolving a disciplined procedure to control malaria among his men. This involved persuading the soldier that he had a key role to play alongside the medical people in beating the malarial curse. Malaria cases subsequently declined to a fraction of their former numbers.[30]

Smith's greater problem was adapting to the differences in fighting in New Guinea compared to his experiences in the Middle East. He later noted that in the Middle East, 'there was always the sense of some-one close at hand if things got out of control... the mass comfort of a brigade fighting together... rather than the isolated small shows in New Guinea'.[31] With his battalion more widespread than any other unit in the theatre his comments were not surprising.

―――――――

By 22 April the Japanese position began to improve as long-delayed rein-forcements arrived at Lae. Astonishingly, within two months of the loss of the Lae convoy, the 115th Regiment had been resurrected. However, it had only two of the original three battalions, the II/115th and III/115th. Major Shimizu's II/115th Battalion consisted of Nos 1, 3, 7 and 8 Compa-nies plus the 2nd Machine Gun Company and the II/115th Gun Platoon. Major Tokuzo Nishikawa's III/115th Battalion consisted of Nos 9, 10 and 12 Companies plus the 3rd MG Company and the III/115th Gun Platoon. Regimental troops comprised the headquarters together with a signalling company and an infantry gun company.[32]

Two companies from the III/115th Regiment plus an artillery piece, a signals unit and engineer unit with three collapsible boats under Nishikawa were sent to hold Markham Point on the south bank of the Markham River. This was a very astute deployment by Nakano as the position would force Savige to keep the 24th Battalion occupied in flank protection throughout the campaign. The remainder of the 115th Regiment and the III/21st Battalion, two machine cannon companies, an anti-aircraft company and part of the 14th Field Artillery Regiment were kept at Lae as a reserve.[33]

Bobdubi Ridge rose like a fortress wall protecting the western flank of the Japanese position at Salamaua. The northern end of the ridge was surrounded on three sides by the bend of the Francisco River, which, unable to penetrate the massive bulwark, had diverted around it. The ridge was named after a small collection of huts near the northern end, a now-abandoned village known as Old Bobdubi. The villagers had since moved down to the river flats west of the ridge and established New Bobdubi village. Since the advent of fighting at Salamaua, both villages had been abandoned, but the north end of the ridge had been occupied by the Japanese since 10 April.

On 1 May Warfe sent a document titled 'Plans for Future Operations' to Savige. Warfe advocated operations against the Komiatum–Mubo line of communication from a base at Namling, operations against the Salamaua–Komiatum line of communication from a Bobdubi base and operations against the Lae–Salamaua line of communication and against Salamaua itself from a base at Kela Hill. Warfe considered that the recommended operations would not only neutralise the Japanese resistance at Mubo but also compel the enemy to withdraw his forces across the Salamaua isthmus to the peninsula. In order to carry out his proposals Warfe requested two infantry companies to secure his own lines of communication as well as the Missim and Hote areas. He also requested four 3-inch mortar detachments and air support, which would be directed by his men. Warfe stressed the need to bring a speedy conclusion to such operations as the ravages of malaria, typhus and dysentery would rapidly erode his unit strength.[34]

Savige did not support the extensive operations that Warfe had proposed, but he did sanction Warfe's action against the northern end of Bobdubi Ridge in order to take some of the pressure off Mubo, where the Japanese defenders were holding firm at Green Hill. However, Savige would allow Warfe to deploy only a single platoon for the operation.[35]

On 27 April, in preparation for a planned attack on Bobdubi Ridge, Peter Pinney led a three-man patrol to observe and map the Japanese positions around Old Bobdubi village. From his position on the west side of the bridge he had watched a five-man patrol from Gunji's 10 Company approach.[36] One man set up his light machine-gun in the open and lay down behind it while another knelt beside him, giving directions and looking in Pinney's direction before rising and turning his back. Pinney 'aimed square at the middle of his broad back and squeezed the trigger. He pitched on his face, and the game was on . . . the LMG gunner hesitated then of all things began getting up to take his gun behind cover. He didn't make it, I shot him.'[37]

Pinney and the other two men scooted back up the track and reported to Warfe at Missim the next day. Pinney noted, 'We were white-haired boys. Our maps were the first authoritative, dinky-die on the spot information they had had.' Two days later Pinney led Captain Wally Meares' C Platoon across the river flats to Meares' Creek, in the shadow of Bobdubi Ridge. From here Pinney continued his reconnaisance work up on to Bobdubi Ridge. On 2 May he wrote: 'Later Sells and I were sent out to recce a Vickers position which would dominate the Japs dug in at the Coconuts, up on Bobdubi Ridge. We located three positions, the most desirable 900 yards from target, out on a kunai spur: nicely out of range there, a Vickers could rake their position and cause them general hell. We slept in the village up there, which is called Buggert.'[38]

Meares' platoon would be used for the attack on Bobdubi Ridge, suitably reinforced with ancillary personnel, including the transport section with the Vickers machine-guns. Lieutenant Ken Stephens' 8 Section would move north down the Bench Cut Track from Namling, along the eastern side of Bobdubi Ridge, to cut off any Japanese retreat from the ridge top and also to stop any enemy reinforcements coming up from Salamaua. Warfe told him to follow the Bench Cut Track along the side of the ridge and 'Stephens did exactly as ordered'.[39] Lieutenant John Lillie's 9 Section would move across the northern end of the ridge as part of an encircling move in concert with Stephens' section. It was designed to sow panic among the Japanese defenders on the ridge so that, when Meares sent Corporal Andrew 'Bonnie' Muir's 7 Section against the position, the defence would break.

Meares' men gathered on the flats below Bobdubi Ridge on the early morning of 3 May, and Peter Pinney pointed out the locations that he had chosen for the Vickers machine-guns. The men then moved off through Buggert to Bobdubi Spur in the late afternoon. As they moved up, they could watch the Japanese digging in astride the main Missim to Salamaua track in the Centre Coconuts area at the northern end of Bobdubi Ridge.[40]

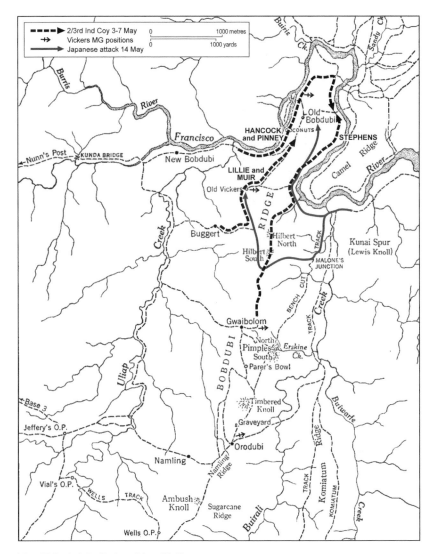

Map 7 Bobdubi Ridge, May 1943

Three main Japanese positions were set up along the northern end of Bobdubi Ridge, each centred on a clump of coconut trees, named South, Centre and North Coconuts. Enemy fire from this area stopped Lillie's 9 Section, which then acted as a holding party while both Stephens' and Muir's sections manoeuvred around the Japanese position. Warfe's encircling plan worked, and the Japanese withdrew to Centre Coconuts.

Photo 9 The northern end of Bobdubi Ridge from across the Francisco River to the west. (Phillip Bradley)

Peter Pinney and George Tropman, who had taken part in the earlier recce, moved up to within 40 metres of the Japanese positions. Then, as dusk fell, Pinney guided Muir's 9 Section up to the first palms area of the Coconuts position, also known as South Coconuts. He noted, 'I stripped off all surplus gear and snuck up to the knoll in almost-darkness. The Nips seemed to know something was going on and opened fire, but they were firing in the wrong direction.'[41] The Australians set up a Bren gun at South Coconuts and waited out the night, standing guard in pairs.

On 4 May Bonnie Muir's 7 Section established a Vickers gun position on a high point of the ridge to the south of South Coconuts, which overlooked the northern end of Bobdubi Ridge. This dominating feature would later become known as the Old Vickers position. The ridge rose sharply in almost a horseshoe shape up to the Vickers position, which, after clearing, had excellent direct fire and observation of the whole of Coconut Ridge except part of South Coconuts clump.[42] The Australian force had taken no casualties and was now in a position to bring machine-gun fire on to the Komiatum Track, the sole Japanese supply route between Salamaua and Mubo.

Lieutenant Lillie decided to open fire on the Japanese positions at Centre Coconuts, and this drew out the location of their light machine-gun positions for the Vickers gun up on Old Vickers. Although he had pulled back from South Coconuts, Peter Pinney was caught in the midst of the firing. 'The Vickers opened up with long strong bursts with ricochets and general hell flying everywhere, and it seemed to be right next to us and we hugged that dirt. The Nips were throwing everything everywhere: heavy and light machine-guns with explosive bullets, .266's and light mortars, grenade launchers.' Under cover of the Vickers fire, Lillie's section pushed forward to attack Centre Coconuts but was fired on from South Coconuts, which the Japanese had boldly reoccupied.[43]

George Head and Ossie 'Tassie' McDiarmid were the forward scouts for Lillie, but as they went forward they walked into light machine-gun fire. Peter Pinney watched them go. 'George Head and Tassie crept off to have a looksee, moving very carefully and slowly . . . and after a few minutes there was a long burst of Jap fire. George came back alone. Tassie was dead . . . we discreetly withdrew.'[44]

As Savige had envisaged, the Japanese had to deploy forces from Mubo to meet the threat to Bobdubi Ridge; sixty soldiers were observed moving north along the Komiatum Track at midday on 5 May. They were engaged by Lieutenant Jock Erskine's engineer section with a Vickers gun and took around twelve casualties. Erskine had followed Stephens' section across the ridge and along the Bench Cut Track with orders to harass the Japanese moving along the Komiatum Track either by ambush or with the Vickers gun. After the ambush he moved his section up to the Graveyard area, the higher position affording better track coverage.[45]

Warfe now received a message from 3rd Division headquarters requesting action against another large group of Japanese troops expected along the Komiatum Track to Mubo. With all three sections of Meares' platoon occupied, Warfe grabbed the medical officer, Fred Street, some riflemen and a Vickers gun, and went up to the Bench Cut Track below Gwaibolom. From here he could see around 250 metres of the Komiatum Track, and the Vickers could readily handle the 800-metre range. As he set up the gun, he saw about fifty enemy troops, probably those already shot up by Erskine one and a half hours earlier, heading up the track towards Komiatum and Mubo. After using a range-finder to get the distance, Warfe ordered a 250-round belt to be fired. About fifteen enemy troops were killed, and the rest were totally confused as to where the fire was coming from, firing wildly at a suspected ambush. At 1430 that afternoon another eighty troops were engaged as they moved south along the Komiatum Track.[46]

On 6 May Peter Pinney led Captain Hancock around the northern end of Bobdubi Ridge. Pinney wrote: 'Hancock and I set off to find a way around to the other side. There was a bit of a pad, rough and a bit dicey in

Photo 10 View east from Bobdubi Ridge across the Buirali Creek valley looking
down on to the track along Komiatum Ridge. The far ridge is Davidson Ridge.
(Phillip Bradley)

parts, squeezing along the bank; no scrub bashing. We found the supply
trail which feeds Bobdubi, too. Nice piece of information: a sneaky route
for an ambushing patrol.'[47] Having found Lieutenant Stephens' section,
Hancock repositioned it to cover the likely route of any Japanese approach
more effectively. In a letter home Hancock noted, 'We managed to get
troops at either side of them on the ridge itself and both sides of the ridge
on the flat thus completely surrounding them. I actually did the first grand
tour right around their position.'[48] Peter Pinney had again demonstrated
his exceptional reconnaissance skills, and Warfe commended him: 'During
this time the recce work by Private Pinney was outstanding.' Keith Myers
put it another way: 'Pinney moved like a ghost.'[49]

Meanwhile, at 0800 on 7 May, after a mortar bombardment, Bonnie Muir led his section on to Centre Coconuts only to find the enemy
troops gone. However, an hour later they came back and made three
counter-attacks, but each was repulsed. When a fourth attack with mortar
support succeeded, Muir once again withdrew his battered section. Brian
Walpole was there: 'I came face to face with this bloody Jap. We were both

surprised. I pointed, he pointed, he was quicker than I am, went to fire, the bloody thing jammed and he started to run away. So, well, that's not so bad, so I pulled out the Colt and shot him.'[50]

Having also discovered the 'sneaky route' up on to the ridge, at 1745 that afternoon Hancock led Lieutenant Gordon Leviston's section up to take control of North Coconuts. This put further pressure on the last enemy foothold at Centre Coconuts, now surrounded on four sides, by Leviston, Lillie, Muir and Stephens. The defenders at the Coconuts were from a 10 Company platoon of Major Tsunendo Takamura's re-formed III/102nd Battalion, commanded by Lieutenant Gunji. With just seventeen men under his command, Gunji estimated that he was being attacked by a hundred enemy troops.[51]

The big blow for the besieged Japanese came in the early dawn of the following day, 8 May, when Stephens' 8 Section, having been repositioned to a more effective location, ambushed a party of sixty Japanese soldiers moving up to Bobdubi Ridge.[52] As they had done earlier on the Komiatum Track, Stephens' men executed a perfect ambush, leaving twenty enemy dead and the rest fleeing back to Salamaua.

Denied reinforcement and supplies, Gunji's men at Centre Coconuts continued to hold out so Warfe organised a night attack for 9 May, with accompanying flares and screaming from a speaker. Hancock wrote: 'Last night we turned on a small nerve raid as a variation from the usual theme.'[53] It was typical Warfe. Savige recollected an occasion when Warfe moved up to a forward section position where the men were speaking in whispers. Warfe asked if the section carried axes and then told them to 'get busy with them and let the bastards know we are here'.[54]

Warfe's bold ploy worked, and the next morning the Centre Coconuts position was found vacant; their nerves had got the better of Toshio Gunji and his men. Warfe was very pleased. 'The Major', Pinney wrote, 'came in tonight pleased as Punch.' With control of the ridge, Warfe's men continued to flay the Japanese columns moving along Komiatum Ridge. Late on 11 May Erskine's Vickers gun opened fire on a column of twelve, killing five of them. The Japanese finally retaliated, first with their own heavy machine-gun fire, then with a mountain gun from Komiatum Ridge.[55]

The Australians now had four Vickers guns set up along Bobdubi Ridge, one at North Coconuts, which could cover the Salamaua–Mubo–Bobdubi track junction, one at Old Vickers, then two covering the track along Komiatum Ridge, at Gwaibolom and further south, at Graveyard. As the Japanese began to work out where the guns were, Warfe would have them moved. Brian Walpole later observed, 'Bobdubi Ridge was the most commanding spot of the lot . . . if we had heavy artillery or something we could have knocked Salamaua off the map.'[56]

———————

The loss of Bobdubi Ridge and the interdiction of the Mubo supply line caused great consternation at Nakano's headquarters in Lae, and troops were allocated to regain control. One infantry platoon, part of a battalion gun platoon and part of a machine-gun platoon under Lieutenant Takeshi Ogawa, the commander of 9 Company of the re-formed 115th Regiment, were to leave Salamaua on the evening of 11 May to attack Bobdubi Ridge. Ogawa's party was to carry ten days of iron rations and join Gunji's men for the attack. Ogawa was ordered to take possession of the high ground on the right bank of Francisco River in preparation for a future attack, relieving the local naval force and taking over their ammunition and provisions. Captain Nobaru Yamada, with one mountain gun, would shell the Australian positions at Bobdubi. The Japanese estimated that the Australians had seventy to eighty men on the ridge with two mortars in support.[57]

Around dawn on 12 May Ogawa arrived at the track junction at Komiatum and assumed command of Gunji's remaining men. These men would be important to Ogawa as they knew the terrain on the ridge. Also on 12 May the Takahashi Battalion in Lae was ordered to form as many men as possible into a composite company to be taken to Salamaua by two large MLCs that night. Staff Officer Sakaki would command the scratch force and commit it against the enemy at Bobdubi.[58]

At 1030 that same day, eighty Japanese troops and Chinese carriers moving south along the Komiatum track were fired on by the Vickers guns up on Bobdubi Ridge, and around thirty were killed. Although the local Japanese command had taken steps to retake Bobdubi Ridge, the fact that troops and supplies were still being sent along Komiatum Ridge in daytime was astonishing, and costly. More astonishing was that, on the following day, as a burial party was still working to recover the bodies of those men who had fallen the previous day, another eighty men moved south along the track and yet another thirty were apparently killed.[59] Ogawa's mission to retake Bobdubi Ridge suddenly became very urgent.

At 1200 Ogawa's men advanced to attack the Coconuts position at the north end of the ridge. At 1330 they made contact with Lieutenant Stan Jeffery's 2 Section outpost position but were forced back. Following

mortar fire, the outpost position was again attacked at 1500, but again
the Australians held. The next day, 13 May, Captain Sekine, commanding an infantry and a machine-gun company from the 21st Independent
Brigade, moved up to Bobdubi and the Australian positions were reconnoitred. Captain Ogura also moved up with one and a half platoons from
Salamaua to reinforce Ogawa and Sekine in an attack scheduled for the
following morning, 14 May. Three mountain guns would also support
the attack. It was thought imperative that the Japanese forces should
recapture Bobdubi Ridge.[60]

Despite inflicting considerable damage, both from well-laid booby
traps and small-arms fire, Jeffery withdrew his section at 1300 to a position 200 metres west, then up Bobdubi Ridge to South Coconuts. An
hour later the Vickers gun on North Coconuts opened up on the following Japanese, stopping them in their tracks. They responded with
heavy artillery fire from guns located at Kela Hill and Nuk Nuk, about
300 rounds of which impacted on the northern end of Bobdubi Ridge.
Heavy mortar fire followed, and the fighting went on all afternoon as the
Japanese attack spread out along Bobdubi Ridge.

On the morning of 14 May Warfe had relocated his headquarters from
Meares' position at Old Vickers down on to the flats at New Bobdubi
village where a new advanced headquarters had been set up with a wireless
and phone centre. As Warfe wrote to the official historian David Dexter,
'We were cleaning up and getting ready for further mischief when the
Jap attack started.'[61] Up on Old Vickers, Captain Wally Meares was
getting ready to tuck into some fresh fish that had been bombed out
of the Francisco River that morning when the Japanese attack came in.
The attackers were from Ogawa's unit, which had been reconstructed
from survivors of the Bismarck Sea convoy and also included some men
from Gunji's 10 Company, which had originally held the ridge positions.
Having failed in a frontal attack on the Coconuts two days earlier, Ogawa
now moved his men to the left, leaving at 0830 and ascending the ridge
unobserved, overrunning Meares' position from the south. Ogawa left
two of his platoons on Old Vickers and pushed another one out to a
knoll to the south. Erskine, who was approaching Old Vickers from
further south, ran into this platoon of Ogawa's men, and Erskine was
forced to pull his section back south along the ridge towards Namling.[62]

Warfe was now forced to use his fighting sections to hold open the
withdrawal routes down off the ridge and across the vital kunda bridge
over the Francisco. This was a precarious, native-built bridge using kunda
vines to support the structure. When Stephens' section arrived, Warfe

placed it with a Vickers gun on a spur 400 metres west of New Bobdubi to guard the bridge and cover any possible withdrawal. At 1645 the vital Vickers gun at North Coconuts was hit by a mortar round and, with the threat of the Japanese getting behind them, all sections were pulled back from the Coconuts area at 1735.[63]

Barney Barron was with 8 Section on Bobdubi Ridge when the attack came in.

> Our sentry, Des [Hore], saw Japs and warned us with a shot. That bullet was like a match thrown into gun powder. Japs opened up with everything they had. The air became thick with bullets, we were trapped, only thing to do, which is what we did best, get out fast and disappear into the protective jungle . . . As soon as we escaped the deadly fire of the Jap machine-guns, they opened up with mortars . . . We heard the continuing crunch of mortars being fired and not knowing when or where they would land . . . We headed for our vital bottle neck, where our retreat track crossed the wide Francisco River over the primitive kunda bridge.[64]

Explosions behind them indicated that the booby traps laid by Lieutenant Jeffery's engineers had 'caused the Japs no end of excitement'.[65]

One of those injured by the booby traps was Major-General Toru Okabe, the Japanese commander whose Okabe Detachment had undertaken the Wau operation. Okabe stepped on a booby trap that put a bullet through his right foot. It had been set up by Ron Young, one of the commando engineers. Okabe was evacuated to Lae by MLC on the night of 16 May, then flown to Rabaul. Major-General Tadakazu Murotani, the 51st Division infantry group commander, took over command on 26 May. Lieutenant Nishida's company finally recaptured the Coconuts position at around 2100.[66]

Warfe had been instructed by Savige to 'avoid becoming committed to further heavy action in the forward area with a consequent risk of suffering heavy casualties', and he therefore pulled his men back off the ridge. Savige later wrote, 'I was content to find enemy reaction and concerned at keeping Warfe and his men alive to fight on another day.'[67] By 2030 all stores and men had returned across the kunda bridge. That night Savige warned Warfe that Japanese aircraft had landed at Lae and that he could expect attention from them on the next day.

After taking back Bobdubi Ridge, Ogawa's 9 Company, with Gunji's men still attached, took over its defence. A reconnaissance patrol led by Lieutenant Nishida was sent down the ridge to New Bobdubi but found no sign of the Australians. On 20 May the Sekine Battalion was withdrawn from Bobdubi, then moved to Lae. The Ogawa unit was to improve defence works on the ridge and, on 26 May, came under the command of the Salamaua unit commander, Major Komagi, who planned to rotate a third of Ogawa's unit continuously through Salamaua.[68]

At 0950 on 15 May ten Japanese dive-bombers bombed Bobdubi and Hote. Peter Pinney watched the air attack with foreboding, then growing amazement. 'Twenty minutes later back came the planes. Judas wept, we'd had the Richard now: we were trapped in the open . . . they could riddle us, like knocking chooks off a perch. But no – they strafed Bobdubi village, blew up our former HQ and what was formerly our stores dump by the bridge. They strafed the bridge where we'd been an hour before.' It was an extraordinary example of poor coordination by the Japanese, as Hancock also observed: 'A very amusing sight the other day was the Nip air force going beserk. Fighters and bombers played merry hell for ages, battling away at wide open (or rather jungled) spaces.'[69]

Savige later noted that Warfe's independent company was the out-standing unit in campaign. 'It was their pre-campaign testing which enabled me to tackle the Salamaua campaign confidently. I tested my appreciation by letting Warfe on to Bobdubi Ridge.' David Dexter, who also served in an independent company, later wrote: 'The 2/3rd Indepen-dent Company was proving that a small, mobile, well-trained force was as necessary in jungle warfare as the battalions with their heavier equipment and hitting power.' Back at 3rd Division headquarters the reality of the situation was appreciated. 'Unfortunately, the role of the Division, the forces available and difficulties of supply, prevented further advantage being taken of the position.'[70]

George Warfe later reflected on his company's achievements: 'I note with pride the efforts of the 3rd Independent Company, which did indeed always carry the fight to the enemy and prowled their section of the jungle like hungry tigers.'[71]

On 12 May Captain Sydney Whitelaw's D Company of the 24th Battal-ion moved up from the Bulolo Valley to assume control of the Bulwa to Pilimung line of communication, thus releasing some more of Warfe's men in line with his early recommendations to Savige. One of the D Company platoons, Lieutenant Leslie Looker's 18 Platoon, moved on through Missim to the village of Hote, assuming responsibility for that sector and guarding against any enemy move from Malolo.[72] On

19 May a ten-man fighting patrol moved out from Hote along the track to Malolo. As the patrol moved up a steep kunai ridge it was ambushed by about twenty enemy troops. The patrol then withdrew to an ambush position outside Hote before pulling two kilometres back to Cissembob, arriving there at 1630. Cissembob was a small village of three huts strung out along a kunai ridge that led to Hote. Lieutenant-Colonel Wilton happened to have arrived at Cissembob that day with Warfe. Wilton, Warfe and Looker proceeded to count 170 enemy troops moving along the track into Hote.[73]

General Nakano had continued to use his newly arrived reinforcements to put pressure on the Australian positions. The Japanese force at Hote was from 8 and 9 Companies of the newly arrived 115th Regiment. The companies had left Salamaua at 1200 on 17 May, moving towards Hote via the Malolo track with the objective of attacking an estimated fifty men eight kilometres west of Hote on 19 May, then returning to Salamaua.[74] The companies had arrived east of Hote at 1530 on 18 May and driven back the Australian patrol before advancing to Hote. They now moved towards Cissembob.

Lieutenant Looker had twenty-five men at Cissembob that evening of 18 May, with one Vickers gun, two Bren guns, three Owen guns and sixteen rifles. The Vickers gun, manned by two of Warfe's commandos, Arthur 'Matey' Crossley and Hilton 'Stumfy' May, had wisely been left behind when Warfe's section had been replaced. Warfe told Looker, 'You should be set here for weeks.' The Vickers gun covered the main track from Hote. At 1700 Wilton requested an air attack on Hote for the following day, but 5th USAAF headquarters refused the request as no air photo was available.[75] Warfe and Wilton left Cissembob at 1745; 3rd Division headquarters had urgently requested Wilton's return as he was required in Port Moresby to receive 'special information' on the planned operations against Salamaua.[76]

Looker's men stood to all night, and booby traps were set up on the approach tracks in front of the Australian position. One of the booby traps, a grenade in a tin attached to a trip wire, went off shortly after dawn, at 0530 the next morning. Soon thereafter three enemy light machine-guns opened up from 700 metres forward of the Australian positions and enemy troops moved up the main track towards Cissembob. Other enemy units moved to the right and left sides of the track.

At 0900 Looker, with Private Daniel Greene and Ormond Hetherington at his side, was watching the enemy advance, indicating targets for the

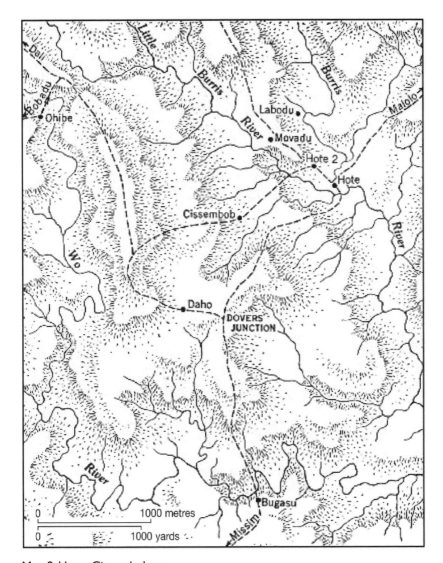

Map 8 Hote–Cissembob area

Vickers gun crew of Crossley and May. Suddenly a Japanese automatic opened up from only 25 metres away, and both Greene and Hetherington were wounded, Hetherington being hit in the head. Looker threw grenades, which knocked out the enemy gun. 'Got the b—, Danny boy,' he told the wounded Greene before dressing the men's wounds. Greene could walk, so he was sent back with three men to Daho. Hetherington would be a stretcher case and would have to wait.[77]

At 1200 mortars opened up on the Australian positions along with more machine-gun fire. May and Crossley, the two Vickers crewmen, were now pinned down. Of more concern to Looker was a large enemy party around a kilometre to the rear of his position, moving to cut his escape route to Missim. By 1300 the situation had deteriorated, and Looker ordered that key parts of the Vickers be dismantled to render the gun inoperable. The lock, slide and firing pin were removed from the gun, then, using the Brens to cover the move, Looker's men pulled out of Cissembob. As Looker's battalion commander later commented, 'It was a case of go before annihilation.'[78]

The wounded Hetherington was carried out on a makeshift stretcher by his 2/3rd mates, Crossley and May. The withdrawal route went across a ridge, in full view of the approaching enemy troops. Having covered around 500 metres, the heavy fire forced Crossley and May to shelter on the reverse slope of the ridge and were unable to move on. Looker told them to stay with the stretcher and hide until dark when he would return to help them back. In the early hours of the following day, Corporal Robert Dovers' section contacted Crossley and May and organised a stretcher party to get Hetherington back to the fallback position at Ohibe.[79]

Looker's men had caused about fifty enemy casualties, more than half of them credited to the Vickers gun, which had fired around 6000 rounds of ammunition. After driving the Australians out of Cissembob, the Japanese withdrew to Hote that night. The Australians returned some days later and, after replacing the locks and slides, made the Vickers once more operable.[80] Back at Missim, Peter Pinney commented on the action.

> It seems the 150 Japs who turned up at Hote were fair dinkum – and
> paid for their enthusiasm. The Vickers gun alone got an estimated
> fifty before it was overrun. Screamer got a bullet in his temple and
> out the side of his head, but lived, and was rescued by a gutsy
> chocko, a 24th Battalion man. Sissimbob [sic] was hurriedly
> evacuated and the Japs could have walked through to Bobadu but
> instead contented themselves with looting some rations left behind
> and retired. Bloody mugs, they didn't even take the Vickers.[81]

Savige was concerned about the vastness of the Pioneer Range–Mount Missim area and the possibility of another Wau-style probe in strength by the Japanese. Therefore the action at Hote caused considerable alarm as the enemy was now in a position to open a route via Dali and Jari all the way to Sunshine and the Bulolo Valley. Despite supply concerns, Savige sent a 24th Battalion platoon up to Dali on 21 May and another platoon from Powerhouse up to Bobadu.[82] The operational area for the campaign against Salamaua was spreading like an ink blot.

CHAPTER 4

SUPPLY LINES

Following the Bismarck Sea debacle, the Japanese command realised that merchant ship convoys to Lae were no longer a viable option. Alternative means of transporting supplies and troops had to be found, and this would require brilliant organisational skill. Destroyers, submarines and landing barges would all be utilised as well as rugged jungle tracks.

Of the almost 4000 troops from the Lae convoy who survived, more than half reached the New Guinea mainland, the rest returning to Rabaul. Around a thousand troops reached Lae by destroyer, mainly those rescued from the first ship sunk, the *Kyokusei Maru*. Other surviving troops who had been landed at Tuluvu and around Finschhafen had made their way down to Lae over the following weeks. On 13 March six Japanese bombers with fighter cover landed at Lae, bringing in unit commanders, one of whom was the commander of the Eighteenth Army, Lieutenant-General Hatazo Adachi.[1]

Supply considerations limited the Japanese force at Lae and Salamaua to 10,000 men. With 2500 of these men from the 7th Naval Base Unit, the army component was limited to 7500 men. The Eighteenth Army Chief of Staff, Major-General Kane Yoshihara, later wrote, 'In the face of the enemy who was making a decisive attack it was as though we were a candle in the wind. It was an agonising situation to command the operations of such an army in this area.' To maximise their effect, Adachi had to ensure the majority of those 7500 men were front-line troops. He therefore ordered the sick and wounded back to Rabaul accompanied by those wasted units that had returned from Buna. However, in order to bring fresh troops the 800 kilometres from Rabaul to Lae he would need to find an alternative to merchant shipping. Eighteenth Army headquarters recognised the imperative to concentrate all available shipping, engineer units and motor landing craft.[2]

An appreciation on 2 April by Australian intelligence observed: 'They are still endeavouring to send troops and supplies into Lae by submarine and by Destroyer Express, but those means cannot cope with the requirements of a main forward base.'[3] What Australian intelligence failed to appreciate was that a Japanese forward base could be maintained on a shoestring of supplies compared to a comparable Allied base. The efficiency of the destroyer and submarine operations and, in particular, the capability of the coastal barge network was significantly underestimated.

The most efficient alternative method of moving troops forward from Rabaul to Lae was by naval destroyer, able to cruise at more than three times the average eight knots speed of a merchant ship. Around 250 troops could be carried crammed into compartments on the ship without using the deck.[4] The Japanese command had used this method with great effectiveness in the Solomon Islands, where the destroyer route from Rabaul was nicknamed the 'Tokyo Express'. The method would now be used to bring the survivors of II/115th Battalion from Rabaul to Finschhafen.

On the morning of 28 March the re-formed battalion left Rabaul aboard the destroyer *Minazuki*, arriving at Kavieng at 1640 that same afternoon. At 1250 on the following day the *Minazuki* and three other destroyers headed for Finschhafen at 30 knots. They arrived during the night of 29/30 March, and within 40 minutes the troops had been landed and the destroyers had departed. It had been intended to bring the troops all the way to Lae but, after the destroyers were spotted by aircraft, they diverted to Finschhafen. Allied aircraft then dropped flares and bombs at Finschhafen and also bombed and strafed the landed units during the day. Seven RAAF No. 30 Squadron Beaufighters took part in these attacks along with USAAF B-25 Mitchells and A-20 Boston bombers. However, the Japanese had efficiently dispersed the troops with little sign of the landings other than an overturned barge in the harbour. On 1 April the landed troops moved to a nearby camp where they stayed until 9 April before commencing a two-week march to Lae.

On 10 April a further detachment of a thousand men from II/66th Battalion and 14th Field Artillery Regiment left Rabaul on four destroyers of the 10th Destroyer Flotilla. Lieutenant Onuki's No. 7 Company had embarked on the destroyer *Minazuki* and First Lieutenant Kitazume's No. 5 Company (of 166 men) on the *Satsuki*. Both vessels left Rabaul at 1230, making a speed of 28 knots in extremely rough seas along the northern route. Although the original destination was Finschhafen, it was decided to land the troops at Tuluvu, on the north-western end of New Britain. Disembarkation commenced at 2215 using motorised landing craft (MLCs) along each side of the ship. As the MLCs came alongside, the soldiers' haversacks were thrown down to them but, with the heavy seas pushing the vessels apart, the troops had great difficulty disembarking and much of their equipment was washed away in the darkness. The MLCs then had to beach well away from the shore but, despite the problems, disembarkation was completed by midnight, allowing both destroyers to depart Tuluvu by 2330.[5]

At 0030 the next morning of 11 April, the other two destroyers arrived at Tuluvu and began unloading in the stormy darkness. They were late because they had initially taken the route around the southern coast of New Britain, then, after being spotted by Allied patrol aircraft, had switched to the safer northern route. It was planned to disembark all troops and supplies in one move using two MLCs, two small motor boats and seven collapsible boats from the 5th Shipping Engineer Regiment. However, four of the collapsible boats could not start their engines and had to be attached to the small motor boats. The two larger MLCs refused to tow the other three collapsible boats, which soon capsized along with one of the towed ones. Many of the supplies were also lost during unloading as the breaking waves crashed into the boats and landing craft, but all boats made it to the shore, the men in two of them using shovels to paddle their craft in. Unable to see the shore landmarks in the dark and rain, the men and supplies were spread out along an eight-kilometre stretch of beach but, apart from three who had drowned, the rest of the men reached shore.[6]

The convoy carrying the Major Sakai Sugiyama's II/66th Battalion departed from Rabaul during the night of 4 May. The unit was carried aboard the cruiser *Yūbari*, and the destroyers *Nagatsuki*, *Satsuki* and *Minazuki*. Travelling close to the north coast of New Britain, the warships arrived and landed safely at Tuluvu before dawn on 5 May. The unit dispersed and camped in the jungle to avoid detection by enemy aircraft, and awaited further orders. Lieutenant Masuo Shinoda, a 66th Regiment officer, later wrote, 'The main strength of our assembled regiment was offered from the following day for airfield duties under those troubled skies.'[7]

On 8 June Lieutenant-Colonel Fukuzo Kimura's III/66th Battalion left Rabaul in four destroyers to join the rest of the regiment in New Guinea. Kimura's men had already seen action in the Solomon Islands, having being sent to Munda, then on to Kolombangara in December 1942. Although the battalion was involved only in airfield construction, the harsh nature of the Solomon Islands took a heavy toll, and almost all the III/66th personnel ended up with beriberi or malaria before the unit returned to Rabaul. The first attempt to evacuate the unit on 16 May had proved disastrous when all three destroyers hit mines off Kolombangara and seventy of Kimura's men were lost. A later evacuation convoy proved more successful and, on 9 June, the troops of Nos 9, 10 and 12 Companies were offloaded at Tuluvu.[8]

On 27 July 300 reinforcements for the 115th Regiment embarked at Rabaul on two destroyers, the *Mikazuki* and the *Ariake* and, after a ten-hour trip, arrived off Tuluvu that same night. However, after the troops disembarked from the *Mikazuki* the ship ran aground on coastal reefs as it turned for Rabaul. *Ariake* rescued some survivors, the troops below being ordered to pack close to make room for more. The *Ariake* then anchored a thousand metres offshore, and all troops disembarked into landing craft.[9]

Both destroyers were still off Tuluvu at daybreak when a flight of fifteen Mitchell bombers arrived to attack the airfield. The flight included the first modified B-25G Mitchell, equipped with a 75mm gun in the nose, and piloted by Major Paul 'Pappy' Gunn, who was carrying out flight testing. Spotting the stranded *Mikazuki* with the *Ariake* nearby in Borgen Bay, the Mitchells swept in at mast height, strafing the two destroyers. Gunn fired four shots from his 75mm gun at one destroyer, the first hitting a chimney stack, the second ricocheting off the deck, the third missing and the fourth hitting squarely in the hull. Before he could try again, the other B-25s dropped their bombs, scoring fourteen hits and leaving one destroyer ablaze. Denied the destroyer, Gunn used his remaining two 75mm rounds to destroy a Japanese transport aircraft that had just landed at Tuluvu airstrip.[10]

The most valuable Japanese naval vessel in New Guinea waters in early 1943 was the humble coastal barge, or motorised landing craft (MLC). These craft were also known as Daihatsu, from the Japanese *Dai-Hatsudokitei*, meaning large motorboat. The building of such vessels

Photo 11 Japanese Motorised Landing Craft. (Watson)

had not been a priority in pre-war Japan, and there were never enough available in New Guinea to carry out the required tasks.

Most of the MLCs used in New Guinea were single-engine boats, 14 metres long and 4.5 metres wide with a crew of seven and a carrying capacity of seventy men. There was also a twin-engine model 18 metres long with eleven crewmen, which carried 120 men. Spare parts were carried on board, and a mobile thirty-man regimental repair section was also available for major repair work. The craft usually travelled in line ahead with a 35-metre gap between boats, but if there were a number of boats, they could travel in a double-column formation with a 70-metre gap between columns. However, due to the more pronounced wake, which showed up clearly at night, this formation was rarely used in New Guinea. The MLCs would travel around 300 metres offshore with lookouts being posted to watch for the distinctive white line of surf that indicated reefs. If enemy patrol boats were seen, the engines were stopped or, if the MLC had been spotted, the craft would beach and the crew would run for cover. If seen from the air, the column of MLCs would rapidly disperse.[11]

There were seventy men in each standard MLC with each man carrying a rifle and 120 rounds. There was a complete disregard for comfort, the men having to stand the entire time; small tins were passed around for toilet use. There were initially no special barge hideouts, and the MLCs were camouflaged with tree branches on shore during daylight hours, hidden in mangroves while the troops disembarked and hid nearby. Staging camps were later set up and native foods made available.[12] Major-General Yoshihara later noted how the Japanese MLCs operated: 'In the daytime, lying hidden in small inlets, river mouths, etc., and in the gloom of night advancing from hiding place to hiding place.'[13]

The southern New Britain transport route had already been used in February 1943 before the Bismarck Sea action. Captain Michiji Ishikawa's company from the 51st Engineer Regiment had taken the III/102nd Battalion survivors from the sinking of the *Nichiryu Maru* to Lae in eight MLCs along the south coast via Gasmata. During the daylight hours the MLCs would lay up in the numerous coastal river estuaries until they reached Cape Bushing. Dampier Strait was then crossed to Finschhafen from where the MLCs moved down the coast to Lae. Most of Lieutenant-Colonel Keiji Matsui's I/66th Battalion followed the same route. In early March an advanced party made the journey from Rabaul to Lae in seven MLCs before 350 troops left Rabaul on 8 May, reaching Lae before dawn on 17 May.[14]

As previously noted, the II/66th Battalion had been taken to Tuluvu on destroyers and would now require MLCs to get across Dampier Strait. To reduce the distance to be travelled across the strait, the troops first marched south across the peninsula to Nigol before a ten-kilometre MLC trip down the Itni River to Cape Bushing near the south-western tip of New Britain. From here the troops were progressively transported by MLCs south-west across Dampier Strait to Finschhafen. Company-sized groups crossed at night in two or three barges and, when reconnaissance planes flew over, the barges cut their engines to avoid leaving a detectable wake. To avoid contact with patrol boats, the onward journey from Finschhafen to Lae traversed the dangerous coastal waters, which were filled with numerous coral reefs. The marine engineers worked tirelessly during the day to repair and prepare the boats for the nightly journey, but the number of available boats steadily decreased. The 66th Regiment headquarters group arrived at Lae on 16 May and moved on to Salamaua the following night.[15]

During April and May 1943 two battalions of the 66th Infantry Regiment were brought to Lae, along with around 750 ancillary troops, mainly artillery and engineer troops, as shown in table 4.1.

Having also being taken to Tuluvu by destroyer, the troops of Colonel Kimura's III/66th Battalion also now required MLCs to cross Dampier

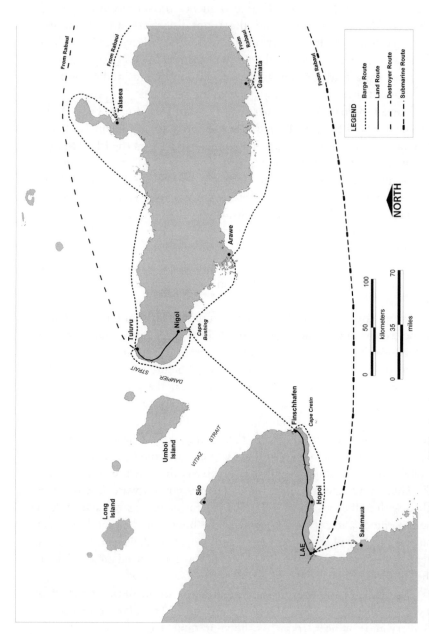

Map 9 Japanese supply route – Rabaul to Lae

Table 4.1: Japanese reinforcements to Lae, April–May 1943

66th Infantry Regiment (less III/66th Bn)	1000 men
115th Infantry Regiment (part only)	200 men
14th Artillery Regiment (part only)	200 men
51st Engineer Regiment	150 men
Miscellaneous	200 men
TOTAL:	1750 men

Strait and possibly move on to Lae. On 13 June Kimura's men and two artillery pieces left Tuluvu with eighty men crammed into each MLC. The men reached Cape Bushing, where they could hide during daylight, 45 minutes up the Itni River at Nigol. On the night of 16–17 June the unit crossed Dampier Strait to Finschhafen and five days later reached Lae. Other units with heavy weapons also needed to be taken by MLC from Tuluvu. In early July the 15th Independent Anti-Aircraft Cannon Company, equipped with 13mm and 20mm guns, travelled from Tuluvu to Lae over four days by MLC.[16]

Unlike Kimura's men, the 115th Regiment reinforcements who had arrived at Tuluvu in late July would have to march south across the Cape Gloucester peninsula before embarking on MLCs for Dampier Strait crossing. Split into groups, the reinforcements, in full marching order with six days' rations, followed a rough vehicle trail and thereafter a difficult jungle track with numerous creek crossings. The troops followed the coastal track for two days, then turned inland before arriving at Nigol six days later. They then embarked for the crossing to New Guinea in large MLCs, which travelled 45 minutes down the Itni River past Cape Bushing and across Dampier Strait. For one group it rained every day and three attempts to board MLCs were aborted because of rain or air raid warnings.[17]

The MLCs were also vulnerable to Allied patrol boats, particularly further down the coast where Japanese forces were moving back along the coast to Salamaua from Buna. At 2300 on 15 March five large MLCs encountered two American PT boats off Mageri Bay. Thinking they were other MLCs, the Japanese vessels approached the PT boats and two MLCs were sunk, one ran aground and another went missing. In another incident, in the early morning hours of 10 July, two large MLCs returning to Lae were attacked by two patrol boats near Cape Cretin, where the Huon Peninsula turns east towards Lae just south of Finschhafen. One MLC was seriously damaged by shell fire and ran aground while the other

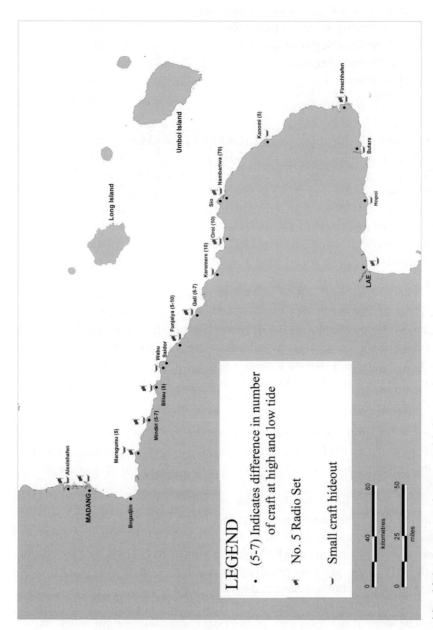

LEGEND

- (5-7) Indicates difference in number of craft at high and low tide

- No. 5 Radio Set

- Small craft hideout

Map 10 Japanese supply route – Madang to Lae

was hit by a torpedo and sank with the loss of nineteen men. Ten days later another three MLCs and one armoured boat were travelling from Lae to Finschhafen when they were attacked from astern by PT boats at Cape Cretin, and six men were killed and another twenty-one wounded. A similar attack took place three days later.[18]

The sea around Cape Cretin was also a favoured hunting ground for Allied aircraft looking to interdict the Japanese barges. During the moonlit nights of 19 and 20 May Allied aircraft took on the barge traffic, and two loaded barges were strafed on the first night. On 20 May fourteen barges were spotted and five of them were sunk, the remainder beaching with eighty men from the II/66th Battalion landed on a nearby island. As the after-action report noted, 'Results confirm the suspicion that these craft move during the hours of darkness, lying up camouflaged by day.'[19]

Another coastal transport program took place along the northern coast from Wewak and Madang to Finschhafen and on to Lae. As part of the Japanese reinforcement of New Guinea, the 20th Division had arrived at Wewak on 23 January 1943. This and later convoys also brought in more landing craft and, by May, 50 of them, operated by the 5th Landing Barge Regiment, were gathered at Wewak. One of the 20th Division's regiments, Colonel Sadahiko Miyake's 80th Regiment, was sent east. Major Otoichi Jinno's I/80th Battalion had marched to Madang by the end of April, and from here it travelled in MLCs via Bogadjim, Sio and Finschhafen to Lae. With around twenty-five men in each MLC, it was an eight-day trip, although some of the companies took much longer. Two artillery pieces accompanied the battalion, 560 men in all.[20]

Major Shobu's II/80th Battalion didn't make it as far as Lae. In early April it had moved to Bogadjim where it had been engaged in building the road up from the coast towards Yokopi in the Finisterre Range. It was not until 20 July that the battalion left Bogadjim via Saidor and Sio to Finschhafen, where the battalion stayed and fought against the Australians in September and October 1943.[21]

Meanwhile, General Adachi had visited the Salamaua front lines in early July and decided that further reinforcements were required. On his return to Madang, Adachi assigned the Shoge Detachment from the 41st Division to move to Lae by MLCs and to reinforce the 51st Division. Major-General Ryoichi Shoge was the infantry group commander, and his force comprised Colonel Kashiwagi's 238th Infantry Regiment and a battalion from the 41st Mountain Artillery Regiment. Elements from the

238th Regiment began leaving Wewak travelling in groups of three MLCs at night, with each MLC carrying fifty men and supplies in sardine-like conditions. Such groups left Wewak every two nights, as the whole regiment was transported east to Alexishafen and Madang. As more MLCs headed east they were replaced on the Wewak-to-Madang leg by small fishing boats or *gyosen*, each of which carried twenty men. In late July Major Shigeru Tashiro's II/238th Battalion moved from Wewak to Alexishafen. No. 8 Company, down to 120 men from an original strength of 200, left Madang on 17 July and on 20 July reached Nambariwa, where it remained for three months before moving to Kanomi.[22]

In early August the II/238th Battalion left Alexishafen, travelling at night by twenty-man MLCs to Finschhafen over five nights, stopping from 0900 to 1500 each day. Due to increasing losses of MLCs and threat of an Allied landing, Nos 5, 7 and 8 Companies remained at Finschhafen while No. 6 Company and No. 2 Machine-Gun Company went overland along the coast from Finschhafen to Lae. The latter unit had been able to carry only six of its twelve machine-guns from Wewak.[23]

On 30 June units from III/238th Battalion also left Wewak in MLCs, travelling by night to Alexishafen, where the unit remained until August when Nos 9 and 11 Companies headed east. No. 11 Company travelled by night in four MLCs, beaching and camouflaging the MLCs during the day and, despite delays of a week at a time, reaching Salamaua on 5 August. Due to the lack of MLCs, Nos 10 and 12 Companies remained at Wewak while all of I/238th Battalion remained at Madang. As the number of available MLCs diminished, other troops used the twenty-man fishing boats to move beyond Madang. Meanwhile, reinforcements for 66th Regiment had arrived at Wewak in July, then moved to Hansa Bay. They left on 13 August for Sio via Long Island in two of the fishing boats, then travelled by the coastal track to Finschhafen, arriving on 6 September.[24]

In line with the increased use of the coastal route from Madang to Lae, the Japanese targeted Australian coast-watchers who could observe the MLC route along the coast to Lae. The coast-watchers had clear indications that a route was being set up along the coast from Madang as Sio had been occupied and building observed at Teliata Point, just east of Sio. An airfield site between Saidor and Sio had also been burned clear.[25]

Two of the coast-watchers, Lieutenant Ken McColl and Captain Lloyd Pursehouse, were located in the mountains just behind Finschhafen with a forward observation post overlooking Vitiaz Strait to the east. They were in an excellent position to observe the Japanese barge traffic into Finschhafen, either from across Vitiaz Strait or along the coast from Madang. With radio communication linking the coast-watchers to Port Moresby, air attacks could be readily called in if any barges were spotted. They would play a vital role in preventing any coastal-based resupply routes to Lae following the demise of the merchant ship convoys. The Japanese command was also aware of this.

On 3 April McColl headed down the track to the forward observation post, leaving Pursehouse resting at the hut further back in the jungle. He was surprised by a Japanese patrol but managed to dash off into the jungle before making his way back to the hut. The Japanese patrol had beaten him, surrounding the hut and firing into it. However, warned by the sound of the ambush on McColl, Pursehouse had gone. The two men met the next day and reached a rear camp where they could radio the situation back to Moresby. Clearly compromised, the men were ordered to withdraw back across the Markham Valley to Bena Bena. After 16 months of sterling service, Pursehouse was to be relieved by Captain Les Howlett, who was already on his way.[26]

The dark mountains that soar above the coastline of the Huon Peninsula provided an abundance of excellent coast-watching positions, and another post had been established behind Saidor along the northern coast, ideally placed to observe any movement of the enemy's coastal barges from Madang to Finschhafen. Lieutenants Lincoln Bell and Ben Hall operated here and, in early March, a party under Lieutenant Basil Fairfax-Ross had made its way across from Bena Bena to supply them. The area around Saidor was one of the staging points for the Japanese barge route from Madang and, as at Finschhafen, the Japanese wanted to ensure that no coast-watchers were in the area. Japanese troops were brought to the Saidor area and were soon able to obtain information from the cowed local villagers. Late in March some of the villagers led a Japanese patrol to the Australians' base, but the party managed to fight its way out. Fairfax-Ross and Ben Hall continued coast-watching, reporting on barge traffic and dodging enemy patrols, before a difficult trek back to Bena Bena, although Lincoln Bell and Lieutenant David Laws didn't make it back, being killed by treacherous natives. Further west at Wewak the coast-watchers had similar difficulties. They found it impossible to operate due to the increased Japanese strength and their influence over the native people in the area.[27]

By the astute use of destroyers and MLCs the Japanese command was able to bring reinforcements to Lae, but regular resupply was another matter. As the Eighteenth Army chief of staff later observed, 'There was no method of doing so other than by submarines.' However, using all the submersible supply capacity of the Japanese navy at the time, there was only sufficient capability to supply a force limited to 10,000 men. To supply 10,000 men Allied intelligence estimated that 150 bargeloads would be required per month, 200 more being required for ammunition and reinforcements. The same report noted that too few barges were available for the task but made no mention of submarines.[28]

Even before the Bismarck Sea battle, submarines were being used as transports. From 10 to 12 November 1942 submarine I-121 took fifteen personnel from the 5th Sasebo SNLP to Lae, transported in the forward torpedo room in place of the four spare torpedos normally carried. Twenty 220-litre drums of rice were also lashed to the deck of the submarine, which submerged by day and travelled on the surface at night using its diesel engine.[29]

After dusk on 22 February 1943 submarine I-36 disembarked at Lae. Able Seaman Kiichi Wada, one of ten naval reinforcements on board, watched as a dozen barges gathered around the submarine. He observed they were 'like ants swarming around their prey, food and munitions were unloaded from the submarine, transported to the shore and disembarked. Trucks were waiting on the shore, where workmen piled up the goods and divided and delivered them to the army and navy.' Ropes that secured drums on the submarine's deck were then cut so that the drums would float free when the submarine submerged. Wada noted, 'Buoys were attached and the drums gathered and secured to the barges by means of a gaff, after which they were taken to shore in tow. Waiting workmen would dive into the water and roll the heavy drums up onto the shore.' Each drum contained two and a half sacks of rice, but about a quarter of each was waterlogged and had swelled up so the contents had to be used immediately.[30]

Following the cessation of the merchant convoys, submarines were making around ten journeys per month carrying ammunition, provisions and, at times, up to forty troops from Rabaul to Lae or Salamaua. The submarines transported all manner of vital supplies, including the 66th

Regiment five-man flag party in May. On the night of 11 June a submarine arrived in Lae carrying a 155mm howitzer and three 105mm guns while a 120mm artillery piece was taken to Salamaua on the deck of another submarine. Until June 1943 six submarines helped carry supplies, but then the number was cut back to three.[31]

The transport submarines employed two unique attachments to enable such loads to be carried. The *unpoto* consisted of two hollow cylinders side by side with a platform on top to which the artillery piece was lashed. Under the platform was a power plant driving two torpedo propellers. The *unpoto* unit displaced 37 tons when loaded and was strapped to the after deck of a submarine. The *unpoto* would be unstrapped when it arrived off the coast and use the motor unit to land the platform on the shore. In contrast, the *unkato* was a sealed cylinder 45 metres long and 5 metres in diameter with ballast tanks at either end of the cylinder and another in the centre. The rest of the space could carry 377 tons of cargo, and the cylinder was towed submerged behind the submarine. Operational problems prevented its use at Lae or Salamaua.[32]

When the 115th Regiment survivors from the Bismarck Sea convoy returned to Rabaul, the units were consolidated and a number of men were sent to Lae via submarine. One such run, from 17 to 19 April, fourteen men were crammed into a compartment on the submarine I-6 for two days with fresh air being available only when the vessel surfaced at night. A SNLP marine made the journey in June on a Type 38 submarine that had been painted black and had its guns removed. After going on board at dusk the marine spent the entire three-day trip forward of the control room with twenty other men crammed into a space 3.6 by 2.3 metres and only 1.7 metres high. There was a separate compartment forward of the conning tower for the men's equipment.[33]

When the submarines reached Lae they anchored offshore and unloaded in three hours using three small MLCs, each making three trips. Navy personnel were evacuated on the return trip while army personnel utilised any MLCs returning to Rabaul. Colonel Koike commanded the Koike Small Craft *Tai*, which controlled the special MLCs used at Lae; these were known as *yammasen*, a faster, sampan-like vessel that carried thirty troops.[34]

On the night of 18 March, the unloading barges were being observed by two spotters from the 23rd Heavy Wireless Section based at the Lae observation post, in the mountains south of the Markham River. They watched twelve barges emerge from their hideout in the Labu swamps and head for Voco Point where they circled until a submarine 'popped up'. A message was immediately sent to Port Moresby, and a bomber soon came over to strafe and bomb the enemy vessel.[35]

Captain Yahachi Tanabe was the Imperial Japanese Navy's most feted submarine captain, who had commanded the submarine I-168 that had sunk USS *Yorktown* at Midway. On the night of 18–19 March, Tanabe's submarine, I-176 stood to 400 metres off Lae with two MLCs on either side for unloading. However, when only half the work had been completed, red flares shot up from the shore and Tanabe called for an emergency dive. At least one USAAF Mitchell bomber strafed the vessel and dropped a bomb astern, killing two men and wounding a number of others, including Captain Tanabe. The torpedo officer, Lieutenant Asakichi Aragi, took over command and managed to beach the stricken submarine at the mouth of the Markham River, repair the many leaks, float off with the high tide, then shelter on the harbour bottom before daylight. On the next night the I-176 headed off on the surface for Rabaul.[36]

By May it was apparent to Allied intelligence that the submarines were making regular supply runs to Lae and, on the night of 13 May, one was spotted by Allied aircraft both coming and going. Two nights later, during the full-moon period, the 3rd Bombardment Group carried out a night attack on Lae harbour, hoping to catch one of the submarines on the surface. Captain John Henebry led five Mitchells on the raid, flying from the new air base at Dobodura. To minimise the chance of being seen, Henebry brought the flight in from the west, with the dark mountains behind them. As the planes came in over the Markham River mouth they spotted a submarine offshore, 'silhouetted against a rising full moon'. The submarine was being unloaded, and the barges were moving between the vessel and the shore. All five planes dropped their four 500-pound bombs, straddling the submarine, but its loss could not be confirmed.[37]

From December 1942 to September 1943 Japanese submarines made ninety-five supply runs from Rabaul to Lae and Salamaua carrying about 2500 tons of supplies. Only one submarine was lost during these operations.[38]

Getting food and ammunition forward to Lae and Salamaua was only one part of the Japanese supply problem.

In mid-April Komiatum villagers told an ANGAU patrol that a thirty-man carrier line was being used to supply Mubo from Komiatum twice per week. It was surmised that only one ton could be carried, and most of this supply was probably food. It was reported that the Japanese were eating leaves and suffering dysentery, and Allied intelligence estimated that the Japanese had food for only 300 men at 16 ounces of rice per day. This was a reasonable assessment as the troops were being issued 22 ounces of rice per day, supplemented by bean paste but with no meat or fish available in the front lines at Mubo. In line with the deterioration of the Japanese position, troops were put on half rations at the end of August 1943.[39]

Lieutenant Shinoda on the breakdown in food supply:

> In the sparsely grassed jungle, the officers and men on the front line
> were picking and cooking the stalk of a wild plant, which was around
> 20 cm long and resembled a sweet potato. This vegetable was given
> the name 'Mubo potato' and was a treasured staple in all battles until
> the end of the war. In the absence of much rice, food at the time
> consisted of dried bread and compressed rations (compressed barley
> which was mixed with water and eaten), supplemented with miso
> powder and powdered soy sauce.[40]

The supply line between Salamaua and Mubo had suffered major disruptions due to the operation of Warfe's commandos. By the end of April the Australians were ambushing the supply lines and, when Warfe moved his Vickers guns on to Bobdubi Ridge in early May, the disruption was complete. Native carriers were also brought across from Japanese-controlled territory to Australian control. Meanwhile, those carriers from villages not controlled full time by the Japanese were deterred from doing so by Allied leaflet drops over the villages. By the end of April, the Japanese had gone from having around a hundred carriers supplying Mubo twice weekly to only six carriers being used three times weekly. A large number of stretcher cases were also returning to Salamaua, requiring further labour. An Australian report succinctly noted: 'Enemy sick and short of rations.'[41]

The lack of native labour or another dedicated labour source meant that front-line Japanese troops had to be pressed into service as carriers. After arriving at Lae in late June, some units of the III/66th Battalion had repaired bomb craters on the main Lae airfield before the companies moved progressively to Salamaua by night. For two days the troops were used to carry provisions from a transport dump around five kilometres from Salamaua, along a narrow path to I/66th Battalion positions at

Old Bobdubi. Each man carried 15 kilograms of supplies before being deployed to the front line on 19 July.[42]

Unable to be supplied, and subject to increasing Allied air attacks, Lae had become untenable as a forward air base for the Japanese in New Guinea. Steps were taken to move air units into Wewak, but this operation would take months, both to build the required air bases and to concentrate the necessary aircraft and aircrew. Allied intelligence noted that at least a hundred aircraft bays had been completed at the two main Wewak airfields in readiness for the new aircraft by the end of March.[43]

No doubt stung by the disastrous Bismarck Sea action, the Japanese air arm showed it was still capable when the navy launched the 'I' operation on 7 April with air missions from Rabaul to the Solomon Islands. These attacks were followed by a major raid of around a hundred aircraft against Oro Bay on 11 April. On the following day, the 106th raid on Port Moresby destroyed more than 3000 drums of motor fuel, about three days supply. Then, on 14 April, Milne Bay was subjected to its 24th raid, delivered by forty to fifty bombers and as many fighter escorts. Three ships were hit by bombs, one of which, *Van Heemskerk*, was sunk. Four days later, on 18 April, the Japanese navy also had a major setback when the aircraft carrying the Combined Fleet commander, Admiral Isoroku Yamamoto, was shot down over Bougainville and the admiral was killed.[44]

Despite the intermittent Japanese air attacks, the 5th USAAF dominated the skies over Lae and Salamaua during the campaign. Table 4.2 indicates Allied air operations during the Salamaua campaign. During this time 364 Allied air support missions were flown, a third of which took place in July during Operation Doublet, the Allied offensive against Salamaua.[45]

Table 4.2: Allied air operations during Salamaua campaign

Target	Bomber sorties	Bomb tonnage	Fighter sorties
Lae	1156	1651	752
Salamaua	1556	2227	954

Source: 3rd Division Operations Report, AWM 54, 587/2/28

The Australians also had major supply line problems. With the decrease in available air supply resources, the Australian command undertook an extraordinary operation to construct a major supply line from the south coast to Wau. Following directions from Blamey, Captain Frank Vidgen and Lieutenant Charles Fox travelled down the Bulldog Track from Wau to Bulldog Camp in July 1942 to carry out a feasibility study. Fox, who had been the mining warden at Wau before the war, reported to New Guinea Force headquarters that the route from Wau to Kudjeru was already of mule track standard and that from Kudjeru for 32 kilometres south such track construction would not be difficult. Construction of a track for 16 kilometres north-east of Bulldog Camp would also not be difficult. However, the area between was treacherous country and a suitable path through the mountains, or, as Fox put it, 'a shelf', would need to be found. Fox and Lieutenant John Ecclestone were then directed to carry out a survey for such a route from the Bulldog end. They arrived at Terapo on 16 August and soon settled on a route following the Eloa River valley north from Bulldog Camp even though it crossed the main range at a higher point than the current track route via Kudjeru. In late November the report was made, and in early December 1942 Blamey directed that a jeep track be built from Bulldog to Wau.[46]

Construction of the road commenced at the Bulldog end on 1 January 1943, supervised by Captain Jack Maynes using 14th Field Company personnel and 450 native labourers under Lieutenant Fox. These personnel also worked to remove snags from the Lakekamu River between Bulldog Camp and the coast at Terapo. This would be ongoing work exacerbated by frequent rising river levels, which brought more snags down from the tributaries. Large trees were the main problem as they had to be cut up *in situ*, working underwater, and the resultant wood stacked above the high-water mark.

Lieutenant-Colonel William Reinhold, chief engineer of the 11th Division, had been appointed to take charge of the challenging project. He left Bulldog Camp on 12 January with Captain Maynes and, after following the track through to Kudjeru, confirmed the earlier opinion that a better route was needed, preferably to link up with the current Wau-to-Edie Creek road. Ecclestone was tasked with surveying a route from Edie Creek through to the Koluron Mountains, crossing at 2900 metres what would later be called Ecclestone Saddle. On the southern side of the saddle a route had to be found back down the range into the Eloa River gorge, a veritable canyon with towering cliffs on either side. Reinhold noted, 'It is a barrier that has to be seen to be believed.' The overriding problem was time, and it was decided to connect Fox Saddle to Centre Camp rather than following a longer but less dramatic route.[47]

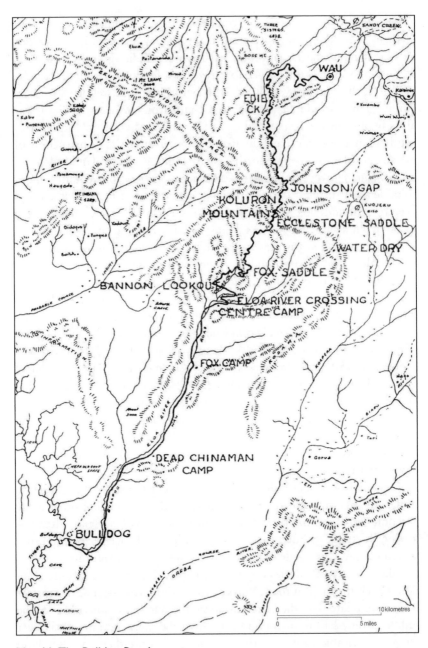

Map 11 The Bulldog Road

A staff directive from New Guinea Force headquarters on 15 February stressed that the completion of the road was 'a matter of utmost importance'. A staged schedule stated that by 15 April the road should be suitable for pack transport, by 15 June for jeep transport and by 30 June for restricted motor transport. To build the road, twenty-six planeloads of heavy road-making equipment, comprising six D4 bulldozers, three D2 tractors and six road-ploughs, were required in Wau by 25 February. On the south coast Hall Sound was being investigated as a possible port for direct shipment from Australia, and new roads from Hall Sound to both Bulldog and Port Moresby were being considered.[48]

On 18 March Ecclestone Saddle was reached. Warrant Officer Roy Bannon, an elderly New Guinea miner who had worked with the Bulolo Dredging Company before the war, then looked for the route to Centre Camp. He decided that the road needed to be turned before running down to Eloa River and the turning point was later named Bannon's Lookout. With the route now determined, Reinhold had to assess the balance between the quality of the road and the need to complete it as soon as possible in order to be of military use. A ruling gradient of 10 per cent and a minimum radius of curvature of 15.2 metres for the road were specified.

Reinhold now deployed his forces. The section from Edie Creek to Johnson Gap would be cleared by 500 native labourers supervised by eight ANGAU men under Lieutenant Charles Johnson. The 2/16th Field Company would carry out the roadwork on this section as it was cleared. Apart from the work on the new road, the existing Wau-to-Edie Creek section had deteriorated and needed considerable maintenance work. The 9th Field Company would work between Johnson Gap and Ecclestone Saddle with seventy-five pack transport personnel and 200 native labourers. Ecclestone Saddle to Fox Gap was a diabolical ten-kilometre section that necessitated following the natural ledges in the rock. The 2/1st Field Company would work on this section and would also have pack transport and native labour support. From Fox Gap to the Eloa River, Bannon would have similar pack transport and native labour resources. From the Eloa River down to Bulldog Camp, a battalion from the US 91st Engineers Regiment would be deployed. The 2/1st and 9th Field Company commenced work in mid-April.[49]

It was planned to bring in a thousand native labourers from Mount Hagen by plane, but lack of fighter cover precluded this move and 400 natives from other areas arrived on 12 May. Papuan labourers, unaccustomed to the cold, were eventually transferred out of the mountain areas and were able to work south towards Centre Camp. This problem was noted in mid-March but, despite the issuing of jumpers and blankets, the lowland natives continued to suffer from the cold.[50]

As work progressed more resources were switched to the difficult mountain sections. The section around Eloa Falls was diabolical, and the blasting dislodged great sections of the rock face, often destroying the bench track. The critical rock sections proved to be a serious obstacle to the completion of the road, and drilling had to be undertaken using a hammer and gad. It was no different from the way Australian prisoners of war were constructing the cuttings for the Thai–Burma Railway. Hand-drilling through hard granite could achieve only 15 centimetres per hour whereas 1.8 metres could be achieved using a compressor – twelve times the rate.[51]

Therefore, when the pilot track reached the critical rock area, Ingersoll Rand compressors would be broken down into manageable loads and carried in from the 24-kilometre peg to the 29-kilometre peg at the Bulldog end of the track. The 2/55th Light Aid Detachment (LAD) set up a camp at the 24-kilometre peg and based four mechanics there to strip five compressors down to portable loads. Another two compressors were stripped down at the northern end of the road at Edie Creek and taken to the 70-kilometre and 67-kilometre (Eloa) sections. The LAD mechanics then accompanied the carriers and reassembled the compressors when they arrived at the desired site.[52]

As the loads were overweight (up to 45 kilograms), relief carriers had to accompany the compressors. In all, fifty-one carriers were used to carry the seventeen parts, the heaviest of which, the engine block, weighed 90 kilograms and required eight of the carriers. Total weight was 785 kilograms with a stripping time of about three hours and reassembly taking ten hours. Despite having a reduced efficiency at the higher altitudes, and only supporting one jackhammer instead of two, the compressors did sterling work and enabled the road to pass through the critical rock ledge sections. The efficiency of the jackhammering was related to the rock type, and in hard granite the bits needed sharpening after only half a metre of drilling. Only an emery wheel or grindstone was available, and the bits could be resharpened only around three times before being discarded.[53]

The native carriers were vital to the construction of the Bulldog Road. At its peak at the end of July 1943, the road construction utilised 2349 natives, 1825 as road labourers and 524 as carriers. One means by which good work was obtained without rancour was for a stretch of road to be

Photo 12 Sappers from the 9th Field Company working on a rock face on the Bulldog Road, August 1943. Photo by Robert Buchanan. (AWM 056210)

marked out by a length of cord with equally spaced knots in it. A stake was then driven in at each knot point, ensuring equal distribution of work. Knowing his exact task and knowing it was the equal of other workers, the native labourer performed admirably.[54] As General Savige later wrote, 'The whole campaign would have been bogged down in impotency but for the native carrier.'[55]

Bridge work was vital and had to rely on what materials were available on site. In all, seventeen bridges were built, thirteen of them single span traversing a gap of up to 20 metres. Three double-span bridges were built, and one that crossed a 29-metre gap required a triple span. Gravel reinforced timber was used for the abutments and suitable timber for the road bearers and decking. A shortage of spikes meant only one spike was used at each alternate spar end to secure the decking.[56]

No matter what the quality of the roadwork, supply also had to be maintained along the Lakekamu River. Supply barges from Port Moresby offloaded to other barges operated by the 1st Australian Water Transport Company at Terapo at the mouth of the river. The first problem was the river bar, then the snags in the river, which increased by the varying river height during the monsoon season after May.

As work progressed, the road from Edie Creek became a clayey quag-mire, and the problem was exacerbated by the lack of suitable road metal quarries nearby. Despite a continuous battle against the elements, the Bulldog Road was completed on 22 August, and the first jeep convoy moved along the road the next day. However, the road was never seri-ously utilised as sea supply was now going direct to Tambu Bay and, within weeks, would reach Salamaua and, not long after, Lae.

The Japanese command was aware of the road's construction. On 18 April seven natives from Kerema arrived in Lae, telling the Japanese that they had been conscripted and coerced into working on the Bulldog Road. Then, on 22 April, a Japanese air recce plane reported that an eight-metre road had been practically completed from Bulldog (Burudokku) to Kudjeru (Kudyiru). In an intelligence report on 28 May it was reported that another road was being constructed between Wampit and Gabensis, which was also confirmed by natives captured during the Hote attack at the end of May. Acting on this intelligence, there was a Japanese air raid on Bulldog Camp on 2 June and, although damage was minimal, the effect on the native labourers was catastrophic, with nearly 700 deserting, many of them taking their tools with them. Other equipment was pilfered by the local Kukuku tribes, one party later seen proudly wearing live detonators as ornaments through their noses.[57]

While work continued apace on alternatives to air supply, the USAAF transport aircraft still provided the essential artery to enable operations to continue against Salamaua. This was not only a matter of supplying those men already in the theatre but also involved bringing in new units. Following Whitehead's gloomy outlook in March regarding the effect of weather and other considerations on his transport capacity, Mackay tried to ensure that he got the maximum efficiency from what transport aircraft were made available to him. The eighteen planeloads that White-head had allocated were only sufficient to bring in the daily requirements for Moten's force. Mackay's first plan, based on Whitehead's recommen-dations, was to build up a 15-day reserve of all the requirements for an operational force of 10,000 men at Wau and Bulolo. To do this he planned with Whitehead to maximise the use of the transports when suit-able flying weather prevailed. Writing to Blamey, Mackay stressed that they must 'use to the utmost every fine spell we get'. Thus, instead of using only eighteen planes, more would be made available if the weather was suitable.[58]

In the 17th Brigade sector, Skindiwai was used as a dropping ground during the early stages of the campaign. However, it was a poor location with a bad approach and with many tree stumps and gullies across the sloping target area. It was used only for emergency dropping, particularly after a transport aircraft was lost on 11 March. Guadagasal was a better option and was set up in March–April when a strip measuring 500 metres by 130 metres was cleared along the top of the ridge. Initial dropping effectiveness varied but, once windsocks and aiming points had been set up and the transport pilots and despatch crews gained more experience, recoveries improved. Guadagasal was used until the fall of Mubo in July 1943, at which point two locations at Mubo were briefly used, Observation Hill and the dry creekbed in the Bitoi River valley. As the fighting moved forward to Mount Tambu and the southern end of Bobdubi Ridge, Goodview Junction became the key dropping point in the 17th Brigade sector.[59] This was a good drop area but was also very close to the enemy lines.

In the 15th Brigade area air-dropping proved crucial to operations due to the difficult supply route across the Double Mountain trail from the Bulolo Valley. The initial sites selected were at Missim, Selebob, Hote and Pilimung, but none of these locations was ideal. Once the Australians were established on Bobdubi Ridge, Nunn's Post, which was in a kunai basin as opposed to being on a ridge, became the key dropping ground for 15th Brigade. The brigade war diary noted, 'The Nunn's Post ground is almost foolproof – it is a long kunai basin and the pilots can't miss.' For three months 15th Brigade was supplied almost solely from the air; only delicate equipment such as radios was unable to be dropped. A lot of food was free-dropped with varying recovery rates but, when parachutes were used, recovery was usually 100 per cent.[60] With access to a ready source of supply, a field bakery was established at Nunn's Post, distributing 120 dozen scones or buns per day to the forward troops.

Parachute drops were made into the wind from around 80 metres at 165 to 200 kilometres per hour along the longest axis of the dropping ground. Free-dropping took place from six to fifteen metres at a slightly higher speed. Drop zones were marked with a unique T sign, set up just before the drop, while dummy drops were carried out at other areas nearby to try to confuse the enemy. To help with recoveries, a coloured streamer was attached to one of the loads detailing the load manifest.[61]

On 26 July an air maintenance company was formed to organise the efficient packing, loading, despatch and delivery of all classes of supplies from the air. Australian Army Service Corps crews flew with the transport aircraft to despatch the supplies. From 4 August these aircraft were based at Dobodura, making dropping much easier as it was not necessary to cross the Owen Stanley Range. B-25 Mitchell bombers could also be used and, although the supplies carried were less, these aircraft did not require separate fighter escorts.[62] However, they had too high a stalling speed to do the job efficiently, and supplies were generally scattered far and wide. The slower RAAF Wirraways, although unable to carry as much, proved better suited to such work.

Free-dropping was used for such items as boots, clothing, blankets, rope, signal wire and rations. Simple tools such as mattocks, picks and shovels were also free-dropped whereas parachutes were used for ammunition, explosives and small arms. The 2/25th Field Park Company produced suitable containers for the Wirraways to use for dropping such items as 3-inch mortars and Boys anti-tank rifles. There was a maximum weight of 90 kilograms per container. Mortar base plates were dropped separately from bomb racks with a single 18-kilogram parachute attached.[63]

On 2 June RAAF No. 4 Squadron was given the task of dropping a mortar at Pilimung. The drop zone was on the side of a range, and the pilot given the job, Flying Officer Ron Dickson, had not previously used it. Another pilot, Flying Officer Peter Ambrose, went along as observer carrying the base plate in his lap. The rest of the weapon was stowed in a sealed cylinder known as a storepedo, which was attached to the Wirraway's bomb rack. Dickson found the drop zone, lowered the flaps and undercarriage to reduce speed, and headed for the clearing, dropping the parachute load without incident. He then returned for Ambrose, who was leaning over the side of the cockpit, to drop the base plate. As he did so there was an almighty thump and the aircraft reacted violently. The spikes that anchored the baseplate had embedded into the aircraft tailplane, resulting in a difficult climb back over the range before the base plate dropped off just before landing at Wau. Dickson's was not the only negative experience involving mortars. Two-inch mortar rounds were found to be arming when dropped, and 2500 rounds had to be condemned after a number of infantrymen had been killed by premature explosions.[64]

No matter how supplies were delivered to Wau and Bulolo they still had to be carried forward to the front line. The maximum load on the Missim

Photo 13 A carrier line forming up at Mubo in July 1943 to take supplies forward to the 2/5th Battalion front line at Mount Tambu and Goodview. Photo by Robert Buchanan. (AWM 055147)

line of communication was 16 kilograms, elsewhere 18 kilograms. Each carrier could transport one of the following:

- ten rations
- three 3-inch mortar bombs
- twelve 2-inch mortar bombs
- one box of a thousand .303 rifle rounds.
- one box of twelve rifle grenades
- one bag of twenty hand grenades
- one box of 798.45 TSMG rounds
- one box of 500 belted .303 rounds.

Ancillary goods required considerable labour. For example, a battery charger including batteries would require eleven carriers.[65] Carrier lines also had to be escorted, usually on the basis of two men per twenty carriers, with more used in forward areas. However, the carrier lines would often stretch back for kilometres, making proper escort impossible, and it was fortunate that the Japanese never seriously attempted to interdict them.

In early April a plan was hatched by Lieutenant George Whittaker, a former Lae planter, now attached to ANGAU, to bring in 400 native carriers from villages around Salamaua: Bobdubi, Namling and Logui. They would be brought to Pilimung and thus deny their use to the Japanese. At the same time the carriers would prove vital in maintaining the supply route back across Double Mountain to the Bulolo Valley. This plan was carried out on 21 April. Brigadier Hammer later wrote, 'Whittaker did a sterling job and helped immeasurably in supplying to the troops.' Supply was a problem that could be lessened by air-dropping, but evacuation of casualties required considerable carrier resources. Hammer rightly noted that it was 'a colossal task'.[66]

The widespread use of native carriers by the Australians might infer that the troops were not unduly burdened. This was far from being the case, particularly given the difficult terrain over which the troops had to operate. The standard loads carried by Australian riflemen, Owen gunners and Bren gunners are shown in table 4.3. The tommy gun was a heavier weapon and had heavier ammunition than the Owen gun.[67] So, while the native carriers were limited to loads of 16 to 18 kg, the poor bloody infantry often carried more than twice that amount.

Table 4.3: Typical loads carried by Australian troops

Equipment	Rifleman	Owen gunner	Bren gunner
Clothing and boots	4.3	4.3	4.3
Pack	9.3	9.3	9.3
Haversack	6.5	6.5	6.5
Web equipment (incl. water)	6.5	6.5	6.5
Weapon	4.2	4.2	10.2
Ammunition (incl. mags)	1.4 (50 rounds)	3.6 (120 rounds)	3.3 (90 rounds)
One grenade	0.7	0.7	0.7
Total:	32.9 kg	35.1 kg	40.8 kg

The battle to maintain supply to the front lines was a difficult and constant one for both combatants, in many ways a greater challenge than the front-line fighting. Following the cessation of merchant ship convoys to Lae after the Battle of the Bismarck Sea, the Japanese had shown great versatility in putting new supply lines in place. The use of destroyers and submarines combined with motorised landing craft enabled both reinforcements and supplies to be brought to the Lae–Salamaua area. With Rabaul threatened as a supply base the Japanese command also acted to set up new bases in the Wewak area. Had the supply problem not been solved then the occupation of both Salamaua and Lae would have been untenable.

The Allied supply system had different concerns. The merchant convoys from Australia to the New Guinea mainland were never seriously threatened, but to move supplies and troops across the Owen Stanley Range to the front lines, the Australians were dependent on USAAF transport aircraft. Air-dropping techniques, pioneered during the Kokoda campaign, were refined during the Salamaua campaign and excellent recovery rates obtained. The reduction in the allocation of transport aircraft had major implications for operations and led to the extraordinary Bulldog Road project. Although the road was ultimately not used, its construction gave the Australian command the flexibility to ensure that the campaign could continue. Closer to the front lines, the Allies had one other major advantage over the Japanese in the supply war: the loyalty of the hard-working native carriers. As they had proven in the Kokoda campaign, the 'fuzzy-wuzzy angels' were indispensable. Without such a resource, the Japanese army was forced to use front-line infantry to carry supplies, taking them out of the front lines.

CHAPTER | 5

MUBO STALEMATE

Although no large-scale offensive was called for in front of Mubo, Moten was encouraged to occupy any vacated enemy positions should the Japanese pull back. At this stage the Japanese had a protective screen at Guadagasal to enable the remnants of the Okabe Detachment to return from Wau. From these positions they controlled the Mubo end of both the Buisaval and Black Cat tracks and prevented any Australian move on to Lababia Ridge. On 7 March another hundred enemy soldiers dug in around Guadagasal, indicating an intention to hold the area, a prerequisite for any renewed move on Wau from Mubo. Despite the loss of the Bismarck Sea convoy, the Japanese command still had designs on Wau, or at least wanted the Australian command to continue to believe so.[1]

Moten's orders to Lieutenant-Colonel Danny Starr, commander of the 2/5th Battalion, were to 'gain contact with enemy and not lose it'. As the month of March began, Starr had two platoons forward, manning observation posts to check on any enemy move up the Black Cat Track. The rest of Starr's men were spread out all the way back to Crystal Creek outside Wau, protecting Buisaval Track. The majority of these men were involved in road construction, the building of accommodation at Skindiwai and the carrying of supplies forward.[2] Due to the limited number of troops in the forward area, Starr considered operations impracticable without sacrificing control of the Buisaval and Black Cat Tracks.

There had been some discussion about bringing up 25-pounder guns from Wau to Skindiwai, from where they could fire on Mubo at extreme range, but the nature of the country made the move impossible.[3] On 20 February Berryman had discussed the use of 3.7-inch mountain guns with Wilton who had used such guns in similar terrain in Burma before the war. Berryman and Wilton then met with Moten in Wau 'and impressed on him the need for getting a section of mountain guns to where he could shell the Nips at Mubo and the Saddle'.[4] By 22 February two 3.7-inch mountain guns, accompanied by three officers and twenty-nine men from the 1st Australian Mountain Battery, had been flown to Wau.

The mountain battery had been formed in July 1942 when it became obvious that Australian army units in New Guinea would require some form of artillery support that could operate in the difficult terrain. The battery was deployed to Papua some months later when a one-gun section was sent to Kokoda and a two-gun section to Buna. These two guns provided vital artillery support against the dug-in enemy positions throughout the Buna campaign.

The battery had brought two Quick Firing 3.7-inch Mk 1 howitzers to Wau. These guns had been manufactured in England in 1923, and four of them had been sourced by the Australian army from New Zealand in July 1942. However, the guns had been modified in New Zealand with the trails welded together and the axles extended and fitted with larger wheels so that they could be used as horse-drawn artillery. In Australia, the guns had to be reverse engineered and new parts fabricated so that the guns could be used in their original role.[5]

The two guns were old and worn and, although two others were cannibalised to keep them in service, the main parts were hand-made to high tolerances and were not interchangeable. Gaskets for the recuperators had to be cut out from the side of army boots to keep the guns operating. Obtaining ammunition was also a problem as it had to be sourced from England and India. The best ammunition originated from Royal Navy stocks as it contained a small smoke charge, enabling the fall of shot to be observed in the jungle terrain. The guns were unsuitable for 'pin-point' targets such as individual enemy positions, yet they would prove invaluable in support of offensive and defensive actions during the campaign. The battery commander later noted, 'The 3.7 How was a miracle gun for accuracy and reliability.'[6]

It would take four weeks to carry the guns along Buisaval Track to the front line. The first gun reached the forward area on 16 March and was emplaced at the Saddle, from where it fired on Observation Hill.

Photo 14 One of Major O'Hare's 3.7-inch mountain guns. Photo by Robert Buchanan. (AWM 054507)

John Tyree noted, 'Between it and its mounting plus a few shells it must have taken about a hundred cargo boys to hump in. It would fire one or two shells in the direction of Mubo every now and then, we would hear this slow whistling overhead then a dull thump somewhere in the bush.'[7] Unfortunately the first gun proved less than reliable and 'constant attention failed to improve its performance appreciably'. When the second gun was brought forward on 22 March, the first was stripped down for service.[8] These two mountain guns would provide the sole artillery support for 3rd Division until mid-July.

The battery was under the command of Major Martin Patrick 'Paddy' O'Hare, who had formed and trained the battery and brought it to New Guinea. The 21-pound rounds used by the 3.7-inch mountain guns were referred to as 'potatoes' and thus the guns became known as 'Paddy's Potato Pushers'. On 30 March O'Hare established new observation posts on Vickers Ridge and Mat Mat Hill, overlooking Mubo, with Lieutenant John Colless as the forward observation officer. Ammunition was a major issue as the expenditure of twenty rounds a day would require 150 native carriers to be constantly employed hauling rounds up from

Ballam's. These carriers could not be spared from other work. Further-more Moten demanded that a reserve of 200 rounds per gun be kept, and therefore the guns could not be used for harassing fire. Only confirmed targets could be engaged and then with only fifty rounds.[9]

On 9 March 26 Japanese bombers made an attack on Wau, dropping their bombs along the side of the airstrip. The 2/8th Field Company was hardest hit with three men being killed and another three wounded. Undaunted, the company proceeded to delouse a number of delayed-action bombs and repair the signal lines around the airfield.[10] The 2/3rd Independent Company also lost a man, struck down by the reawakened terror of a similar attack by German bombers in the Middle East. Peter Pinney wrote: 'He was shellshocked in Greece, and in the middle of explosions straddling us he got up and rushed down a little gully, smack into the middle of a stick of bombs... later the CSM found his blitzed remains. [He] had come through a lot... the bastardry of Greece and Crete, and now this. He lived in mortal fear of bombers.'[11] On the previous day, nine bombers had raided Oro Bay and sunk a transport vessel. The Japanese air arms were obviously determined to re-establish their presence following the Bismarck Sea debacle.

Moten ordered Starr to attack the Saddle area above Mubo, but when Starr requested more of his men be sent forward, he was told that the two companies at Ballam's and Skindiwai would 'continue vigorous road work'.[12] There was a clear recognition that the campaign would be a drawn-out one, and the provision of more substantial supply lines was vital if Mubo was to be seriously threatened.

For the moment USAAF transport aircraft continued to drop supplies at Skindiwai. It was a difficult drop zone, on the southern slope of the Buisaval River valley. The planes had to fly into the valley, then come in low over the small kunai clearing that acted as the dropping ground before flying a figure eight to allow a second run. The planes would come in then swing out, two or three of them at a time, while the men on the ground would stand back on the side of a hill and watch. There was one big tree at the drop zone that could not be felled as it would have fallen across the camp, and this had to be avoided during dropping. On 11 March a C-47 transport plane piloted by Staff Sergeant Elmer Crowley from the 22nd Troop Carrier Squadron hit the top of the tree with a wing. Down below the anxious Australians could hear the roar of the engines as the damaged plane tried to gain height before the stricken bird crashed to the ground.[13] The eleven men on board were killed, six of them USAAF crewmen, together with five Australians helping with the supply dropping.

In a related move, 17th Brigade HQ ordered that troops were not to move forward because of the difficulty in maintaining air supply. On the following day New Guinea Force headquarters stressed that forward supply to the Mubo area would be dependent on the jeep road to Skindiwai. At that stage the bridge at Crystal Creek had almost been completed and the track through to Skindiwai was expected to be operational within a fortnight. Two sections from the 2/8th Field Company with only one tractor, which was often idle through lack of fuel, had done sterling work on this bridge and other smaller ones along the line of road to the Summit. However, despite the optimism of New Guinea Force headquarters, the bridge was not finished until 12 April and the jeephead had only reached Ballam's by that time. The Summit was not reached until 7 June and, as work continued to push the track through to Skindiwai, heavy rain turned the Ballam's-to-Summit section into a bog. Gravelling of the track from the Summit to Skindiwai did not commence until 5 August, but a week later the work was called off as sea supply had been established from the coast.[14]

On 13 March the 2/5th Battalion occupied a deserted Guadagasal Ridge and set up positions commanding the approach to the Saddle. The Japanese withdrawal might have been affected by the accurate Allied air attacks on the Guadagasal area, but the loss of most of the 115th Regiment in the Bismarck Sea was probably the critical factor leading to abandoning the jump-off positions for any further attack on Wau. However, on the same day New Guinea Force headquarters reiterated that Moten 'must not push his operations in the forward area beyond the safe limit of maintenance'. Mackay followed up this directive in a letter to Moten on 21 March that stated: 'It seems to me that with your present force and the difficulty of supply, the occupation of, say, Salamaua, is only a remote possibility. Your brigade is already strung out overmuch and is becoming top heavy in the easterly direction.' The Japanese had also reinforced Mubo with around 600 fresh marines from the 2nd Maizuru Special Naval Landing Party. They represented a much tougher obstacle for the Australians than the wasted remnants of Major-General Okabe's unit.[15]

At this time Major Fergus MacAdie's 2/7th Independent Company was the main unit in contact with the Japanese. The company had built two bridges across the Bitoi River near Waipali, and patrols were operating into the ranges south of Mubo where they found that the Japanese had set up defensive positions on Observation Hill. On 26 March another patrol moving along Lababia Ridge came across the Pimple, a formidable Japanese position adjoining Green Hill above Mubo. This patrol found the track, then discovered that fortifications had been built, the red soil from the digging being obvious. The next day, four of them set up an ambush and fifteen to twenty enemy soldiers were killed during a fierce fight. Private Bob Else and Bob Evans were hit, Evans copping one in the shoulder while a bullet hit a tree next to John Tyree and threw splinters into his eye. Corporal Billy Dunn told the ambush party, 'Let's get out.' However, the wounded Else, in his first action, couldn't be found and never was. Despite the encounter, there was no rest for the weary, and the following day they went out on another patrol.[16]

On 24 March Moten had finally met with, then promptly relieved Starr. The reasons given were: (1) he had consistently ignored Moten's instructions, (2) he had failed to maintain close contact with the enemy during the Japanese withdrawal along the Black Cat Track to Mubo, (3) he had allowed the ammunition reserve of the mountain artillery guns to drop from a requested 200 rounds per gun to four rounds per gun, (4) he had not taken sufficient anti-malarial precautions with his men, who did not have mosquito nets, and (5) he had failed to prepare adequate defensive positions in the Buibaining–Waipali area. Moten later told the official historian that he had 'sacked him [Starr] when he let Japs through after Wau'.[17]

Moten also decided to withdraw the 2/5th Battalion from the front line for reorganisation and replace them with the 2/7th Battalion, although the changeover would take some weeks. Moten requested Lieutenant-Colonel Tom Conroy as the replacement for Starr and, until he arrived, Major Norman Goble would assume temporary command. Conroy, a skilled industrial chemist, had served as a major with the 2/43rd Battalion in the Middle East, then commanded the 2/32nd Battalion from June 1941 to February 1942.[18] During that time Conroy's battalion had been in action at Tobruk in North Africa, but his experience there would not necessarily stand him in good stead for operations in New Guinea. He had been also relieved in the Middle East, and Lieutenant-General Leslie Morshead, his former commander, later questioned General Savige on why Conroy had been given a front-line battalion command. However, Savige had not been involved in the appointment; it was Moten's call. Mackay met Conroy at Port Moresby on his way to Wau and noted, 'He looks a good type and I hope [he] will do well with 2/5.' However, the change did not go down well with the battalion. As the B Company commander, Captain Cam Bennett, later observed, 'Even if the archangel Gabriel had been his successor he would have come in for much criticism.'[19]

Captain Owen Williams, attached to the advanced dressing station at Guadagasal, visited the 2/5th Battalion outpost on Mat Mat Hill on 5 April. He wrote: 'A most peculiar introduction to the front line. We just walked out onto the forward slopes of an open hill – almost clear and I sat down next to a cove who was sitting in the shade of a small tree and looking through a pair of glasses. Yarned for a quarter hour, pointed out Jap positions opposite on Observation Hill – ambushes etc – the closest being 540 yards. Nobody doing anything about it!! A funny war!!'[20]

On the afternoon of 9 April a 2/5th Battalion patrol made contact with the Japanese on Observation Hill. Amid the sound of heavy gunfire, one man could be heard in obvious distress; Harold Feeley was missing and three others were wounded. Despite a bad wound to the shoulder, one of them, Pat 'Digger' Dunne, managed to bring his weapon out with him and another stayed out overnight.[21] The Australian patrol had run into enemy troops from II/102nd Battalion's No. 6 Company, who reported that they had been attacked by six or seven men with automatic rifles but had driven them off, killing one and wounding another.[22] On 11 April another 12 Platoon patrol went out to Observation Hill, which was reached without incident, but as it went further it came upon some timber across the track 200 metres further on. Two men made their way through an archway formed by the roots of a fallen tree, but as the third man, Corporal John Allen, ducked under, machine-gun fire opened up from both sides of the track, apparently killing him.[23] The bodies of Harold Feeley and John Allen remain missing to this day.

Meanwhile, the 2/7th Independent Company was to be relieved after six months in the front line. The unit was on its way back to Port Moresby before being sent to Bena Bena in the New Guinea highlands. Bena Bena was assuming increased importance as a possible base for operations against Madang, Lae and Wewak, and patrols were already harassing the Japanese in the Ramu Valley. Bena Bena also served as a major source of native labour and denied the Japanese use of that resource.[24]

The Australian role at Mubo would now escalate beyond a screening and holding one. Major MacAdie's company was relieved by Lieutenant-Colonel Henry Guinn's 2/7th Battalion. As Savige later observed, 'Guinn is a likable fellow who is, and always was, ultra optimistic which I found overcame prudent action on his part. He always saw the bright colours of the rainbow which he so often pursued in a light hearted manner.' The perceptive Savige also considered that Guinn's second in command, Major St Elmo Nelson, was too similar to Guinn to form a good team.[25]

Captain Bruce Peterson was the 2/7th Battalion medical officer and, after setting up an aid post at Skindiwai, he had gone forward to take over the aid post at the Saddle on 13 April. This post had been dug into the slope of the Saddle, only five minutes from water, and the 2/2nd Field Ambulance's Advanced Dressing Station (ADS) was close by, back along the track at Guadagasal. Major William Refshauge wouldn't allow the Red Cross flag to be used to mark the station despite the fact it had been respected at Wau. Williams wrote, 'We'll have to camouflage it and if we get strafed I'll feel extra poor.'[26]

Once they reached the front, the 2/7th Battalion companies were scattered far and wide: one company was deployed at Waipali and another along Lababia Ridge above Mubo. The other two companies were sent across the Bitoi River, one at Mat Mat Hill and the other at Hill 7, further south. Supplying the medical orderlies at each location was difficult, and Peterson knew that any casualty evacuation would be nothing short of a nightmare. When Sergeant John 'Joe' Law was wounded in the leg while on a patrol down below Vickers Ridge on 16 April, stretcher-bearers could not be organised until the following day and he could not be found. Meanwhile another soldier, Lieutenant James Capuano, had been wounded out near the Pimple. When Peterson got to him he was able to stitch up a dangerous sucking chest wound and administer sulpha drugs and morphine before an improvised stretcher was made to carry him out. One man had to go ahead to hack a track out of the jungle, and the men toiled until they dropped from exhaustion about half way out. A relief carrying party took him the rest of the way, but Capuano would unfortunately succumb to his wounds two months later. Joe Law, having hidden behind the roots of a huge tree with enemy troops coming within five metres of his position, was found and carried out the following day. His first question on being found was: 'Who won the Doncaster?'[27]

There were around 460 Japanese troops in the Mubo area. Most came from a 102nd Regiment formation, the Yamagata Detachment, which had withdrawn from the Buna campaign, together with around seventy SNLP marines. Many of these soldiers had malaria, exacerbated by sporadic supplies from the rear, and their fighting strength waned as the days passed.[28] Although digging in, the Japanese were not patrolling. The Australians maintained pressure by their own patrolling and by limited attacks on the enemy positions. Above Mubo, the Green Hill position continued to prove a difficult nut to crack. Moten had given orders for the 2/7th Battalion to capture the Pimple and Green Hill and thus remove one of the bulwarks protecting Mubo. Captain Frank Pringle's C Company would do the attack. The plan was for the approaches to be secured on 24 April and the main Green Hill attack to be made on 25 April. It would be called the 'Anzac Day Op.'. Vickers guns from the 7th Machine Gun Battalion would be used to support the operation, and O'Hare's two mountain guns were each allocated fifty rounds.[29]

An attack by four A-20 Bostons preceded the 24 April attack with each light bomber making two bombing runs, then four strafing runs. A 2/7th Battalion infantryman, Jack Mitchell, wrote, 'Our bombers were again giving Nip a dust up.'[30] However, the usefulness of air support for the 2/7th Battalion during this period is debatable and a later report stated as much: 'The direct air support of the infantry did not have the desired results.' An enemy prisoner later told how the Japanese would retire to slit trench positions during air attacks, and only one man in his 100-man machine-gun company had been lost due to air attack during a month in the front line at Mubo. With an 800-metre distance between the bomb line and the target in heavy country, if there was any benefit from the air support, it would be nullified before the attack could be launched. At that stage the ground troops would be on their own as there was around a 16-hour delay between a request for an air strike and the operation being carried out.[31]

Pringle's plan was for two sections from Lieutenant Bill Dinsmore's 13 Platoon to make a feint attack astride the main track while 14 Platoon, with one of Dinsmore's sections attached, would try to get around the rear of the enemy position. Captain Pringle would lead the 14 Platoon attack and approach along Law's Track, which bypassed the Pimple to the west. When Pringle's men were in position, he would blow a whistle so that the diversionary fire from 13 Platoon would cease. Once the Pimple was captured both 13 and 15 Platoons would move through to take up positions on the Green Hill track.[32]

Up on Guadagasal Ridge, Owen Williams watched the infantry attack go in. 'To see the start of the big stunt', Williams wrote, 'we stayed on until 1215 listening to the mortars, MMGs, Brens, Tommies, rifles etc and receiving all the latest information. C Coy was to attack the Jap ambush on the Pimple from front and rear as soon as the first bomb dropped.'

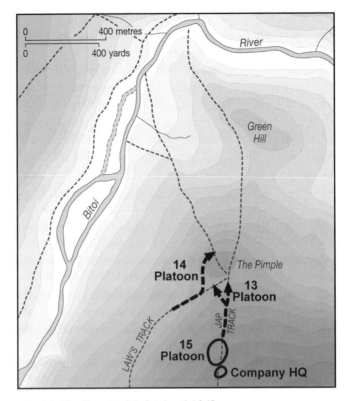

Map 12 The Pimple, 24–26 April 1943

By 1300, 13 Platoon had been pinned down and there was no news from Pringle. Captain Reg Dixon went forward and found that 14 Platoon was also pinned down by heavy machine-gun fire. It came from the northern end of the Pimple position, catching the Australians unaware. As Williams noted, 'The Pimple is about 300 yards long, very steep & terrific jungle.' The Japanese were dug in along the full length of the position.[33] Facing such an extensively developed position, the Australians paid a heavy price, losing six men killed and another eight wounded – the harsh reality of jungle warfare. Guinn observed that the Pimple 'is a razor back with precipitous sides very heavily timbered' and that 'fire lanes have been lightly cleared to enable the whole feature to be covered by fire from MMGs and LMGs'.[34] Yet he had set his men against it.

When the attack was resumed the following day, three more men were wounded without any further progress. Then, with sixty Japanese reinforcements moving down from Green Hill, it was decided to set booby traps and pull back. Don Robertson was killed while he helped organise the withdrawal. Williams wrote, 'C Coy didn't take the ambush yesterday so can't go on to Green Hill today. It's terribly thick apparently and the Nips are dug in and so every time our fellas move they're just hit and never even see where it comes from.'[35] The Japanese defenders, from No. 2 Company I/102nd Battalion, reported that forty-four Australian dead had been abandoned following the attack and, although clearly overstated, this did reflect the failure of the operation. The Japanese losses were reported as five men killed and another five wounded.[36]

The mountain guns tried to try to knock out the Japanese support weapons, then air strikes were made on 26 and 27 April. However, in moving up closer to the bomb line, the Australians had one man killed and five wounded by the bombing. A later C Company patrol found indications that despite the accuracy of the shelling and bombing, the Japanese defenders might have had alternative shelter positions, probably on the reverse side of the Pimple and Green Hill. The artillery was considered to give better support than the bombers as the troops did not have to withdraw from their jump-off positions; however, a lack of suitable observation posts for directing the artillery fire mitigated the effect.[37]

Due to the difficulty of observing the Pimple area under the jungle cover, Lieutenant Colless was ordered to range the mountain guns on his own position and then adjust the fire on to the target. Colless had two signallers with him sending back fire orders via a phone line, and they had run the line well out in front of the Australian front line to the base of the enemy-held ridge. Colless then took a phone line and crawled forward through the undergrowth and got behind a large tree, almost on top of the enemy positions. One of the signallers, Jack Allan, noted, 'After a while I heard the gun fire. A few seconds elapsed and there was an explosion in the tree tops a bit down from where I was sitting waiting. A short while after and another round further down – then silence. I knew he had ranged fairly accurately.' The mountain guns fired seventy-four rounds on to the enemy position that day.[38]

The costly attacks at Green Hill and the Pimple meant more casualties for the medical staff, as Captain Peterson's diary entry for 24 April succinctly noted: 'No rest for the weary.' On the same day Sergeant Bill Russell, one of Peterson's medical orderlies, got to a badly wounded soldier after dark, almost under the noses of the Japanese defenders. The man had a dangerous sucking chest wound and would die without immediate attention. In the pitch dark, using only the glow of a cigarette for light, Russell stitched the wound and lay with the man all night. Peterson later noted: 'I taught him how to stitch them up.'[39] It took special men to fight this jungle war and, as Russell's battalion commander later said, 'VCs have been awarded for much less.'[40]

Close cooperation with the 2/2nd Field Ambulance was vital, and their stretcher-bearers constantly came forward to evacuate the wounded. Casualty care on the battlefield was a stepped process, with the level of treatment increasing with each step in the chain. The first step was the immediate treatment, usually carried out by a soldier with a field dressing. Treatment from a stretcher-bearer came next, and he would also help get the wounded man back to the RAP. In addition to what immediate first aid was required, the wounded brought into the RAP were treated with sulpha drugs, anti-tetanus serum and, where required, morphine. The wound could be further stabilised before the patient was carried by native stretcher-bearers back to the field ambulance where emergency surgery could take place before being carried back to Wau, by air to the General Hospital in Port Moresby and back to Australia as and when required.[41]

One of the C Company men was Sergeant Reg Saunders, serving with 14 Platoon. Reg had been brought up by his grandmother at Lake Condah in country Victoria. His father and uncle had served with the First Australian Imperial Force while his younger brother Harry had served with the 2/14th Battalion and was killed at Gona in December 1942. Reg had enlisted in 1940 and joined the 2/7th Battalion in the Middle East, but it was in New Guinea that his knowledge of the bush made him an outstanding soldier. He later commented: 'I just had the luck, I had good reflexes, I had good hearing, and I had good eyesight – and I could pick the difference between the bushes, the ones they used for camouflage – because they picked them ten feet away, I'd notice the difference.'[42]

Saunders trained the men in the platoon well, imparting his special skills. 'Get off the tracks,' he would tell them. 'Don't walk down those bloody tracks whatever you do, because if you go down the track, he's been told to kill everybody on there – anybody on the track.' Saunders' ability was highly regarded in 17th Brigade and, on 12 April, he had led a 2/5th Battalion patrol down through Napier to the coast at Duali. On another occasion he was out on a recce patrol with two other 14 Platoon men, Jack Gibson and Clyde Stiff. Clyde was the forward scout leading the patrol towards the enemy perimeter at the top of a hill when Saunders suddenly pulled him up, telling him, 'There's a bastard in the tree. Give us your rifle.' The first Clyde saw of the Japanese sniper was when Saunders' shot dropped him from the tree.[43] In November 1944 Reg Saunders became the Australian army's first Aboriginal commissioned officer, returning to the battalion that had fostered him. He would go on to command an infantry company in Korea. He was indeed a special soldier.

On 2 May Guinn had another go at the Pimple, this time with A Company. Six A-20 Bostons, guided in by smoke rounds from O'Hare's mountain guns, bombed the enemy positions before the attack. The experienced defenders had, as anticipated, vacated their defensive positions during the bombing, but rapidly reoccupied them when it ceased. The enemy defence comprised Juki heavy machine-guns with Nambu light machine-guns in front and on the flanks. In turn, the light machine-guns were protected by snipers. The Jukis would provide the first fire, then, as the Australians tried to deal with them, the light machine-guns and snipers would come into play. With the jungle creating echoes from any gun fire and masking gun flash, even identifying enemy positions was a difficult task.[44]

As previously, the attack foundered. Two men were killed, including the commander of 7 Platoon, Lieutenant Laurie Sparke, while another ten men were wounded, one later dying of his wounds. Three Japanese defenders were killed and another wounded. When his section's Bren gunner was wounded, Corporal Doug Smith, the acting section leader on the right flank, moved off to find stretcher-bearers. Separated from his section for only a minute, Smith had to dodge enemy patrols as he moved down the ridge through the Japanese lines and crossed the Bitoi River. Somehow Smith managed to survive on berries and fruit and, when he finally staggered into the Australian lines at Mat Mat 20 days later, he still held on to his tommy gun and magazines.[45]

Captain Vic Baird, the D Company commander, later wrote of the concerns about the costly yet fruitless attacks against the Pimple. 'It was obvious, at least to junior officers of the 2/7 Bn, after the first attack by Pringle's company, that this feature would not be taken without a great deal of prior softening up, and the employment of a force much larger than one under-strength company.' The dissatisfaction went higher. Savige was not impressed by the 2/7th Battalion's actions at Green Hill and the Pimple. 'I was amazed and alarmed as the situation around the Pimple developed...at the first favourable opportunity I called the show off.' Savige also noted that the 2/7th Battalion had been rebuilt following the fighting in Crete and, although the battalion had fought at Wau, the Green

Hill action was the first experience the battalion had of the distinctive nature of jungle fighting. An instruction issued on 4 May stated that 'frontal attacks would not be made against prepared enemy positions'.[46]

Another attack was made on the Pimple on 7 May, this time using flanking tactics. Following a hundred rounds of mountain-gun fire, 9 Platoon advanced on the right flank and got within 40 metres of the main defence position before snipers opened up from tree positions. A section was sent further around to the right flank but was unable to get up the precipitous slopes. On the left flank 7 Platoon came up against two machine-guns and was stopped cold, around 40 metres out. The A Company commander, Captain Vin Tatterson, also tried to get 8 Platoon around on the left, but it was held up by the enfilade fire. At 1430, under cover of heavy afternoon rain, both platoons withdrew. Following the attack, 3rd Division headquarters issued instructions that further attacks on the Pimple were to be discontinued.[47]

CHAPTER | 6

ON LABABIA RIDGE

Following the abortive attacks on the Pimple, Captain Tatterson's A Company had moved to Lababia Ridge, a thousand metres to the south. Tatterson's company was well under strength with only 65 men being available. It was another 400 metres back to Lababia base camp, which was held by a platoon from D Company. At 0815 on 9 May a booby trap went off in front of Tatterson's positions astride Laws Track on Lababia Ridge. Aware that tree branches often set off the traps, Corporal Charlie Broadbent rang back to headquarters saying that it was 'probably another branch. Will let you know.' It would be three days before Broadbent would again be able to contact headquarters. As further reports came in of movement around the right flank, the company stood to. Firing broke out, and soon all of the forward positions were engaged; supporting artillery fire being brought down in front of the Australian positions. However, this attack was a feint, disguising moves to either flank of the Australian position. The main attack came in on the left.[1]

To better support Tatterson, Major O'Hare sent up a forward observation officer, Lieutenant Roy Caterson, with a party of signallers. However, the signal line soon went dead as the Japanese got in behind the Australian position. Late in the afternoon, a report came in from Sergeant Clarrie Hubble that the reinforcing platoon was under heavy attack and was pulling back, leaving Tatterson cut off. An estimated 500 Japanese infantrymen had enveloped Tatterson's company, and Juki machine-guns had been positioned on the flanks and rear of the Australian position,

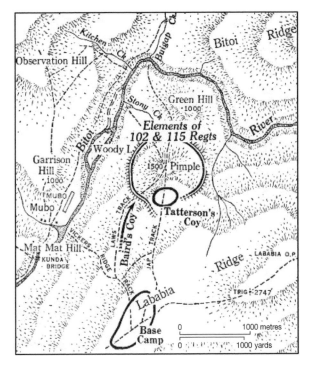

Map 13 Lababia Ridge area, 9–11 May 1943

blocking any relief.[2] Private Charles Germaine, who was in Tatterson's company, later wrote,

> We retreated to a rough line of weapon pits and then they attacked us. I counted twelve assaults in less than an hour. The undergrowth was so thick that we could not see the faces of the Japs, but we got glimpses of them as they wormed their way through the scrub towards us. At times they got within ten yards of us, but every time they were beaten back. It was our grenades which caused the Japs to run in terror. They tried rolling grenades down the hill, but these exploded before they reached our pits.[3]

Len Waters typified the resolute stand by Tatterson's men. His Bren gun came under intense fire from three enemy light machine-guns, losing one bipod leg and having the foresight shot away. On the morning of 10 May the gun was hit again and Waters was wounded in the arm. Yet he calmly repaired the gun and, as he could no longer fire it, handed it over to his number 2. Another Bren gunner, Lloyd Bowen, had his number

2 wounded early on the first day but was able to engage two enemy light machine-guns and silence them. Another Bren gunner, Win Howard, had the magazine shot off his gun by a machine-gun, but after sighting through the bullet holes in the adjacent trees, he rapidly fired off three magazines at the suspected position and shut it down. One of Joe's 7 Platoon mates had a small Bible with him that his father had carried in World War I, and it was a popular read as the men waited for the next attack.[4]

Sent forward late on 9 May to treat one of the wounded men, Captain Peterson and his accompanying bearers came under enemy fire. Ray Pope, one of the bearers, heard a high-pitched order in Japanese and the jungle suddenly erupted with noise. Pope was shot through the thigh but managed to crawl forward with the rest of Peterson's group. They found themselves cut off with Tatterson's company, sheltering in a dip in the ground trying to treat the growing number of wounded in pitch darkness with limited medical supplies.[5]

On 10 May the Japanese put in four more heavy attacks, but A Company held. Tatterson later noted: 'We said to ourselves, we will hold this position as long as water and ammunition holds out.' Fortunately the company had a good supply of ammunition, gathered for the attacks on the Pimple, but water was in short supply. The wounded Ray Pope watched as 'the Japs came on very bravely and resolutely, but our automatic weapons cut them to pieces'. Other wounded continued to gather in the hollows around Peterson, and that night rainwater was gathered off the sides of the tents. As the second night passed plans were made to break bush the following day in an effort to regain the main battalion lines, although Peterson had concerns at getting out more than two stretcher cases. Tim Tyrer, the company cook, shot one enemy soldier who got into his area.[6]

Meanwhile, the rest of D Company under Captain Vic Baird had moved up to support their forward platoon during the night of 9 May. Lieutenant Percy Thomas's two sections moved around the flank on the morning of 10 May while the attached Carrier Platoon pushed down the track, relieving Hubble's section. Later, even the cooks were drafted in to help form the two platoons and, moving forward in bounds, they closed in on Tatterson's besieged company. Paddy O'Hare accompanied Baird as the artillery observer with orders to 'blast your way through even if it takes all your ammunition'. With a signals party laying out signal line back to the guns as they moved forward, O'Hare brought down fire in front of Baird's forward men. Concerned by 'overs' hitting Tatterson's positions, Guinn decided that such a situation was preferable to the relief failing.[7]

The relieving attacks by Baird on the morning and afternoon of 10 May had come up against strong defences astride the track and his company had been held. The following day he moved his sixty men forward in bounds and finally managed to break through to Tatterson's company in the afternoon, led in by the forward scout, Ron Golding. With fresh stretcher-bearers, the casualties were rapidly evacuated. Peterson later noted, 'To see him come down the track is one of the best sights I've ever seen in my life.'[8] Roy Caterson was relieved to see O'Hare. 'He approached with a grin as wide as the Sydney Heads and right hand grasping mine. "Caterson, I never thought I'd ever be so pleased to see your ugly mug again!" The feeling was mutual.'[9]

The enemy immediately counter-attacked, but this failed and the Japanese fell back on the Pimple. Having held eight enemy attacks, Tatterson also pulled his men back along the ridge to a better defensive position but, in doing so, lost one of his platoon commanders, Lieutenant Charlie Ellis, to an Australian grenade. The Australians reported sixty-three Japanese casualties, fifty of them credited to the resolute A Company defence and the other thirteen to the relieving attack by D Company. The Japanese claimed their own casualties to be fifty-four, sixteen killed and thirty-eight wounded, but also claimed that there were fifty-five abandoned Australian corpses as a result of this battle. Australian casualties were actually 16 men, four of whom were killed.[10]

According to Kengoro Tanaka, the Lababia attack had eventuated because Nakano had 'deemed it necessary to dampen the enemy's initial enthusiasm'.[11] On the evening of 5 May two fresh companies, the 3rd and 8th, from the reformed 115th Regiment had left Salamaua, reaching Mubo on 7 May. Two hundred men from Major Takamura's III/102nd Battalion, which had been kept back from the abortive attack on Wau, had also moved up from Nassau Bay on 9 May to support the Lababia attack but, concerned by reports of an Australian patrol moving towards the coast, the battalion returned to Nassau Bay on 13 May without taking part.[12]

On 23 May Lieutenant-Colonel Fred Wood received orders for his 2/6th Battalion to relieve the 2/7th, and the first units moved forward on 27 May. The limiting factor with any relief operation was Buisaval Track, which could maintain only two companies at any given time, one moving forward and one back, and the relief was not completed until 11 June. The 2/7th Battalion went into divisional reserve with two companies located in Wau and two in Bulolo. Guinn's men had had their losses; in the six weeks the battalion had been in the front line, twenty men had been killed and thirty-six wounded in action.[13]

On 27 May the 2/7th Battalion carried out one of its last patrols before relief. Despite having lost so many men in the area, the battalion was again drawn to the Pimple. A log barricade had now been erected by the Japanese in front of the Pimple, and it was clear that they intended to hold the position. Fifteen men under Lieutenant John Mackie left at midday to reconnoitre the area. As they approached the area held by A Company during the earlier battle, a rattling of tins was heard, warning the defenders. One of the forward scouts, George Pincott, was shot in the chest. The patrol took cover, but while firing from behind a tree, the other forward scout, John Sanders, was shot from behind. Mackie decided to get off the track and try to get to Pincott and Sanders. He took Roy Kasper with him but, as he made a run for a tree, he was shot in the shoulder. Kasper sheltered in a depression before heading back for help. Lieutenant Bill Fietz arrived with ten men, but heavy fire made it difficult to spot enemy positions in the jungle. The wounded Pincott called out for the men to wait until dark to rescue him, then he despatched an approaching enemy soldier with a grenade. However, when the patrol reached Pincott and Sanders later that night, they were both dead.[14]

Under instruction from 3rd Division, Moten's 17th Brigade headquarters moved forward from Wau to Skindiwai on 17 May; the wings from the crashed C-47 making excellent table tops for the men's mess.[15] On 29 May Moten was given new orders: to clear the enemy forces from the Mubo area, then to combine with 15th Brigade at Bobdubi Ridge to push the enemy north of the Francisco River. This was part of the Doublet plan with D-Day set for 15 June, although later amended to 30 June. Moten's main tasks would be to capture Mubo and link up with an American amphibious landing at Nassau Bay.[16]

The 2/6th Battalion headquarters was established at Guadagasal with A Company at Mat Mat Hill, B Company at Waipali, C Company at the Saddle and D Company on Lababia Ridge. As early as 9 May D Company had been instructed to move up to support the right flank of the 2/7th Battalion and to carry out reconnaissance operations down off the ridge to Duali and the coast. The company commander, Captain Bill Dexter, had spent two days at Moten's headquarters in Wau going over detailed aerial photos of the coastal area. Dexter noted that Moten 'had specially selected my company from the brigade for this important role'.[17] These patrols were to provide information on any Japanese presence that could interrupt the planned US landing at Nassau Bay. Wood discussed the operation with Captain Henry 'Jo' Gullett, who had led similar patrols behind the lines during the fighting at Wau, telling him, 'I don't want to send a large patrol because I don't want the Japanese to suspect we have any particular interest there. It's a nasty job.' Gullett replied, 'I'll send Gibbons.'[18]

Lieutenant Ernest 'Blue' Gibbons, a tall young redhead, had served with the battalion for four years. He had been awarded the Military Medal for 'outstanding bravery and leadership' during the Wau fighting and, having developed a keen sense for fighting in the difficult New Guinea terrain, had been commissioned in the field. Gullett asked him how he would go about the patrol, and Gibbons told him that he would take only one man, a corporal, and go straight down the main track. 'I shall see them all right before they see me. Like you do,' he told Gullett.[19]

After being briefed by Captain Dexter, Gibbons and Corporal John Fisher left from Napier at 0800 on 7 June and headed towards Duali and the coast. The two men spent the first night at some native huts about two kilometres from the coast; the surf could be clearly heard. At 0630 the next morning they set off on the track along the southern arm of the Bitoi River. Meanwhile, back in the 2/6th Battalion lines, Lieutenant Ernie Price turned to Jo Gullett, who was concerned about Gibbons, and told him, 'Blue should be through the Japanese by now; he always moves fast.' They then heard the ominous sound of gunfire coming up the valley from the coast.[20]

After 45 minutes on the track, Gibbons and Fisher saw fresh Japanese footprints and then, 300 metres further on, shovel diggings across the track. After another hundred metres, Gibbons held up his hand to Fisher, who was close behind him. He then turned his head and told Fisher: 'Japs.' As Gibbons backed away, Fisher noticed the head and shoulders of an enemy soldier in a weapon pit behind a banana clump, only five metres from Gibbons. The enemy soldier, Private Monya Koike, poked his rifle through the foliage and shot Gibbons, who fell. Fisher fired two bursts from his tommy gun at the enemy soldier before another Japanese soldier, Private Uchiyama, opened up on Fisher from the other side of the track. The badly wounded Gibbons waved weakly at Fisher, urging him to flee. Fisher did so, running back 50 metres down the track before sheltering among some banana clumps. Looking back, he saw the wounded Gibbons staggering into another clump of bananas, then heard him fire a burst from his tommy gun. There was shouting from the Japanese, more rifle fire, then a mortar opened up. Fisher moved away and took to the bush. After being swept down the Bitoi River at one stage, he was able to regain the Australian lines at Napier at dusk on 9 June. 'Blue' Gibbons' body was never found.[21]

Japanese documents later captured at Nassau Bay gave further insight into Gibbons' fate. In an order issued on 11 June Takamura referred to a contact that had taken place at the south arm of the Bitoi River on 8 June. A sketch map and other records had been captured 'from enemy who were killed'. Another report told of enemy troops that had appeared in front of the sentry post near Shiraume village (Duali). 'The lookouts fired and killed the enemy at close range of about five metres.'[22] The 'killed enemy' could only have referred to Gibbons.

Another two-man patrol led by Lieutenant Dave Burke took place at the same time, but further south following the general line of the Tabali River to Nassau Bay. After swimming across, the patrol had heard the firing from the Gibbons' ambush but continued the mission, subsequently recommending that the Nassau Bay area was suitable for a landing and later road construction.[23] Meanwhile, Lieutenant Reg Urquhart's 18 Platoon had moved into the Napier area to hold open the link down to the coast. They also built a footbridge over the Bitoi River and blazed a track up to the Bitoi Ridge, in preparation for the American move into the area.

On the other side of the fence, orders had been issued by the Japanese command on 27 May to clear the Lababia–Waipali–Guadagasal area. The orders specified that Lababia Ridge was to be cleared as far as Guadagasal, thus gaining control of the high ground above Mubo, which would make the Australian position on Mat Mat untenable. The 102nd Regiment, which had been in the front line since January and had lost much of its strength in the failed Wau attack, was relieved by Colonel Araki's recently arrived 66th Regiment for the attack.

Two of Araki's battalions had reached Salamaua from Rabaul by the end of May 1943. One of the officers wrote, 'The hopes of the regiment, which had arrived unharmed at the battlefield, were very high.' The first task was to carry forward the food and ammunition for the upcoming attack; this was done at night in single file along narrow jungle trails, which were muddy from the frequent heavy rains. A single track ran up the precipitous slope on to Komiatum Ridge. It was known to the Japanese as Regret Hill, and the hard-working soldiers became more exhausted with each passing day. For example, Lieutenant Shigeru Namura's No. 3 Company spent eighteen days making eight journeys to Mubo carrying supplies.[24]

The arrival of reinforcements in the Salamaua area had not gone unnoticed, and the supply line was subject to air attack. On 10 June 161 men were observed carrying supplies over the Francisco River mouth footbridge, which was bombed by USAAF Mitchells the next day. However, the bridge was back in use on 12 June and, on 15 June, 486 men were counted moving south towards Mubo. Another 163 men moved south on the following day. RAAF No. 30 Squadron Beaufighters strafed Komiatum Ridge, but the carriers tended to move only at night on the open slopes. New Guinea Force headquarters now estimated that there were 1500 enemy soldiers in the Mubo area, although Allied intelligence thought the 66th Regiment was in the Solomon Islands.[25] Having moved up close to Mubo on 17 June, Araki's troops assembled in front of Lababia Ridge by 0800 on 19 June. The newly arrived units had been instructed to conceal their strength from the air with no fires during the day and any movement or digging being undertaken only at night.[26]

The operation orders for the attack noted, 'Three officer and NCO scouting parties who are well versed in the situation and position of the enemy will be attached to the 66th Regiment.' At 0300 on the morning of 20 June, the I/66th Battalion, guided by 102nd Regiment men who were familiar with the ground, began moving around the eastern flank of the Australian position and getting into place for a dawn attack on 21 June. For support, two 14th Field Artillery Regiment mountain guns were positioned on Mubo airfield, while mortars were set up closer to the front lines. The Japanese force was considerable, based around Araki's two fresh battalions.[27]

As the first enemy troops moved up, they noted that 'piano wires are set up everywhere', a reference to the extensive Australian booby-trap systems. Bill Dexter considered that the Japanese detailed one- or two-man patrols to delouse the booby traps, and many were later found with the trip wire cut and neatly coiled out of the way, probably the work of a platoon of engineers that had been attached for the operation. Surprisingly, the deloused Australian grenades were not used by the enemy; Dexter was of the opinion that the Japanese did not understand their mechanism.[28]

Noel Bisset was in a patrol out towards the Japanese lines at the Pimple. The patrol reached a point where the men could see the bodies of Pincott and Sanders, from the 2/7th Battalion, who had been killed on 27 May, their boots since removed. Two three-man listening posts were set up, one on either side of the track. Patrols then found that the main track from the Pimple had not been used by the enemy, but a new track a hundred metres away had been heavily used and had four or five signal wires running alongside. Bisset reported that he 'considered they were preparing for a fairly big show here'.[29]

That same day, 20 June, a patrol was made up from Jock Henderson's section and was about to move out through Corporal Allan Smith's forward section when Private Arnold 'Wattie' Watt told Smith, 'There is movement down there.' Smith took a patrol out for a look and, when they ran into a Japanese officer directing his men beside the track, Smith shot him and bolted back for the main perimeter. In their haste, the Bren gun was left behind, and Arnold Watt went back for it. The bipod was caught up in some roots and he couldn't release it and, with the Japanese coming up the track, he began firing at them. Nine enemy soldiers were killed and another eleven wounded during the action.[30]

Dexter's D Company was holding the Lababia Ridge position above Mubo with four platoons. These were Lieutenant Laurie Roach's 16 Platoon, Sergeant John 'Smokey' Hedderman's 17 Platoon and Lieutenant Ted Exton's 11 Platoon, the latter attached from B Company to replace Urquhart's platoon, which was forward at Napier. Dexter also had Lieutenant Roderic Smith's Tank Attack Platoon of 20 men along with a 3-inch mortar detachment. All platoons were well under strength, giving Dexter only around eighty men. Hedderman's platoon was deployed on either side of the Jap Track down to Green Hill while Exton's was echeloned back along the east side of the ridge behind Hedderman, straddling the Napier track. Roach's platoon was on the west side of the track, also in behind Hedderman and abutting Exton's position.

Dexter's position was further south, but higher up than the position occupied by Tatterson in May. Dexter considered his the best tactical position on the ridge, able to cover all the major tracks. Although the slopes were steep, the top of Lababia Ridge was not a razorback and Dexter could deploy his platoons in support of each other along the edges of the plateau-like crest. When he had taken over, Dexter set out to improve the defences but, as he later noted, 'All around was this bloody scrub.' His view was that 'if you've got to fight them you've got to see them'. One of Dexter's men later recalled: 'He got his men to knock down all the low lying bushes and this gave a pretty clear field of fire. He also put in some fire lanes . . . a couple of yards wide going down the hill

Map 14 Lababia Ridge area, 2–23 June 1943

right in front of our weapon pit.' Dexter observed, 'We had the ground so [we] arranged killing areas around the perimeter.' Wood told Dexter that Moten considered the position should be further forward, but Dexter stood his ground, later telling the Official Historian, 'It would have been madness to go further down the track.' However, Dexter did agree to put a listening post further forward.[31]

At 0630 on 21 June a patrol moved along the track to the Lababia observation post and reported it clear. Jim Kerr was standing by to take the 'kai line' up the track that morning and noticed the phone wire to the observation post jigging up and down in the tree, so he ran over and told his platoon leader, Ted Exton. Exton came up to have a look and said, 'I reckon someone's up there trying to cut the line.' Then, at 0730, the line went dead so Exton cancelled the carriers and had his men man their weapon pits. Kerr noted: 'The next minute's she's on . . . we dived into our pits . . . she was on for young and old.' Further back, Bill Dexter was relaxing at his headquarters 'when thunderous shouting from the direction of the Jap track caused me to leap from my bunk'. The roar from the Japanese attackers was extraordinary; Roach told Dexter that the Australians were facing at least a thousand troops. Dexter told him to open fire. The Japanese were gathering to the north of the Australian positions, and booby traps were going off all morning. At this stage the Australians responded by dropping mortar and rifle grenades on to the likely enemy positions.[32]

The attacks started at 1400 from the north and north-east with machine-gun and mortar fire in support. Kerr observed: 'They started throwing a bit of stuff at us, mostly small mortars . . . exploding in the trees. It sounded like they were behind us.' At 1445 a bayonet attack came in on the north and east sides of the perimeter, getting to within 20 metres of the Australian positions. The first shot from Sergeant 'Tiny' Mann's 3-inch mortar within the perimeter came down 50 metres to the left, and Laurie Roach brought it across to the right. The third round hit the enemy assembly areas, and a great moan went up. After a few more rounds, Roach transferred control across to Ted Exton on the right. However, after the initial success of the mortar fire, the Japanese troops moved too close to the perimeter to enable effective fire, although every round raised the morale of the defenders.[33]

There were three Japanese attacks in the first two hours, all accompanied by the sound of bugles and cries of '*Banzai!*' To Ray Mathers, in Roach's platoon, it sounded 'like a pommy football match'. Bill Dexter later wrote of the roar of noise that would build up from the rear of the enemy lines then progress forward, rising in intensity until the yelling reached the forward troops, who would then move forward, their wild and inaccurate firing adding to the cacophony. It was 'a roaring inferno of screaming and noise of battle'.[34]

Viv Mortyn, a section commander in Roach's platoon, was the first one hit, shot in the side of the head; he died later that night. Dave 'Father' Ryan, who shared Mortyn's pit, was wounded but bravely fought on, taking command of the section. Alongside Ryan, Jimmy Niblett kept firing his Owen gun until the front of the barrel blew off. He then grabbed Mortyn's Owen gun and blew the barrel off that as well. To the right of Mortyn's pit, Ray Mathers and John 'Bluey' Kalms, both from Tom Barlow's section, shared a weapon pit alongside the track. Facing the prospect of being overrun, Ray and Bluey prepared to fight on. The rest of the section, including Barlow, had been wiped out in the initial attack. Mathers was number 2 on the Bren gun at the start of the action before Bluey Kalms was hit during the second Japanese charge, around 0930. The shot had blown off the back of the hand grip from under the gun, forcing it into the palm of Kalms' left hand, taking his thumb off. Mathers wrapped a dressing on him with one hand while grabbing the Bren with the other but didn't finish the job before the Japanese came again. The Bren was still working well enough, and Ray folded up the bipod legs so that the gun was as low as possible as the bullets were just clearing his head, cracking like explosives as they passed.[35]

Mathers' position was at the top of a very steep slope, which helped to protect him, but it also allowed attackers to sneak right up to the crest, crawling along with branches held in front of them. The two Australians never got out of their weapon pit that day and, further back, Pat Meehan and George 'Bunny' Lamont threw ammunition to them. Bunny Lamont had his hair parted by a bullet that left a furrow across his forehead, and Meehan was hit just after he threw the bandoliers. Greg Smith, a platoon runner, ran forward, shot two Japanese and brought Meehan back. Later Smith took some hot soup around and had a bullet hit him in the pocket. Fortunately there was a loaded magazine in there. Smith just looked at it and said, 'That will make a good souvenir. Do you blokes want a drink before I go?'[36]

When Mathers' Bren gun had a stoppage, he slipped the barrel off and put the gun on the number 4 gas blowback setting. The resultant heat from the heavy firing welded the barrel to the gun and, although it glowed red hot half way back to the magazine, the gun kept firing. Then, during the second Japanese charge, Mathers got a tap from Bluey Kalms, who handed him a Bren magazine he had filled by holding it between his knees and loading with his one good hand. Kalms remained all day, helping reload the magazines, before being evacuated that night.[37]

From his weapon pit Jim Kerr noticed the barrel of an enemy knee mortar poking up just above the end of a log. He fired a burst of fire from his tommy gun before enemy machine-gun fire went past, then dropped back into his pit and threw a grenade. The mortar barrel disappeared, and a couple of days later he found drag marks and blood there. Soon after, another machine-gun opened up from downhill to his right, firing tracers across the front of Exton's platoon at Hedderman's. Both platoons opened up on the machine-gun and 'just mowed them down like a bloomin' scythe'.[38]

Corporal Keith Mew's 13 Platoon, part of Captain Bill 'Cocky' Cameron's C Company, moved up at the height of the afternoon attack, arriving in Roach's platoon area. Mew's men were told to get into the nearest vacant foxholes. When a Japanese light machine-gun opened up, Private Clarrie Wilson stood up to have a go at it with his Owen gun but was knocked over within five minutes. Another 13 Platoon man, Private Charlie Hope, was wounded and died later that night. Frank Walsh, the 11 Platoon sergeant, told Ted Exton, 'A Jap's climbing up the tree there, a sniper.' Exton grabbed a .303 sniper's rifle with telescopic sights and fired two shots at a range of 150 metres, dropping the enemy sniper with hits under the arm and through the side of the head.[39]

After dusk, Hedderman told Roach that Tom Barlow's forward section was out of touch. Roach took a section under Sergeant Joe Longmore out into the pitch dark, each man holding the shoulder of the man in front, and found that the three pits covering the track had been wiped out. The bodies of Barlow and his fallen men were removed as Longmore's section took over the positions. It rained all night as the Japanese dragged back their own groaning wounded and deloused booby traps, setting some off. John Hill watched them at work cutting the trip wires, observing, 'They had leaves all over them and had a branch tied on their backs.' At one point Hill shot an enemy soldier who was 'moving forward looking like a tree'. The Australians would throw grenades at any sound but not fire their guns at night. Hill tossed out three grenades their way while Bill Levvell used the extra yoke rifle to send a few out a bit further. Meanwhile, Jim Kerr crouched in his weapon pit with water up to his boot tops and remained awake throughout the night.[40]

On the next day, 22 June, the Japanese infantrymen were probing around the flanks, but the Australian mortar and extra yoke rifle kept them in check. A Japanese mountain gun opened up, but only two shots landed in the Australian perimeter, one destroying Dexter's signals set-up, which was soon repaired and back in action. There were several enemy attacks, but after dusk the Japanese casualties were recovered and the Japanese withdrawal began. They had had enough.[41]

The next morning, 23 June, brought heavy enemy automatic and mortar fire into the perimeter to further cover the Japanese withdrawal. Directed by a forward observer with Roach's platoon, Major O'Hare's mountain guns replied in kind. General Savige later commended the mountain gunners, noting that the guns 'were skilfully and courageously served by O'Hare, an outstanding fighter, who was so ably backed by gun crews of his own calibre'. At midday Wood contacted Dexter and told him, 'I've got a surprise packet for you. Stop the [artillery] and mark your FDLs [forward defensive lines] with smoke.' Then the Beaufighters came over, strafing the enemy positions. 'This was the final nail in the coffin as the enemy broke and withdrew.' 18 Platoon moved out in the late afternoon to re-establish contact with the Lababia operations post.[42]

The Australian strength had been seventy-eight when the Japanese attack began but was down to fifty-five on the afternoon of 21 June before C Company arrived. The Australians lost twelve men killed and ten wounded. Bill Dexter estimated that his men had killed or wounded 240 enemy troops while the Japanese admitted to having forty-two men killed and 131 men wounded. John Hill reported that there were 180 bod-ies in front of the Australian positions, among them three majors and the Japanese commander, found with the attack orders, including maps, still on him. The Japanese losses would cause them major difficulties when the Australians went on to the offensive within a matter of weeks. The Japanese had found the Australian positions stronger than expected, and casualties were significantly higher than anticipated. With no rein-forcements available it would have been difficult for them to hold on to Mubo.[43]

A number of features of the Japanese attacks helped the Australians, provided they held their nerve, to hold their positions. First, the noise the Japanese soldiers made before attacking, which was meant to frighten the waiting defenders, had the benefit of warning the Australians that they were coming. Second, the Japanese attackers had the habit of overdoing their camouflage. As Bill Dexter noted, 'His practice of tying trees to his back is rather indicative as if you see a tree moving towards you, it can only mean one thing.'[44] Third, the Japanese would select one line of attack and continue to press that sector, even if the attack was unsuccessful.

Jo Gullett watched Dexter's men come back to the battalion HQ after the battle. 'They were exhausted, haggard and indescribably dirty; literally covered with red mud from the 48 hours they had stood in their water-logged trenches . . . there was an unmistakable air of triumph about them.' Dexter's men had repulsed five enemy attacks over the three days of the battle. Jo Gullet again: 'Dexter was too exacting a man to be popular, but he was a very thorough soldier, a good trainer of men and a painstaking tactician. In the course of his action, a classic of its type, all these qualities were tested and they endured.'[45] For his effective command before and during the battle, Dexter was awarded the Distinguished Service Order.

The leadership of his three platoon commanders was also outstanding and duly recognised. Lieutenants Ted Exton and Laurie Roach were awarded the Military Cross and Sergeant 'Smokey' Hedderman the Military Medal.

Savige gave a great deal of credit for the successful defence of Lababia Ridge to the battalion commander. 'Wood watched every move and gave instant support to all Dexter's needs. Above all he did not interfere with Dexter's management of the fight.' Moten was also close to the fighting and, like Wood, did not interfere with Dexter. On Dexter's performance, Savige later wrote, 'In this fight he took every trick.'[46]

CHAPTER | 7

ON BOBDUBI RIDGE

While George Warfe's men were playing merry hell with the Japanese on Bobdubi Ridge, plans were afoot to increase Australian presence in the Missim area significantly in order to carry out a new offensive plan, Operation Doublet. The 15th Brigade, comprising the 24th Battalion, the 58/59th Battalion and the 57/60th Battalion, would be deployed. Warfe's 2/3rd Independent Company would also come under 15th Brigade control. The 15th would be the only original brigade from the 3rd Division deployed for the Salamaua campaign.

The new structure of 15th Brigade had little semblance to that which had formed part of the 3rd Division in Australia, both in units and in commanders. The original brigade had comprised the 57/60th, 58th and 59th Battalions. The 24th Battalion had then come across from the 10th Brigade when that brigade had been removed from the division in 1942, and part of the 59th Battalion was merged with the 58th in August 1942. Before leaving for New Guinea, the 15th Brigade commander, Brigadier Alfred Jackson, was replaced by the younger 10th Brigade commander, Brigadier Frank Hosking.[1]

Adding greatly to the brigade's problems was the area over which it was deployed and the tasks the battalions were asked to perform. The 24th Battalion was spread far and wide whereas Lieutenant-Colonel Robert Marston's 57/60th Battalion was relegated to the role of protecting the new airfield site at Tsili Tsili in the upper Watut Valley. The airfield was being built to accommodate fighter aircraft, which would escort the longer-range bombers on planned USAAF missions against the gathering

Japanese air units at Wewak. Whitehead had told the New Guinea Force commander, Herring, 'General, you give us some troops to guard strips at Tsili Tsili and Bena Bena, and we'll knock the Jap air force out of the skies.'[2]

Savige had planned to use Marston's battalion alongside the 58/59th at Bobdubi Ridge and complained that 'Their alleged use to protect the Americans in building the airstrip in the valley was ludicrous...'. He criticised Herring for supplying the Americans with more than a company for the task.[3] His pleas to Herring fell on deaf ears. On 25 June Herring told Savige, 'I decided to put the whole battalion there because the threat to this valley may come down the Ramu and it makes your flank there secure against anything that may come down that way.' The spectre of another undetected Japanese foray to the outskirts of Wau still preyed on Herring's mind. Tsili Tsili also had first priority on air supply at this time and even Herring's staff complained that 'the Yanks are flying in hundreds of transports to Tsili Tsili and only five to 3 Div'. Herring, now focused on the Lae plans, would tell them, 'For goodness sake what do you expect? You ought to know better. It is all part of the big plan.'[4] Clearly 3rd Division's role in the big plan was considered a minor one.

Given these disruptions, all of the brigade's expectations during the upcoming operation would be carried by the untried 58/59th Battalion and Warfe's 2/3rd Independent Company. As Hammer would later write, 'It was a peculiar force.' The airlift of the 58/59th from Port Moresby to Wau required thirty-nine planeloads, and it had assembled at Bulwa in the Bulolo Valley by 31 May along with the headquarters of 15th Brigade.[5]

On 28 April Lieutenant-Colonel Danny Starr, the former 2/5th Battalion commander, was appointed to command the 58/59th Battalion, replacing Lieutenant-Colonel Rupert Whalley. Mackay had asked Savige to use Starr in lieu of one of the three majors who were at that time battalion commanders in the 3rd Division. Both Mackay and Savige had a high opinion of Starr, having had him under their command in the Middle East. Savige also took into account the positive views that the two other 17th Brigade colonels, Wood and Guinn, had expressed over Starr's use of the 2/5th Battalion after Wau. In Savige's mind these views balanced the negative opinion that Moten had of Starr, which had led to his relief on 24 March.[6]

Savige had sent Captain Ted Kennedy's company from the 24th Battalion along the track to Missim to set up a series of staging camps for the 58/59th Battalion. Savige knew Kennedy well from the Legacy organisation and had a high opinion of him.[7] On 6 June the 58/59th's D Company left Bulwa heading for Pilimung and on to Missim, a four-day trek across Double Mountain. The men followed the same punishing route that Warfe's men had pioneered, crossing the range in staggered groups.

Private Harold Hibbert, a signaller attached to A Company, remembered the crossing as 'pretty precarious, hand over hand, had to pull yourself up along the track'. Major Basil Travers went across the track with 15th Brigade headquarters: 'We have been marching nine hours today and it was as cold as charity. I have never seen such a trail in my life. The mud and slush in the moss forest was terrific. The slush in parts was one foot deep.' Damien Parer made his way across in late June: 'Bloody hard climb – ditto descent . . . this stretch is worse than any I encountered on the Kokoda Trail.'[8]

Meanwhile, Major Warfe's men continued to send vital information back from their observation posts, particularly from Wells observation post at the southern end of Bobdubi Ridge. Significant numbers of Japanese troops had been counted moving along the Komiatum Track toward Mubo. On 10 June 161 carriers were observed moving south from Salamaua, followed by 739 troops from 14 to 16 June.[9] Although unknown to the Australians at that stage, these men were from the newly arrived 66th Regiment, moving up to attack the 2/6th Battalion at Lababia.

Warfe also sent out reconnaissance and ambush parties. On 9 June Bart Lamb, Brian Walpole and Les Poulson returned from a three-day recce patrol south-east of Wells. They were able to confirm that there were no enemy troops east of the Komiatum Track, although there were signs that Japanese patrols had moved west along Stephens' Track towards Wells Junction. Another patrol to the same area on 16 June ran into trouble. Five men, including Captain Jim Menzies, the B Platoon commander and Captain Harold Higgs, the 15th Brigade liaison officer, were wounded by an Australian grenade, part of a booby trap set by a previous patrol. The location of the booby trap had been incorrectly reported further south than it actually was. The raid was called off and another patrol sent out to help evacuate the wounded men, one of whom, Bill McDougall, died two days later.[10]

The value of Lamb's earlier patrol was put to good use when a fighting patrol set out on 19 June to ambush the enemy parties moving along the Komiatum Track. Led by Captain Hancock, the patrol found the going more difficult than Lamb had indicated, and they had not reached the ambush position until 20 June. The plan was to capture a prisoner but, when the ambush was sprung at around 1330, the three enemy soldiers were killed. Two of those killed, Sergeant Shimada and Private Chihasa, were from No. 7 Company of the II/102nd Battalion, which had taken part in the failed Wau attack and, since May, had been defending Mubo. Captured documents showed that reinforcements from the 66th Infantry Regiment had been able to move from Rabaul to Lae without a dedicated merchant ship convoy and were now in the Mubo area. Such intelligence was vital in enabling plans to be made to prevent any further reinforcement of Lae or Salamaua.[11]

The 58/59th Battalion had come across to Missim to be part of an intricate three-pronged operation against the Japanese in front of Salamaua, Operation Doublet. The 3rd Division chief of staff, Lieutenant-Colonel John Wilton, had flown to Port Moresby on 23 May and had returned four days later with the Doublet plan and orders to 'drive the enemy north of the Francisco River'. To achieve this goal, the attack on Bobdubi Ridge was ordered by 3rd Division's Operation Order 1, issued on 29 May. Although Operation Doublet had originally been planned to commence on 15 June, it was postponed to 30 June to ensure that the required reserves were available.[12]

The 15th Brigade action would be the second of three punches designed to deliver a crushing blow to the Japanese position in front of Salamaua. Following an amphibious landing by units of the American 41st Division on the eastern flank at Nassau Bay on the night of 29 June, 15th Brigade would attack on the west flank the following day. As the Japanese command tried to deal with these threats, Moten's brigade would attack at Mubo some days later. The enemy force defending Salamaua was estimated by New Guinea Force headquarters as 2150 men, 1500 at Mubo, 400 in the Bobdubi area and 250 at Nassau Bay. The intelligence estimate of total troops was extremely accurate, but the number of front-line troops at Mubo and Bobdubi was actually significantly lower. There were actually 673 front-line troops at Mubo, 127 in the Bobdubi area, 122 at Nassau Bay, 543 at Salamaua, 540 at Malolo and 43 at Komiatum; 2048 troops in total.[13]

The Doublet plan was part of a broader offensive plan in the South-West Pacific Area, Operation Cartwheel, which involved a series of operations directed towards Rabaul like the spokes of a cartwheel. Operation Toenails had the objective of capturing key locations in the New Georgia

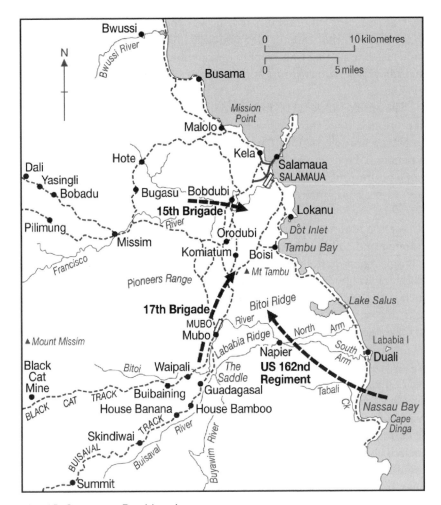

Map 15 Operation Doublet plan

group of islands north-west of Guadalcanal, and the main landings at
Rendova and New Georgia took place on 29 June and 2 July. Operation Chronicle would see landings take place at Woodlark and Kiriwina
islands, providing airfield sites within 500 kilometres of Rabaul. These
landings took place unopposed on 30 June.

On 15 June General Berryman travelled up to Summit camp, between
Wau and Skindiwai, and met with Wilton, Moten and the American com-
mander for the landing at Nassau Bay, Colonel Archibald MacKechnie.
These officers went over the forthcoming operation trying to ensure

that all was suitably coordinated. It was the most intricate operation planned up to that time in New Guinea, involving three separate components, one of them an amphibious landing. Troops for two of three subsidiary operations would still be moving into position on the night of 29 June.

The specific task for 15th Brigade was to move east from Missim to capture and hold the key positions along Bobdubi Ridge, a role given to Starr's untried 58/59th Battalion. If the ridge could be occupied, the Komiatum Track could be controlled by a Vickers gun section from the same positions that Warfe's men had occupied in early May.[14] The ridge was to be captured from the Coconuts position at the northern end to Orodubi, towards the southern end. It was a difficult introduction to battle for a battalion with no front-line experience, little dedicated jungle training and following hard on the heels of such an arduous trek. 3rd Division headquarters estimated that there were 500 enemy troops on Bobdubi Ridge, but 15th Brigade HQ believed that the lack of movement seen around the positions indicated they were only lightly held and that the 500 figure was a 'liberal estimate'.[15] Apart from capturing the key terrain, the 15th Brigade attack was also designed to draw enemy troops away from the Mubo area, making 17th Brigade's task easier when it attacked as the third component of Operation Doublet on 7 July.[16]

On 21 June Henry Guinn had been appointed to the temporary command of 15th Brigade until Brigadier Heathcote 'Tack' Hammer arrived from the mainland. Guinn replaced Hosking, who had not come up to scratch. Berryman later commented, 'Hosking didn't have training and capability to control brigade.' Savige told the official historian, 'Hosking's failure was my responsibility. He looked as though he would be God when I picked him but [he had] no knowledge.'[17] The 15th Brigade headquarters had only reached Pilimung on 9 June at which time it had taken control of all units in the Missim area.

On 14 June Guinn was visiting a friend in Kaindi, on the other side of Wau, and was technically absent without leave. Berryman happened to be visiting Kaindi at the same time and met Guinn 'resting' there. When told of his new command appointment, Guinn had to catch a ride down to Bulwa, then hastily make his way across the Double Mountain track to Pilimung in a single day. He reached Pilimung on 20 June and handed over the letter telling Hosking he was to report back to 3rd Division headquarters. On 29 June, after moving forward to Missim, Guinn sent out a message to his men that Bobdubi Ridge was the key to the area south of Mubo and that the enemy troops there were 'trapped like rats in a trap'.[18]

Two 58/59th Battalion companies would make the initial attack on Bobdubi Ridge. Major Herbert Heward's A Company would attack the Orodubi–Gwaibolom–Erskine Creek position, which dominated any approach to Bobdubi Ridge from the south. Captain Ernest 'Ossie' Jago's C Company would move against the Gardens–Old Vickers position, the key point at the northern end of the ridge. Following in the wake of Jago's company, Captain Frank Drew's B Company had the objective of moving across the ridge to gain control of the Bench Cut Track, which was the major route on to the ridge from Salamaua. D Company, only recently taken over by Captain Harold Hilbert, would be held in reserve at the kunda-vine bridge, which crossed the Francisco River below Bobdubi Ridge. The battalion had carried out a rehearsal in the Bulolo Valley before moving across to Missim, and Starr considered that everyone involved knew their tasks. Patrol reports indicated that the Japanese were not holding the southern parts of Bobdubi Ridge in strength and, according to Starr, 'no special opposition was expected or considered'. Even without the benefit of hindsight, it appeared to be a very naive approach.[19]

Although the frightful track conditions on the march across the range from Bulwa had exhausted Starr's troops, there would be no respite for them. With very little rest, the men set out for the operation weighed down like packhorses. A typical rifleman carried his rifle with the standard fifty rounds and his normal pack, but on this operation also carried 250 extra rounds, one 3-inch mortar bomb, as many grenades as possible and a pick or shovel.[20] With the greatest distance to cover, Heward's A Company set off from Missim on 26 June heading for Base 3 camp. From here the company moved up to Jeffery's observation post and the forming-up point around a kilometre west of Namling. Having not had a break since leaving the Bulolo Valley and having had to carry most of their own stores to the start line, the company now had to go into action.

The 2/3rd Independent Company provided guides for the 58/59th Battalion, but Warfe stressed that they were there only to ensure Starr's men made their way to their start lines and not to get involved in any fighting. Peter Pinney, the guide for C Company, was advised: 'Don't get too far in front: don't get knocked!' Pinney noted: 'It was not until ten p.m. that ammunition arrived, at last we set out for Bobdubi . . . infanteers loaded up with Vickers and boxes of ammo.'[21]

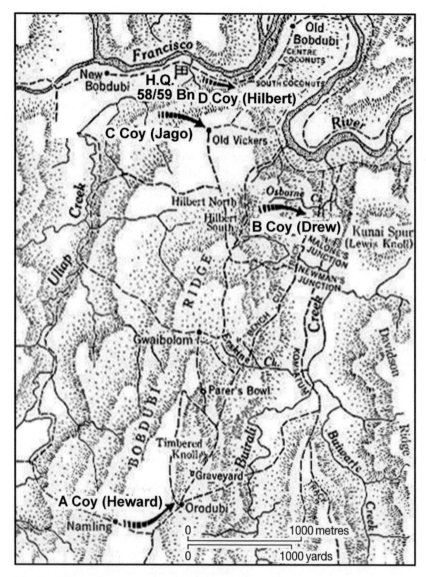

Map 16 58/59th Battalion attack: 30 June 1943

After having waited for the ammunition, C Company left Meares'
Camp at 2230 on 28 June. The night movement prevented the Japanese
observers on Bobdubi Ridge knowing how many troops were involved in
the attack. The troops rested on 29 June before the final approach took
place in pitch darkness. Men grasped the bayonet scabbard of the man

Photo 15 The rickety kunda-vine bridge across the Francisco River. Photo by Damien Parer. (AWM 127969)

in front, and some rubbed phosphorescent moss on to the back of their haversack to guide the man behind.[22] Torrential rain began to fall and, as the steep track became slippery, falls off the track became frequent. Pinney noted there was 'no starlight; it was overcast and pitch dark, and of course the plan was for us to all get down to the flats under cover of darkness'. He was 'anxious to make that steep climb down before it was absolutely dark'.[23]

It was around midnight when the leading units reached the kunda bridge across the Francisco River. Lieutenant Henry Anderson's pioneer platoon had done a sterling job shoring up the bridge to carry the battalion across, although Harold Hibbert observed that it was 'a rough piece of carpentry'. Dave Taylor noted, 'We were all heavily laden with packs, arms and ammunition, and in addition spare mortar bombs which made balance under the conditions awkward.' Peter Pinney put it more succinctly: 'Thank Christ none actually fell in because they would sure as shit have drowned . . . in pitch darkness all these blokes knew was that they were crossing something that swayed and trembled and felt sort of hollow, and there were sounds of running water underneath.'[24]

One man from C Company did fall in when he missed his footing on the slippery kunda vines. He damaged his shoulder but otherwise got out of the river unscathed, helped by the watchful Henry Anderson. Dave Taylor observed, 'He was lucky he got pulled out. Actually we were nearly over…within five yards of the bank when he fell in. But it was pitch bloody black.'[25] Following the fall, further crossings were postponed until daylight and the men tried to get some rest as the rain pelted down, drenching all and sundry.

As first light dawned at 0615 on 30 June the remainder of C Company crossed the bridge, followed by B and D Companies. An anxious Peter Pinney waited by the river bank while the remainder of the attacking force crossed the bridge. 'We kept under cover down there in the valley until 9 am, waiting for the Vickers guns and big mortars to make their way over that gutshot bridge in daylight. No way to hide that little performance from Japs up on Bobdubi Ridge…it should have drawn the crabs: but nothing happened. Anyone who's fought the Huns must find these Japs a picnic.'[26] It would be no picnic for the men of the 58/59th Battalion. The lack of reconnaissance by the officers and NCOs involved in the actual attack was a critical deficiency in the planning. Lieutenant Ted Griff, in charge of 13 Platoon, tasked with taking the vital Old Vickers position, had only a distant view of the ridge before the attack and later reflected that it was 'completely useless as all I can remember seeing was a long hill covered in trees'.[27]

At 0840 the bombing of Bobdubi Ridge commenced. From behind Uliap Creek the 58/59th men watched the bombers come over. Pinney noted: 'Four Liberators; not exactly a second front. They wheeled around in leisurely fashion dropping eggs now and then, a few at least landed where they should, alerting every Jap within ten miles that Here We Come. Then they broke off and flew back to Moresby, and we started climbing up to the attack. There were no Japs guarding the trail and we made fair time.' Ted Griff observed: 'I can recall only one plane over Bobdubi Ridge. This plane dropped only one bomb, which missed the ridge.' At 0900 B and C Companies crossed the start line of Uliap Creek but, as Pinney had observed, any advantage was lost by the distance back to the start line below the ridge at Uliap Creek.[28]

Captain Ernest 'Ossie' Jago was 32 and had served with the battalion for some time. He was a quiet, studious type who never raised his voice,

Photo 16 Looking west from the Coconuts position on Bobdubi Ridge over the Francisco River with Uliap Creek, the start line for the 30 June attack, joining from the left. The dropping ground at Nunn's Post is in the background. (Phillip Bradley)

and this would be his first action. Two of his platoons, Lieutenant Ted Griff's 13 Platoon and Lieutenant Richard Pemberton's 15 Platoon, would make the attack on the Old Vickers position. Pemberton, who was from Rabaul and provided some much-needed local experience, had joined his platoon only at Port Moresby. He had told his men that when they reached Salamaua he would show them where the bank had buried its bullion.[29] His platoon's first objective was Buggert village, on a level piece of ground on the lower western slopes of the ridge. Buggert was only a little village interspersed with trenches that the Japanese were using as an outpost position below Old Vickers.

The plan was for 7 and 8 Sections to flank Buggert to the right then attack when 9 Section opened fire from the front. After positioning the Bren gun with four riflemen on either side, Dave Taylor's 9 Section opened fire on a village hut at around 1100. Two enemy soldiers were killed while another retaliated with a knee mortar. Taylor 'had two shots and missed

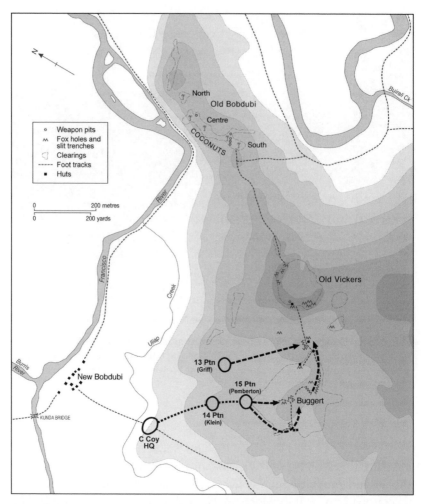

Map 17 Old Vickers – Coconuts position, July 1943

the little bastard and he ran back . . . we all missed him. We must have been excited or something.' The two enemy soldiers killed at the village were not of the small stature normally depicted, one being six feet tall, the other not much shorter and around 13 stone. 'So much for the little men in glasses,' Taylor observed. Corporal Harry Page, in charge of 7 Section, was shot in the jaw during the fighting and made his way back down the ridge.[30]

As 15 Platoon moved up on to the ridge, a Woodpecker machine-gun opened up at close range. Pinney noted: 'It sounded as if it was just a few yards away, but was actually 60 yards off, and well dug in. It was accompanied by .256 fire. Our Bren found cover and started chopping back at the pecker.' Alarmed at the Australian incursion, the Japanese also sent over mortar rounds. Peter Pinney's observation was typical: 'Incredible bloody stuff, you feel as if they explode inside your head. The only one that would have wiped out the bunch of us was a dud.'[31]

Lieutenant Pemberton halted his men behind a large clump of bamboos and looked out over the objective. He saw some movement and asked Jack Shewan if he could see any of the enemy soldiers. 'No, I can't see them,' Shewan replied and handed the Bren over to Pemberton, who had seen something and fired. The Japanese machine-gun then opened up, and Pemberton was killed by the first burst. Corporal Robert Gibson, Pemberton's runner, was hit by the same burst of fire.[32]

Peter Pinney saw the incident. 'I was looking around for Pemberton. He was out left, trying to get a good look at just what the Jap position amounted to – and the 'Pecker [Woodpecker] put a burst into him . . . Bob [Gibson] copped a bullet that went in under the arm and out six inches across the shoulder, so as I was nearby I fixed him up with a couple of field dressings and got him back to a trench.'[33]

Lieutenant Ted Griff's 13 Platoon advanced further left of Buggert village towards Old Vickers, and his men went unnoticed until two of them accidentally fired their Owen guns. Another man fell and cut his leg with a machete as the platoon climbed up through the scrub heading for a clump of bamboos near the crest.[34] As Griff moved forward he saw the ominous sight of Japanese soldiers gesturing in the direction of his platoon, and a Juki machine-gun then opened up, pinning his men down. Griff sent four men from Corporal Alex 'Sandy' Anderson's section around on the right flank, but the last of the four, Bob Woolley, was killed during the move. The other three reached the top of the knoll behind the bamboo clump, and from here they were able to kill a number of enemy soldiers moving back from 15 Platoon. Anderson's party soon drew fire from the Juki but were protected by a slight rise in front. Bert Ashton lost his hat, wryly noting, 'There goes me bloody Stetson.'[35]

Sergeant Jack Clarke managed to reach Anderson and told him to pull his men back. John McDonald was hit in the leg and, as he was being treated, three more enemy soldiers appeared from the direction of Buggert, two being shot by Anderson and Ashton. Meanwhile Griff tried to get at the Juki position but found that all lines of approach were covered. 'It was impossible to move on top of the ridge,' he later noted. Then Jack Clarke was hit in the back, and Griff had to drag him back.

Mortar bombs began to fall on 13 Platoon and, when Griff reported his lack of success to Captain Jago, Jago ordered the platoon's retirement to a defensive perimeter at Buggert.[36]

The remnants of 15 Platoon up on the crest came to the same decision. Peter Pinney was still with them. 'Time passed, we weren't making any further impression on those defensive positions and the mortars were coming close; we were eight men all told and no support was coming, so with my encouragement we all pulled back. No point in being heroes when there's no reward in sight, and one of those shocking bloody mortars is feeling for your throat.'[37]

Both platoons moved back at Buggert where Lieutenant Roy Klein's 14 Platoon joined them. Booby traps were set out, and the company waited out the night. Robert Gibson had died on the way out. Pinney: 'His blokes put him on a groundsheet and started back with him while the rest of us covered their withdrawal. He died even while they were taking him back.' In the late afternoon Starr came forward and told Captain Jago to push on as far as possible by nightfall and, although Griff and Klein apparently supported a further attack, Jago decided to stay put. This was despite a war diary entry mentioning another attack at 1720.[38]

Japanese documents that were captured at the village identified the enemy defenders as Lieutenant Ogawa's company, which had held the position since its recapture from Warfe's men on 14 May. The defenders had been warned that a hundred Australian troops had been seen moving towards Bobdubi at dusk on the previous day so the Japanese were waiting for them. Ogawa was wounded during the attack, and Lieutenant Otojiro Arai, the machine-gun platoon commander, assumed command. The leading elements of Jago's company had reached a position 20 metres from three enemy pillboxes on the southern edge of the Old Vickers position, and they would not pass that position for four weeks. The bunker positions were roofed and mutually supporting, and covered all lines of approach; the 15th Brigade operations report later saying, 'Old Vickers position proved strongly held.'[39]

Meanwhile, at the southern end of Bobdubi Ridge, Major Heward's A Company moved out at 0915 led by Lieutenant Frank Roche's 8 Platoon. Like Richard Pemberton, the 33-year-old Roche had lived in New Guinea before the war. Roche's platoon was followed by Lieutenant Laurie Proby's 7 Platoon, led by Sergeant Henry Barry in the absence of Proby, who had dropped out with beriberi further back along the track.

Barry's men were followed by company headquarters and Lieutenant Bill Houston's 9 Platoon, bringing up the rear. The plan was for Roche's platoon to attack Orodubi then for Barry's platoon to pass through to Gwaibolom while Houston's platoon headed for Erskine Creek. Gwaibolom was named after a local man whose hut was located at this position.

It was estimated that only six enemy soldiers were present in Orodubi, and no support fire from the mortars was used before the attack. One of the platoon's Bren gun sections was sent up to the Graveyard area to provide covering fire for the attack. The Bren gunner saw nine or ten enemy troops in the village and opened fire. These men ran to the rear but were apparently rallied by an officer and proceeded to occupy weapon pits under the native huts.[40] The lack of coordination between the Australian support and attack groups was already apparent and had forfeited any chance of surprise. Despite Roche moving forward after hearing the supporting Bren gun at the Graveyard open up, his platoon was not close enough to the village to engage the enemy troops while they were disorganised.

Roche's platoon, with two sections forward, finally attacked at 1235. The attacking sections had bypassed the main track into Orodubi, rightly assuming it would be booby-trapped, then climbed a kunai slope to rejoin the track at the village. However, the two sections were fired on when 70 metres out. The platoon then closed up to within 30 metres of the nearest hut, but the enemy positions were well hidden and resolutely manned and the advance faltered. The leading Bren gunner, Corporal Brendan Crimmins, was killed and, as Roche took the section further forward, two other men were wounded. The enemy appeared to have at least two light machine-guns in the village as well as supporting riflemen – twenty to twenty-five defenders in all. With only ten fit men remaining in the attacking sections, the attack broke down. Showing great bravery and resolve, an attached stretcher-bearer, Ray Duncanson, went out to the mortally wounded Crimmins and, still under fire from the enemy position, dressed the fallen Bren gunner's wounds. He then went further forward and tended to the two wounded men before helping to bring them out. Crimmins' younger brother, Kevin, serving in the same unit, was shattered by the loss of his brother.[41]

Roche withdrew after 20 minutes, and Major Heward, who had heard the firing, came up to look for other avenues of approach. He proposed an attack with 3-inch mortar support, but as it was now late, he withdrew the men to Namling, leaving a rearguard behind. It was not until 2130 that the first communications were received at battalion headquarters as the 208 radio set had failed in the damp conditions. At 15th Brigade headquarters there was annoyance that no further attack was made or an attempt made to bypass Orodubi. Orders were issued for it to be contained with one platoon while the other two moved to the Gwaibolom–Erskine Creek area.[42]

The later report from 15th Brigade noted: 'A Company attacking Orodubi was diverted from its task by poor leadership.' Poor planning was probably the bigger issue here. The leadership was certainly inexperienced and the schedules were extremely tight and did not allow time for proper reconnaissance, rest and organisation of support before the attack – the same issues that plagued C Company. The report noted the difficulty of deploying more than two sections for the difficult ridge-top attack but suggested that, if those sections came from opposite ends with Bren gun support after a mortar barrage, the chance of success would be high. The frustrating thing was that in this type of fighting if you didn't take your first chance you suffered severe losses in any follow-on attempt. The front line of Bobdubi Ridge was no place to be learning effective jungle warfare techniques, not that 'jungle warfare' was the issue here. In this country, as in the country around Mubo and beyond, the nature of the terrain was the key issue, not the vegetation. On 2 July Savige told Herring that the 'Coy commander sat down, did nothing and was relieved of his command'.[43] In fact Major Heward had not been relieved and continued to command A Company until he was killed on 13 July. The brigade major later wrote that Heward 'was never a particularly energetic officer, but he did keep at it'.[44] Meanwhile, on 2 July, two of Heward's platoons occupied Gwaibolom and the Erskine's Creek area further north along Bobdubi Ridge. His third platoon continued to cover Orodubi and hold the track to Namling.

Concerned at the threat of a Japanese counter-attack, Savige instructed Guinn to redeploy the 2/3rd Independent Company to support the 58/59th Battalion. Savige's concern arose after Japanese barge movement had been spotted between Lae and Salamaua. However, no counter-attack developed over the next two days, and Warfe's company was soon released for operations at the southern end of Bobdubi Ridge.[45]

The failure to secure the Old Vickers position had prevented Captain Drew's B Company from reaching the Bench Cut Track on 30 June. At 1845 Drew reported his company was still in the C Company area, having climbed the hill to the village but supposedly forced back by Japanese mortar fire. The 15th Brigade report put it another way: 'As Coy had no casualties it is considered that B Coy could have carried out task allotted.'[46] Although the Japanese did prevent a move across the Old Vickers position, B Company was not tasked with making an attack there, only to move through for operations elsewhere. The failure had more to do with the terrain and was exacerbated by poor maps and a lack of any preliminary reconnaissance.

On the morning of 1 July Drew's company set out to find another way across the ridge but, after several hours of scrub-bashing, the men carrying the heavy weapons were exhausted. By then the company had reached the headwaters of a creek running east but, as the men followed the creek down the ridge, the way became precipitous. Two scouts went forward and reported the way was impossible for the heavily loaded troops. At 2200, reflecting General Savige's concern that the Japanese might attempt an attack across the Francisco west of Bobdubi Ridge, Starr ordered two of Drew's platoons back across to the west side of the ridge, but the order was countermanded by brigade headquarters. In a report by the brigade major it was stated that 'B Coy's failure to reach its objective may seriously affect the whole situation'. Despite his earlier orders, Starr also stated that his aim was to get B Company into position and that the capture of Old Vickers and Orodubi could be achieved later.[47]

On the morning of 2 July Guinn arrived at the 58/59th Battalion HQ to confer with Starr and replace Captain Drew with Lieutenant Griff. The sacked Drew took over HQ Company.[48] Guinn ordered B Company to move across the ridge via the newly established positions at Gwaibolom and Erskine Creek. Back at 3rd Division headquarters, an exasperated Wilton wrote: 'B Coy 58/59 Bn less one Pl at New Bobdubi instead of objective Erskine Creek! How the hell they got there don't know. Coy Comd has been sacked.'[49]

Three days later than originally planned, B Company, now under Griff, finally reached the Komiatum Track junction east of Bobdubi Ridge and set up an ambush on the morning of 3 July at the junction of the Bench Cut and Komiatum Tracks. In the late afternoon twenty enemy troops, including a machine-gun section, were ambushed as they moved up to Bobdubi Ridge. A Japanese colonel, out in front of his men, was killed first, shot by Corporal Alfred Beaumont, a veteran of the campaign in Malaya.[50] The ambush had killed two officers, the 51st Division Chief of Staff, Colonel Tadao Hongo, and First Lieutenant Kobayashi as well as one NCO, another three men being wounded.[51] As the track junction

Photo 17 Brigadier Heathcote 'Tack' Hammer. This portrait was drawn by Ivor Hele at Nunn's Post in July 1943. (AWM ART22539)

was in a flat swampy area, Griff's company pulled back to a better defensive position on higher ground astride the Bench Cut Track at Osborne Creek. The next day eighty enemy troops were spotted moving up from Salamaua, but they were not attacked; nor were another 102 moving up the following day. Another 120 men moving back were also left unmolested. Griff didn't attack any of these groups because 'they were well dispersed, moving cautiously and with weapons at the ready'.[52]

On 4 July Brigadier Hammer assumed command of 15th Brigade. He had served as brigade major with the 16th Brigade in Greece but had made his mark as commander of the 9th Division's 2/48th Battalion at El Alamein. Hammer was considered 'one of the most original and magnetic leaders of the AIF'. 'Hard as nails' was his motto, 'As you train, so you fight' his creed.[53]

The 38-year-old Hammer had arrived at General Savige's headquarters at Bulolo on 26 June and, after the testing trek across Double Mountain, had arrived at Missim on 3 July, taking up his brigade command from Guinn at midnight. With the 58/59th Battalion attack badly stalled, he was immediately in at the deep end. It did not help the situation that 'Hammer was very full of AIF and 9 Div and Alamein at this stage'.[54] He would need to adapt quickly to totally new circumstances from those of Alamein, with the challenge of different troops, lower levels of support and diabolical terrain.

At 2000 on 5 July Hammer told Starr that the Japanese troops had to be fired on and that 'the offensive spirit must be built up'. Griff's 11 Platoon did carry out one ambush, surprising twenty enemy troops on the Komiatum Track, killing ten and wounding two. At 1430 the next day 12 Platoon killed another ten enemy troops in an ambush of twenty returning from Bobdubi. That night Hammer again stressed to Starr the vital role of B Company to the division's operations, reinforcing a point General Savige had apparently also made.[55]

Griff was not imagining the strength of the forces now being deployed against the Australians as, despite the landing at Nassau Bay, the Japanese had allocated considerable reinforcements to hold Bobdubi Ridge. Major-General Murotani directed the Bobdubi Ridge defence, currently based on 200 men from Colonel Matsui's 115th Regiment. On 2 and 3 July Major Otoichi Jinno's I/80th Battalion had arrived in Lae from Wewak, and two of the companies were also immediately sent to reinforce Bobdubi Ridge. Nakano observed, 'This location is the last key point in the defence of Salamaua.'[56] On the evening of 3 July 146 men and six mountain guns from the 14th Field Artillery Regiment under Major Risuke Suzuki landed at Salamaua to provide much-needed artillery support. The Bobdubi Ridge defence now comprised five infantry companies, two of them fresh, 500 men in all.

Just after dawn on 2 July a Japanese artillery piece fired ten rounds on to the Australian positions at Buggert, followed by twelve more the following day. The gun, nicknamed Kela Kitty, was a Type 96 model 15cm howitzer, and there were two guns of this type at Salamaua. One of the guns had originally been dismantled in Rabaul and brought to Lae by bomber but, due to the weight, the plane crash-landed at Lae. The gun was recovered and taken by MLC to Salamaua from where it was drawn by a tractor to the Kela area.[57] For the men targeted by the gun, it was a frightening experience, but following the initial shock, the large guns were used sparingly. By mid-August the gun positions had been identified, the tractors to move them had broken down and the roads were impassable. The 15cm ammunition supply was also down to less than fifty rounds, and every round fired brought down sixty to seventy rounds of retaliatory fire. Nakano soon ordered the gun to cease firing.[58]

On 4 July D Company went after the Coconuts position at the northern end of Bobdubi Ridge. At 0600, 18 Platoon moved along the north bank of the river to the bend, crossed over and climbed a spur on to the north end of Bobdubi Ridge. Up on the ridge on 4 July, a patrol from 16 Platoon attacked two pillboxes at Centre Coconuts shortly before dawn. Any action at the Coconuts was difficult while Old Vickers was in enemy hands and, when that position opened fire, the patrol was forced to withdraw, having confirmed that North Coconuts was only lightly held. Then, at 1700, a patrol from 17 Platoon under Lieutenant Les Franklin moved up to make another attack. On this occasion, men from C Company fired on Old Vickers as a feint, and by 1750 Franklin's platoon had gained North Coconuts and dug in.[59]

The Japanese had no intention of giving up any ground at the Coconuts and, at 1030 on 5 July, 17 Platoon was attacked by a hundred enemy troops from No. 1 Company of Jinno's newly arrived I/80th Battalion. It was an attack made with a great deal of noise, waving of flags and blowing of bugles. Don Williamson and James Makin were killed and John Watson fatally wounded as Franklin's men were forced out of their positions. The Japanese claimed four Australians were killed and a mortar, machine-gun and eleven rifles were captured.[60] Back at brigade HQ, Hammer was of the opinion that the men could have held their ground longer.[61]

On 7 July brigade orders had specified three objectives for the 58/59th Battalion: to capture Old Vickers, to patrol Bobdubi Ridge between Old Vickers and Orodubi, and to gain control of the Komiatum Track. And so, on 7 July, only a week after the first unsuccessful attacks, the militia had another go at the critical Old Vickers position, later referred to by the Official Historian as 'the thorn in the side of the 15th Brigade'.[62]

For an hour from 1400, six Boston aircraft from RAAF No. 22 Squadron made a supporting air strike on Bobdubi Ridge, targeting the cleared area at Old Vickers first with bombs then with twelve strafing passes.[63] The bombing was considered to be very accurate, with twenty bombs falling on the target area.[64] However, the value of the air attack was limited by the 600-metre distance back to the forward troops, which meant a delay of around an hour before they could follow up. As the air attacks finished, D Company mortars ranged on Old Vickers while C Company moved forward, 13 and 15 Platoons in the lead. The men moved up the steep knife-edged approach into the fire of machine-guns tunnelled into the hill and got only to within 60 metres of the seemingly impregnable pillboxes, dug in and covered by a metre of logs and earth.[65]

Jack Evans and Tom 'Bluey' Roberts were setting up their Bren gun when a shell from the Japanese 70mm mountain gun on Old Vickers landed between them, killing both as well as Joe Bartlett. Fred Bryer was fatally wounded that day as was Ted Butler, the sergeant in charge of 15 Platoon. Dave Taylor was with him behind some bamboo. 'The Japs had us in sight somehow and hearing a swishing sound in the air – we were both standing up – I clearly saw what I thought was one of our 3-inch mortar bombs touch the top of a cane and explode not more than ten feet from our heads.' Jack Shewan and Noel Wain later crawled forward to bring back the ID discs of the fallen men, and that night the bodies were also recovered. Despite the failure of the attack, it had shaken the Japanese defenders, who later claimed that they had been attacked by 600 men. Following the failed attack on Old Vickers one of Jago's platoons established a standing patrol by day across to Taylor's Ridge. All three C Company platoons were now led by sergeants.[66]

There was another attempt to capture Old Vickers on 9 July, following a bombing attack by USAAF Mitchells. Lieutenant Klein's 14 Platoon moved through Sugarcane Knoll, 150 metres from the eastern end of Old Vickers, while the other two platoons fired in support from the knoll. Although this fire silenced two of the Japanese machine-guns, Klein and two of his men were wounded; Sergeant Bert Sutton later died. It was clear that better support would be needed to succeed and, while Sergeant Charlie Moore had adjusted the mortar fuses to try to get some penetration of the top cover on the enemy positions, it was well-directed artillery fire that was desperately needed.[67]

In the A Company area at the southern end of Bobdubi Ridge a section from 9 Platoon was attacked by forty-four enemy troops on the afternoon of 7 July, forcing the platoon's withdrawal. Next morning 8 Platoon occupied a position near Graveyard and contacted thirty enemy troops, killing four. The Japanese were pressing hard at the southern end of Bobdubi Ridge, and on 9 and 10 July fire from a Japanese mountain gun emplaced on Komiatum Ridge killed two men and wounded six more.

A successful ambush on the 2/3rd Independent Company's supply train at the south end of Bobdubi Ridge had emboldened the Japanese and, on the morning of 10 July, Captain Griff's supply line was ambushed on the Bench Cut Track near Gwaibolom. When a sixteen-man clearing patrol from 11 Platoon was sent out to recover the rations, they were also ambushed. The Japanese opened fire as the clearing patrol rounded a horseshoe bend in the trail, a nasty spot where the track cut into the steep slope of the ridge with a steep rise to the right and a steep drop to the left. The two forward scouts were hit, Bill Ryan in the chest and Bob Caspar in the shoulder. Then, caught in a classic ambush, the patrol was fired on from behind. Bill Ware and Bob Cotter were both shot in the leg. Doug Stevenson jumped off the track to the left followed by four other men, all tumbling down the steep slope through a screen of vines.[68]

Sandy Matheson and Ron Williams stayed with the wounded Cotter and Ware on the track while Harry Foots and Michael O'Brien dragged Bob Caspar back. The terrain was daunting, the Bench Cut Track they were on being cut into the side of the steep eastern slopes of Bobdubi Ridge. Matheson and Williams strapped Bob Cotter's legs together and, when night fell, they started dragging him up the precipitous slope. It was so steep that both men had to keep hold of him or he would have slid down again. Despite their devotion, he died early the next morning. At least he died with his mates, Matheson thought. Bill Ware made it back, crawling all the way, his hands and knees badly cut up, his will to live stronger.[69]

Back with the rest of the patrol, Tim Kelly fired back with his Owen gun before he was hit in the chest by return fire. Before he died Kelly handed the gun to Bill Reece, his closest mate, telling him to 'say goodbye to the boys for me'. 'Andy' Anderson continued to fight, throwing three grenades before making a dash up the slope to the crest, a bullet singeing his hair and another taking the tip off his thumb. Sergeant Norm Stenner, Bill Reece, Doug Stevenson and Bill Ryan were with Anderson, and the men worked their way along the ridge, making for Erskine Creek. Just after reaching the creek, Stenner had a fall, was badly injured and was now unable to walk. Reece, Stevenson and Ryan stayed with him, and the next morning, 11 July, Ron Holmes and Vic Perrett also joined up. The party now realised that Doug Stevenson was carrying a wound, and he went off and made his own way back to the battalion. Bill Ryan and Vic Perrett also headed off; the wounded Ryan to his death. The remaining men headed down the ridge.[70]

With the Japanese troops very close, these four men – Anderson, Stenner, Reece and Holmes – stayed under cover, sheltering under ferns in a depression until the early morning of 14 July. They were afraid to go far and, despite having had no food or water in three days, it was not until the next morning of 15 July that they reached the Bench Cut Track. Here they waited until dark when they tried to find food left behind from the original ambush. They were out of luck and, on 16 July, headed downhill to find some water seepage, their first water for five days. But the Japanese were still using the Bench Cut Track, and at one stage the four men had to scramble away down the hillside as the enemy soldiers searched for them. The wounded Holmes could go no further, and the remaining three men – Anderson, Stenner and Reece – headed south and finally reached Erskine Creek, where they gratefully drank their fill. They then followed the creek up the ridge but, after attracting enemy machine-gun fire, again took cover and waited out the day. It was now the morning of 19 July, nine days since the ambush. They continued to follow Erskine Creek up, although now keeping away from the creekbed. It was tough and slow going but, after around three hours, they heard the sound of chopping up ahead then saw a head with fair hair. It was Jack Audley, a 58/59th man. Next day, Vic Perrett also came in.[71]

The Japanese were outmanoeuvring the Australians. Not only had they held the 58/59th attacks along Bobdubi Ridge but also they were now hitting back themselves, and on 13 July there was more trouble along the Bench Cut Track. Starr met Captain Heward at Gwaibolom in the morning. Starr, Heward and Heward's orderly, Private Len Osborne, then moved off along the Bench Cut Track looking for Ted Griff, the B Company commander. Starr assumed that Heward knew the area and, when they arrived at a section post along the track, Heward asked for Griff. The section corporal replied that Griff was not there but would return soon. The party assumed that Griff was further down the track so they kept on, unaware that they had passed the last Australian position. Led by Osborne, Starr and Heward moved around a shoulder in the track, at which point Osborne stopped when he saw a wire stretched across the track. Starr later recalled, 'I looked across to the other shoulder of

Photo 18 Gordon Ayre helping Wal Johnson, the 'blinded digger', across Uliap
Creek. Photo by Damien Parer. (AWM 127971)

the re-entrant, about ten yards away, and saw two troops jump down.
Thinking they were our men, I called out, and was answered by a burst.'
Starr turned and dived back around the shoulder in the track as the gun
continued to fire. He turned to Heward, but he wasn't there; both he and
Osborne had been shot. Starr headed back up the track finally to meet
up with Griff, who had heard the gunfire. Starr passed Harold Hibbert
on the way out, telling him, 'We got jumped.' Heward had been killed by
men from No. 1 Company of Jinno's I/80th Battalion who 'destroyed an
officer's patrol (major), captured materials, code book, map, operations
order etc.' Heward had carried the battalion's Operation Order No. 1
and thus had seriously compromised the Australian operations. Damien
Parer wrote: 'What a terrible mistake to make ... it is typical of this
show – there is no detailed planning – no precise coordinates in this
unit.'[72]

Meanwhile, D Company tried to mount Old Vickers from the north-
west. On 12 July a platoon found a suitable approach and climbed up

Photo 19 Gordon McDonald being brought across the Francisco River on the kunda-vine bridge. He was wounded in the leg at Old Vickers on 9 July. Photo by Damien Parer, who observed that McDonald had been 'four days in no man's land and not a bite to eat'. (AWM 015835)

during the night. It was decided to lie up during the day and attack on the afternoon of 13 July in conjunction with another C Company attack from the south. But at around 1200 the platoon was spotted by the enemy and forced back down the ridge.[73]

One of the wounded men that morning was Wal Johnson. Johnson had been on a two-man patrol that morning, looking at Japanese positions at the Coconuts, when the two men were spotted. Japanese grenades exploded and the Japanese started machine-gunning them. Johnson and the other man were blown off the ridge. Johnson had been badly hit in the arm and had grenade shrapnel wounds to his face. Gordon Ayre took him back to the dressing station at the edge of the river where he collapsed.[74]

Damien Parer, who had been in the area since early 2 July, watched and filmed as 'a blinded digger led by an RAP sergeant stumbles over a stony creek, then squelches ankle deep through the clinging mud of the jungle track'.[75] Johnson was back in action ten days later and again wounded when his mate stepped on a mine, blowing both of them up. His mate was killed and Johnson lost an eye. This time, Johnson was evacuated, ultimately back to Australia.

On the same day some men from C Company returned to the approaches to Old Vickers to try to recover the Bren guns lost in the 9 July attack. Amazingly, they also found Gordon McDonald, close to the enemy positions, with a badly wounded leg that prevented him moving. He had been wounded in the attack and given up for dead.[76] What had happened to McDonald mirrored the fate of the 58/59th Battalion: given up for dead on Bobdubi Ridge.

CHAPTER | **8**

YANKS

General Blamey's planning for an attack on Lae involved landing a force by sea. This in turn demanded the prior seizure of a shore base within a hundred kilometres of Lae, which was considered the maximum range for the type of landing craft that would carry the assault troops. Nassau Bay, midway between Morobe and Lae, was selected as the most suitable area. Its capture would also enable a junction to be made with the Australian forces operating at Mubo.[1] General MacArthur also saw the Nassau Bay landing as a means to ease the logistic situation that was tying up the troop carrier squadrons and native labour resources.[2] Herring wrote, 'It seemed essential that we should get hold of it as soon as possible.'[3] On 27 May 3rd Division headquarters was given orders to secure Nassau Bay using infantry from the United States 41st Infantry Division.

The 41st Infantry Division comprised the National Guard units of the north-western states of the United States. Originally drawn from the states of Oregon, Washington, Idaho and Montana, the division was known as the 'Sunsetters' and had a half-circle sunset motif. The division was deployed to the Pacific theatre in March 1942, and had arrived in Melbourne in three convoys by mid-May. The division had three infantry regiments, the 162nd, 163rd and 186th, three artillery battalions, the 146th, 205th and 218th, as well as ancillary units. The division commander was 56-year-old Major-General Horace H. Fuller. He had served as an artillery officer in France during World War I and had returned to France as the US military attaché to Paris before taking over the 41st Division in

December 1941. General Savige noted, 'Fuller was a dour looking fellow without any sense of humour.'[4]

After an initial training period, the division, now known as the 'Jungleers', moved to the Rockhampton area in July 1942, and training picked up. In August the division was incorporated into Lieutenant-General Robert Eichelberger's I Corps, alongside the 32nd Division. The first 41st Division unit deployed to New Guinea was Colonel Jens A. Doe's 163rd Infantry Regiment with attached signals, tank destroyer, supply and engineer units. Doe's command arrived in Port Moresby on 27 December 1942 and was sent into the fight for the approaches to Sanananda, north-west of Buna. With limited lines of approach through swampy jungle against a determined Japanese foe, the fighting at Sanananda soon developed into a stalemate, and it was not until the Australian 18th Brigade moved into the area in January 1943 that Sanananda finally fell. Like their compatriots in the 32nd Division, the Jungleers had found the going tough.

In late January the 186th Regiment joined the 163rd in an advance up the Papuan coast to mop up the remnants from the Japanese beachheads. In mid-February the third of the division's infantry regiments, the 162nd, arrived in New Guinea. It was taken by sea to Oro Bay in early March 1943 and thereafter relieved the 163rd Regiment further along the coast. The 205th and 218th Field Artillery Battalions followed in April, the 205th losing much of its supplies when two transport ships were sunk at Oro Bay. The 162nd Regiment was commanded by Colonel Archibald R. MacKechnie and, despite not being committed to any action other than patrolling, four months in New Guinea had reduced the strength and condition of his troops. Lieutenant-Colonel Harold Taylor's 1/162 Battalion would be landed on D-Day at Nassau Bay, alongside elements of the 116th Engineer Battalion. MacKechnie would land as the MacKechnie Force commander.

These units would be carried in landing craft from A and D Companies of the 532nd Engineer Boat and Shore Regiment (EBSR), part of Brigadier-General William Heavey's 2nd Engineer Amphibian Brigade. The unit, formed by the army to carry out amphibious operations without relying on the navy, had been assembling and training in Australia since February 1943. Due to space constraints on shipping from the USA, the landing craft had been brought out in prefabricated sections then reassembled at Cairns in northern Queensland. As the landing craft were assembled, the 'amphib' operators retrained, and the first landing-craft detachment from the 532nd arrived at Milne Bay on 28 May. After moving on to Oro Bay on 13 June, the unit trained in night landings in the rough coastal seas, honing the engineers for the task ahead. Corporal Alfred Smith, a machine-gunner with the 532nd EBSR, noted, 'our outfit was getting good. We could handle our boats on any kind of sea or most any type of beach. We were making successful landings through high surf and getting them back off the beach in pitch black nights without ever breaking or upsetting a boat.'[5]

By late June an operational base had been established at Morobe, further up the coast from Oro Bay and 80 kilometres from Nassau Bay. The landing craft were moored under the trees along the edges of an inlet and, despite daily enemy flights over the area, they were not discovered. The landing force would be carried in twenty-nine LCVPs (landing craft, vehicle and personnel), also known as Higgins boats after their American designer, Andrew Higgins. Two LCMs (landing craft mechanised) were also available along with two captured Japanese barges, which would be towed. Each LCVP would carry thirty-six men, the LCM, sixty men and around fifty men in each of the Japanese barges.[6] After assembling at Morobe, most of MacKechnie Force moved another 20 kilometres further up the coast to Mageri Point on 28 June with embarkation taking place at dusk on 29 June. To augment the landing craft, four Patrol Torpedo (PT) boats would accompany them; PT-143 and PT-120 each took on board seventy men, forty below deck and thirty on top, while PT-142 took on ten men. To keep its decks free for action the fourth boat, PT-168, carried no passengers.[7] In all, some 1400 men were to land at Nassau Bay.

On 30 April 1943 the major Japanese unit stationed at Nassau Bay was the weakened III/102nd Battalion, comprising two infantry companies, each of sixty men, the machine-gun company of thirty-eight men and a headquarters unit comprising twenty-two men under Major Takamura. Also at Nassau Bay there was a small engineer unit plus some marine signallers.[8] Allied patrols reported around seventy-five enemy troops at the mouth of the Bitoi River, around 300 at Cape Dinga to the south and only small outposts between the two positions facing Nassau Bay. On the morning of 29 June, with rain falling and unaware of the imminent invasion, Takamura instructed that 'all personnel will rest and take care of the arms and clothing'.[9]

The landing was scheduled for the night of 29 June. Alfred Smith, on landing craft 129, *Old Faithful*, pondered the night ahead with foreboding. 'There was a terrible looking cloud coming up from the north,' Smith wrote. 'For a moment I had the feeling that a greater power than us was taking a hand and was forbidding us to come out on the sea that night.' The convoy formed up as the rain began to fall, and it became heavier as

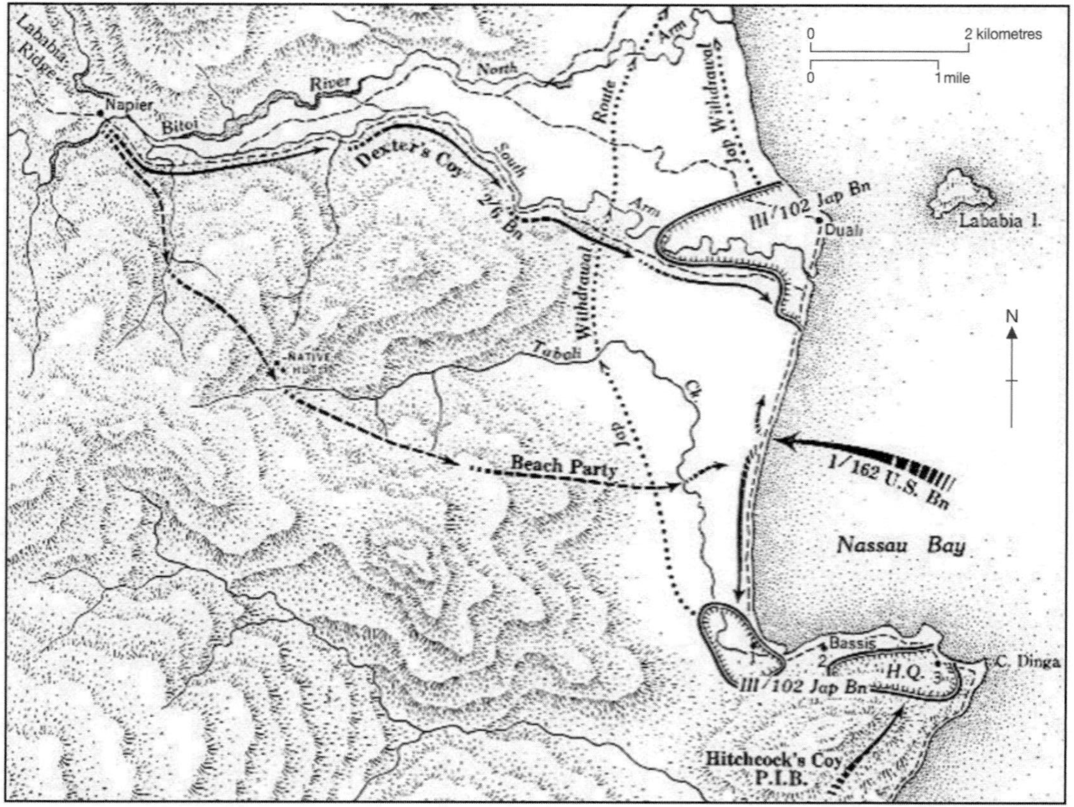

Map 18 Nassau Bay landing, 29–30 June 1943

the landing craft headed further out from shore. Smith observed, 'Here we were out on a terrible stormy sea in a drenching rain slipping up on our enemy.'[10]

The landing waves left Mageri Point at 20-minute intervals. The first two waves picked up their PT boat escort, but the third did not and wallowed along hopefully, piloted by one of the engineering officers on a landing craft. Fred Devenney was on the LCVP with Colonel MacKechnie and, by 2030, they were already having trouble holding formation in the towering swell when the motor failed. A PT boat came alongside and MacKechnie climbed aboard, surmising that a higher viewpoint would make it easier to see the landing lights and enable the best decision to be made on whether to land.[11]

In the stormy darkness, the boats moved cautiously north, unable to see any of the guiding lights laid out on the adjacent islands. Local natives later said that the storm on that particular night was the worst within their memory. The PT boats with a normal cruising speed of 25 knots had major problems in shepherding the convoy as they could not cruise slow enough to maintain position with the eight-knot landing craft. One wave of landing craft lost course entirely and went beyond the landing beach.[12]

Following earlier discussions between their senior staff officers, General Savige and General Fuller had met the New Guinea Force commander, Herring, in Port Moresby on 31 May to reach agreement on the planning for the land phase of the operation. Fuller had requested an Australian battalion in support of the landing but had finally agreed with General Savige that an 'adequate force' would suffice. In Savige's mind that would be a platoon.[13] The Australians would also supply a patrol to deploy lights at the beach landing zone and a company from the Papuan Infantry Battalion to tie down the Japanese garrison at Cape Dinga on the south flank of the landing beach. The escorting PT boats would provide support fire on Cape Dinga to aid the role of the Papuan Infantry Battalion.

The beach party was provided by the 2/6th Battalion and comprised Lieutenant Reg Urquhart's 18 Platoon, led in by Lieutenant Dave Burke, who had previously reconnoitred the area. The plan was to reach the beach midway between the enemy positions at Duali and Cape Dinga on the late evening of 29 June. Three lights were to be set up to provide signals for the American landing, which was scheduled to take place just before midnight. The men proceeded to blaze a track along an ill-defined native pad up the high saddle behind Mount Stewart, then down the far slopes towards Nassau Bay. As they waited behind the coast in the late afternoon, medium bombers bombed and strafed the track around Duali and down to Nassau Bay.

At 1630 the 26-man group waded across the creek and began the two-kilometre move through to the beach. They had to cross a swamp, a difficult task. Corporal John Stephens, attached from 17th Brigade headquarters, noted, 'It was an incredibly evil swamp; the hellish climax to all we had endured in New Guinea.' Men sank up to their thighs as they dragged themselves through the mire; Reg Urquhart called it 'the worst bastard I'd ever struck'. After the group struggled out of the swamp Burke, who as the senior lieutenant had overall command, decided to wait until dusk to cross Tabali Creek and proceed to the beach. This delay was against Urquhart's wishes. The crossing was made in a small inflatable boat, two men at a time.[14]

Dark had now fallen, and it was raining heavily, masking any chance of discovery by enemy patrols, but Burke waited until 2145 to push on to the beach. Half a kilometre of thick scrub remained to be covered and, in the inky darkness of the jungle, it took longer than Burke had foreseen. Using a carefully shaded lantern, Burke and Lloyd Ellen led the group, with each man holding on to the bayonet scabbard or shoulder harness of the man in front. It was some three hours of struggle, ending only when Greg Smith went forward with a machete to hack into the jungle towards the sound of the sea, following a 90-degree compass bearing. It was at least 2315 before Burke's twenty-six men reached the beach, only 30 minutes before the scheduled landing time. However, they had emerged at a point too far to the south, around a kilometre from the base of the Cape Dinga promontory. John Stephens noted, 'The dim promontory forming the right arm of Nassau Bay loomed up much too close.'[15] With four other men, Burke, Ellen and Stephens urgently headed north along the beach. Ellen noted, 'We then tore up the beach to where we estimated the correct position would be.' They set up a red signal light on a high point of sand and another to the north of it, and signalled out to sea with a yellow light between. After 30 minutes, just as Reg Urquhart apparently came up the beach with the remainder of the patrol, the sound of engines was heard and the first landing craft hit the beach. Urquhart had set up other lights further down the bay.[16]

═══════════

Around 0015 on 30 June the first wave of twelve landing craft approached the beach in line abreast. By the flashes of lightning the shoreline could be seen ahead, and the sound of the crashing breakers gave a certain security that the enemy would be unable to hear their approach. To Alfred Smith, 'A landing seemed impossible in that high surf.' As his landing craft grounded, a following wave smashed it into some rock, tearing a gash in the hull. All but two of the landing craft in the first wave foundered, their crews joining the infantrymen on the shore. Smith and another stranded gunner dug a foxhole in the sand and waited for the dawn.[17]

Jack Fleming, serving with the 741st Ordnance Company, had been attached to MacKechnie Force for the landing. In the pitch black night the landing craft were hit by the shore break, and the barges were turned over at the shoreline. The men scrambled ashore and dug foxholes up above the sand at the jungle fringe and waited until the morning to see what they could recover from the barges. They then sent out some scout patrols, directed by some of the Australians in Burke's party who had hurried down to the shoreline to greet the disembarking Yanks.[18] John Stephens observed: 'A difficult business it was, too, in those 12-foot breakers, which hurtled the big square-snouted barges into the beach like so many match-boxes, sideways, and backwards and almost upside down.'[19]

The second wave had no choice but to land further down the beach as the broached craft of the first wave had blocked the designated landing spot. In the second wave, Fred Devenney saw two lights on shore and one flashed the message, 'Let's go.' After waiting up at the direction of a PT boat, the LCVP headed in at 0040, the fifty men on board being ordered to the rear to give the boat the chance to land high on the shoreline. At full throttle the boat hit the beach, the men tumbling out into the water, carting rolls of wire with them up through the surf on to the beach. This second wave also broached, leaving a total of twenty-three grounded landing craft along the beach. Tom McAnally's landing craft was caught broadside and, when it overturned, the Texan engineer had to swim to shore to await the dawn. The crew of each landing craft consisted of three men: a coxswain, an engineer and a deckhand, and all were stranded on the beach as their landing craft broached. Daylight revealed a nearby enemy position, and McAnally's group headed north up the beach to the main landing place.[20]

Meanwhile, Colonel MacKechnie and six men had jumped off the PT boat into a LCVP from the first wave that had managed to retract. As it landed a second time, the LCVP hit the ramp of another barge, but Colonel MacKechnie made it to shore, unlike the battalion commander, Colonel Taylor. Of twenty-four boats in the first two waves, only one got off again to join the eight craft in the third wave that did not land.[21] On reflection, it was most fortunate that this wave didn't land as those boats and a small number in reserve at Morobe would be the only transport available in the coming days.

Twenty-one LCVPs, one LCM and one captured Japanese barge were lost in the landing along with the mortar and reserve small arms ammunition. Of immediate concern, all Colonel MacKechnie's radios were unserviceable. It took three days for Technical Sergeant John Fields to dismantle and dry out radio parts in an oven made from empty cartridge boxes.[22] The landing had been a disaster, mitigated only by the fact that no men had drowned. In all 770 men had landed, 440 of them infantry, 96 from A Company, 166 from C Company and 110 men from D Company.[23] The loss of most of the landing craft meant that the three PT boats carrying troops could not unload, and they returned to Morobe with their men still on board, other than Colonel MacKechnie and six of his staff.[24]

Japanese orders were to oppose the landing, then retire to company or battalion HQ. A six-man observation post resisted but, when they withdrew, found their HQ had already pulled out. This group split into pairs and at least one party, stricken with malaria and trying to survive while cut off in the jungle, was captured.[25] The initial Japanese response was tardy. A captured Japanese captain later noted that the roar of the boat motors, as they sought to get off the beach, sounded like tanks were being landed and his men refrained from immediately counter-attacking. However, there was some enemy resistance on the first night. As dawn broke, Alfred Smith found his foxhole closer to the Japanese lines than to his own men, and the man with him was twice wounded, then killed. Smith noted, 'Japs were closing in very close to us on the south side.'[26]

Colonel MacKechnie acted to shore up his flanks, sending Captain Delmar Newman's C Company south and Captain John George's A Company north. By 0930 a patrol had reached the mouth of Tabali Creek at the southern end of Nassau Bay without encountering any enemy opposition. Meanwhile, in the north, at the mouth of the south arm of the Bitoi River, a patrol from George's company had engaged enemy troops with machine-gun and mortar fire. The Japanese had let the forward elements pass, then shot up the HQ group at the rear, forcing the company to fall back to reorganise. It was a harsh introduction to jungle fighting. Following this, Newman was ordered to leave one platoon in the south and move the other two to reinforce George.[27] Reg Urquhart's 18 Platoon also moved up in support and struck the Japanese on the coastal track before machine-gun fire from the direction of Duali pinned the platoon down. At 1000, as the Japanese apparently moved to encircle the beach defence,

Photo 20 Landing craft at Nassau Bay in August 1943. Photograph by Colin Halmarick. (AWM 055709)

Len Shadbolt moved his section to the right flank. He picked up a Bren gun from a wounded man and, firing from the hip, killed three enemy soldiers. At the same time, Hilary Barwise used a grenade discharger to kill two more enemy troops trying to set up a machine-gun on the beach before Shadbolt's party forced the Japanese withdrawal.[28] The enemy troops were from 12 Company of the III/102nd Battalion, which had lost ten men killed and twenty wounded during the landing operations.[29]

Further south, at the mouth of Tabali Creek, Lieutenant Brown's 2 Platoon from Newman's C Company reported enemy troops crossing the creek and working into his rear. They were troops from the Japanese garrison at Cape Dinga, trying to make their way north. Brown was ordered to pull back and form a new position, but the Japanese were already upon them, a 'bayonet charge' killing at least five of the Americans, including Brown. The supporting machine-gunners pulled back and prepared to fight 300 metres further up the beach, only 200 metres from battalion headquarters. Here, three machine-guns and a line of riflemen formed a position from the beach to the jungle, the one bulldozer that had landed in the centre and rear-echelon men being rushed into the line to shore it up. As darkness fell the line was extended into the jungle. Enemy attacks supposedly went on all night but, apart from a few snipers, there were no enemy troops in the area at dawn. However, nine Americans had been killed that night while twelve were wounded and four more missing. Bob Burns was with Newman's C Company and later recalled, 'The training we had didn't do much for us when we came to the New Guinea jungle.'[30]

Men from the amphibian engineers, although lacking personal weapons, were among those helping to man the southern perimeter. Before dawn, the Japanese apparently made a banzai charge and reached the American foxholes where hand-to-hand fighting took place. The engineers breathed a huge sigh of relief when the first streak of dawn broke over the eastern horizon, but they had not escaped unscathed. Second Lieutenant Arthur C. Ely, who had led his men courageously during the first part of the fighting, was one of seven engineers killed.[31] Although some Japanese soldiers would have been moving in the area, trying to make their way their way to the north, official historian David Dexter believed that a combination of 'itchy fingers', the darkness of the night and nervousness was responsible for the majority of the American casualties around the perimeter; they were self-inflicted. The Australians dubbed it Guy Fawkes' Night.[32]

Meanwhile, following the failure of MacKechnie's communications equipment, General Savige was left very much in the dark regarding the Nassau Bay operation. The morning after the landing, Savige requested that the RAAF No. 4 Squadron army cooperation flight at Wau send an aircraft over Nassau Bay to provide details of the situation. Flying Officer Ron Dickson was given the urgent task and raced down the Wau airstrip to where a Wirraway was being warmed up in the dispersal area. He proceeded to taxi the aircraft to the top of the airstrip where he would also pick up his observer, Joe Werner, when suddenly the motor cut out, the fitter having earlier turned off the petrol cock. On any normal airstrip this would not be a problem, but Wau strip had a 5-degree slope and the Wirraway brakes only stopped the plane rolling forward, not back. As Dickson's plane rolled back down the airstrip, he bailed out and watched as the plane ended up in the drain at the bottom of the airstrip. Dickson and Werner eventually got airborne in another aircraft and were able to confirm that the landing had been made, although nineteen wrecked landing barges were counted.[33]

At the southern end of Nassau Bay Captain Ernest Hitchcock's A Company from the Papuan Infantry Battalion had been keeping the Japanese garrison at Cape Dinga occupied. Hitchcock's company comprised five Australian officers, eighteen Papuan and Australian NCOs, and 119 native Papuan soldiers organised into three platoons. On 28 June the unit had moved north from Buso to Cape Roon by native canoe. From here, the Japanese positions at Cape Dinga could be seen and, following reconnaissance patrols, Hitchcock made his plans to attack and capture Cape Dinga and thus protect the southern flank of the American landing.[34]

Lieutenant Charles Bishop's 5 Platoon would be responsible for securing the heights of Cape Dinga while Sergeant Bob MacIlwain's 4 Platoon would attack the two Bassis villages and capture the observation telescope. An estimated 300 Japanese troops occupied the area so the attack needed to be well planned and executed. The jump-off point would be a creek just south of Cape Dinga. Bishop moved up the ridge line but ran into fierce resistance, and Sergeant Ehava, who had been decorated during the earlier Papuan campaign, helped to keep the attack moving. Meanwhile one of the Bassis villages was found to be deserted while the other was protected by a strong bunker built underneath one of the houses. Combustible material was finally brought up and piled on to the bunker, then set alight, and twenty-six dead enemy soldiers were later found inside. As one of the Papuan Infantry Battalion men later noted, 'We pretty soon cooked him out.' On 1 July Hitchcock's men moved north to Tabali Creek.[35]

On the north flank of the landing the 2/6th Battalion moved to help the Americans. Lieutenant Rod Smith's Tank Attack Platoon, still attached to Captain Bill Dexter's D Company, left for Duali on the afternoon of 29 June. The loss of 'Bluey' Gibbons had shown that the track following the south arm of the Bitoi River down to the coast was covered by Japanese ambush positions, and the platoon's task was to draw them out.[36] The other two D Company platoons would also make diversionary attacks at Duali to keep the Japanese troops away from the landing beach. Following the landing, Dexter's men would then clear the track down to the sea, enabling the American infantry to move through to Bitoi Ridge to help cut off the Japanese at Mubo.

Having failed to make contact on the previous two nights, Dexter's company was now ordered to attack the Japanese position on the Bitoi River following a strafing attack by RAAF Beaufighters. Dexter recalled, 'We advanced through the Japanese position with fixed bayonets and searched the scrub on each side. Everywhere was evidence of a hasty evacuation, dropped equipment and personal rice bags, and evidence of extensive bomb damage. But of the Japs, no sign.'[37] Dexter's men pushed on and, at around 1330, captured the mouth of the south arm of the Bitoi River, then patrolled south to contact MacKechnie. Dexter noted that MacKechnie 'had a bloody great tent, a marquee, on the beach itself'. MacKechnie admitted that his troops were green and asked if Dexter could take care of a pocket of enemy troops down the beach. Dexter refused, having been ordered to hand over responsibility to the Americans. However, Dexter did agree to take a US company with him up to Napier from where the men climbed the Bitoi Ridge.[38]

The Japanese made air attacks along the Bitoi River that day, and Reg Urquhart watched as all the bombs fell in the jungle behind the beach. He noted, 'It was the most harmless air raid of the war.'[39] On the ground, Nakano placed two companies of Kimura's III/66th Battalion, held in reserve at Komiatum, under his direct control. Nakano ordered them to prepare to head overland to Nassau Bay as quickly as possible and, once there, to attack the northern end of the American lodgement and prevent any further advance towards Lake Salus.[40]

On the night of 1 July Lieutenant-Commander Barry Atkins' PT boats covered the landing of reinforcements, mainly from B Company. Eleven landing craft came in under their own power while the PT boats strafed nearby villages, and several more craft were towed in by trawlers.[41] During the daylight hours on 2 July, Second Lieutenant Charles Keele piloted another landing craft to the Nassau Bay beachhead to deliver urgently needed medical supplies. Not long after leaving Morobe, his vessel was strafed by enemy aircraft, badly wounding Keele. He insisted that the mission be completed before returning to the unit base where he could be treated for his wounds, ten hours after the air attack. The selfless Keele died from his wounds five days later.[42]

With the Bitoi River mouth now secured, the bulldozer commenced building a jeep track inland along the south arm of the Bitoi River. Ron Dickson once more flew over Nassau Bay on the morning of 2 July and noted strings of trenches all along the high-water line, seemingly indicating that most of MacKechnie's men were still on the beach. He reported his findings in a message dropped to Moten's 17th Brigade headquarters at Guadagasal. With radio communication now established, Moten impressed upon MacKechnie that he must get his troops moving inland at the earliest possible date. MacKechnie interpreted Moten's impression as 'being substantially an order to begin movement inland on 3 July'. He was right; General Savige was prodding Moten to get the Americans moving. Savige later noted, 'The show on the beach appeared to be sticky. I instructed Moten to act firmly, but courteously, to get things moving.'[43]

Despite the loss of most of the landing craft, MacKechnie knew further troops were scheduled to arrive but was also aware that the Japanese had not yet seriously attacked his lodgement. He therefore left C Company to defend Nassau Bay and headed inland with the rest of his men, comprising Colonel Taylor's 1/162 headquarters plus HQ Company, A Company and B Company, less one platoon. On the night of 2 July further elements did land, including a battery of 75mm guns from the 218th Field Artillery Battalion under Brigadier-General Ralph W. Coane. Following their overnight landing, the four guns had been emplaced at the beach and had commenced shelling targets at the mouth of the Tabali River, Cape Dinga peninsula and the area between Duali and the Bitoi River's south arm. All up, seventy officers and 1042 men had now landed at Nassau Bay, although the Japanese were under the impression that 2000 men had landed.[44]

By the time 10 Company of Kimura's III/66th Battalion reached Lake Salus on the morning of 3 July, Takamura's remaining men had already withdrawn to the same location. With the Americans concentrating on moving up the Bitoi River to get in behind Mubo, the Japanese units now forming a defensive line at the north end of Lake Salus would not be contacted until around 10 July. However, the area to the north was a string of sand dunes with steep cliffs along the coast while, to the west, shallow mangrove swamp extended to the mountains. There was nowhere to establish a position in depth, and the Japanese would soon move into the mountainous terrain further north.[45]

By 4 July three of Colonel Taylor's companies, now known as Taylor Force, had concentrated at Napier, at the junction of the Bitoi and Buyawim Rivers. C Company remained at the mouth of the Bitoi River until relieved on 6 July. With MacKechnie's consent, Taylor Force now came under the command of 17th Brigade and, although Taylor was willing to carry out the important Bitoi Ridge task to help Moten, he had ammunition shortages.[46] Exacerbating his problem, at midday on 5 July a ration party moving up from Nassau Bay was ambushed and three men were killed. Meanwhile, Captain Dexter's company had moved back to Guadagasal after their sojourn on the coast, ready to take part in the upcoming battle for Mubo. On 5 July Savige flew to Port Moresby for a conference, where it was agreed that US operations were to be directed by Savige's 3rd Division headquarters. Due to the difficulty of MacKechnie being responsible to two commanders, Herring requested that General Fuller notify MacKechnie that he was under 3rd Division control.[47]

Fortunately, General Savige had not flown over Nassau Bay that day on his way south. Flying Officers Jimmy Collier and John Utber had done so, piloting two Boomerang aircraft from RAAF No. 4 Squadron out of Wau airfield on a tactical reconnaissance mission to the Salamaua area. However, when cloud cover prevented observation, the two aircraft diverted down the coast to Nassau Bay. Unfortunately the area had been subject to a Japanese air attack earlier that day, and the American anti-aircraft gunners were on guard for another. Collier's aircraft, relatively unknown to the Americans and of a radial engine design similar that of to a Japanese fighter, approached from the north, then dived down to look at the stranded landing barges. At a height of about 60 metres the anti-aircraft fire opened up and Collier's engine was hit, forcing him to carry out a wheels-up landing in the shallows along the beach. The plane hit the water heavily 50 metres offshore before skidding across the beach and into the undergrowth. Tragically, Collier was killed in the landing, striking his head on the aircraft's gunsight.[48]

On the same day the first detachment of C Battery from Lieutenant-Colonel Cochran's 218th Field Artillery landed at Nassau Bay, and on 7 July the four officers and eighty men of the battery began to move inland with their four 75mm howitzers and ammunition. Their objective was eight kilometres up the Bitoi River at Napier, but the jeep track gave out after around a kilometre, then the men had to take over, helped by another thirty-five men from the Service Battery. Rain further upstream soon meant that the Bitoi became impassable for the wheeled guns and they had to be disassembled, broken down into eight parts. The heaviest component weighed around 90 kilograms and was carried on a pole with two men on each end. With each of the 400 shells also weighing seven kilograms, it was a tough haul up the river. The detachment had to cross the river a number of times as well as the adjoining creeks and swamps. Another fifty men arrived from the forward positions on 8 July to help and, by 1600, two of the guns had been emplaced about one and a half kilometres downstream from Napier. The Pimple and Green Hill in front of the 2/6th Battalion positions on Lababia Ridge were the first targets, and the first shell, signed by all the artillerymen, was fired at the Pimple just after 1700 on 8 July.[49]

Increasingly concerned at the delay in getting the Americans moving, Moten sent a message to General Savige on 6 July stating that reports from his two liaison officers, Captain Douglas McBride and Captain Cecil Rolfe, 'indicate conditions on beach are generally chaotic'. In a subsequent message to Herring, Savige suggested that consideration be given to relieving MacKechnie. Herring phoned General Fuller on the morning of 7 July, and Fuller said he would send a senior staff officer to Nassau Bay to appraise the situation. This convoluted command structure did not augur well for future cooperation between the two allies. Moten later directed MacKechnie to return to Nassau Bay, but he would not do so until 14 July. Moten later said, 'MacKechnie was rooted when he reached Napier and I asked him to stay on the beach.'[50]

After a number of delays, Taylor Force was instructed to occupy Bitoi Ridge on 8 July, but the delay in the deployment of the artillery affected this. Taylor's men were on the upper southern slopes of the ridge by 1500 with A Company patrols forward on the crest. However, Taylor's actions were not having the desired effect of prodding the Japanese command into withdrawing from the Mubo area. The Australians would now have to take Mubo by force rather than manoeuvre, a daunting task.

CHAPTER | 9

MUBO FALLS

The primary objective of Operation Doublet was to capture Mubo and link up with the Americans advancing from Nassau Bay. The Allies would then advance to Goodview Junction, Mount Tambu and the adjoining ridges down to the coast, but not beyond that line. Although Operation Doublet included attacks by the Americans on the coastal flank and 15th Brigade on the western flank, the proposed axis of advance would be that of 17th Brigade. Savige later wrote how his former brigade would be 'my spearhead in the attack and my clenched fist to drive home success'.[1]

Brigadier Moten had planned to commence the 17th Brigade operation against Mubo on 5 July but, due to the delays with Lieutenant-Colonel Taylor's US 1/162 Battalion moving inland from Nassau Bay, it was delayed until 7 July.[2] Meanwhile the 2/5th Battalion moved up from Wau to participate in the operation. Three companies, A and B Companies from the 2/6th and C Company from the 2/5th, would take part in the first phase of the attack: to take Observation Hill overlooking Mubo. On the afternoon of 6 July Captain Jo Gullett took B Company down on to a small plain at the foot of Observation Hill where they gathered alongside Captain Mick Stewart's and Captain Bill Morse's companies. A rough hospital had been built by the natives, and a pile of wooden crosses sat nearby. 'I hope they've sent enough,' Lieutenant Ernie Price wryly observed.[3]

At 0840 on 7 July Captain Stewart's A Company headed off to the start line south of Observation Hill. The rain was heavy, and the men had to wade waist-deep through Buiapal Creek in preparation for the steep climb up the side of Observation Hill. Meanwhile Captain Morse's C Company from the 2/5th Battalion, followed by Captain Gullett's 2/6th B Company, moved north to the start line. At 0850 a message arrived at 2/6th Battalion headquarters from Moten. It stated, 'Please convey to Captains Stewart, Gullett and Morse and their men my complete confidence in their ability to capture Observation Hill and thus open the door to Salamaua. Good luck to you all.'[4]

Between 0930 and 1040, heavy air attacks by eight squadrons took place on Observation Hill and adjacent areas. After 106 tons of bombs had been dropped, three white signal flares followed, indicating the end of the air attack. Thick clouds of black smoke rolled up the Bitoi Valley towards Mat Mat Hill, and observers rightly noted 'extremely heavy bombing and strafing . . . the entire Mubo Valley was enveloped in a thick pall of smoke a few minutes after the strike commenced, broken only by sheets of flame flashing across the valley as the Liberators dropped their heavy loads.'[5]

As the air attack finished, the ground troops moved forward, now supported by artillery, then mortar fire. Lieutenant Bruce Lang's 12 Platoon led Gullett's company, striking the main track along the top of Observation Hill, then turning south towards the enemy positions. The forward scout, Tom Bowman, moved around a large clump of bamboo and was killed by enemy machine-gun fire. Lang came up and directed Bren gun fire on to the enemy position, later noting, 'The firing grew very intense. My hat flew off and I watched as a burst went about two inches above the head of my Bren gunner.' Perce Harris later observed how the Japanese light machine-gun position had been skilfully camouflaged with the bush weaved around where the gunner had lain in wait.[6] Stymied, Gullett's company pulled back a short distance and halted in this position.

Mick Stewart's company passed through Gullett's and continued the attack. Jack Bearkley and Richard Nicholson were killed at a barricade across the track just past the bamboo clump. Jack Weeks, who was with 8 Platoon, 'saw Sergeant Jack McNaughton jump over a barricade the Nips had put up across the track. The Nips opened up and Jack got hit on one of his fingers. He came running out cursing. We moved in closer and the Nips opened up with a machine-gun . . . the shots went past my face. I could feel the heat.'[7] Also stymied, Stewart's men took up defensive positions for the night with Gullett's company behind them.

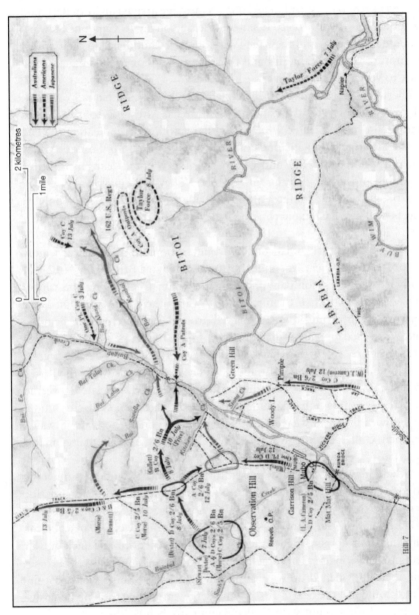

Map 19 Mubo area, 7–13 July 1943

Having climbed Observation Hill on the previous afternoon, the third of the attacking companies, Morse's C Company, sent out a section patrol from 15 Platoon on the morning of 8 July to contact the 2/3rd Independent Company. The patrol, led by Lieutenant Hank Gilbert, headed out along Vial's Track but met only the Japanese, well entrenched further back on Observation Hill. It was a steep approach up to the Japanese position, and the men couldn't even get a foothold. Lou Nazzari asked Gilbert, 'What do you think?' With no chance to get up, the answer was: 'Get out of here.' The enemy took a while to get organised, and Lou's men withdrew to the company a hundred metres back along the track.[8]

Stewart's A Company continued to be held up. Bernie Damm, the broad-shouldered rifleman who had watched his brother die alongside him at Bardia in 1940, led an attack forward. Bernie was wounded, hit above the eye by a grenade blast. 'Get up front, Doug, and see what you can find out,' he told Doug Crabb, who crawled forward to a fallen tree. A Japanese rifleman was on the other side, and he fired first, hitting Crabb in the neck. Crabb crawled back and, along with Damm and Tommy Howard, was carried out. Wood decided to reinforce Stewart and, at 1645, Captain Bill Dexter's D Company, after the killer climb up the hill, reached the kunai patch behind Stewart. Dexter later said, 'This was one of the biggest bastard marches we had ever done – we were absolutely rooted.' However, the arrival of his company was appreciated by Stewart's men, as Dexter observed: 'Weren't A Coy pleased to see the famous Dons arrive . . . Mick appeared very concerned about things and reported Nips everywhere.' Dexter's exhausted men dug in 60 metres behind a flustered Stewart, and Dexter took command of the two companies.[9]

Meanwhile, Jo Gullett's company had moved north across Observation Hill, looking to outflank the enemy position holding up Stewart. However, Jo Gullett had come down with a malarial fever, and Ernie Price had taken command. His men showed extraordinary skill in the thick jungle fighting as they headed cross country. Rod Lee's section was forward when a burst of enemy fire rang out. Lee slid across to a nearby depression with his rifle, followed by Jack Ryan, a tommy-gunner. Lee later wrote, 'These two took turns to rise and fire. They were about four or five paces apart, and as the Jap gunner returned the fire of one, the other immediately rose and took a shot. Suddenly there was silence, and these two climbed up and went ahead. The Japs were gone.' The men pushed on and, at 1400, Gullett sent a message to Wood: 'I have fetched up with a creek on my right and a creek on my left, which I hope to Christ are Kitchen and Buisavella creeks.'[10]

At this stage the Japanese force at Mubo comprised around 950 men of whom 770 were front-line soldiers from the 66th Infantry Regiment and the 14th Field Artillery Regiment. According to Shinoda, 'The artillery intensified again in the morning of 8 July, followed by the advance of superior ground forces.' The Japanese defenders had been from 3 and 8 Companies from the 66th Regiment and 'suffered numerous casualties prior to falling back'.[11]

Further orders were issued late on 8 July for patrols and mortar bombardments to break the Japanese defence. Wood wanted to 'worry them out'. One of Stewart's men, Ron Moss, was heavily involved carrying out his own one-man patrols every day for around seven days. 'I was quite happy in the jungle. Going out on my own didn't worry me one iota. I worked on the theory that if I heard a noise it had to be the enemy...I never went on the track. I always went bush. I could find my way back always.'[12]

Morse's C Company was attacked on both the north and east flanks late on the afternoon of 9 July. The Japanese defenders came during the day, sat above the Australian positions and opened fire with machine-guns. Lou Nazzari was behind the front pits and couldn't use his tommy gun due to the danger of hitting those in front. The platoon sergeant, Bob Shattock, was killed, standing up, trying to take on the Japanese by himself. Perhaps the die had been cast the previous evening as the men had gathered around a native hut, the expectation of battle on their minds. Shattock, from Ballarat in country Victoria, was one of the battalion originals, and he had a fine tenor voice. When the men asked him to sing them a song, he initially refused but, when pressed, chose the song 'Goodbye', and it was the last song he ever sang.[13] At 1730 a platoon from Bill Dexter's company was sent to help Morse.

This was jungle fighting at its fiercest, as Arthur Pearson noted: 'In most cases we were firing blind, but sometimes we were able to pick up the smoke from their rifles.' Pearson had each of his men concentrate on one sector of jungle. With an unhealthy disrespect for the accuracy of the Japanese riflemen, Pearson then jumped in and out of his weapon pit, trying to draw fire. Not surprisingly, Pearson was hit, the bullet passing through the stock of his rifle and damaging his hand before the ricochet killed the lad next to him. Pearson's men raked the area where the shot had come from and killed the sniper.[14]

After a barrage of supporting mortar fire, Stewart's company had another go at breaking through on the following afternoon. When 9 Platoon attacked it was pinned down by at least six automatic weapons

covering the razorback approach. Doug Hansen, Billy Bonsop and Jack
Weeks went forward, and Bonsop, the lead scout, took a full burst in the
chest and was killed. The others tried to reach him but were pinned down
by the intense fire that chopped the bamboo down around their heads.
Bill Dexter was also forward with the attack. 'We had to bite the dust as
Nip's fire fell amongst us.' At 1515 the company withdrew to the former
perimeter.[15]

Out beyond Gullett's position US infantry had cut the main track
north of Bui Alang Creek on the previous day. Lieutenant Marvin Noble's
3 Platoon from Captain George's A Company, accompanied by an Australian guide, Greg Smith, who had done mighty work at Nassau Bay,
had moved up to the high ground near Goodview Junction. The platoon
then dropped down to Buigap Creek and headed south, reaching Komiatum Track late on 10 July. Noble had orders to attack south to join up
with the rest of George's company at midday on 11 July, and sent out
two patrols the next morning, one under Lieutenant Gray to the north
and another, under Sergeant Wayne Fogel south, down the Buigap. Gray
came across at a group of bamboo huts and drove off about ten Japanese
soldiers before running into trouble further on. Soon thereafter Noble's
platoon was also ambushed, near the mouth of Buisavella Creek. Among
the wounded, Noble was hit and one of the medics, James Thacker, was
killed by mortar fire as he bandaged Noble's wounds. Lieutenant Gray
rejoined the platoon and took over command as the men hauled themselves back up the ridge from the Buigap. It appeared that the Japanese
Mubo defenders were using a route north-east along the Buikumbul to
withdraw to Mount Tambu.[16]

At 1730 another patrol from George's company finally contacted an
Australian patrol from Gullett's company. The previous day Lieutenant
Jock Erskine and two other men from Warfe's independent company
made contact with the other flank of 17th Brigade but, although these
junctions had been made, there was no iron ring around the Japanese
defenders at Mubo. Shinoda observed that the stubborn defence of
Mubo had led the Australians to send out a strong flanking party to
threaten the Japanese rear while continuing to attack from the front.
'Not only were we drawing casualties in the desperate fight on the
front line, but were forced to pay attention to our rear positions. Our
troops in the camp repeatedly mounted counter-attacks, thus holding their
position.'[17]

Finally bowing to the pressure, General Nakano ordered the Mubo
garrison to retreat to Komiatum. Lieutenant Shinoda received the order

at 0530 on 11 July but, as dawn approached, the Australians were very close to his lines and it seemed inevitable that they would come under attack after first light. Immediate withdrawal was considered impossible, and the decision was taken to withdraw at sundown on 11 July. The front-line company withdrew at dusk, leaving a token rearguard at Mubo. The withdrawing troops soon realised the enemy troops blocked the main track behind them and had to find an alternative route out. Shinoda wrote, 'We were taking our sick and injured troops with us on the advance through the dark jungle terrain. Climbing and descending through the steep mountainous terrain made our withdrawal operation extremely difficult.' Shinoda's men engaged a small enemy party around dawn on 12 July and, by afternoon on 13 July, had reached the line of well-prepared positions along the saddle from Goodview Junction to Mount Tambu. Casualties suffered during the fighting at Mubo had reduced the strength of each unit by about a third while food and ammunition were in short supply with little prospect of replenishment.[18]

On 11 July Lieutenant Cyril Miles' 17 Platoon moved up to support Captain Stewart's company by attacking the rear of the enemy position. The unit was crossing Buiapal Creek at Mubo when an enemy plane flew over. Cyril Miles noted, 'It was a reconnaissance plane and we were crossing this creek, which was flowing at a hell of a rate. You know you had to take one step at a time and even that was quite dangerous. And this bloody thing flew over.' One of the men turned to Miles and commented, 'Oh, lucky there, Cyril. He didn't see us.' Miles replied that he thought they had been spotted and the plane would be back. The aircraft did a loop, then came back and dropped a bomb killing two men, Geoff Kurzman and Bob Burstall.[19]

Miles' platoon pushed on after the interrupted crossing of Buipal Creek and climbed the southern slopes on to the crest of Observation Hill. Here the platoon was held up by the main Japanese position. Sergeant Charlie Robertson and Charlie Turnbull had a phone line back to the 3-inch mortars and Vickers machine-guns on Mat Mat Hill. As Cyril Miles recollected, they 'directed fire on to this mob that were holding us up'. Fire was brought in so close that Turnbull was wounded by the Vickers, a flesh wound to the arm. The enemy position held and Miles pulled his men back, observing, 'We weren't going to sit there all night on our own so we withdrew.' On the following morning 'they gave them the works again', then found that the Japanese had left in a hurry. There were three large huts at the position that had been shot up by the Vickers gun as well as evidence of buried enemy dead and half-eaten food.[20]

On the American front a patrol from Captain George's A Company sighted a large enemy force withdrawing north-east on 11 July and was able to call down sixty rounds from the 81mm mortars and artillery fire. The artillery support came from the four 75mm guns emplaced near Napier. The gunners observed, 'We had four rounds per gun – sixteen rounds in the air in thirty-six seconds – fired a total of nine rounds per howitzer.' The next day another patrol followed an artillery barrage forward and found forty to fifty dead Japanese and a profusion of hurriedly abandoned equipment in the Buisavella Creek area. More artillery fire on 13 July targeted enemy positions at the head of Buigap Creek. When Captain Delmar Newman's C Company advanced they found 'literally hundreds of dead Japanese'.[21]

Newman's company had moved up from the Bitoi on the right flank of George. On 12 July Lieutenant Ralph Cless took twenty-five men from 1st Platoon plus a five-man light machine-gun crew and three Papuan Infantry Battalion guides on patrol up the Buikumbul Ridge. The aim was to set up an ambush on the Komiatum Track to interdict Japanese troops withdrawing from the Mubo area. The three Papuan Infantry Battalion guides led the way, the men following the rough jungle track in single file. Approaching the summit of the first climb, the jungle thinned to a rocky slope and, just below the crest, the guides called a halt. Cless deployed along either side of the approach trail, and the patrol advanced over the crest of Buikumbul Ridge. One squad then moved up the track that ran along the top and another down it. Both squads soon encountered resistance, and an enemy flanking attack had to be beaten back.[22]

Lieutenant Ralph Robson's 3rd Platoon moved up behind Cless and formed a strong perimeter at the track junction. More Japanese troops also joined the fray, with machine-guns now in operation on both flanks and bombs from Japanese knee-mortars dropping on the American position. The American infantrymen soon found out what the Australians had already noticed: that a significant percentage of the Japanese mortar bombs failed to explode. However, Lieutenant Robson was badly wounded by machine-gun fire while scouting the flanks on the left, and soon thereafter the Japanese made a strong attack and broke into the American lines. Cless called up Robson's reserve squad, and they managed to reinstate the position before the increasing enemy pressure on his left flank forced Cless to pull back off the ridge. The Japanese did not follow; these were the troops withdrawing from Mubo and their destination was the new defence line on the heights from Goodview to Mount Tambu.[23]

In the late afternoon of 12 July the Pimple, which had resisted persistent Australian attacks in April, was finally captured without opposition. Green Hill went the same way, and Observation Hill was also reported clear. It was apparent that the Japanese defenders had finally pulled back after holding Mubo for almost 11 months since August 1942. Too late to prevent the withdrawal, B Company of the 2/6th Battalion joined Newman's Americans on the night of 12–13 July. Lieutenant Ernie Price had taken over command of B Company on 10 July after a malaria-stricken Jo Gullett had been carried out. On the next morning, 13 July, a small American patrol went back to Buikumbul Ridge and found it was still in enemy hands. At 1000 an artillery observer arrived and directed shell fire on to the ridge and, when the Americans next went up, they found twenty-two enemy graves. That afternoon a relieved Moten informed Savige, 'Woody [Island] is cleaned bowled 0900; Green Hill 1140; Yanks now batting on the Buigap; no further scores to luncheon adjournment.'[24]

These actions meant that Mubo was finally in Australian hands, but the failure of the Americans to shut the gate detracted from the victory. The American artillery had undoubtedly caused heavy casualties to the retreating Japanese, but the inability of the infantry to hold an effective blocking position across the Japanese line of retreat meant that those forces would be able to dig in around Mount Tambu. Many of the American infantrymen, who should have fought the withdrawing Japanese to a standstill on Buikumbul Ridge, would later be lost trying to attack near-impregnable positions on Mount Tambu.

Meanwhile, Jo Gullett had gone back to Australia to contest his father's former seat of Henty in the federal election. Captain Bill Quinn helped him decide to go. 'He wanted someone to talk to. We walked up and down, up and down. He didn't want to leave the battalion.' Quinn told him that he could do more good for the troops if he was in politics than he could if he stayed. 'We can soon replace you here but we can't get a good man in politics.' Wood had the same advice, and Gullett went back but failed to be elected. He was later sent to England as an exchange officer, landing in Normandy on D-Day.[25]

On 11 July, following the fall of Mubo, Herring signalled Savige, 'All good luck in your next push. You can and I know you will drive the enemy over the Francisco River.' Savige surmised that he was to push on to Salamaua and asked Herring for clarification, noting that 'future intentions of higher command regarding Salamaua are not known'. At this stage Savige was apparently unaware of the plan to use Salamaua as a magnet for Japanese troops, drawing them away from Lae where the decisive blow would fall.[26]

Herring was certainly aware of the plan. Blamey had informed him of the 'Salamaua magnet' plan on 15 June, stating, 'Salamaua should not be seized; it should be bypassed.' Blamey went on to provide three convincing reasons for this approach. First, if Salamaua fell, enemy troops would reinforce Lae. Second, Salamaua could be controlled if Komiatum Ridge was held by the Australians. Third, Salamaua would fall without a fight once Lae had been captured.[27] As Herring later wrote, 'Salamaua could not help being a blind for Lae. The Jap commander was bound to assume that we had committed ourselves to Salamaua.'[28]

On 29 July Savige had a clear indication that the Salamaua operation was now a secondary one when he received a message from Herring requesting that the use of aerial supply should be limited due to operations planned against Lae. Herring also restated that Savige's role was to drive the enemy forces north of the Francisco River. The capture of Salamaua, although 'devoutly wished', was not to interfere with planned operations against Lae. Hence Savige's role was to hold as many enemy troops as possible in the Salamaua area. Savige later wrote that he was not directly informed that Salamaua was not to fall before Lae until Berryman told him and Wilton on 20 August.[29]

Meanwhile, the fighting continued.

CHAPTER | 10

'A BIT OF A STOUSH'

While the 58/59th Battalion struggled to achieve its objectives at the northern end of Bobdubi Ridge, Major George Warfe's 2/3rd Independent Company moved against its southern end. Warfe's role in the Doublet plan was to establish a strong blocking position at Goodview Junction 'to prevent the escape northwards of enemy forces in the Mubo area'.[1] This would be the anvil to complement the 17th Brigade hammer that would strike at Mubo.

Warfe moved down from Missim with two of his three platoons, accompanied by 200 native carriers. The party followed Uliap Creek, then made the steep climb up Bobdubi Ridge to Namling, arriving on 5 July. Meanwhile, B Platoon moved into the Vial's Post area to cover the track up from Observation Hill, which abutted Warfe's right flank. To cut the main Japanese supply route behind Mubo, Warfe would take eighty-five native carriers further forward to carry the considerable supplies required to maintain his blocking position. This included two of Warfe's beloved Vickers guns, a 3-inch mortar, ammunition, rations and medical supplies. C Platoon led off from Namling along the track up on to the ridge and on towards Wells Junction in single file. The carriers followed with accompanying escorts from the engineer section while sixteen men from A Platoon under Lieutenant John Barry brought up the rear.[2] The rest of A Platoon, including the commander, Lieutenant John Lewin, was still on the way from Missim.

Warfe was determined to move in strength on Goodview, but he was hampered by the failure of the 58/59th Battalion to secure the

186

Orodubi area on his left flank. Much of Warfe's previous success had come from bold movement and on showing his strength, but on this occasion he was almost contemptuous in underestimating his enemy. The Japanese had a clear line of sight from Orodubi to the track along Bobdubi Ridge up to Wells Junction. At 1000 on 6 July, after C Platoon had passed through, Warfe's carrier line was ambushed astride the track. The native carriers dropped their cargo, which included two Vickers guns and one 3-inch mortar, and fled. Peter Pinney was forward with C Platoon, having already passed through the ambush site, when 'fierce fighting broke out behind us, and stopped... A Platoon had been ambushed.'[3]

Young Tom 'Curly' Tregaskis, one of the carrier escorts, was killed in the ambush and, when John Barry's section counter-attacked, the Japanese were waiting for them. The Bren gunner, Wal Dawson, had his gun hit in the butt, and the splintered wood struck him in the head, knocking him off the side of the ridge. Alan Ives was kneeling down firing when he was hit in the leg, and Alan Besley copped one through the wrist. Nev Swadling fired off a magazine from his tommy gun, then yelled to 'Lofty' Moran, 'Get going! We are the last two.' They dashed into the jungle and set up a blocking position further along the track towards Wells Junction. When they sighted a sword-carrying enemy officer, happily eating a captured chocolate bar, he was shot down.[4] The remaining carriers were sent back towards Vial's Post.

The ambush had been sprung after the Australians had climbed a dominant feature on the south side of the saddle following the track up from Namling. This position would now become known as Ambush Knoll with the ambush site along the ridge where the track split, heading in one direction for Goodview and the other to Wells observation post. Warfe's men had been attacked by troops predominantly from I/66th Battalion, two of whom were killed and another two wounded. Japanese sources reported that a mortar, two automatic rifles, a phone and medical supplies were captured.[5]

Lieutenant Ron Garland's section from C Platoon was sent back to reopen the track. Peter Pinney:

At the actual ambush site we found A Platoon had withdrawn; but there was no one to tell us where the Japs were. If they had any sense they'd be gone by now too... so one moved very quietly, with big eyes and with care. There were two dead Japs on the track and I souvenired a sword one of them had... Down a muddy slope now:

twenty yards or so down, the trail began to climb again to a knoll
more sensed than seen through fairly heavy foliage. If the Japs were
going to be anywhere, that's where they would be.[6]

Garland, who had only just joined Warfe's company, was very con-
scious of the need to spot an ambush before leading his men into it, but
was only ten metres away when he spotted a Woodpecker machine-gun.
For Garland, 'Time seemed to stand still.' Garland and Pinney fired bursts
from their tommy guns and jumped over the steep slope on the right side
of the track with bullets whistling by. Both men got back to the section,
and they formed a defensive perimeter for the night across the track.
Pinney wrote, 'We put in a lousy night. It was cold, we had no shelter
other than groundsheets draped loosely over us, rain belted down and
made rivulets under us, whenever it ceased raining for a spell the mossies
swarmed about us, we were drenched and shivering and ate our iron
rations in the rain.'[7]

That night Hammer ordered Warfe to leave a force to secure Wells
Junction but to proceed to Goodview to carry out the original role.[8]
Warfe detailed eight men to hold the knoll at Wells Junction and bluntly
informed them, 'If the Japs are here when we come back you'd better
be dead or you'll be court martialled.'[9] George Warfe clearly had his
difficulties, later noting, 'Hammer was constantly on the phone, the rain
was incessant and my temperature was 104 degrees . . . we were all hungry
and confusion reigned supreme.'[10]

When Garland's section went back to the enemy ambush position the
next morning of 7 July, the Japanese had gone and the mortar, machine-
guns and stores could be recovered. Although the mortar sight bracket had
been damaged, the weapon could still be used, unlike one of the Vickers
guns, which was missing the crosshead.[11] Warfe's men now occupied
Ambush Knoll, although Hammer did not miss the opportunity to berate
Warfe over the setback. 'Careful planning is NOT a general attribute with
this Coy. Warfe for instance was adamant that Jap troops would never
move on the tracks where on [6] July they ambushed part of his force.'[12]

In preparation for the Goodview operation Warfe had arranged for
another track to be made above Stephens' Track. Brian Walpole had
helped to blaze the new track, via which it was hoped to take the enemy
defenders at Goodview by surprise. As Walpole said, 'George reckoned
that the Japs knew everywhere we'd been along. In other words he

reckoned they would have people say at Stephens' Track, they'd have people everywhere. He wanted somewhere completely new and that's when he sent me out. He didn't say where, he said the other side of Stephens' Track would probably be all right. That's jungle, it's thick jungle, dense jungle.' The three men in Walpole's party had machetes but stopped using them because of the noise that might have alerted the Japanese. Walpole observed, 'We bush bashed . . . just bashed through the virgin jungle.'[13]

Following the correct route was difficult for Walpole's party with only Mount Tambu providing a reference point when the jungle allowed. The steep and curving terrain at the head of the valley meant that a compass was of little use, and Walpole tried to keep to the highest ground possible. His party finally came out to Goodview Junction, overlooking the Komiatum Track, noting, 'It was the most perfect spot you could ever find.' From this commanding position he could clearly see enemy troops below and 'was itching to toss a couple of grenades down, could have got the lot. George would have cut my bloody throat or something, so I didn't.' Then a large party of marines came along, bigger men than most. 'They were having the time of their lives there, rotten bastards, just enjoying themselves there, no guards or anything, you know, just happily.' The next day Walpole's party returned down their new track and 'jazzed it up a little bit more'.[14]

Despite the setback at Ambush Knoll, Warfe got on with his role at Goodview Junction and issued orders for an attack by two platoons for 8 July. Captain Wally Meares' C Platoon would use Stephens' Track, and Captain John Winterflood's B Platoon would use the recently blazed Walpole's Track. Lieutenant Hugh Egan would take up a blocking position with seven men around 800 metres south of Goodview Junction overlooking the main track along Buigap Creek to Mubo from a dominant crag. On 7 July Meares' platoon moved east along Stephens' Track and settled at Stephens' Hut for the night, around 400 metres west of Goodview Junction. Peter Pinney noted, 'At [Stephens'] Hut we bedded down in pouring rain after a frugal tea, on sodden ground, in darkness, half an hour from the Komiatum track . . . rain poured down all night. We got up at 4.30 and grateful to bring this travesty of rest to an end, packed drenched things in saturated packs, shaking and shivering with cold.'[15]

Winterflood's B Platoon moved off at dawn towards Goodview Junction along Walpole's Track. Norm Bear observed, 'It's very steep. To get along there it was single file. You couldn't have a broad frontal attack.' Fred Taylor led the men off the track and around the left flank of

Map 20 Goodview Junction, 8–10 July 1943

the Japanese blocking position; the rain deadening the sound of their approach. Fortunately the Japanese guard with the machine-gun was asleep as Taylor slipped a grenade into the pit beside him. This brought out the rest of the Japanese squad only to be met by Australian gunfire. Taylor led the charge with his blazing tommy gun, and the position was taken. Les Poulson observed, 'We cleared the ridge and took up positions covering a track junction below.' Poulson was also in the action, using a Bren gun in a sniping role on a party of Japanese trying to set up a machine-gun. Norm Bear later said, 'He killed seven of them before they woke up to the fact that they shouldn't be trying to do it. Sniping with a bloody Bren gun, single shot, bloody incredible.'[16]

In the afternoon, under the cover of mortar and machine-gun fire, the Japanese counter-attacked Winterflood's position from both flanks. Robbie Roberts had just brought up some rice for the men when a Japanese officer blew a whistle and the attack began. Roberts later wrote, 'They started to fire from all around us but their aim was too high as their bullets were hitting the trees above us and showering us with twigs and leaves.' Winterflood's men accounted for twenty-five enemy soldiers, but the platoon's position among a bed of roots was untenable and he soon pulled back 300 metres up Walpole's Track. Norm Bear said, 'We didn't have any support. They had trench mortars, they had a mountain gun, they had half a regiment. We were totally undermanned, not in the race.' Bear was hit as B Platoon pulled back. 'I got hit with a bloody bit of mortar shell. A mortar bomb burst, an air burst, and it threw me to buggery getting whacked against a tree and put a hole in my bum, but I was okay. We got out.' However, two men, Tommy Kidd and 'Pancho' Stait, who had been out on the flank, missed the order to pull out and were left behind. Next morning, after Stait had taken his tommy gun apart to clean it, he heard enemy voices on top of the hill. After warning Tom Kidd, he quickly reassembled his gun and the two men took off into the scrub chased by enemy grenades. Being good bushmen, they were able to rejoin the unit two days later.[17]

To the left of Winterflood, Wally Meares' platoon had moved up Stephens' Track before dawn on 8 July. Ron Garland's 8 Section, now down to eight men, went with them. Garland observed, 'We adopted a fast pace as I wished to hit the Japs as early as possible. I didn't know whether the Japs manned their defences at first light, as we do.' When Garland's section reached the kunai clearing that marked the Mule Track junction just after daybreak, the Japanese machine-gunners were waiting. Peter Pinney wrote, 'Thirty yards away was the bench-cut Komiatum track we'd heard so much about. The forward scouts and first few of the patrol darted across it safely and vanished in a jungled gulley, then suddenly an LMG opened up and swept the track with a long burst.'[18]

With Garland's section engaged by the strong enemy position at the Mule Track junction, the other sections bypassed to the right and reached the main Komiatum Track only to find another enemy post. The Japanese defenders had formed a strong position based on the triangle formed by Komiatum Track, Mule Track and Stephens Track. It would prove a tough nut to crack. Peter Pinney: 'Climbed up a spur around a gully and found ourselves, Section 9 and part of Lewin's, at the junction of [Stephens'] Track and the Komiatum Track. We were still flopping round like a bunch of chooks in a dust bath, selecting defensive positions where we wouldn't shoot each others' heads off, when Troppy saw the leader of a mob coming. Seventy Japs passed us less than ten yards off, happily yodelling to each other like "Hi-ho" in *Snow White*. And somewhere close by a few hundred yards off, their mates with the LMG are being murdered by rascally intruders. Strange animals, these Nips.'[19]

Meares now attacked the first enemy position from the east and killed thirteen defenders. Pinney wrote:

> Fighting to our rear was changing position and we couldn't tell if the Japs had been reinforced, or how the patrol was doing, so we began to circle around towards them . . . we attacked three times, and three times we withdrew. It's not our forte, belting in frontal assault through fixed defences, and I don't know why we bothered to try. Babe was fired on from a range of four yards and was not hit; he did some savage work with his Bren. It was confused fighting in too much cover where hardly anyone, once they went to ground, could see anyone else, and anyone who poked his head up copped a concentrate of fire.[20]

Scouts then observed ninety Japanese reinforcements moving up to the area and also heard enemy movement from further east, towards Mount Tambu. At dusk Meares withdrew to a blocking position on Stephens' Track.[21]

Late on 8 July Hammer told Warfe he had to hold at Goodview Junction and to throw all available men into the fray. 'Max no personnel possible MUST be concentrated in fight for Komiatum Track. Possession must be gained 9 July for success of ops.'[22] Warfe stripped Wells Junction back to three men and the track force to ten men. The rest were sent to Goodview Junction where his men were now fighting a full-blown infantry action better suited to an infantry battalion. Signallers, cooks and carrier escorts were brought forward and added to the two front-line platoons. By 1800 on 8 July Warfe had 102 of his men in the Stephens' Track area and forty-six at Goodview Junction. Peter Pinney spent the night at the Stephens' Track junction. 'Each of us put in two hours on listening posts through the night, and slept in pelting rain. You couldn't have seen a Jap admiral at three paces.'[23]

The next day, 9 July, started well for Peter Pinney. 'The everlasting rain cleared, and early morning was ablaze with glorious sunlight, steam drying the patch of open space we own. We stayed where we were, presumably an anchor point to secure the escape route out of this melange of confusion; and though we could hear Japs digging and digging through the morning, we relaxed and laid our clothes to dry and revelled in that sun.'[24] That morning, Winterflood's B Platoon attacked frontally and was pinned down by heavy fire, suffering four casualties. Norm Bear later said, 'The next morning it was decided by brigade that we'd go back and that we would take Goodview Junction, with the same men, except that George [Warfe] came. George always carried a revolver on each hip. I mean, you might as well have had a pea-shooter in that situation. And, because it's a narrow defile, naturally the Japanese have got a machine-gun set up on fixed lines and the first bloke to shove his nose around the corner was killed, Les Prentice, and the whole exercise was called off, recognised of course by George that it was just a wasteful, stupid exercise. And it was.'[25]

At 2050 Winterflood's platoon was heavily attacked and brought under fire from Juki machine-guns and mortars on commanding ground. Unable to dig in, the platoon retired with three wounded. Hancock set out at 1000 with his section along Stephens' Track then south, parallel to Komiatum Track, but could not get close enough to support Winterflood. The next day Hancock's men attacked a party of Japanese, killing eight and dispersing the remainder. It now appeared that the Japanese were using a supply line further to the east of Goodview Junction.

With the opportunity to block the Japanese withdrawal from Mubo now fading, Hammer had become increasingly concerned about the possibility of another enemy thrust into the gap between the 58/59th Battalion and Warfe's company out on a limb at Goodview. The 2/5th Battalion was ordered to take over Warfe's blocking position at Goodview. Morse's C Company and Cam Bennett's B Company joined up as 'Bennett Force' and relieved Warfe on 14 July. Switching his focus, General Savige ordered Hammer to capture Bobdubi Ridge from Namling to Old Vickers.[26]

The supply situation for Warfe's men was now critical. The 58/59th Battalion was using most of the supplies that could be brought in via the tenuous Missim Track and from the evolving air-dropping operation around Nunn's Post. Further away from this source, with declining carrier capacity and ammunition a priority, Warfe's men were almost starving. Hancock elaborated on the dire situation in a letter home: 'We have had a higher authority which appears to think troops can fight without rations. Our last meal was yesterday's breakfast and prior to that we ate about the equivalent to one meal a day for three days.' On 12 July a carrier line arrived at Wells via Base 3 Camp from Mubo; 17th Brigade would now be responsible for supplying Warfe's men.[27]

Having been relieved, Warfe pulled his company back towards Wells on 14 July. However, the Japanese had moved quicker and had reoccupied Ambush Knoll or, as they knew it, Uma Nose, two days earlier and had been busily digging in since. It would need to be retaken by the Australians. John Winterflood's B Platoon moved off at first light around the precipitous eastern flank while Wally Meares' C Platoon left Wells at 0700 and moved down the main ridge top track towards the enemy position. H Hour would be at 1345, and the attack was preceded by half an hour of support fire from two Vickers guns and a 3-inch mortar. Bren guns had been used to shoot a hole in the trees for the mortar to fire through, while an observer up a tree called down with corrections for the mortar and machine-gun range.[28]

The C Platoon attack at 1400 was a frontal assault along the narrow ridge-top track. The track rises in a gradual slope up to Ambush Knoll and is about 25 metres wide at that point. There were only sixteen men in the attack, but what men. They had only gone about 20 metres when they reached the timbered area where the Japanese were well dug in behind a bamboo barricade with what looked like pillboxes covering the track. Keith Myers later said, 'The ridge was a gradual slope. The ridge would have been 30 metres wide, I suppose. They were right on the top and they were well and truly dug in. They had been there for days.' Keith 'Digger' McEvoy had helped supply the supporting 2-inch mortar fire when his section was asked for a volunteer to join the attack. Thinking that the mortar bombardment had cleared the position, 'and it would only be a matter of picking up the souvenirs', McEvoy volunteered. He would later tell the official historian, 'We all make mistakes at some time in life . . . that would be one of my biggest.'[29]

Keith Myers was one of the five men who got over the barricade with McEvoy. He observed, 'We tried to sneak in the side . . . he and I went in to the right, to where the Nips were; that's when they opened up of course. Luckily there was a rise . . . you'd get down. Fire was going over the top of us more or less and there was blokes getting hit all the time.' Digger McEvoy later recalled, 'When I got over that barricade with half my shirt ripped off my back by a machine-gun burst and four bullet grazes across my ribs I realised it was no place for Mrs McEvoy's little boy.' He then saw that Ron Collins was alongside him and he was shouting, 'Come on, Mac, let's go through the bastards.' Meanwhile, Claude Wellings was doing outstanding work with the Bren gun, standing up to fire the gun from the hip to clear the enemy positions at point-blank range. Keith Myers had helped one of the wounded men back who had 'got hit, hit through the thigh, with a machine-gun. I carried him out and I put him down the track. I came back; somebody else got hit. It was bedlam, you know.'[30]

Garland's 8 Section followed up the first attack, the eight men charging forward in a line before the heavy enemy fire forced them to ground. The attack had stalled, and soon the adjutant, Lieutenant Frank Harrison, crawled up alongside Garland to get things moving again. 'Let's charge the bastards,' he told Garland. But, as he went forward, Harrison was badly hit and soon died. Next, Wally Meares came forward, bringing a 2-inch mortar with him, which Garland directed from further forward. On the third shot, the mortar bomb hit an enemy trench and Garland yelled back, 'On target, rapid fire.' Unfortunately there were not many bombs available and dusk was approaching.[31] But not before John Winterflood arrived.

Winterflood's approach across the side of the ridge through thick jungle had been a nightmare. Robbie Roberts noted, 'As we neared the track on the ridge leading from Orodubi to Ambush Knoll, we left our packs and heavy equipment near a creek, to be collected after the attack . . . Bullets flying from C Platoon's attack were flying over our head.' At 1730 Winterflood's platoon attacked the eastern side of the knoll. The men moved to get behind an enemy bunker covering the track up from Orodubi. The Japanese saw them and threw an Australian grenade, wounding Dudley Woods and Bart Lamb. Lieutenant John Lillie had also been hit, suffering a serious wound to the neck. With night falling, Winterflood pulled his men back to the track where Vic Wright, who had been badly wounded in the knee, died that night.[32] It was a hell of a fight, and the attacking sections had taken terrible casualties. Like Meares' men, they were caught in a difficult position, still below the knoll but having crucially cut the enemy supply line to Ambush Knoll.

During the night of 15/16 July one of Winterflood's men tried to get down to the creek for water but ran into a party of Japanese. Little did he know that they were probably the former defenders of Ambush Knoll; they had withdrawn during the night. The position, encircled by a hundred metres of trenches with two log bunkers, had been defended by a platoon of engineers alongside an infantry section. Japanese sources stated that four of the engineers had been killed and another forty men wounded in the fierce fight to hold the position from two attacks. When the Australians took over the knoll, they found ten dead Japanese defenders, and there were signs of several stretchers having been made up to carry out the wounded. Garland wrote, 'The place was a shambles.'[33] Two sections from C Platoon were given the job of holding the captured knoll; Hugh Egan's 7 Section was positioned at the northern end and Garland's 8 Section was to cover the southern approach track from Wells.

The previous day had been a tough one for 9 Section. Peter Pinney, who knew all the boys, caught up with some of the survivors back at Missim where he was laid up with swollen feet. 'The results of attack yesterday include Harrison killed, Buge concussed, and Bren gunner Babe with five bullets through his arm. [Kendall] and Troppy, Monty and Curly Young and Sig Buckley all got shrapnel wounds. A bullet wounded [Lillie] in the neck; Spr [McGuiness] got a dose of shrapnel too . . . it's bad news about Harrison; a nice bloke, recently married. He copped a gutful of LMG.'[34] The loss of Frank Harrison, an original member of the company, was indeed a tragic one as he would never see his unborn daughter, Frankie Louise.

With Ambush Knoll apparently back under Australian control, Hammer looked further north to where the Graveyard position overlooked the saddle. He would use Captain Albert Jackson's company of the 58/59th Battalion for the main attack while Lieutenant Jack Barry's A Platoon section would apply pressure along the ridge top from the south. Other 58/59th attacks would take place further north around Erskine Creek. Barry and ten men, later reinforced with another six, attacked up the steep slope at 1050, and by 1700 they were on the objective, having killed five defenders and beaten off two counter-attacks. Corporal Garth Neilsen played a major role in the success of the action. Neilsen accounted for eight enemy troops with his tommy gun as he cleared a number of weapon pits, and that night he played a key part in the defence of the position.[35] This section action was an outstanding example of the drive and skill in battle of Warfe's men but, with so few men, Barry feared he might struggle to hold the position. With 119 enemy troops counted moving north through Komiatum, that was an understandable concern.[36] Despite having considerably more resources, Jackson's attack with A Company had failed, twice, so the required reinforcements were not forthcoming. Under increasing pressure, Barry reluctantly pulled back from his hard-won gains the following morning. The inability of the 58/59th to match the 2/3rd Independent Company's success must have frustrated Hammer but perhaps not as much as Warfe's men.

The loss of Ambush Knoll rankled with the Japanese command. With the fall of Mubo and the movement of the front line to Goodview Junction and Mount Tambu, Ambush Knoll was a key point in securing the Japanese western flank. Already a Japanese mountain gun was firing at the knoll from Komiatum Ridge, and there were other ominous signs. On the afternoon of 19 July Ron Garland took out a patrol to set booby traps in the rear of the Japanese defences at Orodubi, returning at dusk. As he looked back over Orodubi he could see the whole side of the hill blinking with small lights and reported this to Warfe, who rightly seemed anxious. Later, Garland heard some of the booby traps go off, then, at 2015, firing broke out from further down the track to Wells.[37]

Following artillery support from across on Komiatum Ridge, fresh troops from Jinno's fresh I/80th Battalion counter-attacked.[38] Using the light of a full moon, around sixty of Jinno's men had come up the ridge in the early evening. They crested the ridge further south towards Wells, then immediately turned north along the ridge to attack Ambush Knoll. Garland's section waited for them, also concerned that the first men they might see approaching could be Arthur Malone's standing patrol. Indeed Malone and three of his men were the first to appear, a welcome addition to the defence.[39]

Taking full advantage of the cover offered by the Japanese trenches dug around the Ambush Knoll position, Garland's men waited for the attack. Garland had put a man out in front in a listening post, and he soon came back with the simple observation, 'The Japs are coming.' Garland told his men to wait for his own gunfire, then to open up with a 'broadside' at waist level along the narrow approach track that followed the top of the ridge. When Garland heard a twig snap and bushes move in front of him, he opened fire.[40] The situation in which Garland had found himself some days earlier was now completely reversed, and the Japanese attackers

Photo 21 Vickers gun at the northern edge of Ambush Knoll. The troops are from 2/3rd Independent Company with Lieutenant Hugh Egan, who was later killed, on the left. Photo by Damien Parer. (AWM 127970)

soon withdrew. Garland sent out the listening post again; the next attack might be better organised and he would need that early warning.

Back at Namling, Warfe had heard the attack on Ambush Knoll and immediately sent two sections from Winterflood's weary platoon to help. He let Garland know they were coming and would arrive by morning. Other help was closer at hand as the Vickers guns now arrived. No doubt the crews had heard the sounds of the first attack, and that had driven them up the steep approach, carrying their weighty loads. Two Vickers guns were brought up with their transport section crews. One gun, manned by 'Matey' Crossley and 'Bunny' Sides, was emplaced in the forward pit covering the main approach up Sugarcane Ridge from Buirali Creek. The other gun, manned by Col Luke, Bob Brown and Claude Govers, was allocated to Garland's sector, covering the southern approach track along the ridge from Wells Junction. 'They jumped into an empty trench and rapidly prepared for action.'[41]

They were none too soon as the listening post came back and reported, 'The Japs are coming in large numbers.' At 2100 hours, under the full

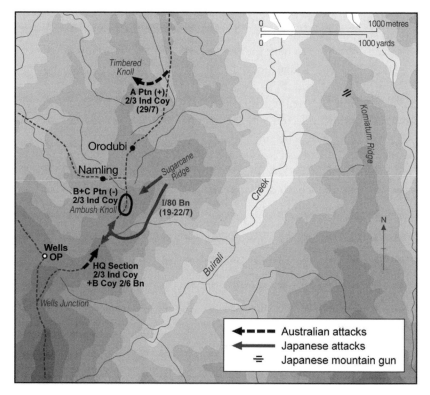

Map 21 Ambush Knoll, 6–23 July 1943

moon, the second Japanese attack came in only to run into an unexpected wall of fire. Once again Garland tried to time the opening burst to catch the enemy on their feet. The weight of fire from the Vickers guns was of immeasurable help, the guns being put on loose mountings and used to 'hose' the attacking enemy waves.[42]

At dawn on 20 July Winterflood's weakened platoon reached Ambush Knoll. Once again, Warfe's company was trying to carry out roles that would normally be allocated to a battalion. To augment Winterflood, Warfe had sent all the men he could scrape up, many carrying much-needed Vickers gun ammunition. At 0900 the phone line back from Ambush Knoll to Namling went dead; the Japanese were using the same tactics that lost them the knoll in the first place: cutting off resupply. Fortunately, Winterflood still had a radio to maintain contact with Warfe. At 0920 the enemy attacked again and again Garland's sector beat them back. Woodpecker machine-guns from Orodubi and Sugarcane Ridge

now fired on Ambush Knoll, closely followed by mortar fire and continued shelling from the mountain gun on Komiatum Ridge. Norm Bear
observed, 'We used to hear the thing go pop and get in a hole.'[43]

From Namling Ridge, John Lewin could see the Japanese attackers
moving up from Orodubi to Sugarcane Ridge, their base for the attack on
Ambush Knoll. Sugarcane Ridge acted as a wide approach ramp straight
up to Ambush Knoll, and a Vickers gun at Namling was used to fire on
any movement on it. The gun was fired on fixed lines on to positions only
50 metres from Ambush Knoll, and this flanking fire helped to break up
the attacks along Sugarcane Ridge. But it was the fire from Ambush Knoll,
straight down the length of Sugarcane Ridge, that caused the most damage. The Vickers gunners, Bunny Sides and Matey Crossley, could hear
when the Japanese moved up through the bamboo and would open fire
accordingly. They were soon targeted by enemy light machine-guns, and
the Vickers was moved ten metres to the right, giving better protection.
Further down the knoll, Henry Couldwell fired at the light machine-gun
muzzle flash, only for the light machine-gun to swing across on to his
position. Couldwell was shot in the neck; Bunny Sides went down to
bring him out.[44]

Having been stymied in at least fourteen attacks on the previous day,
the Japanese began more attacks before dawn on 21 July against the
north end of Ambush Knoll. The Australians' ammunition supply was
becoming critical, and the order came through to switch to single-round
fire, including the Vickers gun. The men awaited a dawn attack with
trepidation, but it never came. What did come was a supply line up from
Namling, the photographer Damien Parer being one of the carriers. Jack
Arden later wrote, 'It was pitch dark and raining heavily. We had to carry
cases of ammo, grenades, food, tins of water and medical gear. At least
we knew the direction, it was always up.'[45]

Brian Walpole, who had just returned from a reconnaissance trip
across to the American lines, had found the route up through the Japanese
lines. Warfe had told him, 'Wally, the poor bastards haven't got any food
and they're running out of ammunition and so forth. Would you go and
see if you can find a way we can get up there without the Japs knowing?'
Observing that the main approach was covered by the Japanese, Walpole
'looked at this other side . . . and it's just straight up . . . and nothing there,
virgin jungle.' He went back and told Warfe. 'So he sent everyone he
could up there to take stuff up . . . I went up with them when they went up
there. Carried some food, ammo and your own gear . . . you reckon someone would do it for you so why wouldn't you try and do it for someone?'[46]

At 1300 there was another enemy attack, and Lieutenant Hugh Egan was killed. Allan Oehlman was Egan's signaller, the two men normally occupying a two-man trench back from the edge of the ridge, the communications centre for Ambush Knoll. Egan and Oehlman were further back at the 2-inch mortar position when the enemy mortar bombs began to fall. As they made their way back to their trench, Oehlman got there quickly but Egan was only walking and, as he went to get in, a mortar bomb exploded on top of him.[47] Death came randomly. Basil 'Basher' James and Norm Bear were in the same weapon pit and, when a mortar shell burst overhead, James was hit and killed while Bear survived.[48]

Winterflood told Oehlman to dig a new hole next to the Bren gun pit, and he stayed there from then on when he wasn't out keeping the signal line intact. Late in the afternoon he went out with 'Peter' Blencowe to fix one break caused by enemy mortar fire but found they were now the target. Oehlman wrote, 'Peter and I tried to fix the line but every time we could be seen or even shook a bush it drew machine-gun fire and mortar bombs.' They therefore decided to run a new line out of sight of the Japanese. More mortar fire opened up and, with dusk falling, Blencowe lost touch. Next morning Blencowe was found down at the bottom of the ridge. Oehlman noted, 'He looked a wreck, face grey and drawn and you could see that he must have been through a traumatic experience.' Blencowe had been dazed and disoriented in the jungle, probably blown off the ridge by a mortar shell. He then followed a track until he had heard a Japanese patrol before hiding in the bush until found.[49]

Meanwhile, Keith Myers was positioned with a Vickers gun back along the track towards Wells Junction, watching the enemy build up around the knoll. 'There was bamboo just this side of Ambush Knoll, a heap of bamboo, and the Nips came round the bottom through the bamboos . . . a real moonlight night. This was while our blokes were on the ridge . . . there must have been around about fifty Nips. I didn't know what they knew or anything else. They opened up with a machine-gun on the bamboo which we were behind . . . no way they could hit us, but they poured some ammo into us. All of a sudden they all just – we never fired – stupid to – they dispersed. They didn't try to go forward – disappeared. Real moonlight – you could see them clear as day.'[50]

Hammer was concerned that the Japanese pressure on his 15th Brigade front was greater than against the 17th Brigade front. He therefore wanted Moten's stronger brigade to take over responsibility for Bobdubi Ridge as far as Namling. General Savige agreed; Wood's 2/6th Battalion was to move to Wells.[51] Brigadier Moten also agreed with the decision, although it would upset his own planning. Lieutenant Ernie Price's B Company was immediately ordered to Wells Junction.

Keith Myers was at Wells Junction when Warfe approached and told him, 'I've got a job for you, Myers. 2/6th Battalion, they don't know where we are but they're coming to reinforce us. I want you to go and find them.' He then asked Myers, 'You'll be right on your own?'

'Yeah, I'll be right,' he replied.

The first man Myers met was a lieutenant he knew from Lismore, who asked Keith, 'Good God! What are you doing here?'

'Same as you,' Myers replied.

A few of the other 2/6th blokes enquired, 'Are you having a bit of trouble? Can't you handle it, Snow?'

Myers quietly replied, 'You'll find out when you get there' before leading them to Wells, arriving soon after midday.[52]

On arrival, Ernie Price reported to headquarters. Major Basil 'Jika' Travers, the brigade major from 15th Brigade, was there and ordered Price to attack down the track to Ambush Knoll without delay. Price argued that his written order from Wood was to set up a base at Wells Junction. Travers later wrote, 'His orders were 24 hours out of date and based on two premises that were outdated.' These premises were that Price had been told not to fight and that he didn't know that 17th Brigade had been given responsibility for the ground through to Namling from the next day, and this included Ambush Knoll. Warfe stressed that the knoll would be Price's worry from the next day and, if Price did not help on this day, then Warfe could not guarantee it would be held. Travers directed Price to organise an immediate relieving attack on the knoll. Wood observed, 'Travers was correct as he was the senior officer on the spot and there was no time to lose.'[53]

Lieutenant Bruce Lang, commander of 12 Platoon, had been resting with his exhausted men while Price reported the company's arrival. 'It was a grim company commander who returned. We had been ordered in, almost immediately.' So Bruce Lang readied his fifteen men; his weakened platoon had literally drawn the short straw. Two of Warfe's men guided Lang's platoon in along the track while Ernie Price took the remainder of the company out to the right in a flanking move.[54] Also that afternoon the 2/6th Battalion's 13 Platoon moved up the supply track from Namling to directly reinforce Ambush Knoll, arriving around dusk.

Back on the ridge, Perce Harris was acting as forward scout for Allan Leverett's 7 Section in Lang's platoon, leading the unit along the track towards Ambush Knoll at around 1400. Moving along the side of the ridge just off the track, the alert Harris noticed a slight movement ahead near a large bamboo clump, and he went to ground just as the enemy opened fire. Mick Cummins was hit in the shoulder as he rolled off the track before Allan Leverett came forward with the Bren gun, got behind the bamboo clump and opened fire on the Japanese position. Bruce Lang also decided to go back but had moved only three paces when he too was hit, shot through his left knee. Lang wrote, 'I felt as though I had been hit by a steam hammer, not to mention the pain.' Behind Lang, 9 Section moved up and was fired on by snipers, Jack Ryan being killed and Jim Smith fatally wounded. Jim Andrews and Cliff Hirst dragged the wounded Lang off the track. Jimmy 'Gabba' Sier was another hit. Later in the afternoon Private Rod McNeill was killed and Frank Doyle and Jack Quinn wounded when their 2-inch mortar exploded. Perce Harris later commented that it was 'a particularly nasty day'.[55]

Having held the relieving attack, the Japanese continued their attacks on Ambush Knoll. At 1815 another attack was repelled, and at 2210 a night attack, the eighteenth and heaviest yet, was held. The Japanese infantry advanced to within six metres of the Australian positions before being driven off. The attacks continued throughout the night, with two more occurring before dawn on 22 July. Phil Mumford was with Winterflood's platoon in a position on the south-east side of Ambush Knoll alongside Bill Newport, Claude Wellings and Bob Spratt. Looking down into a jungle ravine in the night they could hear the Japanese digging in, so they fired in their direction. Grenades came back, most going over or wide and exploding harmlessly before one landed in the pit between Newport and Wellings, badly wounding both men. Mumford and Spratt got the men back to the medical orderly. Jack 'Cheesy' Green and Mumford, who had also been hit, helped take Bill Newport down the steep supply track to Namling that night. Hammer's comment to Savige was that there was 'a bit of a real stoush going on'. The problems now were the acute manpower and ammunition shortages.[56]

As dawn broke on 23 July, a 2/6th Battalion patrol moved north along the track from Wells Junction and found that the track was clear. Garland and his men were standing to for another attack at dawn, but had also been warned that the infantry might be on their way. The first man Garland saw was his commanding officer, George Warfe, followed by Lieutenant Vic Maloney's platoon. There had been no enemy resistance; the Japanese had gone. Price's men reached Ambush Knoll at 0700, passing seventy enemy weapon pits along the track between Wells Junction and Ambush Knoll. At least sixty-one enemy troops were killed during the attack on and defence of Ambush Knoll. At 0730 the C Company HQ and 15 Platoon also reached Ambush Knoll followed at 1300 by the rest of Price's company. They had only one Vickers gun with them so Sides and Crossley stayed behind with theirs. Ron Garland gathered his ravaged section to move out, observing, 'They looked older and gaunt. Their eyes seemed to have shrunk into the backs of their heads. They hadn't washed, shaven, slept or had clean clothes for some time.'[57]

Despite giving up the attacks on Ambush Knoll, the Japanese troops were still entrenched on Sugarcane Ridge. The next morning, 24 July, a 2/6th Battalion patrol moved out along Sugarcane Ridge and cleared the forward slopes, killing two enemy soldiers. By midday 14 Platoon had occupied forward positions on Sugarcane Ridge and reported nearly a hundred enemy troops moving north off the ridge. At 1445, C Company opened up with a 2-inch mortar, but another defective bomb exploded and Frank Bubb and Mal Paul were killed. Following the earlier incident with mortar ammunition at Ambush Knoll when Rod McNeill had been killed, Bubb knew the risks. He refused to let others use it, knowing that it was likely to blow. 'If anyone gets blown up, it will be me,' he told the others. It did. A 2-inch mortar bomb is normally primed by the action of being fired from the mortar tube, the pressure releasing the detent springs. When the 2-inch bombs had been air-dropped, the shock of the drop caused the detent springs to go across, thus priming the bomb. When it went down the barrel, the whole thing blew up.[58]

After an earlier frontal attack on 26 July had failed in the face of heavy enemy machine-gun fire, the 2/6th Battalion had another go at Sugarcane Ridge on 28 July. With support fire from the 2/6th Field Regiment guns on the coast at Tambu Bay as well as two 3-inch mortars, four Vickers guns and extra yoke rifles, B Company made the assault. Lieutenant Clive Trethewie's 10 Platoon moved down the main track from Ambush Knoll in a frontal attack while 12 Platoon, now under the command of Sergeant Stan 'Stagger' White, was on his right. Lieutenant Ted Exton's 11 Platoon was further right again, almost at 180 degrees to Trethewie's line of advance. Sergeant 'Tiny' Mann directed the hundred 3-inch mortar bombs fired in close support. Trethewie's men 'drew the crabs' and Don Matheson was fatally wounded, apparently by a 'Jap wearing an Australian hat'. One of Matheson's section, wary of White's platoon coming in from the flank, had cried out not to fire. The Japanese had actually advanced towards Trethewie and were thus vulnerable to enfilade fire from White's platoon advancing to the right. Ernie Price later wrote, 'They were quite unprepared for an attack on their flank due to sheer slope.' Perce Harris was with White and later observed, 'I have never heard a man shout so much as he urged us up a near vertical slope.'[59]

White's men fired as they went over the crest of the ridge into the enemy trench network. Cliff Hirst used his tommy gun with effect while, alongside him, Jim Dall dropped his webbing and flung grenades at the enemy position. Unprepared as they were for White's flanking attack, the Japanese defenders were overwhelmed when Exton's 11 Platoon then came in at the rear of their position. Exton's men were helped by a display of enemy bayonets poking out above a trench, giving away their location.[60] The attack had been opposed by 50 defenders, and a Japanese counter-attack just before dusk was also defeated. Great credit for the success must be given to Ernie Price who planned the show, using the terrain to the attacker's advantage. He had pinned the defence in place both physically and mentally with Trethewie's attack, then come in from the flank with White and from the rear with Exton.

After handing over Ambush Knoll to the 2/6th Battalion, Warfe's A Platoon had taken over an area from the 58/59th Battalion. It was an unsatisfactory position on the reverse slope of the Japanese-held Timbered Knoll. Hammer decided the enemy-held knoll should be attacked by Warfe's men to maintain the initiative. In mid-afternoon on 29 July, Ron Garland and twenty men took over from John Lewin's A Platoon at Parer's Bowl. This enabled Lewin's men to move out to attack Timbered Knoll, about 250 metres south along the ridge. Bob Silva, 'Digger' McEvoy and Garth Neilsen made a reconnaissance of the position before the attack. McEvoy was leading when he spotted the barrel of an enemy machine-gun. He shouted, 'Jump!' and the three got off the track. It was going to be a tough nut to crack but support was available. At 1600, artillery and mortar support commenced a 15-minute barrage with the 2/6th Field Regiment guns that had landed on the coast at Tambu Bay, giving Warfe's men their first artillery support since the fighting at Wau. A third of the preparatory fire was directed on to the ridge leading south-east from Timbered Knoll as it would be via this approach that any Japanese reinforcements would come.[61]

The attack was made by Johnny Lewin's A Platoon supported by 7 Section from C Platoon. Damien Parer went in with the men, creating an astonishing record of the attack. He filmed as machine-gun fire hit Bill Robins as he reached the top of a grassy ridge. Robins was hit in the chest

Photo 22 Private Len Mahon from 2/3rd Independent Company during the attack on Timbered Knoll. Photo by Damien Parer. (AWM P00928.005)

area, spun around and was hit again in the back by the same burst of fire. He called out for Roly Good, the unit medical orderly, as he rolled back down the hill. Parer filmed it all, later writing, 'I saw Robbie wounded in the back, groaning, yellowing, white in the seeming interminable wait for the stretcher to come. Roly worked deftly – Robbie let a cigarette dangle unheedingly from his mouth. As the stretcher bearers were taking him he turned and winked at us much as to say, "I'll be home before you anyway."'[62]

The first attack up an open steep ridge side had faltered, and 1 Section was pinned down by machine-gun fire. The first attack was costly with three NCOs being killed: Percy Hooks, Don Buckingham and 'Bonnie' Muir. Parer wrote, 'On the right, three men have been killed. The lanes of Jap fire are too accurate from this side. They pin us down. Swift realisation follows. A chap dashes down the slope to the side of our leader, Johnny Lewin. He decides that we'll have to go round to the left.'[63]

With the first thrust parried, Lewin took Lieutenant Sid Read's 3 Section via the Bench Cut Track to attack the other side of the defences. The commandos were faced with a steep razorbacked ridge with heavy

Photo 23 Burial service for the fallen from 2/3rd Independent Company on Timbered Knoll. Photo by Damien Parer. (AWM 127986)

covering fire from pillboxes and trenches. Wal Dawson went forward with his tommy gun and grenades and opened the way. When Lewin's men reached the crest they saw the remaining Japanese facing the opposite direction and firing at the original assault. They fought on the ridge line along the knoll, clearing 20 metres of foxholes, mainly through the use of hand grenades. Parer observed, 'We moved around to the Jap's position feeling out the pits with grenades. Just rolling them in and ducking before the grenade went off.'[64]

Parer had gone in to film the action. 'Johnny [Lewin] gets the boys around, then once more the slow advance. When they are about eight yards from the Jap weapon pit, the boys throw their grenades, ducking to avoid their own shrapnel. The way looks clear so they advance to the top. The ridge is theirs.' The assaulting troops linked up with 1 and 7 Sections and left eighteen enemy troops dead on the position.[65]

George Warfe now wanted to press on to the Graveyard area, but Hammer, in a textbook example of operational command at brigade level, kept Warfe's men in check. He did not want to open any sort of gap to the 58/59th Battalion along the ridge to the north by moving Warfe

Photo 24 A plaque on Timbered Knoll in remembrance of the fallen men. (Phillip Bradley)

further south. Hammer's concern at an enemy thrust between his units on the ridge would prove to be well founded in the coming days.

The three dead men were buried on the misty knoll on the following morning. Damien Parer watched as 'they prayed with sincerity their homage to their three fellow comrades'.[66]

CHAPTER | 11

THE FORBIDDEN
MOUNTAIN

Following the fall of Mubo, the 2/5th Battalion was ordered to occupy the Goodview area on the high ground north of the Bitoi River. This would enable a shorter supply line from the coast at Tambu Bay to be opened, relieving the strain on aerial supply and on the hard-pressed native carriers bringing supplies from Wau. On 10 July Conroy had received orders to move two companies to relieve the 2/3rd Independent Company at Goodview Junction. Captain Bill Morse's C Company moved forward along Vial's Track from Observation Hill towards Goodview Junction on 12 July and, the next morning, Captain Cam Bennett's B Company followed; the two companies combined late that afternoon to form Bennett Force. Bennett also provided food and ammunition to Warfe's hard-pressed men. Captain Mick Walters' A Company and Captain Lin Cameron's D Company moved up behind Bennett Force over the next few days. Captain Delmar Newman's C Company from the US 1/162 Battalion was also attached to Conroy's command.[1]

Captain Vernon 'Mick' Walters was a 23-year-old Tasmanian who had enlisted in 1939 and had been commissioned in July 1940. He had arrived in the Middle East in 1941 as a 2/12th Battalion reinforcement but had been transferred to the 2/5th Battalion soon thereafter.[2] When his battalion had been deployed to New Guinea, Walters had flown into Wau and fought that battle in command of 17 Platoon before being promoted to captain and given command of A Company.

On the late afternoon of 16 July Mick Walters led the sixty men of his under-strength company up a steep track leading to the southern crest of

209

Photo 25 Captain Mick Walters. This photo was taken at Buigap Creek on 23 July after Walters' company had taken and held the crest of Mount Tambu. Photo by Robert Buchanan. (AWM 056749)

Mount Tambu, the most dominant feature in front of Salamaua. Walters' scouts reported that the Japanese occupied two knolls just over the crest and were busy digging weapon pits. With barely sufficient room to deploy the thirty-eight men in the two forward platoons, Walters sent them into a bold attack on the crest. As Arthur 'Unk' Carlsen commented, 'Once we encountered the enemy, we attacked straight away.' Walters later recollected that surprise was complete: '... the forward scouts shot a Jap having a crap'.[3]

When Lieutenant Tim McCoy's 9 Platoon was pinned down on the right flank, the other forward platoon of twenty-two men made a shallow encircling move to the left and stormed the Japanese position. Leading from the front, the platoon commander, Sergeant Bill Tiller, wiped out an enemy machine-gun post as his men took the eastern of two slight knolls at the southern end of Mount Tambu. Twenty enemy defenders lay dead in their wake, many others fleeing north across the mountain

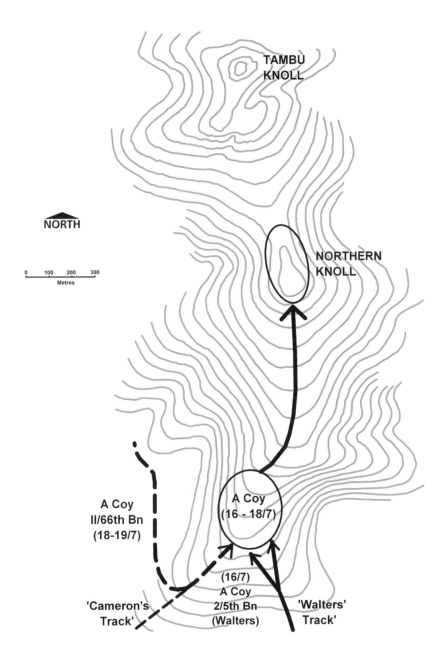

Map 22 Mount Tambu, 16–18 July 1943

plateau. Hot on their heels, the twenty-two men from Lieutenant Eddie Reeve's platoon then took another slight knoll to the west. As he had done during the battle for Wau, Reeve went in hard and fast with his men. Cam Bennett painted him as 'a tough guy and natural leader'. Another saw him as 'very cocky and very, very aggressive in his job'.[4]

It was an extraordinary coup; the enemy defenders had built positions for more than a hundred men, but only a single platoon was manning them when the surprise attack came. Most had bolted after a few shots, leaving the positions to the Australians, who had neither time or tools to dig their own defences. A number of the weapon pits had been reinforced with layers of coconut logs and earth, and Walters' men would make good use of them. However, the Japanese, who were from the II/66th Battalion, remained on higher ground further north with jungle between.[5]

That night the Japanese, determined to recapture the position, made eight separate attacks on Walters' men. They crawled up close through the undergrowth before making screaming charges backed by heavy enemy mortar and mountain-gun fire. Around 120 mortar bombs were dropped on one of the Australian positions, and a searchlight from Salamaua was even directed towards the position to aid the attackers. By daylight the Australian riflemen were down to five rounds and the Bren gunners down to two magazines; they had to ensure that every round met its mark. Walters wrote that the 'fighting was thick and furious during these counter-attacks and the small arms fire was the heaviest I've known'.[6]

In the forward weapon pit of McCoy's platoon Unk Carlsen, the number 2 on Jack Prigg's Bren gun, was up to his waist in empty cartridges. His job was to reload the Bren magazines quickly and correctly so that the Bren gun would have no stoppages. Carlsen said that Prigg 'used that weapon with devastating effect'. Meanwhile, Ivan Gourley moved between the positions with bandoliers of ammo ensuring that men like Carlsen could continue to fill the magazines. The Japanese were creeping up to within a few metres, throwing their grenades, then retiring. It would go on and on through the night, and Carlsen thought that if they had pressed harder the Australians would have been overrun. As the pressure built, one of McCoy's section leaders panicked and withdrew his men only for Walters to order them back immediately. A week later that same section leader was killed as he sought redemption, standing up in his weapon pit to direct the fire of his men. Carlsen later wrote in a simple poem that 'all that night we lay there, in the darkness and the rain, while the Japs hurled bombs and bullets, but we hung on to our gain'.[7]

Photo 26 View of Mount Tambu from the north-west. (Phillip Bradley)

With Walters' depleted company desperately hanging on, Captain Lin Cameron managed to get the two available platoons from D Company and a 3-inch mortar crew up on to Mount Tambu the next morning, also bringing supplies for the besieged Walters. The company came up using a new track from the south-west, and Cameron later observed, 'This track was much shorter and of better gradient than the old Jap track.' As a platoon commander Lin Cameron had shown his drive, intelligence and bravery during the fighting at Wau where he had been awarded a Military Cross for leading his men into the heart of the enemy positions, breaking their defence. He had then been given command of D Company. He was a single-minded officer and set very high standards for his unit but, in return, gave his men everything. His former company commander, Cam Bennett, knew him as well as any: 'Lin himself was tall, dark and intense and, during any show, completely without emotion. He led his men coldly and quietly and set an amazing example of efficient leadership. After a show he got on with the reorganisation, coldly and practically, but with tears streaming down his face.' Ron Beaver also saw the two sides of Cameron, saying, 'If he lost a man it used to take him days to get over it . . . he was that sort of a bloke and yet – jeez, he was a good soldier.'[8]

When D Company arrived at 1030, Cameron attached Lieutenant Howard 'Tiddly' Martin's 18 Platoon to Walters' overstretched company, and these men were deployed on the western flank of the defence line. With little ground available on the crest, Cameron positioned 16 Platoon further back and put the men to work carrying up the vital supplies which would ensure that the Australians could maintain their hold on the southern half of Mount Tambu. At midday there were more Japanese attacks, and Ernie Pike's newly arrived 3-inch mortar helped to repel them. Pike was a boxer and now found himself in the fight of his life. 'We have fired so many rounds at these little blighters that they must be bomb-crazy by now.' In the afternoon, until dusk at 1800, the Australian riflemen targeted enemy troops moving in from the north. Sergeant Fred McCormack crawled out in front of the lines and sniped at the Japanese soldiers in their forming-up area, killing eight. Doug Kirwan, who would be killed the following day, accounted for another four. More Japanese troops gathered, and Reeve's platoon was attacked at dusk by 200 of them supported by a mountain gun or heavy mortar. Although outnumbered tenfold, Reeve's men continued to hold their ground, helped by Pike's 3-inch mortar section. As an indication of how close the mortar fire had to be ranged in to help stop the attacks, at least three of Walters' men were wounded by the mortar bombs.[9]

Over the 36 hours in which Walters' company had held the key position there had been twenty-four separate Japanese attacks, but those waves broke on an immovable shore; Japanese losses were in the hundreds. At this stage, 'the Australians were standing up in their trenches throwing grenades and firing with utter disregard for their safety, and using the most picturesque language'. The jungle between the two forces had now disappeared under the intensive fire.[10]

Such fighting was ravenous on ammunition supply, Walters' company having already fired 17,000 small arms rounds. Everyone at battalion headquarters was used to carry supplies up for the besieged company. The regimental sergeant major, Len Byron, organised the supply lines that came up from Buigap Creek. A stern character, Byron was nicknamed 'Laughing Lennie' by the men, but his steely determination came to the fore under these trying circumstances.[11] It was a three-hour climb up the near-vertical track on to Mount Tambu, each man carrying around 14 kilograms of supplies. By the time the first supplies arrived, Pike's men were down to only three mortar rounds. Further back, A and C Companies from the 2/6th Battalion were drafted in to get the supplies forward from Mubo to Buigap Creek.

Lance Copland was in a twenty-two-man party carrying small arms ammunition and grenades up on to Tambu. To maximise their load they carried only two tommy guns between them and, as night fell, the party set off along the unfamiliar track. Copland wrote, 'We struck a mountain stream, which marked the beginning of the nightmare ascent.' The party climbed up razorback ridges where 'precipitous sides trailed off into deep ravines'. The strength of the men ebbed as they climbed, then the rain began, making the steep climb that much harder. The loads became unbearable, and the men draped the bandoliers of ammunition across their shoulders, freeing both hands for climbing. Two men dropped out while the rest pressed on until they heard the sound of battle. 'The final hill up to the forward position tested us to the limit', Copland wrote, 'for, at this stage, we were actually marching by sheer will-power.'[12]

Bill Swan, who was one of two signallers attached to A Company, used five kilometres of signal cable to set up the vital link from Walters back to battalion headquarters. Swan noted, 'That three miles was, I think, the worst march or climb through the most foul mountain country I've ever done.' Meanwhile, Captain Hugh Busby, the 2/5th Battalion RMO, set up an aid post under two large American tent flies just behind the forward lines. From here the wounded were carried down to the 2/2nd Field Ambulance post at Buigap Creek.[13]

Savige had instructed Moten not to make further attacks until all preparations were in order. He mentioned that artillery would be available from the coast within a few days and that Moten should wait for it. The two Australian mountain guns moved to the junction of Buigap and Buieo creeks late on the afternoon of 16 July, and one gun was ranged and firing on 17 July.[14] Meanwhile, the American guns were being hauled up to Green Hill and, on 18 July, the wait for artillery support was over.

On that morning, heavy concentrations of mortar and artillery shells were fired into the enemy positions, then, at 1000, just when the defence had been tested to the maximum, Walters attacked. The 17th Brigade war diary stated that Walters attacked along a razorback, but this was not the case. The top of Mount Tambu is plateau-like for a thousand metres from its southern edge up to Northern Knoll, a 300-metre-long feature where the ridge narrows before rising steeply to Tambu Knoll 200 metres further north. Northern Knoll was a knoll only in name, it was just an extended length of ridge with gentle slopes to the north and south and the steep mountainside on the east and west sides. There was a gentle slope all the way up from Walters' position at the southern edge of Mount Tambu to Northern Knoll, and it had to be taken to shore up the Australian position on Tambu. Walters had to attack frontally, but he was attacking on a reasonably broad front and could spread his men out.[15]

Taking advantage of the support from the heavy mortar and mountain-gun fire, Mick Walters' men moved forward and gained Northern Knoll at the top of the slope. One of Tiller's section commanders, the lanky Jimmy 'Lofty' Jackson, single-handedly captured one enemy position, using three grenades to clear the bunker and his tommy gun to take care of the three occupants. The attack had been another outstanding success for Walters' men. Walters later wrote, 'We dug in on the new ground and shortened our perimeter to the narrowing plateau.' Enemy losses were eighty-two killed and many more wounded while the Australians had six men killed and thirteen wounded.[16]

According to Japanese accounts, Walters' men had taken the sentry post in front of the main Japanese position back on Tambu Knoll. The Japanese estimated that 400 men backed up with six mortars had attacked the sentry post on the high ground in front of Tambu Knoll, forcing their sentries back. A Japanese report to 51st Division headquarters stated: 'Although we secured key point by driving the enemy back at Tambu, we finally withdrew when we were again attacked by the enemy (100 men having 3 trench mortars). Although the first line company of that area made a counter-attack, the enemy has not been dislodged as yet. We are still holding the ground against the enemy.'[17]

Late on 18 July after a long trek from Observation Hill, the remaining platoon from Lin Cameron's company, Lieutenant Cyril Miles' 17 Platoon, arrived on Mount Tambu. As Miles finally attained the crest of the mount after climbing up Cameron's Track, Cameron was there to greet him. Cameron was a tough soldier, yet even he could see that Miles and his men were spent after the fierce climb. With the front line now further north along the top of the mount, Cameron told Miles, 'Well, you've done all the hard work. I'll put you in reserve. I'll take 16 and 18 Platoons ahead where they're likely to attack.' With his platoon being positioned in behind the two forward platoons with sheer mountainsides protecting them on the flanks, Cameron told Miles that there was no need for his platoon to dig in, just get some rest. The men dropped where they stood, taking just long enough to cut some branches to spread on the muddy ground beneath them, and their day was done.[18]

When a severe earth tremor shook the area that night it seemed that something was amiss. At 0300 heavy rain followed, falling in blinding sheets across the ridge as the men huddled under their rain capes, miserable and tired. However, the troops knew their business and some men remained on guard. Just down the track, Jim Regan and his Western Australian mate, Fred Allan, tried to keep as dry as possible under their rain capes. They listened to the rain and wind, then another sound: the sounds of movement along the side of the ridge. Fred Allan heard voices; there were enemy troops out there, at one with the night. 'Cyril, Cyril, there are Japs out there,' Regan hissed back to his platoon commander. Yet Cyril Miles couldn't fathom it; he had looked down over the near-vertical sides of the spur on the climb up, and there was no chance that any enemy troops could get in behind his position.[19]

It was around 0340, as the signal line was cut, that the first cries came from out of the night, then the gunfire, a veritable hail lashing the exposed Australian positions. Regan and Allan replied; firing straight down the track; there just was no other possible approach route. How the hell the Japanese had got there was not now the concern; they were there and they were charging the Australian position. Fortunately, Allan and Regan knocked out an enemy light machine-gun, and all attempts to retrieve it were stymied. Miles later said, 'I don't know the strength of the force that hit us. But it sounded like a hell of a lot . . . it was pitch black dark.'[20]

Cyril Miles was one of the casualties, a bullet going through his arm, then killing his batman, Doc Doherty. Miles' platoon was almost wiped out, but his men held. 'I had seven killed and six wounded in a matter of half an hour . . . so there weren't too many left.' Both Fred Allan and Jim Regan were wounded, Regan losing the tip off a finger and Allan hit in the right eye by the blast from a grenade. One of the men doing great work in looking after the wounded was the stretcher-bearer Les 'Bull' Allen. Allen had been decorated during the fighting at Wau and within a few weeks would be at it again, earning legendary status among the front-line soldiers. A wounded Cyril Miles later said, 'That was the morning that Bull Allen did a sterling job carrying out the wounded.'[21]

The Japanese lost half the forty men involved in their attack, which had almost unhinged the Australian hold on Mount Tambu. The attack had been carried out by Captain Kunizo Hatsugai's 9 Company, which had been attached to the II/66th Battalion the previous day after the fall of Northern Knoll and ordered to undertake a flanking manoeuvre on the enemy position. Three separate attacks were mounted during the night of 19 July but, as the attacks occurred in the dark, and in mountainous jungle terrain, the attacking parties found it difficult to maintain contact with each other. Commenting on the Australian defence, the Japanese troops observed how well the Australians were able to judge the location of the attackers and instantly pour fire down, resulting in numerous casualties.[22]

Up at Northern Knoll, Walters' men had also suffered from the elements during the wet night but stood to, listening to the battle raging behind them. One man had frozen stiff in his exposed position but refused to leave his post, recovering only with cup after cup of hot water. By morning the men knew that the threat to their rear had been held, but in the afternoon the frontal attacks continued. With most of the men bringing up ammunition, only two men occupied the forward post, Percy Friend with a Bren gun and Jack Prigg with a tommy gun. They held for 20 minutes until the rest of the section returned, then it was once again Bill Tiller, a colossus among his men, who went at the enemy with grenades and dispersed the attack.[23]

More attacks came that afternoon; the attackers crawling up close to the Australian pits, then running screaming out of them. Like so many of his brave men, Mick Walters was wounded as was his faithful lieutenant, Eddie Reeve. But the Australians held them; in a test of wills they would not relent. 'By 2.30 pm that day we knew we had him. Our men stood up in their trenches and sometimes out of them, yelling back the Jap's own war cry and often quaint ones of their own.' Walters wrote, 'It developed into absolute slaughter of the Japs.'[24] Once again, Bob Beddome held his section together, moving around the weapon pits, then crawling out under enemy fire with two others to reach four men who had been killed. Although unable to drag the bodies back, Beddome's party recovered their weapons.[25]

During the fighting the mountain guns had fired 129 rounds in support of Walters' beleaguered company, and not one shell dropped short. As Major O'Hare commented, the sturdy 3.7-inch mountain gun 'was a miracle gun for accuracy and reliability'. The fire was directed by Lieutenant Mal Cochrane, calling back his fire orders from within 50 metres of the Japanese positions. Meanwhile, as Ron Beaver remembered it, the mortars continued to 'supply the music'. Cameron later noted, 'Our mortar and later, artillery, broke up Japanese assaults before they got under way.' Mick Walters observed, 'After three days of fighting the thick jungle on the top of the mountain was cleared.'[26]

At 1730 Cameron's company finally relieved the remnants of A Company, which moved back to the southern edge of the mount. As Moten sent his congratulations to Walters' men for their defence of Mount Tambu, the first American units, Captain Newman's company, moved on to the mount to take over Cameron's supporting role.[27] That night every spare man was used to bring up supplies, toiling up the mountainside with their vital loads in the inky darkness.

The Australians had lost fourteen killed and twenty-five wounded by that stage. Japanese losses were considerably higher. A body count on 20 July revealed 282 enemy dead around the Australian positions on Mount Tambu. The total enemy strength around Komiatum and Tambu was estimated at 1100 men, although next day this estimate was revised down to 350, still around three times the Australian strength.[28] A Japanese report hinted at the losses: 'We again counter-attacked, applying skilful hand-to-hand fight by small forces and holding the hill line positions firmly.' According to a Japanese reconnaissance patrol to the south side of Tambu, there was a substantial concentration of Allied troops, seemingly preparing to attack. The Japanese believed these troops to be those who had landed at Nassau Bay.[29] The Japanese command was determined to hold Mount Tambu and, on 19 July, Kimura's III/66th Battalion moved into the front line. The battalion, which had returned from the Solomon Islands, had been arriving at Salamaua nightly in company groups and progressively assembled to the south of Komiatum to form the divisional reserve. Kimura's battalion helped fortify Mount Tambu, and was also charged with carrying supplies and munitions to the front line.[30]

The remaining Japanese position on Tambu Knoll was like a castle keep, complete with a ravine for a moat and near-vertical walls as well as tunnels deep within the knoll to strengthen the fortress. Tambu peak held ten log-reinforced bunkers connected by tunnels, which could shelter half a battalion, and a chain of weapon pits was set up on the ledge below. When the defences were later investigated, the overhead cover on the weapon pits was found to be up to four logs thick, and all pits were interconnected by crawl trenches. Dugouts for sleeping and cover had been built three metres down while the main headquarters had living quarters and office space built beneath around seven metres of soil cover. The Japanese defenders would emerge like ants from the ground, climbing up long bamboo ladders from well below ground. Many of the weapon pits had been carefully sited within the roots of large trees, making them almost impervious to the Allies' support fire.[31] The tunnel entrances were dug into the side of the peak directly behind the defence positions, allowing the defenders to shelter underground, then return to their positions within seconds. The remains of the ledge dugouts and adjacent tunnels are still evident more than 60 years later.

Ernie Pike, the mortar sergeant, later inspected the defences and commented, 'Our boys need to be equipped with ploughs as well as tommy

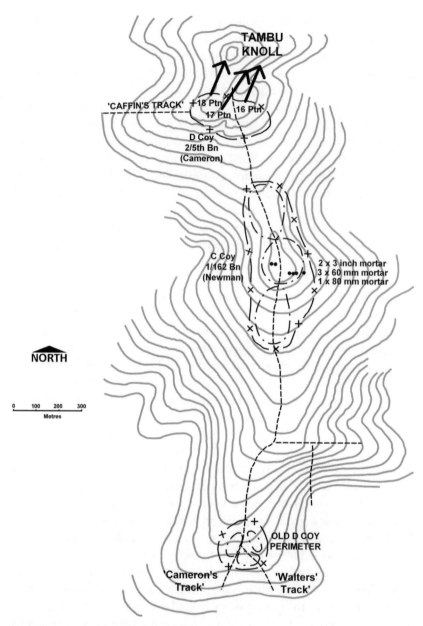

Map 23 Mount Tambu, 24 July 1943

guns to get the Nips out of these funk holes.' One of the Japanese defenders of the place they called Buyu Mountain later wrote, '. . . the company's faces are pale, their beards long and bodies dirty with red soil from the ground. We are just like beggars.'[32] But they fought like demons.

On the afternoon of 23 July Conroy received orders from Moten for his battalion to attack and capture Mount Tambu the following morning. He passed the order on to Cameron, who immediately requested a delay to enable reconnaissance to be carried out, 'to ascertain whether such an order was practicable'.[33] The plans issued by Conroy stated that 'the attack will be a partial encirclement'. Cameron would attack on his left flank with two platoons forward while A Company, with 4 Platoon under command, would move up Caffin's Track on the west flank of Mount Tambu and attempt to cut the main Japanese supply route back to Komiatum. Caffin's Track, blazed by Sergeant Max Caffin and two other men, began at Buigap Creek south of Goodview Junction and followed a steep razorback ridge up to Tambu.

Covered by Corporal John Smith and another rifleman, Cameron crawled forward before dawn on 24 July. He counted seven enemy bunkers in two lines and watched as shovels of dirt were thrown out from inside; the enemy defenders were still digging in. Sharpened bamboo stakes had been set into the ground in front of the bunkers on the left flank. Cameron then advised Conroy that a flank attack had the best chance but was told by Conroy that 17th Brigade had ordered that a frontal attack also be made. With three officers and fifty-four men up against perhaps 400 defenders entrenched on a precipitous knoll, Cameron would have had few illusions regarding the likely outcome.[34]

On 24 July the Allied artillery, then the mortars, closely directed by Sergeant Charles Robertson, lashed the ridge. At 1130 Lin Cameron led his men forward with Sergeant Alvin 'Hungry' Williams' 16 Platoon on the right and Lieutenant Bernard Leonard's 18 Platoon on the left. Cameron hoped to drive a wedge into the line of bunkers, then use Lieutenant Howard Martin's 17 Platoon to move through and clear the top of the knoll. Cameron, accompanying Williams' platoon on the right, approached within 20 metres of the enemy bunkers 'before all hell let loose'. One of the men in the forward section was killed, and Cameron was wounded, his right elbow being shattered by a machine-gun bullet. As he saw his men hesitate, the wounded captain shouted, 'Forward! Get stuck into them!' The Japanese bunkers were constructed with logs, then

Photo 27 As the mortar fire lifts, the first section moves out on the morning of 24 July. Photo by Robert Buchanan. (AWM 056770)

covered in soil, leaves and ferns with just a narrow firing aperture in front. 'Hungry' Williams found them difficult to spot until he was almost on top of them but, with plenty of hand grenades on his belt, he managed to get in close enough to drop grenades through the apertures. Close at hand, Vic Carey provided effective covering fire. With his men falling around him, Williams then carried out Harry Hine, who had been shot in the leg.[35]

On the left, Bernie Leonard's platoon knocked out two bunkers before heavy enfilading fire forced his men to ground. With his right arm useless and his eyesight blurring, Cameron handed over command to Lieutenant Martin, who put John Smith in charge of 17 Platoon. The solidly built Smith took the eleven-man platoon through to follow up Hungry Williams' success, heading for the crest through three lines of enemy bunkers. 'Follow me,' the courageous, blonde-haired Smith called back as he pushed on. Cameron's last view before staggering out was of 'Smith heading up Tambu with the bayonet'. Three men managed to stay with Smith, but Japanese grenades soon caught them as they broke through a third line of bunkers. Although also hit, Smith kept on and soon stood on the top of Mount Tambu with his back to the enemy yelling, 'Come on, boys! Come on, boys!'[36]

Without further support, and with no indication that A Company had made progress on the left flank, Martin had to pull his men out. Under cover of machine-gun and mortar fire they gave up the hard-won wedge into the enemy defences. Two of Cameron's men had been killed and fourteen wounded. Again it was 'Bull' Allen who helped to get the wounded out and dress their wounds. The gallant Smith was dragged out and would die of his severe wounds two days later, Cameron noting that there were 'some forty odd the Doc told me later'. Smith had been decorated for showing similar bravery in Syria in 1941 where he had cleared out three machine-guns at a roadblock and, despite being badly wounded at Wau, he had come back for more. One of his former comrades later remarked, 'Death held no fears for him.' Cameron later requested that some of his men be recommended for awards but was told there was 'not much hope with our Brig for such to go through when the attack was a failure'. Did that diminish John Smith's bravery? His proud father thought not and wrote to Prime Minister Curtin, pointing out that 'he sought not to save his own life'.[37]

Meanwhile, Max Caffin led Walters' depleted company up the steep track from Buigap Creek while the attached tank-attack platoon took up a blocking position across the main Japanese track to protect the left flank. Things began badly when five Allied artillery shells from Mubo heading for Goodview Junction burst in the overhead trees, killing one of Walters' men. Caffin went forward with Bill Tiller and a scout to look at the Tambu Saddle track and spotted two enemy soldiers but, as the rest of the company came up, so did a company of 125 Japanese infantrymen, moving from Goodview to reinforce Mount Tambu in response to Cameron's attack. Outnumbered, Caffin allowed them to pass. Soon thereafter the artillery support barrage opened up, and Walters' company moved into the attack, striking strong enemy positions along the saddle. The brave Bill Tiller was killed by fire from a well-concealed enemy position that they had bypassed to the west and, soon thereafter, the attack was called off.[38]

Although the 24 July attack never captured Tambu Knoll, it achieved more than it could ever have been expected to with such a small force. Even had Walters' men got behind Tambu Knoll, Cameron's men would still have had the near-impossible task of storming the Japanese bunker lines. The fierceness of Cameron's assault can be gauged from the Japanese account, which claimed that 400 troops had attacked supported by

mortars and mountain guns. Any trees still standing after days of contin-
ual bombardment were flattened during this attack. The impact of John
Smith's action is clearly recounted in the Japanese records: 'One portion
of the enemy, fiercely throwing hand grenades, counter-attacked repeatedly and fiercely advanced into our position.' The Japanese defenders had
twenty killed and twenty-four wounded in the action.[39]

Four days after the failure of the latest attack, the Australians moved
out of the front line on Mount Tambu. Damien Parer met Mick Walters
at Wau hospital after the latter had been wounded on 29 July. He told
Parer that a different approach was required on Mount Tambu, espousing
the use of flammable explosive against the bunkers, delivered from the
air perhaps using aircraft belly tanks. Although not yet available, napalm
bombing would be introduced later in the war. Savige also met Walters
at the end of July and said that the brave company commander 'was
full of praise for the gallantry of his troops but it was evident he had
lost confidence in his CO and was bitter about some frontal attacks the
battalion was ordered to undertake'. The attack on 24 July had been
ordered by Conroy bereft of any first-hand knowledge of the terrain and
the condition of his attacking companies. Moten was also at fault as
he wanted Mount Tambu taken at any cost. Moten later deflected the
criticism back to Conroy, saying, 'Conroy was trying to run the battle
from too far back and I had to give him a kick in the pants.'[40] When
asked to comment after the war, Conroy declined.[41]

How much can you ask of any troops? Walters' company was only
sixty men strong when it stormed Mount Tambu on 16 July. Then, after
fighting off twenty-four Japanese counter-attacks over 36 hours, it was
again ordered to attack on 18 July, when the Northern Knoll was taken.
Another eighteen of Walters' men became casualties in that attack and in
holding the position against more counter-attacks. Cameron's depleted
company relieved them but also suffered, particularly Cyril Miles' platoon. Yet Cameron was ordered to make a frontal attack on the toughest
position on Mount Tambu. With the arrival of the American relief imminent, perhaps Moten and Conroy were trying to upstage the Americans?
Whatever the reason, Walters' and Cameron's companies paid the price
in spades, bled white on the slopes of the *tambu*, or forbidden mountain.

On 28 July Captain Newman's American company took over the Australian front line, a hundred metres south of Tambu Knoll. Lin Cameron's
company continued to hold a firm base of fire on the left, 75 metres behind

Photo 28 US infantrymen on Mount Tambu, 11 August 1943. Photo by Gordon Short. (AWM 015521)

the Americans, while the 1/162nd Battalion's D Company held the southern end of the mount. Here the American 81mm mortars were deployed alongside the Australian 3-inch mortars.[42] Ron Beaver was with the 3-inch mortars and watched the Americans come up. 'One morning things were nice and quiet and all of a sudden these bodies started to come up this track and – there seemed like a million of them, but there was only a thousand of them. Can you imagine a thousand blokes reinforcing twenty-odd blokes?'[43] Around 400 American troops were now on Mount Tambu, up against a similar number of enemy troops. All told, there were 743 enemy troops in the Tambu–Goodview–Komiatum area, mainly from the 66th Regiment.[44]

Just before dusk on 29 July, the eight 105mm guns from B and C Batteries of 218 Field Artillery as well as the five 25-pounders from the Australian 2/6th Field Regiment opened fire on the Japanese-held knoll. B Battery and the Australians, who both had their guns down at Tambu Bay, directed their fire on to the south-east slopes of Tambu Knoll while C Battery targeted the south-west slopes from their position down in the Buigap Creek valley. Having ranged in on Tambu Knoll, the artillery recommenced firing at 0730 the next morning, despatching more than 200 rounds per gun in a fierce one-and-a-half-hour barrage. During a three-minute hiatus at 0840 an enemy machine-gun opened fire in retaliation, a deadly portent of what could be expected when the infantry advanced. At 0843 two 75mm guns added their weight to the barrage, directly targeting the nearest slope up to Tambu Knoll. The mortars also joined the final bombardment, then two .30-calibre Browning machine-guns on the far left flank opened up against the enemy bunkers on the far right.[45]

The artillery observation post was only 80 metres from Tambu Knoll. It was a difficult target to hit as any rounds dropping short threatened the American troops waiting to advance. Bombardier Clyde Paton was one of the Australian artillery observers, sheltering in a shallow depression in the ground: 'As I crouched lower and lower, I removed my hat on to the bank of the depression. It subsequently managed a neat slice out of the brim.'[46] From further back Ron Beaver watched this display of American firepower. 'They blew the shit out of the place . . . they burned barrel after barrel out of their Brownings . . . the jungle was disappearing at a hell of a rate; everything was chopped down.'[47]

As the artillery fire stopped and the Brownings started up, the three thirty-man platoons of C Company moved out from their assembly position behind the command post. Newman's 2 and 3 Platoons moved up on the right flank while 1 Platoon remained in reserve. After around 45 minutes the two lead platoons had moved 150 metres obliquely across the Japanese front towards the right shoulder, another 50 metres on. The first terrace on the slope up to the knoll had eight bunkers, and six of these were knocked out, along with two heavy machine-guns, the victims of rifle-fired anti-tank grenades. Then, as the lead men moved up on to the first terrace, the defenders on the second tier, three metres higher, opened up with a deadly fire. Grenades were also rolled down the slope on to the Americans, and a machine-gun opened up with enfilade fire along the terrace from the far left. Using the extensive tunnel and trench system, other defenders moved back into some of the previously neutralised pillboxes on the left, adding their fire. The two American platoons were now unable to move. Clyde Paton had watched as the attack progressed: 'After the barrage we stood up and watched as the Yanks moved in, or rather up. Down they went on our side of the neck, were lost to sight, and then slowly climbed a further side, steep and impossible really, as hand grenades were rolled down upon them.'[48]

Newman's reserve platoon now moved forward, climbing up the slope on the left of the earlier attack, straight towards the centre of the Japanese stronghold. Like the earlier two platoons, it was held up by the fierce enfilading fire from the left flank, and a move against the left flank was needed if the attack was to progress. Captain John George's A Company was given the task, and its 1 Platoon moved forward at 1200. To protect their left flank one of the Browning machine-guns was moved even further left to fire into the key bunker on that flank. However, as the platoon moved down into the ravine at the base of the knoll, another Japanese bunker, even further around to the left, was now able to open fire on them. The supporting Browning machine-gun could not bring effective fire on to it, not least of all due to the American infantry now masking its line of fire. The platoon commander, Lieutenant Barney Ryan, and one of his corporals were immediately hit and, within 25 minutes, four men had been killed and another twenty-one wounded; only six men were untouched. Lieutenant James Clarke, who was with Ryan's platoon, lay down as flat as he could and wondered how he would survive. It was murder.[49]

Now forward with his men, the gallant Captain Newman saw machine-gun rounds pass through his shirt sleeve and take the pockets off his webbing belt. Having seen both companies stopped, the battalion commander, Colonel Taylor, ordered a withdrawal at 1242. The mortars laid down smoke rounds to cover the move back, causing another seven casualties from a drop-short smoke shell. By 1330 the three C Company platoons had extricated themselves, but Ryan's shattered platoon on the left flank had not moved. More smoke and machine-gun support was called for and, by 1600, the remnants had returned to the American lines. The mortars waited for any enemy counter-attack, ready to open up on the ravine where most of the American wounded also lay. Ron Beaver later said, 'Had the Japs attacked the Yanks would have lost the rest of their blokes because we would have killed them all . . . that was the order and our mortar was then ready with the HE.'[50]

The Japanese had waited out the barrage in their tunnels, then came out as the American attack reached the ravine. Although Newman's men took the first line of bunkers, the assault ended in carnage, with a third of the force being killed or wounded trying to break through the well-echeloned enemy bunker lines. Shinoda later wrote, 'On this occasion, the camp was secured owing to the efforts of our machine-gun company and a platoon from the battalion artillery unit. Our defending troops had become familiar with the method of attack of the enemy, who would advance after close artillery support. Consequently, we would ride out the artillery inside bunkers then our ground troops would pour down

Photo 29 Les 'Bull' Allen bringing in one of the wounded Americans on Mount Tambu. Photo by Gordon Short. (AWM 015515)

withering fire on the attackers.' During the desperate fighting the commander of 8 Company, Captain Mami Tetsuo, was killed, and Major
Sugiyama was forced to commit 7 Company to the fighting.[51]

Two American medics, Byron Hurley and Samuel Sather, were killed
trying to bring in some of the thirty-six wounded Americans. An Australian stretcher-bearer, the 2/5th Battalion's Les 'Bull' Allen, stood tallest,
responding to the plaintive cries of 'Bull, Bull, Bull'. Clyde Paton watched
as 'Allen came ploughing hurriedly upwards through the slippery mud.
He brushed past me and then was lost to view . . . Shortly, back came
Bull Allen with a soldier draped over his shoulders. Under the weight he
staggered a little and then lowered the body to the ground right before
me.' Paton watched Allen go out again facing the prospect of being shot
like the men he rescued; however, 'providence watched over him'.[52]

Twelve times Allen went forward and brought back the wounded
Americans across his broad shoulders. Lance Copland watched as Allen

Photo 30 The prize: the view north from Tambu Knoll over Komiatum Ridge, Bobdubi Ridge and the Huon Gulf (Phillip Bradley)

brought in his last man; he was at the end of his tether. Ron Beaver observed, 'He had about seven touches altogether but he had holes in his hat, he had holes in his sleeve, he had holes in his pants, he had holes under his shirt... Jesus Christ... and each time he went out, the Yankee O Pip blokes... were having bets of "How much?" "Do you think he'll make it this time?"' Allen would be awarded the American Silver Star to go alongside the Military Medal he already held for similar work during the battle for Wau. No Australian award was made, despite Australia's first Victoria Cross having been awarded to a medical officer, Captain Neville Howse, who went out into no man's land during the Boer War and brought in a wounded man across his back. Then, at Pozières in World War I, an Australian stretcher-bearer, Private Martin O'Meara, received his Victoria Cross for repeatedly going out into no man's land and bringing back wounded men. Perhaps saving Australian lives was a prerequisite for any Australian award, although the most recent Victoria Cross recipient, Trooper Mark Donaldson, was awarded the honour partly for the rescue of an Afghan interpreter. As the gallant Donaldson noted, 'If someone's been knocked, you go and get them, no matter who they are.' Ron Beaver put Allen's action into perspective: 'That bloke should have got a case of medals.'[53]

Following the American attack the Japanese extended their defences on either side of Mount Tambu. Shinoda noted that, from the latter part of July, daily raids supported by artillery were carried out on the Japanese positions to the east and west of Mount Tambu. On every occasion, however, the small number of defenders fought desperately and did not yield. 'The enemy would face our counter-attacks and fall back, then renew the artillery barrage and, going into August, artillery became for us a part of everyday life.'[54]

Moten now realised that Mount Tambu could not be taken frontally. He later reflected, 'After the two failures I said to Savige that it was too hard a nut to crack and we must find a way round.' Savige probably got in first, instructing that there be no more frontal attacks and the position be surrounded and cut off. He later wrote, 'We were up against factors which would deny success in that area.'[55] Success would come from elsewhere.

CHAPTER | 12

ROOSEVELT RIDGE

On 3 July Herring had met with MacArthur and obtained permission to deploy a second battalion from Colonel MacKechnie's 162nd Regiment to Nassau Bay. Two days later Herring met with Major-General Fuller, the 41st Division commander, to discuss the possibility of moving that second battalion north to Tambu Bay to secure that area for the deployment of artillery. Herring, a former gunner, appreciated that artillery emplaced at Tambu Bay could be used to support the attack on Salamaua.[1]

The 3/162nd Battalion began landing at Nassau Bay on 6 July. The battalion commander was 50-year-old Major Archibald B. Roosevelt, the fourth child of the late US president, Theodore Roosevelt. Serving as a first lieutenant with the US 1st Division during World War I, Major Roosevelt had been thrice wounded and awarded the French *Croix de Guerre*. Due to his age and his previous discharge with disability, Roosevelt was exempt from active service in World War II, but he had successfully lobbied his cousin, the incumbent US president, Franklin D. Roosevelt, for permission to undertake active service.

On 12 July a separate command, Coane Force, was created to drive north as directed by Herring. Coane Force was commanded by Brigadier-General Ralph W. Coane, the commander of the 41st Division artillery. The 51-year-old Coane had enlisted in the army in 1918, had served in France on active service and after the war had served as an artillery officer in the Californian National Guard.[2] New Guinea Force headquarters had requested that an infantry company from the 2/162nd Battalion be sent to Nassau Bay to take over defence of the beachhead and thus allow

Photo 31 Major Archibald Roosevelt (right) discussing the finer points of the Australian-designed Owen gun with Corporal Ralph Jones. Photo by Gordon Short. (AWM 015385)

Lieutenant-Colonel Harold Taylor's 1/162nd and Roosevelt's 3/162nd battalions to fully deploy forward. The request included the advice that 'for clarification all concerned all units MACK [MacKechnie] force are under operational control of 3 Aust Div.'[3] When MacKechnie returned from Napier to Nassau Bay on 14 July he found that two-thirds of his regiment had been allocated to Coane, who outranked him.

Meanwhile, Moten had signalled Major Roosevelt with orders for the move north, but Roosevelt had apparently been told by General Fuller that he was not under Australian command. A cocksure Roosevelt bluntly informed Moten, 'For your information I obey no orders except those from my immediate superior.' MacKechnie tried to smooth things over with Moten, but at this stage he was still unaware that Roosevelt's battalion was not under his command but under General Coane's. General Fuller then tried to clarify the situation by putting Coane Force under Major-General Savige's 3rd Division control. Fuller also dismissed the unfortunate MacKechnie partly because, by relinquishing command of his men to the Australians, he 'thereby failed to protect American interests'.

That American interests differed from those of the Australian commanders on the ground was a concern. Despite that, Savige now instructed
Coane Force to secure the beachhead at Tambu Bay, provide artillery
support at Komiatum and Bobdubi, and advance northwards along the
coast towards Salamaua.[4] Lieutenant-Colonel Charles A. Fertig replaced
MacKechnie.

The first contact with the Japanese force at Tambu Bay involved Captain Ernest Hitchcock's company of the Papuan Infantry Battalion, which
had scouted ahead of the Americans. By 14 July Hitchcock's patrols had
confirmed that Tambu Bay and Dot Inlet were occupied and fortified by
the Japanese. Lance-Corporal Bengari and another Papuan Infantry Battalion scout moved to the mouth of the lagoon, three kilometres south
of Tambu Bay, where they observed that the Japanese had a five-man
observation post set up on the northern side of the lagoon and that
200 Japanese soldiers, half of them fresh marines, were dug in at Boisi,
expecting a landing at Tambu Bay. The native reconnaissance was quite
accurate; a platoon of Japanese marines was deployed at Boisi alongside
III/66th Battalion troops and an artillery battery, some 250 men in all. In
addition, those men retreating from Nassau Bay and Mubo had gathered
at the ridge overlooking Tambu Bay, later known as Roosevelt Ridge.
As the Japanese reserves sent to Lake Salus had observed, the coastal
area was difficult to defend and the surrounding mountain ranges offered
much better prospects. Meanwhile, a company from the 2/162nd Battalion landed unopposed on Lababia Island off the coast of Tambu Bay on
15 July, guided by an Australian signaller, Sergeant Frank Parmiter.[5]

The American advance on Tambu Bay commenced on 18 July when
Captain Colvert's and Captain Kindt's companies moved north along an
inland track and Captain Fred Gehring's K Company moved along the
coast. All companies used guides from the Papuan Infantry Battalion,
but the companies taking the inland route found the going tough while
K Company had to halt halfway between Lake Salus and the lagoon.
On 20 July a Papuan Infantry Battalion platoon attacked a Japanese
outpost south of Boisi, killing four men before Gehring's men continued
the advance, reaching Boisi without further opposition. The Japanese now
harassed K Company with gun and mortar fire from Roosevelt Ridge,
killing five men and wounding Gehring.[6]

Roosevelt Ridge extended westwards from the sea for 1800 metres,
forming an imposing bulwark that shielded the northern end of Tambu
Bay, and, until the ridge was taken, Tambu Bay would not be secure.
The Australian Broadcasting Commission correspondent, Peter Hemery,

Photo 32 View north-east to Roosevelt Ridge with Tambu Bay on the right. (Stephen Darmody)

described the ridge as 'a piece of old style razor blade jutting into the sea'. According to Japanese sources, 'The area around Boisi had a lay of land most suitable to the arrest of the enemy advancing northward along the coast.'[7]

With Gehring's company occupying Tambu Bay, Major Arthur Lowe's 2/162nd Battalion began landing there that same night, having being brought up the coast from Nassau Bay. Anxious to have Tambu Bay secured, General Savige suggested to Coane that Roosevelt Ridge be attacked from the western end and rolled up to the east from the higher ground. Coane did send a Papuan Infantry Battalion platoon up that end of the ridge, but he made his major move at the eastern end, with an attack by Gehring's K Company and Kindt's L Company. The men climbed up the steep side of the ridge hand over hand but were hampered by grenades and mortar bombs rolled down from above. As the men neared the crest, enemy machine-gun and rifle fire broke out from well-concealed enemy positions and the attack failed, as did another attempt later that day. Both companies were forced off the ridge two days later.[8]

General Savige's liaison officer, Captain Alex Sturrock, could not get information from Major Roosevelt on when the ridge might be secured, and Roosevelt also refused any offered advice. Sturrock observed, 'If the show continues as it is now going I can't see them getting very far.' Savige was annoyed that his advice had been ignored, and a chastened Coane belatedly sent I Company on to Scout Ridge at the western end of Roosevelt Ridge. Scout Ridge ran north-east from Mount Tambu towards Salamaua, essentially parallel to the coast with a number of ridges running off it towards the sea. Roosevelt Ridge was the first of these, and subsequent ridges were alphabetically designated B to E. Scout Ridge was separated from Roosevelt Ridge by a deep ravine. Kimura's III/66th Battalion was defending the area, along with III/102nd Battalion and another 250 men from the 115th Regiment.[9]

The deployment of Allied artillery was now a priority. On 18 July a two-gun battery of 25-pounder field guns from the 2/6th Field Regiment under Major George Thwaites was landed at Nassau Bay. The guns had been moved up from Buna by landing craft, set up so that they could fire while at sea, but there was no need. By 20 July four 25-pounders had been landed, ready to be moved up to Tambu Bay once it had been secured. With artillery support urgently required but enemy observers still up on Roosevelt Ridge, it was decided to land two of the 25-pounder guns on the night of 21 July. However, once landed, the guns were isolated outside the American defence perimeter when the American infantry withdrew for the night. Two more 25-pounder guns from the 2/6th Field Regiment landed on 24 July along with 1500 rounds. Despite great efforts from the gunners, equipment was still on the beach when day broke; the Japanese observers were only a kilometre away on Roosevelt Ridge and further north on the Salamaua peninsula.[10] Meanwhile the Australian forward observation officers, Lieutenant Roy Dawson and Lieutenant Charles 'Dick' Lord, had already left for the 15th and 17th Brigade sectors and would soon be utilising the Australian guns.

On 25 July the first rounds were fired by the four 25-pounders of the 2/6th Field Regiment. A Boomerang aircraft from RAAF No. 4 Squadron directed the fire on to the Orodubi area at the southern end of Bobdubi Ridge. Radio communication with Dick Lord was finally established around midday. Despite some initial problems with ammunition, the four 25-pounders fired 1200 rounds during the 27 July bombardment of the Old Vickers position on Bobdubi Ridge. A few retaliatory enemy 75mm rounds landed in the vicinity of the guns but caused no problem as the guns had been well camouflaged under a clump of bamboo.

The second troop of 2/6th Field Regiment guns was landed around a week after the first. With 200 rounds available per gun per day, constant harassment of the enemy positions was now possible. The 25-pounders worked well particularly for counter-battery work, and different fuses could be used depending on the fire task. Fuses 117 and 119 gave good airburst results in jungle terrain while fuse 231 was used against dug-in positions. However, the 25-pounders had their limitations when firing on reverse slope targets such as those on the west side of Komiatum Ridge and Colonel William D. Jackson, the American artillery commander, soon allocated the higher-trajectory US 105mm howitzers to that role.[11]

The Americans were also organising their own artillery support. General Coane had moved two batteries, each of four 75mm guns, to positions north of Lake Salus and another battery of four 105mm guns to an area south of the lake. Ultimately the Americans had three batteries of 75mm and two of 105mm guns deployed. On the early morning of 24 July ten landing craft carrying the four 105mm howitzers of C Battery, 205th Field Artillery Battalion landed at Tambu Bay. Using four tractors, the guns were dragged into position that morning and surprisingly attracted no enemy fire. The first gun was ready to fire at 0945 and, by 1100, had registered a number of rounds. Enemy shelling began later and continued sporadically while a lone Japanese bomber dropped three bombs on the area at night. On 27 July a hundred enemy rounds fell on the battery area and another thirty the next day as the battery fired on Mount Tambu. Three men were wounded by the enemy shelling, but there was no damage to the guns. Due to the thorough mapping of the battle area, the 2/6th Australian Survey Battery had significantly increased the effectiveness of all the artillery. Targets could now be fixed via the new survey map, enabling accurate fire by prediction without registration rounds.[12]

On 27 July the Americans had another go at Roosevelt Ridge. A hundred men from E Company moved in single file up through the jungle, following a creek that parallelled the ridge to the south. One commented, 'Dark Roosevelt Ridge's jungle towered above us to our right.' Turning off the track to the right, the lead scouts looked for an undefended way on to the crest of the ridge, finally finding a path along a spur leading to a small knoll on the crest. Here enemy fire stopped further advance, but the company firmly held a shoulder slightly below the top of the ridge. F Company joined up on the left but was also unable to gain the ridge top in an attack the next day. As one of the men noted, 'That night, F flattened miserably in red-clay foxholes while Jap tracers stabbed close to their helmets.' The company continued their attacks over the following days, losing more men without gaining ground. 'We managed to bury some dead where they fell. An old map bears these crosses . . . up and down the twisting contour lines of that shoulder.'[13]

The Japanese also saw the danger of the American lodgement on Scout Ridge, which threatened the adjoining bulwark of Roosevelt Ridge. The attack on I Company by Japanese troops charging uphill was held by the Americans, but nightly attacks continued through to 3 August when Bald Knob, a blasted knoll further along Scout Ridge, was also secured. A Japanese raiding unit of four men under Second Lieutenant Tanaka infiltrated the American lines on the afternoon of 7 August, severed phone lines in the Scout Hill area and returned at sundown on 9 August. Nakano awarded the wounded Tanaka a watch for his brave action.[14]

The failure of Coane and Roosevelt to secure Roosevelt Ridge was frustrating the Australian command. Herring had written to Savige on 4 August urging him to 'drive Coane on to the capture of Roosevelt Ridge' and offering to take up any command issues with higher authorities. Taking Herring at his word, Savige requested that both Coane and Roosevelt be relieved. He also informed Coane that the ridge must be secured forthwith 'irrespective of difficulties'. Now MacArthur became involved. Savige later wrote, 'MacArthur asked me for my views ref Coane and Roosevelt and I gave them strong . . . I had my bags packed but MacArthur supported me.' Coane was replaced in command of the 162nd Regiment by the resurrected Colonel MacKechnie, whose regiment was now detached from the 41st Division and would be directly controlled by New Guinea Force.[15] The trying Major Roosevelt was also on his way out, replaced by Major Jack E. Morris. However, he would resume command of 3/162nd Battalion after the Salamaua campaign.

The inability of the Americans to secure Tambu Bay had become a much bigger issue than the security of the units deployed there. Plans were progressing for Operation Binocular, the operation against Lae, which would require much of the air transport resources currently allocated to supply the Australian units via Wau and the forward dropping grounds. The air transport squadrons were already in demand for the training of the parachute regiment that would take part in the operation against Nadzab. The 7th Division commander, Major-General George Vasey, would also require a thousand native carriers to be assembled in the Watut Valley by 20 August, and these would have to come from Savige's resources. A secure Tambu Bay was urgently required as the major supply point for the Australian forces in the drive for Salamaua.

On 1 August, 3rd Division headquarters had informed Coane that an Australian battalion, the 42nd, would be landed at Tambu Bay and put under Coane's command. The battalion's major task would be to prevent Japanese reinforcements and supplies from reaching Mount Tambu from the north and north-east.[16] The 42nd Battalion was the first of the 29th Brigade battalions deployed. The brigade comprised three Queensland battalions, the 15th, 42nd and 47th, and had moved to Buna from Milne Bay in mid-July. The brigade commander was Brigadier Raymond 'Bull' Monaghan, an imposing, determined man, who had formerly commanded the 2/33rd Battalion and the 2/2nd Pioneer Battalion in the Middle East. His divisional commander saw the 'hard bitten infantry complex' in Monaghan 'but he was never very stable'.[17] Until the arrival of Monaghan's headquarters, his troops came under the command of 17th Brigade.

The 42nd Battalion commander, Lieutenant-Colonel Charlie Davidson, had enlisted as a private with the original 42nd Battalion in World War I and had then rejoined the battalion in 1938 as a lieutenant. He was the only battalion commander in the brigade who had kept his job following Monaghan's arrival as brigade commander. Monaghan had taken the original battalion commanders for walks up and down the hills around Townsville until he had broken them. He didn't break Davidson.[18]

The battalion moved in coastal vessels from Buna in three waves leaving on 5, 6 and 7 August, transferring to landing craft at Morobe. The first two waves landed at Nassau Bay before marching to Tambu Bay while the third wave was taken directly to Tambu Bay.[19] When the first group landed at Nassau Bay at 0200 on 7 August, Coane requested that Davidson immediately march north. Davidson refused until his exhausted men got a hot meal and a sleep but started the march north that afternoon. When Davidson reached Duali that night Major Stephen Hodgman was waiting with orders stating that Moten had operational command. Coane was only to supply communications and rations. When Davidson reached Tambu Bay the next day, 8 August, he met Coane, who was annoyed that he would not be able to employ Davidson's battalion against Roosevelt Ridge. Coane told him, 'If I can't do as I want with you, I don't consider you under my command at all.'[20] It was soon after this incident that Coane was relieved of his command by MacArthur.

The second party from the 42nd Battalion arrived at Nassau Bay late on 8 August, while the third, after almost landing in enemy territory at Dot Inlet, landed at Tambu Bay early on the morning of 10 August. The first company from the 15th Battalion also arrived at this time. On 9 August the 42nd Battalion was ordered to occupy Davidson Ridge, named after its battalion commander. In order to better introduce the new battalion to the theatre, D Company and the machine-gun platoon from the 2/5th Battalion were temporarily attached. Moten indicated that Davidson should use the three platoons from D Company to help foster his three leading companies in the art of operating in the difficult country around Mount Tambu. Moten also stressed that the unit was to act as covertly as possible in the occupation of Davidson Ridge and was not to patrol west of Buiwarfe Creek, which flowed between Komiatum and Davidson ridges.[21]

Davidson was also told of Moten's plan to encircle Mount Tambu, with the 42nd Battalion to be the right arm of the pincer. To hold open the line of communication back to Boisi, C Company from the 15th Battalion was also attached. The companies moved up into the ranges on the morning of 10 August, and the steep climb up the slippery track saw many bits and pieces discarded. All helmets and respirators had already been dumped at Boisi. Bob Dillon observed, 'It was a stupendous climb. For the most part there seemed to be no grade at all, but just straight up and down.' By 1100 on 11 August the 42nd Battalion had occupied positions on Davidson Ridge, and on the following day B and D Companies moved to Scout Ridge.[22]

Despite being able to observe the Allied artillery batteries from Roosevelt Ridge, the Japanese had failed to prevent them from operating. Lieutenant John Iredale later said, 'Japanese use of both artillery and MG fire was poor. They could have made the artillery positions untenable by skilful artillery or even machine-gun fire.'[23] Although the Japanese claimed that their gun batteries had destroyed two Allied guns and neutralised another four at Tambu Bay on the afternoon of 11 August, the truth was very different.[24] This could not be hidden from the front-line troops, who were subject to increasing Allied shelling, so it was decided to send an infantry raiding party to knock out the guns.

Major Ichisaburo Oba would command the formation, known as the Oba raiding unit. Oba was commander of the III/102nd Battalion, having replaced Major Takamura following the retreat from Nassau Bay. All

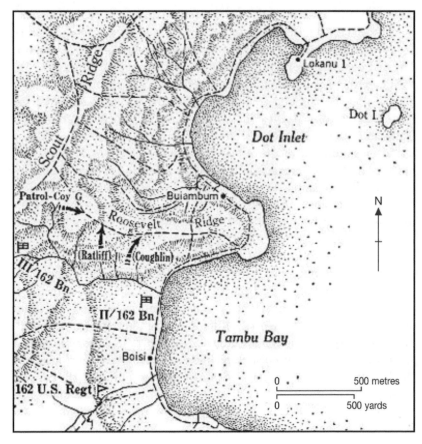

Map 24 Roosevelt Ridge, 13 August 1943

three 102nd Regiment battalion commanders had been replaced at this time, along with the regimental commander, Colonel Maruoka.

The 243 officers and men of the unit formed up at Salamaua with the intention of raiding Allied artillery positions at Tambu Bay. However, at least sixty-three of them were designated for flank protection duties. There were three attack units; Lieutenant Shinnojo Gamo and Lieutenant Ohashi commanded two of them. Each of the three units contained ten engineers from the 30th Independent Engineer Regiment for the demolition work as well as a platoon of infantry for protection. Each platoon carried three light machine-guns and a grenade discharger, the rest of the men being equipped with rifles. Two medical officers accompanied the raiding party.[25]

The guidelines for the attack were simple: 'Determine the location when the guns are firing and attack when the guns are silent.' Lightly dressed, with around eight days rations, the infantrymen carried small arms and the engineers had slabs of explosive. The tactics were to attack at night following wide flanking movements through the jungle.[26]

After leaving Salamaua, Oba's unit camped at Komiatum on 10 August, then near Mount Tambu on 11 August, before crossing the Allied lines to the east of Tambu the following day. A three-man patrol from Colonel Taylor's 1/162 Battalion saw them cross Boisi Track, moving south-east along a re-entrant on their right flank. Oba's unit was heading in the direction of Bitoi Ridge, and artillery units in that area were warned. At 1400 that afternoon 29th Brigade headquarters, moving north from Nassau Bay, received a phone message from Major Ron Hughes, the New Guinea Force liaison officer with Coane Force. Hughes stated that 150 Japanese troops were moving towards the gun positions, and he ordered the headquarters troops to be deployed to protect the guns.[27]

A Papuan worker had also spotted evidence that around forty Japanese troops had crossed the Boisi Track, and Colonel Taylor ordered Lieutenant Wendell Messec's platoon from B Company to follow. Of Taylor's four companies, B Company was in the best shape, having missed the initial Nassau Bay landing and the main attack on Mount Tambu. The thirty-two men of Messec's platoon were strung out along the jungle tracks following the trail of abandoned enemy equipment, 12 hours behind Oba. Messec covered around 12 kilometres on the first day, accompanied by signals linesmen, but with only one day's rations. Messec's first estimate of the enemy's strength was fifty, but when his platoon came across the enemy bivouac areas, 85 sleeping places were counted in tight perimeters. Messec then realised that his platoon was chasing about a hundred enemy troops, double what they expected and triple his own troop numbers. Messec's signalmen had soon run out of signal wire, but they remained at the end of the line, phoning back to battalion headquarters for a food resupply. The platoon kept on; as Messec later wrote, 'We alerted again [sic] to the green jungle wall of death ahead, dragged our weight of steel over confusing ridges.' At 1700 on 14 August, with Lake Salus in view, Messec's lead scouts made contact with an enemy outpost and routed the five enemy soldiers there.[28]

That same afternoon, Lieutenant Wilf Hoffman's 16 Platoon from the Australian 47th Battalion, the first units of which had landed at Nassau Bay on 10 August, had arrived north-west of Lake Salus on the march north. Hoffman's tired men prepared to set up a firm base, some troops

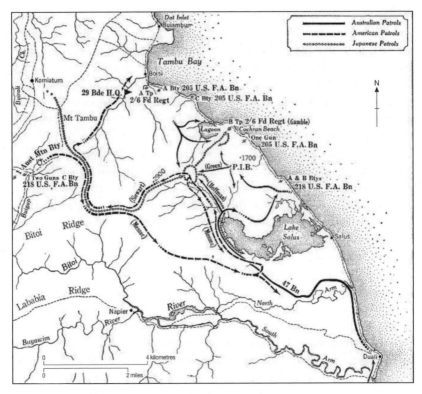

Map 25 Tambu Bay – Lake Salus area, August 1943

cutting fire lanes and some going to the creek to wash while others stood guard. The cutting party had put down their weapons and commenced work when enemy troops opened fire with rifles and light machine-guns from the left flank at 25 metres range. The covering party returned fire, but three men were almost immediately wounded and the fighting continued until dark. On the next morning Hoffman set off alone but was shot in the arm when he clashed with a party of enemy troops. Sergeant Richard Camp, an American messenger on his way to the coast with three local guides, heard Hoffman call for help and was able to get him to safety and bandage his shattered forearm. Two of Camp's accompanying native guides, Myra and Tomanda, used grenades to help deter any Japanese follow-up. The next morning Camp's party managed to get Hoffman down to the coast. Here Hoffman found fourteen of his men, although another fifteen remained missing, three of them arriving back at Nassau Bay with Messec two days later. Hoffman estimated that the enemy force comprised two parties, each of about fifty men, one of which had ambushed his platoon and the other had been spotted the next morning.[29]

Meanwhile, Messec's platoon had finally received some supplies and, on the morning of 15 August, moved down a deep ravine and cleared two villages where the enemy had passed. They then found the victims of the enemy ambush on Hoffman's platoon, six dead Australians, shot and bayoneted; two of them still under their mosquito nets indicating the surprise of the attack. Apart from two Japanese bodies that had been left behind, Messec's men found two automatic weapons as well as food, indicating that the enemy party had moved on swiftly after the clash.[30]

On 16 August Messec's men headed back north along the edge of the salt marsh, moving through the jungle away from the main tracks. They finally found the main body of Oba's unit and, after a brief contact, formed a perimeter on a small knoll overlooking the main track. Messec massed his automatic weapons, two Browning automatic rifles (BARs) and eight tommy guns to cover the main track. About a hundred Japanese soldiers came up single file in a long line, and Messec ordered his men to hold fire until they were within 20 metres range. The BARs opened up on either end of the line before the tommy guns and M1 rifles joined in. Thirty-five enemy troops were killed before they began probing for the American flanks. Almost out of ammunition, Messec pulled his men back, losing touch with one of his sections in the night. Messec took his men down to Nassau Bay, his sixteen men arriving at midday on 17 August, while a detached section under Staff Sergeant Meier made it out to Tambu Bay that same afternoon.[31]

By the morning of 16 August Oba's force had divided into the three attack groups. The plan was for the infantry to attack the gun positions, clearing the way for the engineers to place the charges under the guns. However, after the incidents with Hoffman's and Messec's platoons had diverted Oba's raiders from their task, only two of the three raiding parties made an attack on a gun position. Captain Wilton Stewart's D Company from the 47th Battalion, deployed to protect US artillery positions north of Lake Salus, was attacked three times in the early morning hours of 16 August. Each attack was only minor and soon repulsed and, just after midday, some Papuan Infantry Battalion men ambushed part of this gun-raiding party, killing three soldiers and a native guide.

At the 2/6th Field Regiment battery position at Cochran Beach, around three kilometres north-west of Lake Salus, Lieutenant Ian Gamble's troop of 25-pounders had received a warning of the possibility of attack on the previous evening. Twenty men from Lieutenant Lee Grove's 47th

Battalion platoon had been allocated to help defend Gamble's position. In the pre-dawn darkness of 16 August, the enemy raiding party attacked through the swamp from the west. Grove's men took the brunt of the attack as most of Gamble's gunners were busy moving ammunition that had been landed on the beach during the night. The main assault was accompanied by a second attack on the lightly defended rear area while an enemy machine-gun on the beach prevented the unloading party getting back to the guns.[32]

Lieutenant Gamble was woken by noise, then woke Lieutenant Johnny Bryant, who shared the two-man tent with him. With a hand over Bryant's mouth, Gamble whispered 'Japs' and told Bryant to warn the rear details, 400 metres down the track. When Bryant got there, no one was about, so he returned to Gamble. The two men and Gamble's signaller then joined another gunner in a nearby slit trench as the Japanese opened fire, a machine-gun firing just over their heads. Gamble's position was where the edge of the beach rose steeply from the sea 30 metres north-east of number 1 gun. Two Japanese soldiers crept along the line of sand-filled metal ammunition boxes beside the guns, and one threw a grenade, wounding Bryant in the right shoulder. The guards had also been warned by Gamble and had just grabbed their weapons when the attack came in. In the number 1 gun pit, Mick Speer was badly wounded in the legs by a grenade tossed over the gun shield, and Johnny Wilkinson, after shooting the enemy sergeant, braved machine-gun fire to drag him further back. Sid Stock then fired his Bren gun into some gun charges, setting them on fire and thus providing some illumination, but the raiders entered the command post and smashed the wireless and other equipment. Lieutenant Grove and Gunners Frank George and Harry Johnson were killed as they tried to break through to the gun position from the ammunition party. Another two men, Gordon Gates and Tom Howells, were wounded and had to dive into the surf for some cover.[33]

With an officer and sergeant dead, the Japanese withdrew after around 45 minutes, leaving behind slabs of gun cotton with fuses attached. Amazingly, none had been detonated. The ABC war correspondent Bill Marien walked through the area half an hour after the attack and reported, 'At the muzzle of one gun lay a Japanese sergeant. He was shot through the head and he had fallen on his face on to a ten-pound package of TNT. Three yards from the command post lay a lieutenant and in the bushes just back of the guns was the body of a captain.'[34]

The raid was causing ructions back at New Guinea Force headquarters. On 18 August Herring sent a message to Savige, heavily criticising the effect of the 'small Jap raiding parties'. Herring stated he was 'shocked to find you making major alterations your positions at expense of getting on with main battle'. Herring went on to suggest that the artillery units should be responsible for their own defence and railed against the use of 29th Brigade troops in the defence role. Wilton wrote, 'Further stupid signal from Herring regarding Jap raiding party and our counterarrangements, shows he has no conception of the situation nor the method by which it is handled.' Herring's message upset Savige, who justified his position in great detail, barely concealing his venom. He summarised his position by telling Herring that 'this episode like many others inseparable from jungle fighting did NOT nor will it interfere in any shape whatever with my general control of my forces for offensive ops'. The Japanese command was disappointed by the lack of success. Oba told Nakano that the unit was 'lacking in willingness and courage'.[35]

While Oba's raiders caused concern behind the lines, Lieutenant-Colonel Harold G. Maison issued orders for yet another attempt to capture Roosevelt Ridge. Major Lowe's 2/162nd Battalion would make the main effort on the right flank while Major Morris's 3/162nd Battalion would attack on the left. A 2/162nd Battalion patrol had established an outpost position on the ridge crest on 12 August and, at 0700 the next morning, artillery opened up in front before switching to the flanks. More than 2000 rounds were fired in an hour and a half before the infantry went in.[36]

Captain Ratliff's F Company attacked on the left while Captain Coughlin's E Company made a diversionary attack on the right. That day thirty-nine Japanese troops were killed whereas the Americans had twenty-five casualties. Enemy reports stated that their line had been breached at three points and that Colonel Kimura's men were fighting desperately to hold the ridge. On the night of 13 August, 200 men from Lieutenant-Colonel Toshio Sakata's III/238th Battalion were sent along the coast by boat to reinforce Kimura. The reinforcements, units from 41st Division, had come by barge from Madang, arriving at Salamaua on 8 August. As one wrote in his diary, 'I shall defend till my death.'[37] Early on 14 August Ratliff's and Coughlin's companies linked up as the Japanese forces pulled back to the eastern end of the ridge.

Having established a lodgement along the crest at the western end, the remainder of the ridge would be left to the gunners and bombers to clear any resistance. The intense shelling included Bofors guns that had been dragged up the rough track on to a knoll adjacent to the ridge. The gun barrels were lowered and fired on a horizontal trajectory directly into the Japanese positions. It was a display of American firepower utilising pattern bombardment, as the Australians observed: 'Section by section the target was laid bare. When one section was devastated the guns were trained on the next section . . . the whole deadly show might have been controlled by a switch.' Bombers followed and 'those who watched from the beach saw the top fourth of the ridge lift perceptibly into the air and then fall into the waiting sea'. One of the 15th Battalion men observed, 'Where once was heavy jungle you could only see scorched earth.' Although Roosevelt Ridge had fallen, Colonel MacKechnie considered a further advance to capture the Scout Ridge junction impractical until Colonel Taylor's battalion, still on Mount Tambu, was available. Total combat strength of the two American battalions on Roosevelt Ridge was fifty-five officers and 620 men, but they suffered from an average daily loss of twenty-six men.[38]

With Allied observers now on Roosevelt Ridge, the artillery began firing observed rounds on Salamaua and its approaches. Lieutenant Stephen King directed the four 105mm guns from Captain Ted Helmer's battery at Tambu Bay. In true American fashion the four C Battery, 205th Battalion howitzers were named Salamaua Suzy, Blood and Guts, Tombstone and Scatterbrain. Day and night the guns fired, expending 17,638 rounds over six weeks of shelling. The building of a small airstrip suitable for artillery spotter planes was also commenced at Tambu Bay to improve the effectiveness of the shelling. In late August two 155mm M1A1 1941 guns, christened Peter and Paul, were emplaced at Tambu Bay, manned by Australian gunners from the 56th Battery, part of 2/6th Field Regiment. The guns fired a massive 95-pound round to a range of 22,500 metres, ideal to neutralise or destroy the Salamaua defences, but in the end used only for harassing fire tasks.[39]

The Americans now pushed patrols further forward. On 16 August I Company was back in action, down two-thirds in strength and reorganised as a single platoon. The men crept forward to hurl grenades at the enemy positions while Sergeant Warren directed supporting mortar fire. The Japanese retaliated that night, attacking from dusk to dawn, but the grenades and mortar fire kept them back. It was the start of two weeks of such attacks on the I Company platoon as the unit held four key foxholes guarding its position on Scout Ridge.[40]

The enemy positions on Scout Ridge were stronger, being set out in depth back towards Salamaua. Scout Ridge provided the Japanese defenders with many ideal defensive positions along its crest and along the four intersecting ridges behind Roosevelt Ridge, extending back to Lokanu. On 18 August K Company made a frontal attack along the ridge, but it foundered at a high barricade covered by Japanese machine-gun fire. Three of the Americans were killed and another seven wounded, including one of the selfless medics, before they pulled back behind the barricade. If Scout Ridge had to be taken, there would be many more casualties.[41]

Night brought no respite for the American frontline troops; booby traps were set and empty ration tins spread around the perimeter to give warning of any approach. Lieutenant Robert Pope observed, 'Nearly every night the cans tinkled. And always someone shot or grenaded; others caught the fear and blazed away. On 22 August, for example, we threw forty grenades during 1900–2030 hours, results unreported.' Daybreak brought no respite. 'Rain fell almost every afternoon. We drained drinking water from shelter halves into our helmet. We could not bathe; many feared to take off their shoes. Red mud was everywhere, coloring us reddish brown all over our scraggly uniforms and getting into our skin pores. Food bored us: C and J rations, some Aussie bully beef and biscuits. We ate them cold mostly; smoke could draw Jap shells.' There was also danger from the American artillery, the shells barely clearing the American ridgeline positions in searching for the enemy mountain guns beyond. Four American medics were wounded by drop shorts.[42]

Captain George's A Company was sent forward on 27 August, moving east to contact Captain Garlyn Munkres' platoon on C Ridge. The men followed a trail on a connecting ridge, later named George Ridge, and cut the Japanese supply line. They dug in for the night and set up an ambush, sending out riflemen to shoot at the Japanese and try to bait them into following the American troops back to the ambush position. Despite losing men to the rifle fire, the Japanese held, then counter-attacked the next night, leaving nine dead behind. The following night a further nine attacks came in. George: 'We began to feel chill in the stomach. Every rush meant firing a few more clips, throwing a few more grenades. As the dark suddenly quietened, our hands counted blindly the few clips left in our belts, the last grenade or two on the parapet – like a thirsty man in the desert checking his last water. For when ammo ran out, they would overwhelm us – waves of many Japs with long bayonets. Home was a long way off indeed, over dark waters to Oregon.' The fighting became hand to hand, foxhole to foxhole, men fighting on as they succumbed to their wounds and four of them dying. George knew the position could not be held, and the next day four rifle shots signalled permission for his shattered but unbowed command to withdraw.[43]

George's infantry action typified the American infantryman's experience in the South West Pacific theatre during World War II. Throughout the war 32 per cent of casualties in this theatre were caused by small arms fire and 17 per cent caused by artillery fire. The comparisons to the casualty rates in the European theatre were stark: 19.7 and 57.5 per cent respectively.[44]

For the Americans at Salamaua the campaign had been very much a learning experience. The performance in battle of some of the smaller units, such as Captain George's company at Scout Ridge and Lieutenant Messec's platoon against the Oba raiding unit, was outstanding. However, the majority of American commanders were unable to come to grips with the nature of the fighting in New Guinea. In many cases a small, well-led force acting quickly and decisively could achieve more than an entire battalion with artillery and air support. However, the Americans placed too much reliance on their artillery blasting away any Japanese opposition before sending in the troops. Alternative infantry tactics were seriously lacking. The deficiencies of the 41st Division commanders would come to a head the following year when General Fuller would be relieved of his command during the fighting for Biak in the Dutch East Indies.

CHAPTER | 13

OLD VICKERS

July had been difficult for the Australian 58/59th Battalion. With Brigadier Hammer's other two battalions engaged in ancillary actions away from the main stage at Bobdubi Ridge, there was no relief or reinforcement for the hard-pressed 58/59th. Although the battalion's presence along Bobdubi Ridge had released the 2/3rd Independent Company for operations against the southern end of the ridge, its own lack of operational success had repercussions. It meant that the Japanese command had been able to maintain the vital supply line up the Komiatum Track to the critical defensive positions at Goodview Junction and Mount Tambu.

The failure of the 58/59th Battalion to achieve its operational goals soon led to considerable criticism. According to Starr, this criticism was mainly from 15th Brigade headquarters staff and was condoned by, if not originating from, Hammer. Starr later noted, 'The loudly expressed opinion of the brigade command was gleefully taken up by members of the brigade staff, and the battalion signallers frequently had to listen to contemptuous remarks bandied back and forth on the one and only line.' As Lieutenant Ted Griff observed, 'The whole area was on a party line and all conversations were heard by signallers wearing headsets.'[1]

Starr also considered that his own and Hammer's ways to win the war were 'diametrically opposed'. Starr favoured preserving his force for the main task, which he believed was to get strong units across the Komiatum Track to snare the enemy forces retreating from the 17th Brigade attack at Mubo. Starr believed Hammer wanted to kill his men *'pour encourager les autres*'. The obvious tension between the two men was general knowledge within the battalion and could only make the 58/59th's task ever more difficult. Hammer told Savige that he thought Starr was incompetent and should be replaced. Savige, the consummate man manager, preferred to believe that Starr was suffering from the harsh conditions of war in New Guinea and, in mid-August, had him replaced on medical grounds. Lieutenant Laurie Proby, who was twice awarded the Military Cross for bravery, later wrote that Starr 'was used as a scapegoat – to satisfy an ego'.[2]

George Warfe, who would later replace Starr, and who knew the battlefield intimately, had his opinions on the battalion's deficiencies, noting, 'Their officers were bewildered, particularly by the early casualties and conditions of living. This was reflected in the troops' utter lack of confidence in their leaders and their supply organisation.' Lieutenant-Colonel George Smith, who had fought in the Middle East, hit the nail right on the head when commenting on the lack of battlefield experience in his own 24th Battalion. 'What a godsend a few hardened NCOs and privates would have been on loan from the [Middle East] tried units to mother them over their first action,' he observed. Lieutenant Russell Mathews, who didn't reach the battalion until August, sagely noted, 'The AIF battalions had the grain separated from the straw in the Middle East, but the 58/59 Battalion was not able to get rid of its incapable officers until the Salamaua campaign had sorted them out.'[3]

Knowing how to react in those first moments when a battle was won or lost was not a quality that was naturally present in the platoon and section leaders of any unit; it had to be forged in battle. Ted Griff told the official historian, 'I think that lack of experience, in command, on active service, was our weakness.' A bitter Laurie Proby rightly stated, 'All 1939–45 Aust tps [troops] had to learn the arts of war, and such learning takes some time no matter how well trained units appear to be.' Proby also questioned, 'Why is it so hard for cmdrs [commanders] to truly appreciate the difficulties of fighting in such terrain?' He considered that Hammer 'had lots of drive – however at this stage he did NOT realise the difficulties of forward troops in the jungle'. Ted Griff added, 'I think 58/59 Battalion had no hope of getting its head above water during this period. It got no credit for jobs similar to those which other commanders were writing up as successes.'[4]

Other units in the campaign certainly suffered similar setbacks in their first encounters. During the battle for Wau, Warfe's independent company had taken three days to take the Woody Island positions while two companies of the 2/6th Battalion had failed to join up and block the Japanese route to Wau. More recently the 2/7th Battalion had got nowhere and had taken heavy and needless casualties during a number of futile attacks on the Pimple in April. Yet Moten described it thus: 'Outstanding in the battle for Mubo, were the attacks by companies of 2/5, 2/6 and 2/7 Battalions in turn on the Pimple.'[5] In the Doublet operations at Observation Hill above Mubo, Moten's companies had also struggled to make headway while the Americans had failed to carry out the blocking task they been allocated.

Hammer had no such opinion of what was a similar situation with the 58/59th Battalion at Old Vickers. On 26 July he sent Starr a letter detailing his vehement criticism and, to back it up, he cut Starr out of many of the command decisions. As Laurie Proby noted, 'Far too many orders were sent direct to company and even platoon commanders – this is surely contrary to normal practice.' Ted Griff checked some of Hammer's orders with Starr, 'only to find out he wasn't in the picture'.[6]

The 58/59th officers took their share of the blame for the earlier failure. As B Company's James 'Sandy' Matheson observed, 'We changed officers as often as most people change socks.' However, it was not a simple matter; if new officers were brought up from Australia they would also have to be tested in the front line. The best option was to use those few who had already performed well under fire. Recognised for his drive and ability following his role in the capture of the North Coconuts position on 4 July, Lieutenant Les Franklin was given command of C Company. He brought that same drive to the task of capturing the Old Vickers position, briefing every officer and man involved in the attack on their specific roles as well as detailing the terrain and enemy dispositions that they would face.[7]

The inability to capture the Old Vickers position at the northern end of Bobdubi Ridge was at the heart of the 58/59th Battalion's problems. Although the Japanese defenders had held the position since retaking it from Warfe's commandos on 15 May, they were under considerable strain. On 23 July Sergeant Kobayashi, who served with 11 Company of the 115th Regiment defending Old Vickers, wrote in his diary, 'The situation grows worse from day to day... this is the 71st day at Bobdubi and there is no relief yet. We must trust our lives to God. Every day there are bombings and we feel so lonely. We do not know when the day will come for us to join our dead comrades. Can the people at home imagine our sufferings? Eight months without a letter. There is no time even to dream of home.'[8]

Following the failure of the poorly planned and executed attack of 30 June, the 58/59th Battalion had adopted a more measured approach to the problem of capturing Old Vickers. It was difficult to estimate what strength the enemy had on the position as the Japanese defenders rarely made any movement during the day and did not fire on the Australian lines of supply up to the ridge from the kunda bridge area. Reconnaissance patrols of the area showed that the defenders appeared to shelter on the reverse slope and occupy their main defences only when directly threatened. The recce also showed that more resources would be needed to crack Old Vickers; C Company was down to only one officer and sixty-one men.[9]

One platoon from A Company, the twenty-three men from Lieutenant Laurie 'Butch' Proby's 7 Platoon, would also take part in the attack. The other two A Company platoons would hold a firm base in the Gardens area and carry forward supplies for the attacking units.[10] The attack, originally scheduled to take place on 26 July, was delayed for two days until A Company, having been relieved by Warfe's men, was available.

The most telling addition to the attack plan would be artillery support, provided by the 2/6th Field Regiment's 25-pounder guns down at Tambu Bay. The artillery forward observation officer, Lieutenant Roy Dawson, moved to Sugar Cane Knoll from where he could direct artillery fire on to the Old Vickers position. It was a difficult fire task as the rounds would have to cross Mount Tambu on the way to the target, and there were some early drop shorts. A frustrated Hammer, accustomed to the desert war where no such barriers existed, told Dawson that 'the guns should move to meet infantry demands'. However, the gunners managed to thread the needle and, on 27 July, after two ranging shots straddled the target, Dawson brought down very accurate shell fire, plastering the Japanese positions on Old Vickers. The cane on Sugar Cane Knoll was four metres high, and the artillery shells were flicking through the cane above Dawson on their way to the target.[11] For the Japanese defenders the accurate shelling of the 25-pounders must have come as a great shock. It would certainly have driven them deep into their underground shelters and on to the reverse side of the position to escape it. The fact that there was no follow-up attack after the initial shelling would also have a major influence on the battle the next day when the attack would go in hard on the heels of the shelling.

————————

Les Franklin had hoped for a late morning attack but, after a number of changes, it was decided that the attack would take place at 1500.[12] The 15-minute bombardment commenced at 1445 using two 25-pounders firing from Tambu Bay, each with a hundred rounds, plus two 3-inch mortars. Mortar and Vickers gun fire was also directed on to the Coconuts area further north along Bobdubi Ridge to prevent enemy reinforcements moving up to Old Vickers. The final five minutes of the artillery barrage was delivered as a creeping barrage to give the infantry the best chance of getting at the enemy positions before the defenders could recover from the bombardment. The mortars also joined in at this stage with both high-explosive and smoke rounds and, as the barrage stopped, two Vickers guns opened up.

The attack would start even before the support fire ceased. This was a classic infantry tactic, used to great effect by Australian infantry in World War I when German defenders would emerge from their shelters after a bombardment to discover the Australian infantry already in their trenches. Seven months earlier at Gona, after a number of costly and fruitless attacks, the successful breakthrough had come when courageous infantry from the 39th Battalion had attacked even before the artillery had ceased firing. On Old Vickers the Australians would cross their start line at 1455, as the crucial last five minutes of the support barrage commenced.

Franklin's plan was to have three platoons simultaneously attack Old Vickers from three directions. Butch Proby's 7 Platoon would attack across the exposed ground at the centre of the position while Lieutenant Jack Evans's 13 Platoon attacked on the left. Both these routes were narrow approaches that allowed only one or two men to deploy at the head of each platoon. Meanwhile Sergeant Vic Hammond's 15 Platoon would attack up the steep slope on the right flank while Sergeant Alex Anderson's 14 Platoon would be kept in reserve. A section from Anderson's platoon moved well out on the right flank to create a diversion while the other two sections added support fire from the Sugar Cane Knoll area. Franklin later noted that '. . . success appeared to hinge on getting on to the objective quickly with the bulk of my force'.[13] However, despite Franklin having four platoons available for the attack, all were well under half strength.

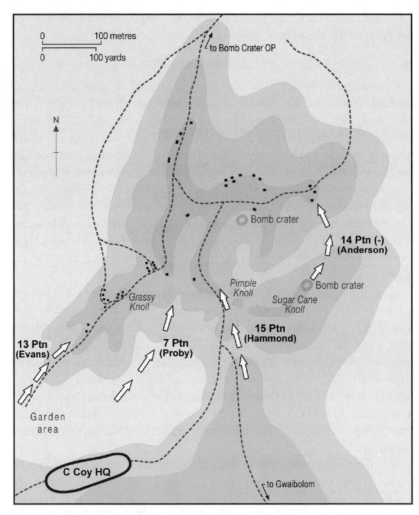

Map 26 Old Vickers position, 28 July 1943

Not all the enemy defenders were in their defensive positions when the attack went in. Many were in dugouts in a gully behind the main positions that was well protected from the artillery and mortar fire. When the bombardment finished, the Australians were cresting the slope in front of the enemy positions. As the enemy machine-guns opened up the Australians were already among them, the sound of their exploding grenades crashing out across the position. Laurie Proby later noted, 'I don't blame Nippon for keeping his head down.'[14]

Photo 33 Ivor Hele's painting of the 28 July attack by the 58/59th Battalion on Old Vickers. Hele had originally been sent to Bulolo to paint General Savige's portrait, but Savige suggested he go forward to the front lines to find his subjects. (AWM ART27543)

Photo 34 A recent view across the slope at the southern end of Old Vickers from a similar point of view to that depicted in Hele's painting. (Phillip Bradley)

Dave Taylor led 15 Platoon's 9 Section down the slope, across the deep intervening gully. 'As soon as the bombardment finished we went straight down ... it was straight down and up.' Hearing a rustle nearby he turned to see Damien Parer beside him and, although he held his fire, Taylor didn't miss with his advice for Parer to stay put. Parer and the war artist Ivor Hele had moved up behind the troops to record the action, Parer noting, 'After artillery show today the boys went in and from this position we could see a wonderful battle panorama of smoke & men advancing. We were both as excited as hell.' As 9 Section crested the ridge, there were no Japanese defenders in place; the artillery had done the trick. Taylor observed, 'As soon as we got up this bloody great bomb crater was in front of us ... right on the edge of the crest where the Japs were.' The crater gave good cover from the enemy defenders as they started to come out of their burrows. Taylor later noted, 'the first bloke I shot was playing doggo. My mate had jumped over the trench and I saw him move and I fired from the hip. I can still see it ... a little brown spot like a cigarette burn on his shirt.' Taylor then watched as a machine-gun opened up on 13 Platoon across to the left, mowing down one of the closely bunched sections.[15]

Lieutenant Evans's 13 Platoon had run into trouble as soon as the men crested the ridge, with heavy fire forcing the lead elements to seek cover. The men had to move along the narrow approach spur from the Gardens area, and it was well defended, as it had been for the past month. Corporal Bill Lawry's section led in, followed by Bert Ashton's. Ashton's section was hit hard by the enemy fire, with three of the five men in the section being killed, including Ashton. Another was badly wounded while the fifth man, Ray Wyatt, who was at the back of the section, went at the enemy position with rifle and grenades. Jack Evans was then killed as he went back to get more magazines for the lead section's Bren gun. Meanwhile Ray Wyatt continued to fight with a fury, using his sniper's rifle to pick off any enemy soldiers who showed themselves. Sergeant Joe Peers was helping the wounded Bill Robertson when Wyatt yelled, 'Got the bastard, Joe. He was taking a bead on you.'[16]

Butch Proby's platoon had been allocated the direct approach, across the gully at its steepest point, then up a steep and narrow spur with room for only one man at a time. 'During the bombardment we approached as far as possible,' Proby later wrote.

> What a high climb we have to gain our objective ... on the way up
> the ridge, it is obvious that our request for lots of smoke has borne

results . . . by pressing on we were able to reach the crest quickly . . . the smoke was so thick we had the chance to organise near the top of our spur and extend for our final charge . . . on the approach ridge we struck three bunkers which were grenaded – just in case – although they had not fired at us . . . we surprised Nips coming up from underground positions tossing grenades to which we retaliated with the same medicine – ours was the best obviously.[17]

With grenades being thrown on both sides as well as from Taylor's section on the right it was a dangerous place. The blast from one grenade caught Proby, wounding him in the hand, arm and head. Proby's left hand section lost touch, and the section leader, Corporal Tom Archer, was killed at the head of his men.

The Australians chased the rest of the defenders off the top of the ridge. In doing so, Dave Taylor and Vic Hammond came across enemy positions around the side of the hill joined by a tunnel. One of the defenders came out to fire a shot, then ducked back inside. According to Taylor, 'I was looking down the hill and I suddenly sensed something and I actually threw myself backwards.' Then, as he yelled a warning to Vic Hammond, another shot whistled by. The two Australians then threw a few grenades in at each end of the tunnel. Further ahead, a Japanese 70mm mountain gun had been captured. Dave Taylor noticed a broom handle sticking out of the barrel and, presuming that the gun was booby-trapped, he removed the barrel and threw it down the slope.[18]

Another defender in a trench down the slope opened up with a light machine-gun, firing a burst then ducking down again. Franklin called out to Dave Taylor and Ian Ross to keep the defender's head down while he crept up on him. However, another burst of fire caught Franklin in the leg before other men from 15 Platoon managed to shoot the Japanese soldier. Corporal Mo Gardiner's reserve section from 15 Platoon, as well as Alex Anderson's 14 Platoon, soon moved up in support. The men watched in amazement as Proby appeared at the head of 7 Platoon, his head swathed in a trailing bandage. A medical orderly had started bandaging Proby, who had headed off before the job was complete. Jack Shewan passed the wounded Proby, who told him, 'Keep going, Jack. Get the bastards.'[19] Proby later retired, leaving Sergeant Ron Farrelly to take over the platoon while Warrant Officer Noel Pigot organised boxes of grenades to be brought forward to clear out the remaining enemy positions. At 1635 Pigot fired the success signal, and picks, shovels, ammunition, food, water and a Vickers gun were carried up to the newly captured position.

Four pillboxes and fifty-seven weapon pits were found on the Old Vickers position. All of the weapon pits had overhead cover up to a metre thick and provision for sleeping underground or in adjacent trenches. One Type 92 70mm gun, twenty-two rifles, four light machine-guns and one Juki machine-gun were recovered along with 300 shells for the mountain gun and 9000 rounds of ammunition for the Juki. Seventeen enemy dead from Ogawa's unit were also found on the position.[20] Many more had fled and, as Laurie Proby observed, 'a number were seen scrub bashing towards the Coconuts'. The Australians lost one officer and four men killed during the assault with another two officers and nine men being wounded. Lieutenant Albert Jackson temporarily took over C Company from the wounded Franklin. Hammer was impressed, commenting on the 'determination and vigour' of the men in following the artillery barrage.[21]

Hammer believed that the Japanese 'would react violently to our capture of Old Vickers', and he also had concerns that 'the weary 58/59 may not stand up to a series of determined counter attacks'.[22] He relieved the 58/59th Battalion companies on Old Vickers with those from the newly arrived 2/7th Battalion. The battalion headquarters and Captain Septimus Cramp's A Company had moved up to Bobdubi Ridge via Mubo while Captain Fred Barr's B Company had moved from Bulolo across Double Mountain to Missim, then to Bobdubi Ridge, arriving on 29 July. On 30 July Cramp's company took over the defence of the Old Vickers position. It was apparent from captured documents that it was a key enemy position, part of both the outer and inner defence perimeters for the defence of Salamaua. Enemy counter-attacks were expected, and a second native supply train brought up more ammunition and supplies.

Having captured Old Vickers, only the Coconuts position at the north end of Bobdubi Ridge remained in Japanese hands. Following a reconnaissance patrol, the 58/59th Battalion prepared to attack the position, which was a series of three closely spaced knolls, named South, Centre and North Coconuts, each being progressively higher to the north. These positions covered any movement along the ridge-top track while any flanking move would be via precipitate slopes. On North Coconuts there was an enemy bunker with the embrasure facing south along the ridge top, and harassing fire was being directed on to the Old Vickers position.[23]

Having been relieved by the 2/7th Battalion, Captain Ted Griff's B Company moved to Buggert and made preparations to attack South

Photo 35 Lieutenant Roy Dawson firing the captured mountain gun from Old Vickers on to the Coconuts. Photo by Damien Parer. (AWM 015838)

Coconuts on 30 July. The attack was timed for 1430 following an artillery barrage, but when Griff contacted Starr to confirm the support, he was told that 'the guns within range were out of ammunition and the guns with ammunition were out of range'. The Australians improvised, with Lieutenant Dawson using the captured Japanese mountain gun on Old Vickers by sighting down the barrel to fire on to North Coconuts. Damien Parer observed, 'Roy Dawson with the zest of a school boy had great fun with the captured mountain gun.' However, Griff saw little benefit, noting, 'In actual fact it was useless.'[24]

Griff's company moved down the track following the narrow top of the ridge until fired on when 80 metres from the South Coconuts position. He moved men off the ridge top to either flank, but the enemy defenders just rolled grenades down on them, forcing them back. Nonetheless, the forward weapon pits on South Coconuts were captured and, although many grenades were thrown at them from Centre Coconuts, most failed to explode. John Quirk and Alf Stone occupied the most forward position and noticed an enemy soldier with foliage attached to his helmet pass across their front. As they shot him, they exposed themselves to machine-gun fire from further along the ridge, and both men had to withdraw with bullets thudding around them.[25]

Patrols were despatched to look for alternative routes on to Centre Coconuts. Late in the afternoon one of the platoon commanders, Lieutenant Bill Hough, decided to go forward along the side of the ridge to spot the enemy machine-gun position. Sandy Matheson was in the forward position as Hough went past, and he told the lieutenant, 'You're bloody stupid if you go down there.' Hough continued on his way but never came back.[26]

Ted Griff also went forward to look at the options and realised there was no chance of a successful attack along such a narrow ridge line, which was well covered by machine-guns. The three Coconut knolls were in a line, each of which could fire on the preceding one, and the Australians were on the lowest one. Griff moved a platoon to the left flank but, with an almost sheer slope to traverse and dark falling, the operation was called off and his men prepared to defend South Coconuts.[27]

Starting at 0300 the next morning, 31 July, there were three Japanese counter-attacks on South Coconuts, accompanied by much noise and clamour. All were repulsed, but seven men were evacuated with stab wounds, reflecting the closeness and ferocity of the fighting. Matheson was in the thick of it that night trying to spot the Japanese probes in the moonlight, picking off a few of them with the Bren gun as they showed their silhouettes.[28]

At dawn a 2/7th Battalion patrol came down to South Coconuts to retrieve six boxes of captured ammunition to use with the Juki machine-gun on Old Vickers. Soon after, at round 0720, a fourth Japanese counter-attack with a hundred men finally overwhelmed the Australians. Sandy Matheson covered their withdrawal with his Bren gun, firing at some enemy troops coming up the track from down near the Francisco River. He stayed behind with Alfie Stone and, as Alfie came through, Sandy asked him, 'Any bastard behind you, Alf?'

'Any behind me?' Alf replied. 'All fucking Japs.'[29]

Before Matheson could move, an enemy machine-gun opened up from only 25 metres away and Matheson hugged the ground. 'By Jesus it whistled some lead over my head,' Matheson observed. He had the Bren gun's legs down and was lying in the scrub as all the shots went over, missing the magazine on the gun by centimetres. If they had hit, the gun would have been put out of action. Matheson fired back. The shells from the Bren bouncing off the dirt were hot on his arm, but he couldn't stop. Fortunately he always wore his sleeves down, but even they nearly burned off. Once he had quietened the enemy gun, Matheson pulled out along the track back towards Old Vickers, covered by Alf Stone, who was waiting further back. When they got back to the company position, Ted Griff asked what kept them. 'I tickled some ribs,' Matheson replied.[30]

Now down to two officers and thirty-six men, B Company had withdrawn north to a position between the track junction and the Old Vickers position. In the attack on the Coconuts, two men had been killed and six wounded, and Lieutenant Hough was still missing. Hammer had decided to withdraw B Company because the enemy force for the expected counter-attack on Old Vickers was expected to come up Stevens Track and would have cut off the men at South Coconuts. This information had been gleaned from documents captured on Old Vickers.

Griff's depleted company took up positions along a grassy ridge in the Gardens area, just south of Old Vickers. Lieutenant John Bethune's 12 Platoon occupied a position on their eastern flank, later known as Bethune's Post. Lieutenant Henry Anderson's 10 Platoon occupied Sugar Cane Knoll, but with only nine men remaining in the platoon, four other men were attached from the 2/7th Battalion. The unit had been provisioned for three days in anticipation of an enemy attack cutting them off and, with good foresight, Griff arranged for two Lucas signalling lamps to maintain communications. Vickers guns were also brought up and used to fire on the Japanese routes of attack.[31]

———————————

At dawn on 1 August enemy troops to the east opened fire on the Old Vickers position. It was the start of a determined Japanese bid to recapture it. By 0645 the signal lines had been cut by Japanese troops who had come in overnight. They had taken up positions in the gully and along the side of the Old Vickers position in defilade from the defenders on top. Further down Bobdubi Ridge a 58/59th Battalion ambush position had been attacked during the night and forced back up the ridge in the morning. Dave Taylor: 'It rained all day and we were tired so did very little but set out about eight two-man positions.' The Japanese were watching and fired on the positions that night. At least three men were killed and at least seven others wounded. The attackers had been fresh troops from Major Sugiyama's II/66th Battalion who had moved on to Bobdubi Ridge to join Jinno's I/80th Battalion in the counter-attack. Jinno was wounded when a mortar bomb hit his headquarters on 1 August.[32]

Lieutenant Lindsay McDonald's platoon was just the other side of the gully in front of the Old Vickers position. Griff had sent a runner up that morning to warn McDonald and ask for a reconnaissance patrol to see how many enemy troops had infiltrated. Sandy Matheson went out with

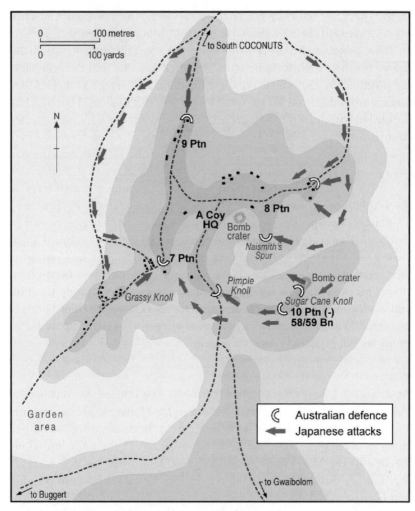

Map 27 Old Vickers position, 2–4 August 1943

two other men to do the recce, working along the ridge to the south of Old Vickers, where he took up a position in the scrub. Having carried up his Bren gun and about eight full magazines, Matheson proceeded to fire on the enemy positions and, although the enemy troops fired back, they didn't know exactly where Matheson was. He kept moving, spending only a few minutes in one place. He moved around along the top of the ridge from where he could look down on the enemy troops in the gully or on the slope below the Old Vickers position, preparing to attack.

Matheson fired for around half an hour, 'till I ran out of Japs', before returning to Griff and telling him what had happened. When the Japanese attacked Old Vickers the next morning Matheson once more climbed the ridge behind them and again took a considerable toll with his Bren gun. A later Japanese report said that the attacking troops were unsuccessful in attacking the enemy position on account of many men falling off the cliffs in steep terrain.[33] Sandy Matheson certainly helped a few on their way; dead men fall easily.

Despite their losses while getting into position, the Japanese attacked Old Vickers at dawn on 2 August from the Grassy Knoll area to the west. The attack hit 7 Platoon, which held on with the support of 3-inch mortar fire from within the perimeter. A bugle call signalled the enemy withdrawal as thirty reinforcements arrived for the Australians. Soon thereafter, the 58/59th Battalion brought Vickers-gun and mortar fire to bear on the enemy positions west of Old Vickers.[34]

In the afternoon there was accurate and effective enemy light machine-gun fire on to Sugar Cane Knoll. Wire communications were cut, and a Lucas lamp was used to provide communication back to Old Vickers. A patrol was later sent out, moving a hundred metres forward of the former positions to investigate the Japanese incursion route. Private Heinrich Forst, who was leading one of the sections, soon came under heavy fire, forcing the section back to better cover. Forst then realised that two of his men, Richard Gray, who had been shot in the chest, and Herbert Hoffman, a 58/59th man, had been wounded and remained under enemy fire. Forst went out 'under a hail of LMG fire' to drag Gray back, then returned to bring Hoffman in. A brave man, Heinrich Forst.[35]

The Japanese counter-attacks came in from the north-west, north along the track from the Coconuts, the north-east and the south-east. Two factors helped the Japanese: first, they knew the ground very well and second, the Australians didn't; the 2/7th Battalion had occupied the former Japanese positions only on the previous day. The attacking troops used these advantages to move very close. However, the Australians had the great advantage of having the well-built and well-sited former Japanese positions available for their use.

Corporal Alan Naismith, a former RAP sergeant who had dropped a stripe to return to the front line, was the acting commander of 8 Platoon, deployed at the southern end of Old Vickers. There were only twelve men in the platoon, and Naismith, the only NCO among them, split the men

Photo 36 View west across the steep southern slope of Old Vickers towards the Gardens area. (Phillip Bradley)

into three reliefs of four. Naismith's position would take the brunt of the Japanese attacks. The Japanese were only 15 metres away down the slope, and the Australians set up a Bren gun pit at the top of the crest a few metres in front of the other weapon pits to stymie any attack. Don Finn was the Bren gunner on one of the reliefs, and most of the attacks took place while he was on duty. As Jock Sym, the company sergeant major, observed, 'Don was the perfect jungle sentry, didn't trust his eyes much but his ears were tuned to catch the slightest foreign sound.' Finn's alertness was helped by the Japanese trait of fixing bayonets before each attack, thus giving Finn a vital warning sign. He would immediately throw a couple of grenades down the slope into the Japanese positions, then call out, 'It's on again, boys' before opening fire with the Bren. Sym noted, 'Each attack was washed out, even in the short distance of 15 yards.'[36]

The first Japanese attack had hit Naismith's sector, and his men would be under fire for four days and nights. The nature of the position meant that any attackers had to ascend the steep slopes of the Old Vickers position, making the grenade the best weapon for defence, and the men would stick the grenade pull rings into the side of their weapon pits to keep score. When any attack came in Naismith would be one of the first to appear, tossing more grenades down over the crest at the Japanese attackers. Sym would prime the grenades, then hand them to Naismith. As well as their own, the men used 200 Japanese grenades during the defence of the position, many of them obtained by crawling out to the enemy dead. On one occasion Naismith surprised five enemy soldiers priming grenades, killed the lot and took the grenades.[37] A captured enemy machine-gun was also used in the defence of the position. In all, twenty-five enemy soldiers were killed during the first day of attacks.

Knowing full well the dominating nature of the Old Vickers position by day, the Japanese now concentrated on night attacks. At 2115 on 2 August they attacked with fixed bayonets in the dark and rain but, as Sym wrote, the 'hysterical chanting and screams gave warning of the enemy's intention'. Once again 8 Platoon bore the brunt of it, and some enemy troops died in the pits they were attacking, the rest fleeing back down the slopes. Meanwhile, mortar and Vickers-gun fire helped stymie the enemy attacks from Grassy Knoll.

Wally Bayliss was in a forward pit on Naismith's Spur and, as he heard the enemy approach, he fired his Bren with one hand and threw grenades with the other. This broke the enemy attack long enough to enable to rest of the unit to stand to. Alan Naismith rushed from position to position and gathered more enemy grenades to be used in the defence. Some days later, Naismith was shot in the right shoulder but, using his left hand, the former RAP sergeant stitched a comrade's wound before heading off on the trek down the ridge to have his own wound seen to. Although some of the fighting was at close quarters, only one bayonet wound – to Private Hyram Lethlean – was treated following the attack. Although Lethlean might not have agreed, Captain Peterson observed that he had 'a harmless laceration to the scrotum'. He could have been the man wounded during an extraordinary action where a Japanese soldier threw his rifle and bayonet like a spear at the Australian positions.[38]

Another in the thick of it was Win Howard, a Bren gunner with 7 Platoon. As at Lababia Ridge in May, the bipod for Howard's Bren gun had been hit, but Howard was clever enough to take sightings from the bullet holes along the top of the trench. He spotted the enemy light machine-gun on an adjacent knoll, giving off some smoke as it fired and providing a good target. At night the two men in Win Howard's weapon pit slept two hours on and two off. Howard and his mate used all of their 4-second grenades, then switched to using the 7-second grenades normally used with the extra yoke rifle, counting to four before throwing them. His mate had a sniper rifle and was picking off enemy troops at long range while, at shorter range, Owen guns were used, one so much that its barrel melted and had to be chopped off with a hacksaw, resulting in quite a spray of fire.[39]

After three days of frontal attacks without success, the Japanese moved further south along the ridge and dug in between Old Vickers and Buggert village at the bamboo clump area where the ridge-top track branched off down the western side of Bobdubi Ridge. Ted Griff was ordered to attack the position with two 58/59th platoons to restore the line of communications to Old Vickers. With Henry Anderson's platoon cut off on Sugar Cane Knoll and Bethune's platoon holding Bethune's Post, he had only Lieutenant Lindsay McDonald's platoon available. Therefore Lieutenant Bert Murphy's tank-attack platoon was attached for the task. Murphy and his men had arrived only the previous afternoon after an extraordinary journey via air to Dobodura, truck to Oro Bay, schooner to Nassau Bay, then a trek up the Bitoi River, across Observation Hill and thence via Dierke's Post to the 58/59th Battalion headquarters. As Griff's men would have to attack uphill, he suggested that A Company should make the first attack from Old Vickers. That attack failed, and Captain Vin Tatterson was killed leading it.

Under the cover of 3-inch mortar support, Murphy's platoon attacked on the left flank at 1630, with McDonald on the right. Murphy's men charged up the slope while the mortar rounds were still falling. Ted Griff had heard Murphy moving up after only three mortar rounds had fallen and therefore ordered the mortar fire to stop and for McDonald to get his men moving. Both platoons met at the top just before dusk.[40] Following Griff's thrust, twenty-seven dead enemy troops were found. These troops were from Major Jinno's I/80th Battalion which, by daybreak on 4 August, had moved around the ridge from the north and 'captured the central part of the enemy's main position'. Japanese records note how they met with concentrated enemy fire from three directions and were forced to withdraw.[41] After dusk, Griff's men made contact with the section from 14 Platoon that had been isolated for three days on Sugar Cane Knoll.

On the morning of 5 August Griff organised a mopping-up party, including Sandy Matheson who noted, 'All the Japs were in foxholes. You might only see a foot. If you put a bullet in it you knew if he was alive or dead.' They went from one pit to another dropping in grenades, holding them for a second or two to ensure that they were not thrown back before exploding. Eight Japanese soldiers were killed, making a total of fifty enemy dead and seven light machine-guns captured in the area south of Old Vickers. When the patrol finally reached Old Vickers the defenders were very happy to see them.[42] All told, eighty-seven enemy dead were found and buried around Old Vickers, although total enemy casualties were much higher than that. The bodies of many of those killed during the first twelve attacks had already been cleared. One of the enemy identification tags recovered from the Old Vickers area depicted a rising sun with anchors, indicating that Japanese marines had taken part in the action.[43]

As they had proved when the battalion had stormed Old Vickers a week before, the 58/59th Battalion was composed of fine soldiers and, when led with intelligence, drive and courage by men like Franklin, Proby, Griff and Murphy, the battalion was as good as any in the Australian army. However, this opinion was not one held by Hammer, who now relieved Starr of his command, to be replaced by Warfe. Captain Hancock would replace Warfe in charge of the 2/3rd Independent Company while Major Keith Picken would administer command of the 2/7th Battalion in the absence of Guinn. Hammer had requested Guinn be temporarily relieved after he had to be ordered to bed for seven days on his return to the forward area on 26 July. On 5 August Guinn was evacuated for what Hammer suggested should be an extended period of recuperation.[44]

Following the successful defence of Old Vickers, attention again turned towards clearing the remaining Japanese positions on Bobdubi Ridge at the Coconuts. The 2/7th Battalion would be used, and patrolling commenced to discern the layout of the enemy positions. It was soon found that any approach along the ridge top could get no closer to South Coconuts than 75 metres.[45] Artillery fire on to the Coconuts was having little effect, and the infantry would have to go in and take the ground. Japanese sources confirmed that view: 'Although we are bombarded all day by enemy artillery, we have suffered no losses.'[46]

Captain Andrew Rooke, who had commanded the 2/7th Battalion platoon at Bena Bena for four months until May, had arrived at Bobdubi Ridge only on 10 August. Now in command of C Company, he had been given the opportunity to lead a composite A Company platoon, known as the Bena platoon, in the attack on the difficult South Coconuts position. After a reconnaissance up the steep eastern approaches to within 25 metres of the enemy positions, Rooke reckoned that his men could take the feature. To support Rooke's men, 9 Platoon would move directly

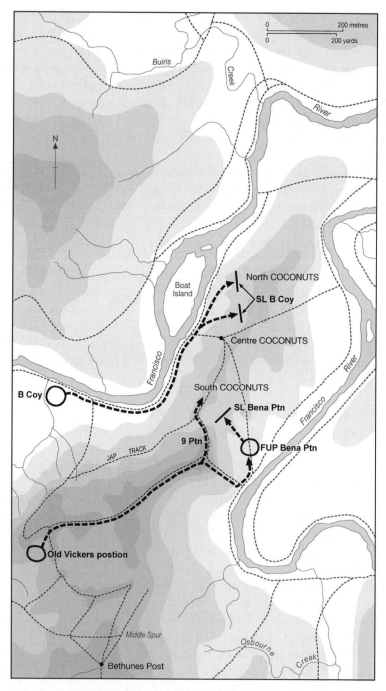

Map 28 Coconuts position, 13 August 1943

along the narrow ridge-top track from Stevens Track junction and simultaneously attack the position. Captain Fred Barr's B Company would make the attack on the North Coconuts with Lieutenant Henry Mallett's 10 Platoon. Backing them up would be 11 Platoon with Lieutenant Bill Fietz's 12 Platoon in reserve. One of Barr's men, Jack Mitchell, wrote in his diary, 'We are to attack the Coconut ridge tomorrow.'[47] Meanwhile, Lieutenant John Lewin's platoon from the 2/3rd Independent Company would move down the eastern side of Bobdubi Ridge to ambush any enemy reinforcements moving up from Salamaua.

Heavy air support from twenty-two B-24 Liberators and seven B-17 Flying Fortresses was laid on for the attack. From 0930 on 14 August the first three Liberators released their bombs on the Coconuts and, 'with a noise like the rushing of a great wind', the bombs passed over the heads of the waiting assault troops. 'Trees, logs and other rubbish flew through the fall [sic] of dust which now cloaked the target.' The observers at Old Vickers observed, 'It seemed that nothing could have lived in the midst of devastation loosed by the planes.' At 1010 the forward observation officer began directing a one-and-a-half-hour artillery barrage accompanied by fire from six 3-inch mortars.[48]

As the artillery fire ceased, the mortars continued to cover the approach with smoke bombs. Then, as Axel Olsen later wrote, 'came a terribly fierce raking with Vickers guns firing through the haze from smoke bombs'. To keep enemy heads down, Vickers guns on Old Vickers targeted North Coconuts, and other Vickers guns out to the west of Bobdubi Ridge fired across on to Centre and South Coconuts. Olsen watched as some Japanese, 'cracking under the terrific blasting, began to scuttle out of their dugouts and flee into the jungle . . . then from the tattered jungle came the figures of Australians moving deliberately, unhesitatingly, up the steep soft slopes of the bomb craters, their guns blazing at the Japanese pillboxes.' However, the approach was treacherous as the bombing had blown away the cover from the formerly reconnoitred lines of approach, and the western ridge face was now a sheer slope of loose earth enfiladed by Japanese machine-guns.[49]

Although the North Coconuts position was guarded by two pillboxes connected to weapon pits by crawl trenches, the area had suffered in the bombing, and the Australians soon managed to capture it. As Olsen wrote, 'There was the bark of grenades as they were thrown into pillboxes, then quiet. We had captured the northern and most important knoll.' The men then moved south along the ridge and found that the Centre Coconuts position had been almost obliterated by the bombing and that many of the

Photo 37 View south along the ridge from the edge of a bomb crater north of Centre Coconuts. (Phillip Bradley)

Japanese defenders had been buried in their tunnels. Japanese accounts reported the fierce artillery fire had completely destroyed the defences of 2 Company, I/80th Battalion here. The position also fell but was untenable for the captors while the South Coconuts position remained in enemy hands. Jack Mitchell, who was Captain Barr's runner, was moving up to make contact with Mallett's 10 Platoon when he was pinned down by a machine-gun sited in a big clump of bamboos. Working his way along the ridge side, he then came up behind the Japanese position and tried to get close enough to throw a grenade. Just as he threw it there was a thump and an enemy grenade dropped only a metre away. As his own grenade exploded he was 'up and off as hard as I could go till I reached cover'.[50]

Meanwhile, Bena Platoon and 9 Platoon moved down to the Stevens Track junction from Old Vickers. While 9 Platoon formed up on the main track for the attack on South Coconuts, Rooke moved his men to their start line on the east side of the ridge level with, but below, South Coconuts. When Rooke's men advanced at 1227 they immediately ran into difficulties. As Rooke later wrote, the bombing had 'destroyed the covered approach for Bena Force, and we literally had to make our way over a sea of broken branches and trees'. Despite this obstacle, his platoon managed to move up the ridge. In front of Rooke his experienced forward scout, Corporal Jim Hughes, was hit by the first shot from the defenders, and heavy fire immediately broke out from both sides. Three more men were soon wounded, and Rooke sent Corporal Charles Berry's section to his right flank to occupy a bomb crater astride the ridge at Centre Coconuts. However, the area was thick with well-entrenched defenders, and grenades soon began falling into the confines of the crater, killing one and wounding two of Berry's men. The wounded John McPherson reported back to Rooke that the crater position was untenable, then returned to Berry with orders to pull his depleted section out. Meanwhile Rooke had been injured by a grenade blast as had the already wounded Hughes, who would die on the way out.[51] Andrew Rooke was among the ten men from his platoon who had been wounded, and he was taken out using a stretcher made up from his and the two stretcher-bearers' shirts.

Back up on the main track, 9 Platoon waited until 1300 before also attacking South Coconuts. However, two Japanese light machine-guns, each well protected by log bunkers, began firing down the track, stopping any approach. At the same time, down on the river flat below the ridge, B Company headquarters came under fire from the same position, and Captain Barr was shot in the upper arm. Even as Barr bled to death his second in command, Lloyd Walker, was shot in the head by an enemy sniper. Sergeant Bill Russell went up from the aid post at about 1330 to find the wounded Walker in a foxhole and managed to get him back to a safer spot where he died. Russell then stitched up Max McDougall's chest wound, and McDougall made his own way back to the RAP. Another man, Corporal Ernie Fox, was arm-chaired down off the ridge having being shot through both thighs.[52]

When Jack Mitchell returned to company HQ, the first thing he saw was 'the bodies covered over with groundsheets'. Shocked, he found the signallers sheltering further back. He rang through to battalion HQ and told them he would go to fetch Lieutenant Bill Fietz to take over. Mitchell then went back up the ridge to find Fietz, one of the platoon commanders, an experienced soldier who had been commissioned in the field in Crete. Mitchell told him, 'Look, Bill, take over – the CO and 2IC are dead.' Fietz headed back to the company HQ with Mitchell and the wounded Rex Byrne. Fietz then sat down behind the bamboo clump with the phone and manned the 3-inch mortars to direct fire on to the enemy positions on South Coconuts. 'Up a little, down a little,' he told the mortar crew as

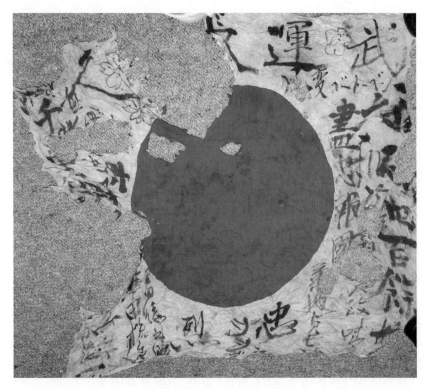

Photo 38 The tattered Japanese flag taken from the South Coconuts position and still held by Jack Mitchell. 'Best wishes for victory' is emblazoned across the top. (Phillip Bradley)

they sent up bombs at a fast rate. Then there was a hell of an explosion among the enemy positions; one of the mortar bombs had hit home.[53] Meanwhile, with B Company at Centre Coconuts, an attack was made in concert with 9 Platoon on South Coconuts at 1705 but was unsuccessful. A listening post was then left at Centre Coconuts, and B Company pulled back to the more defensible North Coconuts position. It had been a tough day for the 2/7th Battalion; nine men, including two officers, had been killed and another 17 men wounded.

When South Coconuts was finally evacuated by the enemy some days later, Jack Mitchell was one of the first men to reach the position. He found two intact enemy bunkers, formidable constructions with one containing artillery and mortar shells, the other small arms ammunition. A tattered battle flag still flew from one of them.[54]

The fighting at Old Vickers and the Coconuts was some of the most intricate of the Salamaua campaign. The terrain has defensive character-istics that not even the legendary French fortification engineer Sebastien Vauban could ever have replicated. Whether you look at this northern end of Bobdubi Ridge in profile, from above or at ground level, it is obvious how dominant the Old Vickers and Coconuts positions are. Once the ter-rain is understood, the reason the Australian operations foundered here also becomes apparent. Even today, equipped with map, compass and GPS, it is difficult to discern the twists, turns and precipitous nature of the slopes around these positions. Although Warfe's commandos had pre-viously captured these positions in May, this only prodded the Japanese command into realising just how vital the northern end of Bobdubi Ridge was to the security of Salamaua. From then on, the defence of this area became as important as that in the Mount Tambu area and, as at Mount Tambu, it would be only through the application of tried and tested infantry tactics that the positions would fall. Such tactics included proper reconnaissance, intelligent planning, focused support and the drive and courage to carry through the successful assault.

CHAPTER | 14

KOMIATUM RIDGE

In the 17th Brigade sector, where the peak of Mount Tambu remained in Japanese hands, operations shifted to the Goodview area. On 4 August Conroy's 2/5th Battalion staged an attack with two companies south of Goodview Junction. Captain Cam Bennett's B Company had the major role. Damien Parer said of him: 'Cam Bennett is great – big & easy & calm – the real AIF.' Bennett handed Lieutenant Brian Hodge's 12 Platoon the task of capturing the Japanese razorback knoll position that overlooked the junction of Walpole's and Mule Tracks. Bennett charcterised Hodge as being 'tall and lithe, with startling light grey-blue eyes. He got on well with and was absolute boss of his platoon and was a complete enthusiast.'[1]

By 0900 Hodge's men had gained a foothold on the position now known as Hodge's Knoll. The platoon held all day against steadily increasing enemy pressure that culminated with a heavy attack from three sides at 1630. Bennett's other platoons had attempted to get up on to the knoll to assist Hodge but were unsuccessful. Lieutenant Bill Lind's 10 Platoon tried to push down Walpole's Track on Hodge's right but was stymied by enemy pillboxes astride the track. Having lost seven men killed and ten wounded in the heavy fighting, Hodge's platoon withdrew, leaving behind twenty-eight Japanese dead.[2]

George Comber was one of those wounded in the fighting. Damien Parer, who was unable to film due to the low light levels, helped carry Comber's stretcher out. He wrote, 'As I watch George with broken leg & bullet through groin in pain – game – white – cigarette hanging

274

Photo 39 Private Herbert Escreet, 2/5th Battalion, 3 August 1943. Photo by Gordon Short. (AWM 015377)

from his lips – yet cracking a joke, I almost cried. This cream of Australia is just going on and on and we're losing them every day.'[3]

After Hodge had pulled his men out, the Australians called down mortar fire on the lost position. After several bombs had been fired it was suggested that the range be reduced, although the mortar observer recommended against it. Sheltering in a shallow weapon pit nearby, Chuck Ryan heard the next round descend on the Australian position. The explosion stunned Ryan, and he staggered from the weapon pit and grabbed the phone yelling, 'No more, no more.' As he later said, 'It was a hell of a mess.'[4] Five American artillerymen, setting up a forward observation post, had been killed along with a 2/5th Battalion corporal, Ron Bush.

Meanwhile, the Japanese had emplaced a mountain gun on Komiatum Ridge that fired across valley of Buirali Creek on to the 2/6th Battalion positions at Sugarcane Ridge and Ambush Knoll. Each day during the first week of August the gun, dug into the ridge for protection from counterfire, would fire no more than twelve rounds at a time before being returned

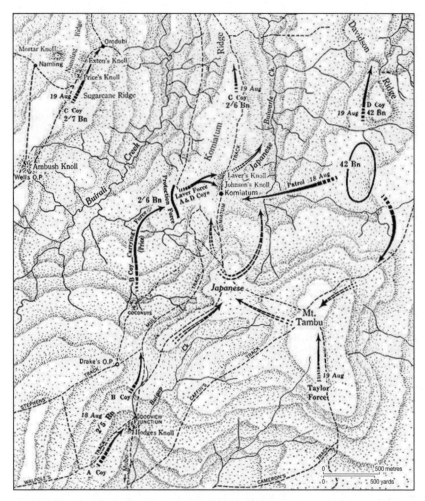

Map 29 Komiatum Ridge area, 16–19 August 1943

to shelter. The gun was so close that the first shot arrived before the men on the ridge heard the gun go off. Jim Gatt, who was one of the casualties, observed: 'I heard one explode and then felt what seemed like a kick from a mule.'[5] The gun caused eighteen casualties to the men on Sugarcane Ridge, two of them fatal, before Captain Gordon Edgar, who had taken over B Company from Ernie Price, reorganised the men. Edgar observed, 'It became so hot that we had to move back and only occupy our positions with one section by day, moving in again at night with the full company.'[6]

The 2/6th Battalion was by no means passive. Regular patrols were sent out with a view to finding the best way to get the battalion on to Komiatum Ridge. Moten had told Savige that ten days would be needed to organise a flanking route on to the ridge. This critical task was given to D Company, which had moved forward on the morning of 4 August. With Captain Bill Dexter now back in Australia on a training course, Captain Harold Laver had taken over command of the company. Leaving on 5 August, two reconnaissance patrols, one led by Sergeant 'Smokey' Hedderman and the other by Lieutenant Les Johnson, tried to find a suitable route on to Komiatum Ridge north of Goodview. Johnson's route, which was the closest one to Goodview, was rejected as it was considered impassable for a company of infantrymen. Although also difficult, Hedderman thought his route, which emerged from the jungle near Komiatum village, would work.[7]

Hedderman's confidence in the route and Wood's trust in his judgement was a critical turning point in the fight to isolate Mount Tambu. Savige later wrote: 'By the 8th [of August] it was apparent that the key to Mount Tambu was in Wood's hands, but the trouble was to find the keyhole.' On 10 August both Savige and Moten visited the 2/6th Battalion positions to observe the 'frightful country' over which the critical advance would take place. Savige put it into perspective: 'In my experience covering two wars this was the toughest operational problem I ever faced.'[8]

The Coconuts position, a separate feature from that at the north end of Bobdubi Ridge, was selected as the forward base for operations, and a supply track was cut to it. The plan was for Laver's men to attack on 16 August in concert with the 15th Brigade attacks to the north-west. Moten originally wanted to get the whole battalion on to Komiatum Ridge but 'Wood insisted on two companies only and he was right'. It was also planned to use the artillery, mortars and Vickers guns to protect the area around Laver's lodgement. Moten said, 'I reckon this would safely hem in Laver. I also reckoned the Japs, wanting their rations, would try to break out on the third day.'[9]

At daybreak on 16 August Bennett made a diversionary attack at Goodview Junction to hold the Japanese front line in place. It totally surprised the enemy defenders, as Bennett observed: 'They stood in a group at daylight, listening to an officer before retiring to their log bunkers.' Caught out in the open, eighteen of them were killed. Chuck Ryan, who was on signals duty, realised, 'We had the buggers.' The next thing the phone rang, and Conroy ordered Bennett to 'withdraw immediately, brigade commander's instructions'. Bennett did as ordered but was 'boiling mad' when he later reached battalion headquarters. He fronted Conroy and told him, 'I had 'em, I had 'em in the palm of my hand, and you called me off!'[10] Moten's focus was on his other plans, but how Bennett's success could be perceived as not increasing the pressure on the Japanese defence positions at Komiatum is puzzling. Moten's order had been for Bennett to send out a fighting patrol to maintain the pressure, and the seizure of the key position put even more pressure on the Japanese defence.

Also at daybreak on 16 August, under cover of artillery fire, Captain Laver's men made their move up to Komiatum Ridge. Most of the enemy defenders had fled due to the artillery fire, and the knoll was in Laver's hands by 0710. His company soon had a 3-inch mortar in action, firing defensive tasks using the ammunition brought up by B Company, each man carrying three 3-inch mortar bombs in his haversack. These men returned with a second load the same day. Even before Laver's men had dug in, Lieutenant Les Johnson's 17 Platoon occupied another knoll, 150 metres further south, now called Johnson's Knoll. The Japanese had already dug perfectly sited defensive positions, which Johnson's platoon eagerly took over.[11] At 1830 enemy fire was directed against Johnson's Knoll, but two enemy counter-attacks were held. That night the 42nd Battalion, positioned on Davidson Ridge overlooking Komiatum Ridge, was ordered to provide harassing fire from mortars and Vickers guns, and this kept further enemy probes at bay.

Before dawn on 17 August there was a third enemy counter-attack on Johnson's Knoll. Sergeant James Gibson said, 'They attacked for three hours before moonrise, throwing everything they had at us . . . we hurled grenade after grenade and pasted them with everything.'[12] The Japanese got within metres of the Australian positions but were held. Artillery and mortar support continued throughout the day to keep the Japanese at bay, and the Japanese retaliated with twelve artillery rounds fired on to Laver's Knoll. There were two further Japanese attacks from the south after dusk but, with Vickers machine-gun support fire from Davidson Ridge and the Coconuts, the position was held. The Vickers gun fire was so accurate that 'had we stuck our arms out of the pits they would have been shot off'. Two men were killed in the action. One of them, George 'Bunny' Lamont, was struck down by machine-gun fire at around 2000 as Captain Laver was giving him a message to take forward.[13]

Also on 17 August a 42nd Battalion patrol adjacent to Mount Tambu was engaged, and three men were killed. George Eddleston did a lot of damage with his Bren gun but also drew return fire and was one of those

Photo 40 Aerial view north down Komiatum Ridge. (AWM 128384)

to fall. Larry Read from the 2/5th Battalion took his place behind the Bren but, after a few bursts, he was also shot. The big six-footer, John 'Bill' Greene, then charged up the slope firing his Owen gun, and an enemy light machine-gun got him as well.[14] Meanwhile, a Vickers machine-gun was brought up to Laver's Knoll, and Laver's men linked up with a 42nd Battalion patrol from Davidson Ridge.

Major-General Berryman arrived at 17th Brigade headquarters on 18 August. He had flown across from Port Moresby to Nassau Bay and thence travelled by boat to Tambu Bay the previous day. Moten told him that there were indications that the enemy was withdrawing from his positions at Goodview. Berryman listened to Moten's explanation of the operation and commented that it was 'a perfect plan . . . [It] is the best bit of tactical surprise I've seen in the campaign and will crumble the Nip front.' Wilton agreed: 'This little battle has been the perfect action, everything went exactly according to plan. Jap encircled and made to attack us during which process he was mown down by our [defensive] fire both MG and [artillery].'[15]

Following orders from General Nakano, the remaining Japanese defenders withdrew from Mount Tambu during the night of 18–19 August via the steep valley between Komiatum Ridge and Davidson Ridge. On the next morning a 42nd Battalion patrol established that Mount Tambu had been evacuated, although there were still enemy troops in the area; ambushes that afternoon and after dusk killed five of them and drove more away. Having being urged forward, Taylor's Americans found the final knoll on Mount Tambu unoccupied and moved in. At 1820 the 42nd Battalion's Captain Frank 'Punchy' Greer made contact with Taylor's men and guided them down on to Scout Ridge.[16]

Early on 19 August patrols from 2/5th Battalion also found the enemy positions at Goodview Junction deserted. Moten was informed, then he 'woke Berryman who came in his pyjamas to my bamboo hut. At the same time I sent a signal to Conroy telling him to push up to join with Laver.' Moten, Berryman and Conroy, together with twenty headquarters staff, then went forward and joined Bennett and his forward platoon. Berryman was impressed by the work of the forward platoon, noting: 'Leading section on making contact took up a position on either side of track, rear section working around flank on high ground – all done quickly, quietly and almost automatically.'[17]

Cam Bennett was not so impressed by the audience, being constantly asked what was happening. 'A pause while the three of them poked around the bushes with their pistols and on we would go . . . to my horror and rage had General Berryman and the brigadier at my elbow.' Bennett soon let Berryman know his displeasure, telling him, 'I wish to God you would go to buggery and take the brigadier with you.' Berryman looked at Bennett rather hard for a minute, then threw back his head and roared with laughter before telling Moten, 'Come on, Moten, we must be worrying Bennett.' Both men then retired for their midday meeting with General Savige.[18]

Now unhindered by the higher command, Bennett's men pushed forward and captured two mountain guns, three heavy mortars and a number of machine-guns left behind by the fleeing Japanese. By 1430 Bennett's men had contacted Laver's. Both A and C Companies of the 2/6th Battalion now also moved on to Komiatum Ridge from the west.[19] Later the same day, after the Berryman meeting, Savige and Wilton also made their way down to Laver's Knoll. Both men would soon be on their way out of the theatre, and both wished to savour the success of Laver's company. Savige later recalled, 'That short period we spent with those fellows was a tonic.'[20]

The meeting between Berryman and Savige was always going to be an interesting one, and Savige expected trouble despite his adherence to Herring's orders. On 29 July Herring had sent a message to Savige outlining the operation against Lae, planned to commence by the end of August. The message stated, 'These operations for your own private ear only involve an attack on Lae from both E and W.' Herring went on to confirm Savige's role of driving the enemy north of the Francisco River and to state, 'The capture of Salamaua is of course devoutly to be wished but no attempt upon it is to be allowed to interfere with the major operation being planned.' Herring went on to specify that the role of 3rd Division was 'to hold in the Salamaua area, if not already in your hands, the maximum number of the enemy'.[21]

According to Moten, 'Berry came up to give a bowler hat either to Savige or me if unsuccessful or to Herring for not knowing what was going on... Berryman said that the main drive should have been along the coast and that Mount Tambu should have been bypassed. Savige stuck to his guns and he was a successful general. He had a watertight show and Berryman hastily stowed away the bowler hat when Savige tackled him.'[22]

Savige and Wilton showed Berryman a message from Herring urging Savige on. This followed a visit from Herring's chief staff officer, Brigadier Roy Sutherland, on 26 July expressing Herring's concern at the failed attacks on Mount Tambu and at Komiatum Ridge on 24 July. The latter attack had not even taken place, which unmasked the 5th USAAF air support officer who was feeding information – in this case incorrect – direct to Herring at New Guinea Force headquarters. Berryman thought that Herring's signal was most unjustified, particularly as no senior New Guinea Force officer had previously visited the front line. Berryman later made some pertinent comments to the official historian about Herring 'not giving Savige a fair burl... Savige having to fight Herring as well as Japs'.[23] Despite his support for Savige, Berryman now told the 3rd Division commander that his divisional headquarters was to be relieved by Major-General Edward Milford's 5th Division headquarters. General Blamey thought highly of Milford and later wrote that he 'at once showed qualities of force and drive in this, his first period of operational command, that marked him as a leader of quality'.[24] Milford would relieve Savige on 25 August. Milford had been told that the main reason for Savige's demise was Herring's annoyance that the supply line to the coast had not been opened so as to free supply aircraft for the upcoming Lae operation. Herring had also told Milford that Savige had never visited the front line as he was too old.[25] This was incorrect; Savige had visited Mubo in the early days of his command and again before and following Laver's attack at Komiatum. Wilton had visited the 15th Brigade sector, thus ensuring that Savige's operational decisions were based on an understanding of the terrain.

With the change in command, Savige's right-hand man, John Wilton, would also be replaced and sent to Washington. Wilton accompanied Berryman and Savige down to Tambu Bay, then by barge to Nassau Bay. Here he met Milford 'on his way to take over from Stan – full of plans he has made from the map – he will learn!'[26] Back in Port Moresby Berryman told Blamey and Herring that 'Savige had done well and we had misjudged him'.[27]

Savige later wrote, 'I expected to be prevented by Herring from being able to enter Salamaua. I had forecast to Griffin and Wilton in June that I would be relieved on the line when it was simple to enter Salamaua. They were astounded that when Jap resistance [was] broken at Komiatum, Berryman came up and gave me letter.' Savige later noted that Blamey's first words to him when he returned to Port Moresby were that 'you look fit and so did Wilton'.[28]

Down at Tambu Bay the 25-pounder guns of the 2/6th Field Regiment supported the Australian drive. Heavy shelling continued day and night on 19 August and for the next two days. On 21 August Brian Gomme noted, 'All guns are keeping up incessant fire on Salamaua. It is impossible to sleep at night. The noise is deafening.' The gunners got little sleep and had to fire more than a thousand rounds a day with 'sweat streaming from aching bodies, while all else became a blurred reality'.[29]

On 20 August the 2/5th Battalion took over operations on Komiatum Ridge, and the 2/6th moved back into reserve. Four days later the 2/5th Battalion was also relieved, this time by the newly arrived 47th Battalion. Both relieved battalions then moved down to Tambu Bay to be evacuated. Conroy was also on his way out, relieved of his battalion command.

Following the loss of Mount Tambu, the keystone position in the new Japanese line south of the Francisco River was now Kusa Yama, a severe peak towards the northern end of Davidson Ridge, known as Charlie Hill to the Australians. From Charlie Hill the line ran east along Yamada Yama (Scout Ridge) to the coast at Lokanu and also north through Kunai Spur, then across the Francisco River along the ridges of Ogura Yama (Rough Hill), Hyotan Yama (Arnold's Crest) and on to Tusukaba Yama (a prominent feature two kilometres south-west of Malolo) and the coast near Malolo. Reinforcements from the 115th Regiment, which had just landed in Salamaua, also moved up to Charlie Hill, digging weapon pits along the crest. On 24 August Nakano told his men, 'If this line cannot be maintained, the division is to be honourably annihilated.'[30] Nakano would have had in mind General Adachi's comments to him regarding Salamaua: 'In light of the great importance of this place, it is my hope that it can be held till the very last, just like the Soviet Army did at Stalingrad.'[31]

Meanwhile Davidson's 42nd Battalion patrolled forward towards Nuk Nuk. On 21 August C Company pushed north along Davidson Ridge crossing a creek then climbing up towards Bamboo Knoll, the feature in front of Charlie Hill. As the steep climb levelled out at the knoll, the Australians made contact with the forewarned enemy positions. As dusk fell, the two lead platoons consolidated below the knoll, and the position was taken the following day without loss. From the top of the knoll the men could look at the accusing finger of the Salamaua peninsula pointing over the blue waters of Huon Gulf.[32]

The next morning, the Japanese counter-attacked Bamboo Knoll from the east. The attackers set up a light machine-gun within 25 metres of the C Company position and later positioned riflemen in the trees on the western flank to snipe at the Australians, killing one of the section leaders. Captain Rod Cole moved among his men ensuring that the perimeter was tightly held, then moved out behind Frank 'Shorty' Deal to clear the enemy snipers. Three of them were shot out of the trees and the rest dispersed. Meanwhile, one of the stretcher-bearers, Les Gatton, went out to the forward weapon pits to treat the wounded while another bearer, Arch Little, was fatally wounded carrying out the same task. Artillery support fire was then brought down to the east, and a platoon was sent out to clear the enemy. The sweep was a success with 20 enemy soldiers killed, but three Australians also fell and another would later die of wounds. The enemy withdrew in the afternoon as Captain Frank Greer's B Company moved up to support Cole.[33]

Meanwhile, a small enemy force moved between Davidson Ridge and Scout Ridge and attacked the A Company headquarters area. The

Australians were caught unawares, with only two sections of 9 Platoon present alongside company headquarters. Captain Ted Pattingale and two other men, Hector Wedge and George Francis, were killed in the opening exchange of fire. There was a thought that the approaching Japanese might have been mistaken for Americans due to the similar helmets. Lieutenant Gordon Friend took over the defence with sixteen men and, helped by the support of a Vickers gun on an adjacent knoll, the position was held.[34]

On the morning of 22 August B Company of the 58/59th Battalion had crossed the Buirali Creek, and a patrol had later advanced north along a heavily timbered ridge, the approach to Kunai Spur. This was a dominant position that blocked any move along the Francisco River to Salamaua and was well defended by the Japanese. Two men from the patrol were killed and another six wounded before the Australians withdrew. Three simultaneous attacks were made on Kunai Spur the next day, by Captain Cramp's 2/7th company from the north, Sergeant Tom Potts' 58/59th platoon from the west and Lieutenant Russell Mathews' 58/59th platoon from the east. The approach was very steep, but Mathews got his men on to the spur, only to be confronted by a machine-gun which could fire along the spur from higher up. Corporal Les McFarlane was killed and Lieutenant Mathews was among those wounded during the grenade duel that eventuated; the Gibraltar-like position would be a tough nut to crack. Even the battalion headquarters came under fire and was then attacked by seven enemy soldiers trying to get through from the Bobdubi side. A party led by Warfe chased them off through the scrub.[35]

On 25 August a 2/7th Battalion platoon outflanked an enemy position near Buirali Creek but was then fiercely counter-attacked. Win Howard was sent back to get permission to withdraw and 'when I returned Japs had bought up a Woodpecker and were really belting us'.[36] Two Bren gunners, Private Bernie Finn and Private Wal Bayliss, covered the platoon's move back across Buirali Creek. As the men pulled back, Bayliss told them, 'I am old, I can die. It is better that I die than the company complete.' Although down to their last dozen rounds, Finn and Bayliss also made it out, leaving forty-nine enemy dead behind them.[37]

The third 29th Brigade battalion, the 47th, had landed at Nassau Bay on 10 August, then marched north to Tambu Bay. It arrived at Komiatum on 23 August and took over the 2/5th Battalion positions. The battalion commander was Lieutenant-Colonel Ken 'Monty' Montgomery, considered a bit of a larrikin by his men but also a stern disciplinarian. One of his men noted, 'He was the boss. If he said something, do it.' On 25 August the 29th Brigade commander, Brigadier Monaghan, met with Warfe and Montgomery. Warfe noted that the command post was under fire from Kunai Spur with 'bullets chopping the bamboos about four feet over our heads'. Montgomery's battalion was ordered to take over the forward positions at Kunai Spur now renamed Lewis Knoll after the forward company commander, Captain Eric Lewis. A patrol under Lieutenant Len Barnett soon contacted the first enemy bunker position. Unable to fire at it from ground level, Reg Domin stood up to allow his Bren gunner, Tom Tobin, to balance the gun on his shoulder, in effect acting as a bipod. Tobin fired four magazines into the bunker embrasure to knock out the enemy position before the crossfire from two more bunkers forced Barnett's men back. An enemy counter-attack killed two men that night while another two were killed during a night patrol.[38]

Following another two days of intense patrolling, A Company attacked at dusk on 28 August with Sergeant George Pitt's 9 Platoon on the left and Barnett's 7 Platoon on the right. There was hand-to-hand fighting for one position, and Barnett was twice wounded as his men were again forced back. On the left flank Pitt's platoon met heavy machine-gun fire from well-dug-in log bunkers and was also forced to withdraw with two men killed and another wounded.[39] On 30 August C Company had a go but was also forced back by the heavy fire, Major Idris Leach and Sergeant Bill Eisenmenger being killed and four others wounded. The loss of Leach was especially tragic; he had five children. Leach had served under Hammer with the 2/48th Battalion in the Middle East but had been allowed to return to Australia to train militia units and had been transferred to C Company from HQ Company only that day 'to give it a kick along'. As Hammer later observed, 'The willing horse usually cops the lot in war.'[40]

In the end, the required kick came from the artillery with 200 rounds being fired on to the enemy position the next day. An even greater weight of fire was brought down on 1 September and, after five hours of shelling, two platoons attacked. Vickers gun support fire was also used for the last few minutes, firing across the crest of the ridge above the climbing men. The machine-gun officer, Lieutenant Doug Griffith, counted down the last ten seconds of the firing over the phone line to Captain Lewis before calling, 'OUT!' Griffith noted that 'on that instant the attacking force came over the edge of the ridge'. During the attack the lead platoon commander, Lieutenant Ernest Anzac Walters, as the inscription on his grave notes, 'gave his life for Australia'. The objective was gained by late afternoon with many enemy defenders fleeing their positions, leaving others to be dealt with by Owen gun and grenade. Some died by their own hand, as Captain Lewis later noted: 'Several underground explosions were heard and felt, indicating that a few who had "got away alive" were taking the easy way out.' Japanese losses were sixty-two men, many of them from the devastating barrage.[41]

Meanwhile, to the east, the 42nd Battalion confronted Charlie Hill, protected by a steep gorge across the southern approach. As with Davidson Ridge, it had been named after the battalion commander. One of the men later noted, 'On the map it had no name; to the boys it was Charlie Hill.' At this stage of the campaign the priority was to pin Japanese defenders in place where they were found, and they were well ensconced on Charlie Hill, part of the inner defence perimeter for Salamaua. Papuan Infantry Battalion patrols had already discovered that the enemy troops were busy digging in on the position and, at dusk on 24 August, Captain Arthur Jenks' D Company had moved part way up the hill and dug in on a narrow ledge just below the Japanese positions. Next morning the first 42nd Battalion patrols moved towards the top of the hill. Two men were soon killed and another two wounded without any idea of where the enemy fire was coming from. Jenks called for artillery support, and Captain Lloyd McElroy directed the shellfire in from Tambu Bay. When Captain Jenks' company again moved forward, more men were killed without seeing the well-camouflaged enemy positions. Water was limited to one bottle per man per day and had to be brought up from the creek, a half-hour trip down but a two-hour climb back up. Jenks' company was 'fighting on biscuits'.[42]

To take the pressure off Jenks, the battalion second in command, Major Charles Crosswell, had been sent out on 27 August with A and C Companies to get around Charlie Hill. The men scrambled along the steep side of Charlie Hill between two enemy positions before mortar fire sent them to ground. More men were wounded as they lay down and tried to dig in, while those who stood up attracted sniper and light machine-gun fire in the limited area. As the battalion historian noted, 'The two companies were stacked together like the proverbial sardines.' Moving east along a creek, C Company had to divert up a spur to avoid the artillery fire, dropping short on its way to the crest. Patrols continued the next day, one of them making contact with the Americans to the east. The Japanese command considered Charlie's Hill to be impregnable

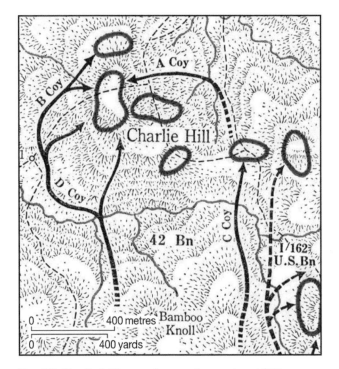

Map 30 Charlie Hill area, August–September 1943

and had even withdrawn some troops on 27 August to recapture another key defence position at Arnold's Crest, across the Francisco River.[43]

Although Colonel Davidson and Brigadier Monaghan now agreed that Charlie Hill could not be taken front on, General Milford, who had a penchant for artillery, insisted it could if enough support fire was laid on. That morning, Brigadier Monaghan rang Davidson and said he could not overestimate the importance of taking Charlie Hill. Davidson passed the imperative on to Captain Jenks, who advised he would use one platoon to attack, another to mop up and the third platoon for fire support. A platoon from B Company would take over Jenks' current position and another platoon would carry ammunition forward following the attack. One of Jenks' men later noted, 'They knew it was going to be tough; the hill was back-breakingly steep, the jungle and vines so thick, the Japanese so hard to see. The artillery might blast a path for them. They hoped so.' At 1130 on 29 August, the US 105mm howitzers opened up with 2000 rounds, followed by 3-inch mortar and Vickers machine-gun support from Mortar Knoll.[44]

When the support fire ceased, Captain Jenks told his men, 'It's time to go up, lads.' Lieutenant Bernard Garland's 17 Platoon led the attack, and three men were wounded as the lead section moved slowly up the narrow main spur, which had steep gorges on both sides. Jenks reported, 'Hill steep as side of house and covered with fern and vines.' It was the perfect defensive position, and every move forward was met by fire from above. Bernard Garland's men were at the bottom of a fern-covered clearing 50 metres long, which rose steeply up to the Japanese positions. At least four well-camouflaged light machine-guns covered the Australian advance. With Garland's platoon held up, a second platoon tried to work around the flanks, but the way was too steep and the Australians were still pinned down on the ridge at 1730. With the forward section unable to move forward or back, Garland opened fire to draw attention, thus allowing the other men to scramble down the hill, followed by the gallant Garland. Davidson ordered Jenks' men back to their former perimeter for a night of rain and little sleep.[45]

To reduce pressure on the D Company attack, Crosswell had been ordered to make a support attack with one of his platoons from the eastern flank. Lieutenant Paul Steinheuer's platoon made the attack but was held up by the artillery support fire as it moved up Charlie Hill. The men almost reached the crest when they noticed occupied enemy bunkers so they moved around the hill to the west, trying in vain to contact D Company. Meanwhile, Lieutenant Roy Winter's 14 Platoon was to cut off the Japanese supply track that supposedly ran from Charlie Hill east to Egg Knoll, then on to Scout Ridge. As Winter's platoon advanced towards the track junction, Len Hoare and Norm Mortleman were killed, and a later attack by Winter, supported by Lieutenant John Ramm's 13 Platoon, was recalled at dusk. As Crosswell observed, 'The Japanese positions were difficult and well defended.' The C Company commander, Captain Rod Cole, and five other men were wounded by two grenades inside the perimeter at dusk. Cole had to move back to have his leg wound treated, and Lieutenant Merv Andersen took over the company. The brigade major later ordered both A and C Companies to move forward with 'utmost aggression'.[46]

With Jenks deadlocked just below the top of Charlie Hill and Crosswell struggling on the eastern side, Captain Frank Greer's B Company moved off on 1 September around the west side of Charlie Hill, intending to cut off the Japanese supply line. Davidson had told Greer, 'I want you to go around the other side of Charlie Hill and sit on the Nips' *kai* [food] line.' Greer's company crossed the creek and later established a perimeter

Photo 41 View north-east to Charlie Hill. (Phillip Bradley)

for the night, having not encountered any enemy troops during the day. Next day Greer's company crossed two spurs and found a well-used track 200–300 metres from the crest of Charlie Hill. An ambush position was set up, later killing two enemy soldiers.[47] Next morning the company was attacked by two small enemy parties from east and west. Four enemy soldiers were killed and another two wounded, who were later found and shot. In the late afternoon a second ambush was established on another track a hundred metres further east. The Japanese soon responded with more attacks, this time supported by machine-gun fire from the crest of Charlie Hill. Greer's men held despite continuing harassing fire from the Juki machine-gun on Charlie Hill.

Also on 2 September A Company, after a difficult day struggling through the thick undergrowth on the east side of Charlie Hill, reached a saddle where another access track was located. The company established an ambush position, and the next morning, when two enemy soldiers approached from Charlie Hill, one was killed. Soon after, another four soldiers approached from Salamaua and two more were killed. After an unsuccessful enemy counter-attack at midday, A Company moved west to try to contact B Company and thus seal off Charlie Hill. The next day Lieutenant Fred Birch's 8 Platoon led out and, despite striking some opposition along the supply track, contacted B Company outposts soon thereafter. It was decided that A Company would remain to the east of the track, complementing B Company to the west.[48] Meanwhile enemy troops had occupied the vacated A Company position, and Charles Barker was killed as he moved forward with a supply party. An A Company platoon was sent back to hold the position.

The morning of 4 September brought a major change to the strategic situation at Salamaua. At dawn the Australians on the ridges observed warships in Huon Gulf, part of an Allied invasion force destined to land on the coast east of Lae. However, the purpose of the fighting around Salamaua – to hold the enemy in place – became even more important with the critical battle now taking place at Lae. Already Nakano had been ordered to return to Lae, and some of his front-line troops accompanied him on barges from Salamaua on the night of 4–5 September.

Lieutenant Genkichi Usui was the commander of a company from I/66th Battalion charged with the defence of Charlie Hill, along with Lieutenant Shigeru Namura's company. On 5 September he reported to his battalion commander, Captain Masamitsu Numada, that the telephone line had been cut the previous afternoon and, when he had sent out linesmen that morning to fix it, the Australians prevented it. Usui now had to rely on runners, but of two runners sent back to Numada the previous night, one was missing and one had returned without getting through. Usui had plans to cut the Australian supply line at the rear of Charlie Hill that day, once reinforcements had arrived. If the wind was favourable Usui also planned to light fires that would burn towards the Australian positions, thus forcing them out.[49]

The Japanese NCO who was carrying the maps and documents from Usui did not reach his commander that morning because he was killed at the A Company ambush astride the main track down the hill. However, soon after, a party of fifteen Japanese troops carrying supplies up to Charlie Hill managed to pass the A Company positions; the two companies ensconced behind Charlie Hill had left gaps and confusion. This was confirmed when a party from A Company was mistaken for Japanese and fired on by B Company, wounding two men including Major James Ross, the company commander. It was not until mid-afternoon that A Company finally took up the correct position to block the Japanese supply tracks.

Photo 42 The entrance to the Japanese command post in the Komiatum Ridge area. Photo by Harold Dick. (AWM 015678)

The Japanese could also set ambushes, and the extended B Company supply line around the west side of Charlie Hill offered a perfect opportunity. At 1300 an accompanying native Papuan Infantry Battalion soldier escorting the supply line turned and whispered to the supply line leader, Private Glenn Cousins, 'Japan man ahead.' The Japanese ambush position was cleverly positioned on a higher ledge overlooking the supply route and would need to be bypassed while a platoon from Jenks' company was brought up to clear the site. Sergeant Merv Blow led the supply line around the ambush position to the west but returned to the main track too soon and was fired on. The native carriers dropped their loads and ran off downhill, and no supplies got through to B Company that day. Brigadier Monaghan, who was forward with Greer's company taking in the views to Salamaua, was also cut off from his headquarters.[50]

The next day, 5 September, 18 Platoon, having had to work forward by sound in the thick kunai grass and bracken, made slow progress against the higher Japanese ambush position and finally gave up in the late afternoon. Meanwhile 8 Platoon, coming from the other end of the track, also had difficulties, coming under heavy fire and losing one man, Arthur Sherlock. However, the supplies had been lifted and, after a wide deviation, finally delivered to B Company early that afternoon. Usui's ambush plan had been very successful, preventing supplies and Vickers guns getting through to the north and diverting two platoons from offensive operations against Charlie Hill.

Tit-for-tat cutting of supply lines continued the next day when B Company's 12 Platoon moved to cut the Japanese supply line but, at 1700, a kunai fire forced the platoon out. Another of Usui's plans had worked a treat. When 10 Platoon reoccupied the same position the following morning, 7 September, it was also burned out, and a fire break had to be cut around the new position. The platoon was then ordered to reoccupy the initial position before last light, but when the men tried the next day, the Japanese were already there. The platoon finally dug in on a knoll a hundred metres further west.[51]

The nature of the terrain meant that A Company was now underneath the path of the artillery rounds shelling targets further north in front of the 47th Battalion. That morning the men heard the distinct click as shells brushed the trees above them, but before the signaller could get the shelling stopped, a shell hit a larger branch and detonated, fatally wounding Jack Dalrymple. On 8 September, as 9 Platoon made plans to assault Charlie Hill on the following day, the Japanese beat them to it. That night Charlie Hill was evacuated. When Davidson's troops finally moved on to Charlie Hill they discovered that the enemy position had been set out over four perimeters, and parts of a 70mm mountain gun were found. Below ground, the Japanese had constructed an intricate tunnel system to protect the troops and supplies from the extensive bombardments. The entrance shaft was served by a vine-covered ladder that went down six metres. Galleries branched off the main tunnel like catacombs with benches cut into the side for sleeping and small rooms holding signal equipment, ammunition and stores. There was room for at least a company of men to shelter below ground.[52]

By 9 September such positions were no longer useful to the Japanese; the defenders to man them had been ordered out.

15

ACROSS THE FRISCO

Further afield, the 24th Battalion had been operating in the vast spaces north of the Francisco River, fanning out as far north as the Markham River and east to Huon Gulf. On 7 August the battalion commander, Lieutenant-Colonel George Smith, had been told by General Savige that recently captured documents indicated that a battalion of Japanese troops was being tied down in the Buang Valley by 24th Battalion patrols. As Savige stressed, 'The enemy is there and must be kept there.' Such operations were not without hazard. On the afternoon of 15 August the Japanese reported an ambush on a six-man Australian patrol at close range and claimed all killed. The Australians had sent two patrols out that day, six men moving along the north bank of the Buang River and another fifteen under Sergeant Wally Fox on the southern bank, heading for the river mouth to lay booby traps. Fox's men crossed three undefended barricades on the main track before being ambushed as they tried going around a fourth, set up between the river and a steep cliff. Fox was killed and Lieutenant Alan Saunders fatally wounded while Private 'Pop' McKenzie was wounded in the thigh. Trevor Russell and Sam Manning stayed with McKenzie until they were all found the next morning. The rest of the men pulled back before Harry Paxino and Jack Hourigan returned to get Lieutenant Saunders under cover, staying with him until he died around dusk.[1]

On 12 August Warfe assumed command of the 58/59th Battalion from Starr. Hammer had been pressing Savige to relieve Starr for some time but, in his uniquely considerate manner, Savige maintained his respect for Starr's previous military record and had the burnt-out colonel replaced on medical grounds. Savige had 'a desire to see justice done to a man who rendered good service in the field in the past'.[2] Warfe made an immediate impression, later noting, 'When I took over from Starr, two companies in the Erskine Creek area had not been supplied with a hot meal for seven days.' Warfe arranged for the men to get two hot meals a day and also set up a rest camp for them behind the front line. Concerned at the problem of accidents that had bedevilled his previous command, he also had grenade booby traps replaced by harmless rattle traps.[3]

Hammer now ordered that the Komiatum Track be occupied at its junction with the Bobdubi-to-Salamaua track. The initial objective was to cut the Japanese supply route on to Bobdubi Ridge then, if possible, reach the Komiatum Track junction. This would interdict the vital Japanese supply line up Komiatum Ridge that enabled Goodview Junction and Mount Tambu to be held. It would also divert Japanese resources from the 17th Brigade action further up Komiatum Ridge, designed to also cut that supply line. The 2/7th Battalion and the 2/3rd Independent Company would furnish the men for Hammer's operation.

On 14 August, forty-seven men from the 2/3rd's A Platoon reached the junction of Stevens Track with the main track from Bobdubi to Salamaua, cut the enemy signal wire and set up an ambush position. Four enemy parties were ambushed that afternoon and another early the next morning. The Japanese finally reacted when thirty men attacked the ambush position, but were driven off with the help of mortar support, leaving four dead behind.[4]

Up on Bobdubi Ridge Captain Hancock indicated targets to the Vickers gun, mortar and artillery observers for attention before the attack. Unfortunately, air support had to be cancelled due to a major USAAF operation against Wewak designed to neutralise much of the Japanese air power there.[5] Captain John Winterflood's B Platoon moved off Bobdubi Ridge down to the Francisco River where they joined Lieutenant John Lewin's A Platoon, a hundred men in all. The sixty-six men from Captain Vic Baird's D Company moved with them; zero hour for the attack was 1130, following the preparatory barrage.

The plan was for the two commando platoons to attack first, then for Baird's infantry company to pass through and occupy the important track junction where the Komiatum Track left the track from Salamaua to Bobdubi. However, the thick belt of jungle that ran across the line of advance would channel any attack along the main Salamaua track. Due

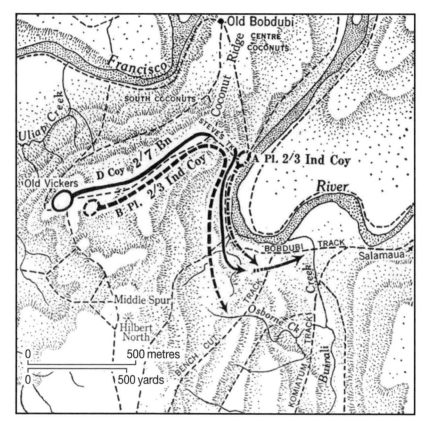

Map 31 Junction of Bench Cut and Bobdubi Tracks, 17–18 August 1943

to the close nature of the country, two men had already been wounded when a reconnaissance patrol stumbled across Japanese positions.[6]

At dawn on 17 August the Australians attacked south from their positions below the eastern side of the ridge. Lewin's A Platoon was on the left following close behind the support fire and soon contacted enemy bunkers running along Buirali Creek, astride the main Salamaua track.[7] Five men, including Lieutenant Jack Barry, were killed and eleven men wounded, one of whom would later die. One of the men killed was 21-year-old Private Cyril Robb, who had been with the platoon since the landing at Wau more than six months earlier. A few weeks earlier he had written to his family in Lismore, saying, 'Owing to matters going wrong a little up here it is going to delay the homecoming a little or I hope it is only a little.' His mother received the letter three days after his death.[8] Up

Photo 43 Looking north down Buirali Creek to the Francisco River junction. (Phillip Bradley)

on the ridge, Hancock could hear the fire fight: 'The din was absolutely terrific, masses of lead flying about and in such an enclosed area, it was a nightmare.'[9]

At 1145 Winterflood's B Platoon contacted enemy positions on the right flank at the foot of Hilbert's Spur, along which the Japanese supplied Bobdubi Ridge. However, Winterflood's men were soon surrounded by a strong enemy force coming down the spur from the west. Norm Bear, who was with 4 Section, was moving through the dense undergrowth when he was shot in the right arm. Alongside him big Len Thomas was also hit, fatally. Thomas, a former Aussie Rules footballer, had been wounded earlier in the campaign and had only just come back to the company. Private Bert Nordin from 5 Section was also killed before Winterflood's men pulled back to the next spur to the north. As Cliff Crossley later noted, the river flats were 'a bewildering tangle of marshy stinking jungle – visibility five yards, until . . . terrific small arms fire literally cut a clearing'.[10]

Major Picken ordered Lieutenant Percy Thomas's 16 Platoon, with Lieutenant Stan Jeffery's 2/3rd Engineer Section attached, to move between the two commando platoons. Having found the gap in the enemy line 150 metres to the right of Lewin's position, Jeffery and Thomas reached a Japanese staging camp without encountering any opposition. There the two groups split. Jeffery's section pushed on to the south before turning east, cutting an enemy signal wire on the way. The section then came to a clearing where they came under heavy fire from a machine-gun bunker about 70 metres away, covering the track junction up to Bobdubi Ridge. Although there was not a single bush between the now-prone men and the enemy machine-gun bunker, the headstrong Jeffery gave the order to charge.

Before the section got half way to the gun position seven or eight men had been hit. The enemy machine-gunner knew his craft and had kept his aim low, cutting up the Australian attack. Then Jeffery was hit and went down, calling a halt to the suicidal charge, at which time the enemy machine-gun also stopped firing. Vin Maguire and Joe Wills had managed to get reasonably close before the order came to stop but were able to get back. The wounded men were also dragged back to shelter as dusk came. Five men, including Jeffery, had been badly wounded, and there was no chance that the five unwounded men could get them back to the main lines. Two other men were dead, one of them after being shot while helping to bring in Des Hughes, who had been hit in the legs. Maguire fired at the bunker as he withdrew and the machine-gun opened up again, hitting the man alongside Maguire. The section survivors then managed to get into some thicker cover, finding a crater-like depression to shelter in. They lay in a circle and stayed there all night, unsure of what to do.[11] For the 2/3rd Independent Company it had been the most tragic day of the war.

Meanwhile, Lieutenant Thomas had sent his runner, Bill Cowie, back to Baird to let him know that there had been casualties and that 16 Platoon was returning. However, Cowie spotted the Japanese moving in behind to set up an ambush and returned to Thomas to warn him. In the fading light, Thomas decided, 'Bugger it, we'll fight our way out.' As the platoon advanced, the men were met by a wall of fire in the darkness; Thomas was wounded in the thigh and Bill Clues hit in the jaw. However, both men, along with five others, got through in the dark and spent the night close to the ridge before reporting in the next morning.[12]

After some time Baird brought his remaining two platoons forward, and they took up positions at the western edge of the Japanese camp with the two commando platoons on either flank. Thomas's and Jeffery's men were still isolated out in front, somewhere amidst the dense undergrowth that covered the area. Next morning Baird sent Lieutenant Wallace Fleming out with a patrol to try to contact the missing men. Fleming did manage to locate some of Thomas's men in the undergrowth, but other men were still cut off by the enemy ambush positions. As they tried to move back, the Japanese began an attack all along the line: 'The noise of small arms and the thumping of thirty-six grenades grew to a roar as though the Jap were attempting to scare the troop out by an impressive demonstration of fire.' The Australian mortars and Vickers guns added their weight of fire, and the enemy attack was repulsed. The remainder of the isolated platoon, all of whom had been wounded, were finally contacted the following day.[13]

The survivors from the engineer section back in the scrub continued to die. During the night Peter Maher heard a sound and threw a grenade that hit a tree and rebounded, killing him. The youth and inexperience of some of the men was telling. As the Japanese searched for them in the undergrowth the next morning, two who had come too close were shot. In the afternoon Vin Maguire headed back with three others to try to get help and reached the 2/7th Battalion lines that evening.[14] Twelve men were still missing.

Next morning, Lieutenant Ron Garland led another patrol through the thick undergrowth looking for the missing men, guided by one of the returned sappers. He brought Garland to a wounded soldier, who was being sheltered by his mate. The enemy were close but the men kept quiet, particularly the wounded one, who was now lifted on to a stretcher. Carrying him out was difficult as it involved negotiating a bamboo clump where the stretcher got wedged between trees. The closeness of the enemy also meant they could not hack their way through so the wounded man had to get off the stretcher. He did so without a murmur, although he later died of his wounds. Other men were found sheltering in the bomb crater, with the wounded in the centre. Phil Mumford stayed with them while the others went back for medical help. The medical officer, Captain Fred Street, came up with the stretcher-bearers, but on their way back they tripped a booby trap, which wounded Mumford and Angus Torpey. More of the isolated men made their way back in the following days, among them Private James Fisher who, despite wounds to his abdomen, had endured.[15]

On 20 August Hammer issued his third plan in 24 hours, setting out the following tasks for his brigade: (1) make a firm base on the Komiatum Track; (2) capture Kunai Spur; (3) cut Salamaua Track; (4) capture the Salamaua–Komiatum–Bobdubi track junction; and (5) move north over

Francisco River and occupy high ground at Rough Hill–Savige Spur–Arnold's Crest.[16]

On the same day, as part of Hammer's drive, Baird's company attacked enemy positions astride the Buirali Creek junction but, as with the earlier operation, it foundered on the enemy bunker system. Four men were wounded, and mortar fire was called down. The Japanese defenders had also lost heavily, twenty-three bodies, including the commander of I/80th Battalion, Major Jinno, being found around the track junction. With the Komiatum Track now cut at Laver's Knoll by the 17th Brigade, the Japanese pulled back to positions further east at Charlie Hill and Kunai Spur that night. Dawn patrols the next day found the Komiatum Track abandoned, and Captain Cramp's A Company moved through Baird's company and attacked the new enemy position. By evening A Company had two platoons east of Buirali Creek. Eight men were wounded, including Lieutenant Roy Smith, mortally so.[17] However, the reduction of the new enemy positions at Kunai Spur and Charlie Hill would now be left to others. The main thrust of the 2/7th Battalion would be to the north, across the Francisco River.

General Savige thought that the pressure on the Japanese to defend Salamaua on the south bank would 'cause him to leave the back door open for an advance on the coast north of Salamaua which would isolate his troops'.[18] He was also trying to fulfil the main goal of the campaign: to drive the enemy north of the Francisco River. Moving his men across the river would certainly also stretch the enemy forces in front of Salamaua, forcing them to remain and perhaps drawing reinforcements from Lae.

On 21 August Lieutenant Henry Mallett's 11 Platoon from the 2/7th Battalion crossed the Francisco River at the south end of Bobdubi Ridge. The platoon moved up a razorback spur towards Rough Hill, where it was held up by enemy machine-gun fire. Another platoon was brought up by the company commander, Major Harry Dunkley and, by 1500, had taken the position, the weapon pits of which were only 12 hours old. Faced with a steeply rising approach along a razorback ridge, the tactics were designed to best utilise the terrain and the firepower. Three pairs of Bren gunners were used, with one on the crest and one to either side. Two pairs of Owen gunners advanced in support, using fire and movement, while the rest of the men passed the ammunition. The third B Company platoon protected the river crossing. That afternoon a composite platoon under Lieutenant Owen Edwards advanced further and occupied a dominant hill feature without opposition. Early the next morning, C Company moved

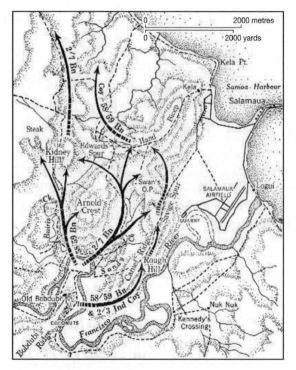

Map 32 15th Brigade operations, 26 August –
10 September 1943

up to reinforce the position, now named Arnold's Crest after Captain Ted
Arnold, the C Company commander.[19]

As the last major features in front of Kela Ridge, the loss of Rough Hill
or Arnold's Crest would unhinge the Japanese defence plans. However,
the wonderful opportunity offered by their capture would, for strategic
reasons, be refused. The next day Savige sent a message to Hammer
explaining: 'Situation most satisfactory but on no account undertake any
operation which may influence the enemy to evacuate Salamaua.'[20] The
cat was now very much out of the bag, the rationale for the Salamaua
operations now clear. But for Hammer and the men of the 2/7th Battalion,
poised to strike at Kela Ridge and thus render Salamaua untenable, it must
have been heartbreaking.

With Hammer switching his attention to the north, Brigadier Monaghan's 29th Brigade took over operations south of the Francisco River.
It was around this time that an edgy rivalry developed between Hammer
and Monaghan. Hammer later noted how Monaghan had telephoned

Photo 44 Aerial view north over Bobdubi
Ridge and across the Francisco River bend
to Arnold's Crest. (AWM 128385)

him after the 29th Brigade had moved into the front line south of the
Francisco River. He had apparently told an astonished Hammer, 'Don't
worry, Hammer, you can relax. Leave the battle to us and we will clean it
up for you!'[21] Major Travers observed, 'There began a race between Hammer and Monaghan to see who could reach Salamaua first.' In response,
Hammer told Monaghan that he 'had come in at the death knock'. As
Travers noted, 'There was great jealousy between them.'[22]

Relieved of his south bank duties, Hammer was now able to reinforce his north bank lodgement, then wait for the enemy to react and
join battle. He needed to hold the Japanese in place. On the morning of
22 August Captain Charles Newman's C Company from the 58/59th
crossed the Francisco River and occupied the Sandy Creek and Buiris
Creek junctions unopposed. That afternoon Arnold's company grabbed
another feature north of Arnold's Crest, stretching the line. Captain
Baird's 2/7th company crossed late in the afternoon and, when they

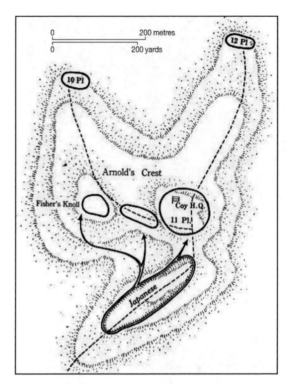

Map 33 Arnold's Crest, 27 August 1943

advanced the next morning, struck sixty enemy troops who were coming down Sandy Creek to attack Newman's lodgement. Hammer also
deployed Lieutenant Clyde Egan's platoon from the 24th Battalion into
the Rough Hill area, where it patrolled to the east and broke up another
enemy patrol.

Hammer moved more men across the river. On the morning of
26 August the 58/59th's A Company crossed over and proceeded to
Camel Ridge while Lieutenant John Bethune's B Company crossed at
the Buiris Creek junction and moved up to Arnold's Crest to take over its
defence. Captain Cramp's A Company also finally crossed the Francisco
to join the rest of the 2/7th Battalion. Although he now had most of his
brigade across the river, Hammer clearly considered that progress was
difficult and in a message to Savige he confided, 'Must admire Jap resistance this area.'[23]

On the morning of 23 August, the Japanese had reported that 150
Australians were at Hyotan Yama, as the Japanese called Arnold's Crest.

Nakano ordered a counter-attack, and 420 men from three battalions struck on 27 August.[24] That morning Private Dick Schultz observed enemy movement a hundred metres south of Arnold's Crest, and the signal wire back to battalion headquarters was cut. A five-man patrol sent to the south was heavily engaged, and Eric 'Snowy' Hanel was mortally wounded by a grenade burst. When three other men dashed out to help extricate the patrol, one of them, Les Parry, who had joined the battalion only that day, was hit by a burst of machine-gun fire and also killed.[25] Arnold's Crest was cut off.

At 1125 a patrol from the south tried to break through to Bethune's isolated company but was stopped by a strong enemy ambush astride the track. Contact was finally made via a runner; the company was practically surrounded and almost out of ammunition. Two other 2/7th Battalion patrols sent out to contact Bethune were also ambushed, and five of the eight men in one of them were wounded, James Walters mortally so. Private Stan Blythe was with Baird's D Company bringing forward ammunition when he noticed enemy forces gathering on a spur near the forward platoon and, using a grenade discharger, he put down accurate fire. This, together with mortar fire well directed by Sergeant Basil Sinclair, helped to break up the enemy concentrations. The Japanese had a strong ring around Bethune's company. That night Picken watched from Bobdubi Ridge as his 2/7th Battalion companies fired off flares in sequence so that he could determine exactly where they now were.[26]

With his company down to thirty-four men, John Bethune would need every one of them to hold Arnold's Crest. The company cook, Corporal Max Fisher, led a five-man section that captured a dominant knoll on the western flank, now known as Fisher's Knoll. Bethune's men held a Japanese attack from the south and also took a toll on enemy parties trying to move around the northern perimeter. With pressure building on all sides and serious ammunition concerns, a five-man party under Corporal Bill Webster was sent west to contact battalion headquarters. At dusk the two outlying platoons were then pulled back to a final redoubt around Bethune's headquarters and Fisher's Knoll, with a section being deployed along the connecting saddle. That night enemy troops could be heard gathering to the south: 'Led by a cheer leader, they squawked and carried on well into the night.'[27]

At dawn on the next morning of 28 August the Japanese attacked, from east, south and west, advancing with fixed bayonets and using separate grenade-throwing parties. The heavy machine-gun support was accompanied by the standard yelling and screaming, but Bethune's gallant band drove the attackers off, leaving 40 dead behind. By drawing in his two out-lying platoons, Bethune had given himself a chance to hold the position, but another violent thrust from the east now broke into the Australian perimeter. With ammunition rapidly running out, and with four men dead and another six wounded, Bethune withdrew from Arnold's Crest. With Lieutenant Les Marsh and Murray Hicks acting as the rearguard, the company moved north-east away from the main lines of attack. Although this also put Bethune's men further away from the main Australian lines, they had successfully broken contact by 0700. Bethune then moved his men north-west along a creek line before turning due west along the 00 grid line to Buiris Creek and reaching battalion headquarters the following morning.[28] The Australians knew from captured documents that Arnold's Crest was an important part of the Japanese defence system around Sala-maua, so the reaction to its capture was not unexpected. The Japanese would now hold the eastern side of Hyotan Yama (Arnold's Crest) and Hohei Yama (Kela Ridge) until their withdrawal on 11 September.[29]

Seemingly blinded to the realities of the situation, Hammer had sig-nalled his new divisional commander, General Milford, that 'unreliability of 58/59 Bn [troops] has forced me to withdraw to hold a tighter line Buiris Ck'. Almost surrounded by a company of enemy troops, down to less than thirty men, with wounded to carry out and nearly out of ammu-nition, Bethune's company had, on the contrary, shown extraordinary reliability. One of the other company commanders, Newman, noted that Hammer 'had weak companies flung out into the blue where they could not be reinforced or supplied'. After some reflection, Hammer later signed off a recommendation to award John Bethune a Military Cross in which he wrote, 'Displaying grit and determination Lt Bethune tenaciously held the area until shortage of amn [ammunition] and supplies forced him to withdraw.'[30]

Lieutenant Garland's section from C Platoon had been sent up to help the 2/7th Battalion by infiltrating the rear of the Japanese position to carry out an ambush. However, penetrating the Japanese lines proved difficult until Bob Silva and Norm Buglar found a way through on 2 September. The route went along Buiris Creek where the creekbed was blocked only by barbed wire but not covered by the defenders on the ridges on either side. Silva and Buglar then pressed on and found a suitable ambush site along a well-used track that carried an enemy signal wire alongside it. They returned after dark.[31]

Photo 45 Decorated men from the 58/59th Battalion's Salamaua campaign (left to right): Ray Duncanson, Alex Anderson, Laurie Proby, John Bethune, Gordon Ayre and Charles Newman. (AWM 063147)

Garland arranged to have Arnold's Crest shelled the next morning to keep enemy heads down and to drown out any noise while his men infiltrated. Leaving at 0900, the thirteen-man section moved along the creek between the Japanese positions and established an ambush along their supply track by 1100, at which time the shelling stopped. Garland observed: 'My men made their way forward through the jungle canopy like deadly green ghosts. I never heard a sound as they moved forward and adopted their ambush positions.' Garland positioned his men on the southern side of the track with around ten metres between them, covering more than a thousand metres of track, watching while hiding; a difficult balance. Garland noted: 'You soon learn to look through the jungle, by slightly moving your head from side to side, whilst preserving your concealment.'[32]

After two hours of waiting, the signal came from the left flank at 1300 that an enemy party of twelve was approaching from Arnold's Crest. In the centre of the line, Garland watched the enemy troops move across in front of him, oblivious of the danger: 'They were so close they looked

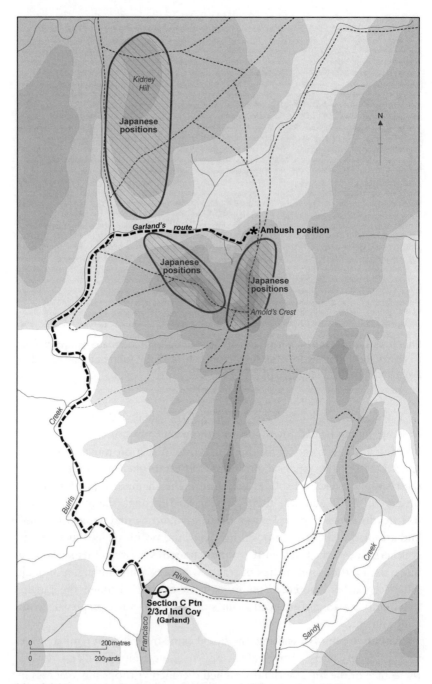

Map 34 Lieutenant Garland's ambush patrol, 3 September 1943

huge. They looked tired and dejected . . . They were about five yards apart
and their heads were down.' The first shot would come from the Bren gun
on the right flank, ensuring that as many troops as possible would be in
the ambush zone at the time. At the first sound of the Bren firing down
the track, the other men opened up, already tracking their targets; the
ambush killed eight of them. Garland's men now switched their attention
to Arnold's Crest, opening fire on the position to keep the troops there in
place. They then scrambled off through the jungle to a rendezvous point
before carefully exiting the enemy lines using the same route along the
creek as they had used on the way in.[33]

As in the other sectors, the observation post on Old Vickers reported
considerable barge activity in Huon Gulf on the morning of 4 September:
the Lae invasion force carrying the Australian 9th Division.

Despite the Lae landing, the Japanese continued to fight for the positions north of the Francisco River and now added considerable artillery
support, firing off the remaining rounds. However, the ammunition was
faulty; the 2/7th Battalion reported that only six of thirty rounds exploded
while less than half the fifty-eight shells fired at the 58/59th exploded.
Lieutenant Roy Dawson, the Australian artillery forward observation
officer, had now joined the 58/59th Battalion and, on the early morning
of 5 September, he directed the Allied artillery fire on to Rough Hill.
Then a fighting patrol moved to within 200 metres of the crest where a
bunker atop a steep cliff stymied any further approach. Another fighting
patrol, from Lieutenant Bob Lane's 7 Platoon, was fired on by a pillbox
and weapon pits that covered the only feasible approach track to Rough
Hill. Any attack on the hill was going to be a very difficult affair. On
8 September Lieutenant Bowers, a US interpreter attached to 5th Division, moved up into no man's land and occupied an abandoned weapon
pit to broadcast to the enemy up on Rough Hill. He told them that they
had been left to die by their commanders, who had already abandoned
Salamaua. He also mentioned that Lae had been surrounded and that
they could safely surrender by coming forward in twos or threes with
arms raised. It was stressed that no names would be forwarded to Tokyo
and thus no disgrace attached. Although the enemy troops listened and
did not open fire, there were no takers for Bowers' offer.[34]

The 2/3rd Independent Company had also moved on to Rough Hill.
On 10 September Lewin's A Platoon moved up Savige Spur, to the north
of Rough Hill. The platoon attacked from the south-east and killed three

enemy soldiers, drove other defenders from their bunkers and established a defensive position near the top of the hill. That same morning the 58/59th Battalion attacked Rough Hill. Following artillery support, each platoon – Bob Lane's 7th, Ted Griff's 8th and Arthur O'Rourke's 9th – advanced up a separate spur, with Lewin's commandos on a fourth, but all approaches failed. However, later that morning, 170 enemy troops were seen moving back towards Salamaua, and the next morning another attack finally broke through and Rough Hill was taken, the formidable defences being abandoned during the night.[35]

Meanwhile, Major Harold Dunkley led thirty-three men from the 2/7th's B Company out towards Kela Ridge. The men waded up Sandy Creek to keep out of sight of the enemy positions and, late in the afternoon of 10 September, moved on to an open kunai knoll to bivouac for the night. The next morning Dunkley took over at the head of the patrol and followed an enemy track across a series of open knolls below Kela Ridge, heading for Salamaua. As the men reached a kunai patch on one of the knolls, fire broke out and the company went to ground. However, the position was without cover, and the Japanese mortars, grenades and machine-gun fire lashed the exposed Australians. Five men were killed and another eight wounded, including Dunkley, who was shot in the chest.[36] They were the first deaths in the battalion since 31 August and would also be among the last. Salamaua was about to fall.

CHAPTER | 16

SALAMAUA FALLS

General Milford's 5th Division was advancing on Salamaua on three fronts, the third of which was the coastal route along Scout Ridge. On 30 August Milford moved Lieutenant-Colonel Jack Amies's 15th Battalion on to the coastal flank of the American 162nd Regiment with orders that 'the crest of Scout Ridge must be secured at all cost and with least possible delay'. Captain Don Provan's D Company moved across Roosevelt Ridge that night.[1]

This use of the 15th Battalion was much to the chagrin of the 29th Brigade's commander, Brigadier Monaghan, as the 15th was one of his three battalions but it had been retained under the direct control of 5th Division. Milford later noted, 'I could not commit the 15 Bn anywhere west of Scout Ridge because they could not be supplied', but this caused Monaghan to 'go off the deep end'.[2]

The service numbers of Lieutenant Doug Matthew and his brother George were consecutive; they had joined up together. Having served with the 2/5th Battalion in the Middle East, both men had been commissioned and transferred to the 15th Battalion and both now commanded a platoon, George with 14 Platoon and Doug 18 Platoon. Early on 31 August Doug Matthew led his platoon up the precipitous slopes to the kunai-clad Bamboos position, a separate feature from that on Davidson Ridge. This was the position where D and E Ridges intersected just before joining Scout Ridge. Once there, Matthew's men were stopped from moving further by mortar and machine-gun fire from Scout Ridge, which overlooked

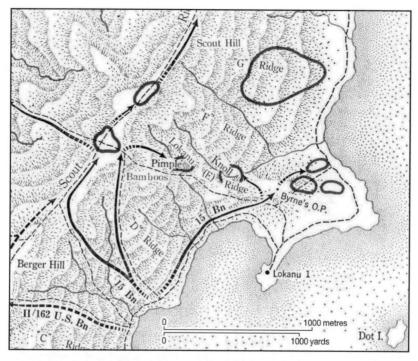

Map 35 Scout Ridge area, August–September 1943

and dominated the position. Without support, and faced by more precipitous slopes, 18 Platoon managed to advance another 75 metres before
being halted by grenades from the ridge above.[3]

Captain Provan came up to organise another attack at 1300, although
still without artillery or mortar support and limited by the terrain, which
meant that only one platoon could be deployed. Again Doug Matthew
led 18 Platoon forward, and eleven men were wounded in this attack, the
courageous Matthew among them. Matthew had been shot in the leg, and
men from his brother's platoon helped carry him back to the aid post at
Dot Inlet. He told his brother George on the way out, 'About six weeks,
I think.' George figured that all would be OK, later recalling, 'I didn't
worry too much about it. I thought one of the family has got out of it.'
Doug Matthew died the next day.[4]

Captain Percy Proctor's C Company now moved up in support. Provan
attacked again the next day, 1 September, with Lieutenant Laurie Best's
platoon leading. Another twenty-one men were wounded, including Proc-
ter, his second in command, Captain Alan Struss and two of his platoon

Photo 46 Aerial view down the coast south of Salamaua.
(AWM 128382)

commanders, Best and Ken Rattray. The remaining officer in the company, Lieutenant Les Thirgood, clung to the precarious lodgement gained
by Matthew's men while the mortar platoon sergeant, Maurice Whitlam,
came right up to the edge of the enemy position to provide what support he
could. He registered mortar rounds that helped the Australians hold three
Japanese counter-attacks throughout a desperate day. Although wounded
himself, one of the stretcher-bearers, Ervine Sallaway, attended to the
growing list of casualties throughout the action.[5]

On 2 and 3 September artillery and mortar shelling continued on Scout Ridge before George Matthew's 14 Platoon tried to gain the crest for which George's brother had died. Again the strong defence and limited approach stymied the Australians. When the Japanese finally withdrew it became apparent that the original position was on a false crest and that the true crest was 200 metres further back and even higher. Heavy mortar and artillery fire was brought down on the Japanese positions along the crest and, on 3 September, a recce patrol reported that the crest was clear. Two B Company platoons moved up to occupy it, but the Japanese counter-attacked before they could do so. The Australians were up against Japanese marines from Commander Takeuchi's 5th Sasebo SNLP, tough fighters who would not give an inch.[6] As General Milford later said, the Japanese 'had no initiative but were not frightened to die'.[7]

Amies now turned his attention to Lokanu Ridge, which dominated the right flank at the eastern end of E Ridge. On 3 September Lieutenant Tom Cavenagh, the A Company commander, ordered Lieutenant Les Byrne's platoon to grab the eastern end of Lokanu Ridge. Byrne was a former artillery officer with no infantry experience, yet he would be awarded a Military Cross for that day's action. He took both 2/6th Battalion scouts, Arthur Dehne and Allan Rose, with him as well as Frank Kane. The two 2/6th Battalion privates were from a group of men who had remained in the front line to foster the inexperienced 15th Battalion platoons after their own battalion had been relieved. One 2/6th man was attached to each section. The patrol made contact with the Japanese and knocked out a bunker containing three enemy marines. Under cover of artillery fire Byrne managed to creep up close to the unoccupied positions on the crest and capture them. Byrne then sent Kane back to bring up the rest of his platoon.[8]

On the night of 3 September enemy barges were heard entering the bay to the north on three occasions, and next morning newly dug enemy positions were found on the northern side of Lokanu Knoll. Two enemy guns were also located, in a valley 500 metres north of Byrne's OP and firing across the ridge towards Tambu Bay. Private Keith Ross, another of the attached 2/6th Battalion men, was able to use the land line to connect with the US artillery for counter-fire. They got one gun that day while the enemy gunners hurriedly pulled a camouflage net over the other.[9]

On 4 September the fighting around Salamaua became strictly secondary as the Allied amphibious forces landed east of Lae. In a letter written on 7 September following the successful landing, Herring wrote that 'the

Salamaua show has drawn down quite a number of the enemy's reinforcements as we hoped it would'. In the end Nassau Bay had not been used as a staging point for the smaller landing craft that had originally been detailed for the Lae landing. For some time the idea had been growing that such vessels would not be sufficient for the operation. However, there were difficulties with MacArthur who wanted to control his own amphibious force, independent from the navy. The broaching of the boats during the Nassau Bay landing had helped the Australian command to persuade a stubborn MacArthur that the navy must be brought in. As Herring later said, 'With disaster to small boats on 30 June and time lag it became obvious that the bigger boats would be better . . . using Nassau Bay as launching pad for Lae with little ships would have been hazardous and would have lost us every element of surprise.'[10] The rationale for the American landing at Nassau Bay had been shown to be a false one, but by making that error a potentially catastrophic landing at Lae had been averted.

Despite Lae now being the main objective, the Australians kept the pressure on at Salamaua, wanting to hold the Japanese troops there. On the afternoon of 5 September 12 Platoon, from Lieutenant Albert Farley's company, attacked the Pimple, a prominent feature near the middle of E Ridge. It was a razorback approach along the ridge from the Bamboos, on a three-man front with no possibility of a flank move, and three well-placed enemy light machine-guns quickly brought the attack to a halt. One Bren gunner and one Owen gunner were killed and the section commander and one other were wounded in the attempt. It was reported that the Japanese had used some captured Australian grenades with great effect.[11]

Meanwhile, Lieutenant Byrne's platoon sent out a reconnaissance patrol. Keith Ross led three men along the ridge, but did not get far before a shot whistled past him. He replied with an Owen gun burst then, as the men made their way back, they set up three grenade booby traps 20 metres apart along the ridge-top track. The traps were readily set by almost removing the pin and connecting it to some signal wire strung across the track to a tree on the other side. Shortly after, the booby traps went off, one by one, accompanied by howls from the unfortunate victims. Now closing to around 30 metres, the Japanese patrol opened fire, but the Australians, wary of disclosing their positions, did not reply.[12]

After some mortar fire during the night, the Japanese attackers crept to within 10 metres of the Australian lines before stopping to cock their weapons. According to Keith Ross, the Japanese hadn't put any bullets in the spout because they were frightened one of their men would prematurely fire a shot and thus let the Australians know they were there. However, as Ross observed, 'When they charged the magazines they made a hell of a racket and we realised they were there.' The Japanese then attacked with fixed bayonets along the track that ran along the top of Scout Ridge. In the forward Bren-gun pit, Herb Troughton and Roy Gill put up a wall of fire until a grenade blast dazed Troughton. However, the other riflemen and grenades from Gill held off the attacking marines. Keith Ross's Owen gun and an adjacent tommy gun added their weight of fire. Although they had crept close, the Japanese marines did not reach the Australian positions, and Ross later counted fifteen of them lying dead out front. With their charge halted, the marines set up a light machine-gun firing down the track. However, the Australian Bren-gunner, Herb Troughton, the big guy who stuttered, was the more accurate. Ross and Rose later went out and dragged two dead marines back, one an officer with white scarf and gloves. For most of the 15th Battalion men it was their first sight of the enemy. That same morning Keith Ross and his two 2/6th mates were recalled to their battalion. They wished the militia boys well and headed for Tambu Bay and a boat back to Australia, where the 17-year-old Ross was discharged as underage.[13]

On 9 September the 15th Battalion made another attack on Scout Ridge, as much to continue to pin the enemy troops in place as to gain the position. At 1420 Les Thirgood's platoon moved up a spur and reached the crest of Scout Ridge soon thereafter. At 1540, after a mortar and artillery concentration, the main Japanese position was occupied. Meanwhile 9 Platoon moved east and occupied Lokanu Knoll, noting signs of hasty enemy evacuation. The Pimple area was also occupied and, by day's end, the battalion held the ridgeline from Lokanu Knoll on the coast back to the crest of Scout Ridge.[14] To the left of Colonel Amies' battalion, the Americans had limited their operations to a holding role since Captain George's company's travails at the end of August. On 8 September E Company made an attempt on Berger Hill, another difficult position on Scout Hill, but it proved to be beyond the men. The next day, F Company took the position unopposed and moved forward to contact the Australians at the Bamboos. Milford saw this lack of drive for himself when he came across a US platoon going into bivouac for the night at 1400 in the afternoon.[15]

Astonishingly, despite the landings at Lae, the Japanese command continued to stress that Salamaua must be held. However, following orders from General Adachi, at noon on 8 September Nakano issued his orders to commence the Japanese withdrawal from Salamaua. Units on the south bank of the Francisco were to retreat across the river on the night of 9 September, then make another move at sunset on 11 September, regrouping in the Kela, Malolo and Busama areas. All units were to be in Lae by 20 September.[16] Milford had opposing aims when he met with his brigadiers at Colonel Davidson's 42nd Battalion headquarters on 9 September. That afternoon he ordered a general advance on Salamaua to commence at first light the next day, but the Japanese beat him to it with their withdrawal that night. Heavy rain during the night helped to mask the withdrawal and, by the morning of 10 September, all organised enemy resistance south of the Francisco River had ceased. Unfortunately the heavy rain also prevented the Australians from crossing the Francisco River that day. It was ironic that, even with the Japanese defenders gone, Salamaua's natural defences still protected it from capture.

The next morning Captain Alfred Ganter's B Company from the 42nd Battalion finally got across the river. Private Roy Urquhart crossed first with a signal cable, which was used to help the others across. Ganter's company then moved north-east across Salamaua airfield without opposition and, at 1315, reached Kela radio station, capturing a machine-gun and a mountain gun as they went. Following concerns from Milford, a party under Captain Ganter moved across to Logui I village at the northern mouth of the Francisco River, but found nobody there. Continuing, Ganter and his six men became the first Allied troops to enter the ruins of Salamaua.[17]

Salamaua was a shell; the Allied bombing had been particularly destructive. Ted Griff observed, 'The isthmus was lined with bomb craters.' Peter Hemery reported that 'not a building is left standing – just an occasional heap of scattered wreckage'. Jack Glynn wrote, 'Salamaua was a shambles; a building wasn't left standing, by the look of the place it was very good bombing.'[18] It had indeed been very good bombing and, despite sheltering in slit trenches or fleeing to the hills at the approach of the bombers, 200–300 Japanese had been killed in Salamaua by the Allied bombings and many supplies destroyed. The evacuation of Salamaua had come as a relief for the Japanese troops stationed there.[19]

The aim of the Allies now was to drive north for the coast and thus cut off any remaining enemy troops in the Salamaua area. On the morning of 11 September the 58/59th Battalion had put in another attack against Rough

Photo 47 Salamaua following its capture in September 1943. Photo by Colin Halmarick. (AWM 057553)

Photo 48 Salamaua in 2006. (Phillip Bradley)

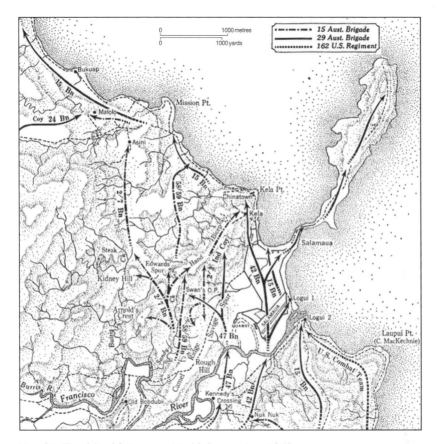

Map 36 The fall of Salamaua, 11–13 September 1943

Hill only to find that the defenders had evacuated during the night. Along with the 2/3rd commandos and the 2/7th Battalion, the 58/59th headed north for the coast. Charles Newman recalled: 'The Nips had flown by daybreak so we kept going with orders to swing around to the coast north of Salamaua and cut off retreat.' However, when the company reached the coast, the enemy had gone. The 58/59th Battalion had been in continuous contact for 77 days and had lost as many men killed as days served. General Savige later paid a great compliment to the battalion: 'The way the 18 and 19 year olds of 58/59 Bn from 30 June – 13 September kept at Japs was one of [the] outstanding feats of both wars.'[20]

When Milford met the 2/7th Battalion on 17 September he expressed his pleasure to see a battalion from the 17th Brigade complete the eight-month campaign from Wau to Salamaua. However, the infantry companies of the 2/7th Battalion had been reduced to rumps; A Company, those veterans of Lababia Ridge, Old Vickers and the Francisco River flats, being reduced to only twenty-one men. They were all that was left of the 120 men who had walked in from Wau in April 1943 as well as another forty reinforcements since. B Company had fared no better, losing many of its remaining men in the last days at Kela Ridge and being down to 20 men at the end.[21]

The 2/3rd Independent Company had been continuously engaged in operations since it had landed in Wau on 30 January 1943. In those eight months fifty-seven men had been killed, nine of them officers. The willing horse had certainly copped his lot.

On 12 September Brigadier Hammer accompanied a commando patrol across Kela Hill to the coast at Salamaua where he met Monaghan. Hammer then established his headquarters at Kela Hill, which was 'away from the stinking Salamaua and awaited further orders. Our task was ended.'[22] The next day the 15th Brigade was withdrawn to divisional reserve while the three battalions of 29th Brigade pushed on towards Lae.

On 13 September the remaining Japanese units of 51st Division left Malolo by MLC, 120 men from Nakano's headquarters being the last to leave. The fleeing Chinese labourers were abandoned, and one of them walked for four days before he was captured on the fifth. The 500 patients at the Japanese hospital at Malolo left on the following night, carried by Captain Sadaichi Teramura's three Daihatsu barges to Finschhafen, moving past the Allied landing fleet east of Lae in the dark.[23]

In a letter written on 7 September following the successful landing at Lae, General Herring wrote that 'the Salamaua show has drawn down quite a number of the enemy's reinforcements as we hoped it would'.[24]

At a parade on 16 September Hammer addressed the troops, and an army chaplain, Lieutenant Vernon Sherwin, raised the Australian flag over Salamaua. The tattered emblem had been taken from Salamaua in March 1942, as Japanese troops landed, and Sherwin had carried it ever since. A satisfied Sherwin turned away, but when he looked back moments later, he was dumbfounded; the flag had gone. 'I'll shoot the man who's taken it,' a distraught Sherwin cried out.

'It's all right, Vern,' a brother officer said as he touched him on the back. 'That flag would have been too good a souvenir. I had it taken down. You'll find it in your pack.'[25]

PLACE NAMES

Australian name	Japanese name	Iwal name
Ambush Knoll	Umanose Hill; the Horse's Back	Rauvap
Arnold's Crest	Hyotan Yama; Mount Gourd	
Buiwarfe Creek		Buiumboi
Charlie Hill	Kusa Yama	Buiemuakual
Coconuts, the		Bobdubi
Francisco River		Buiyouth
Goodview	Kanshi Yama; Tiger Mountain	Eiduravo
Green Hill	Minami Yama	Eigotogimil
Gwaibolom		Weramdubi
Kela Ridge	Hohei Yama; Artillery Mountain	
Komiatum Ridge	Hill of Regret	Namumal
Lababia Ridge	Left High Point	Sikolol
Mat Mat Hill		Eikete
Mount Tambu	Buyuzan	Uspo
Observation Hill	Mukai Yama; Right High Point	Buimaliel
Old Vickers	Oldbicars	Buiwerbabalodabe
Roosevelt Ridge	Boisi Highland	Buisdubi
Rough Hill	Ogura Yama	
Scout Ridge	Yamada Yama	Muaeigodo
Sugarcane Ridge		Eirembaboldubi
Tambu Bay		Bassis (Solong)
Timbered Knoll		Eukiadubi

NOTES

1 Death in the Bismarck Sea

1 Yoshihara, *Southern Cross*, chapter 9. Also spelt Yoshiwara.
2 Dexter, *The New Guinea Offensives*, p. 4.
3 For complete details of the Japanese operation against Wau see Bradley, *The Battle for Wau*.
4 ATIS interrogation reports, AWM 55, 6/3, IR141.
5 US Army Japan, *Japanese Monograph 37–18th Army Ops*, vol. 1, p. 118.
6 ATIS enemy publications, AWM 55, 5/1, EP-05.
7 Ibid., 5/1, EP-05. ATIS interrogation reports, AWM55, 6/1, IR012 and 6/4, IR184.
8 ATIS enemy publications, AWM 55, 5/1, EP-05. ATIS interrogation reports, AWM 55, 6/3, IR082, IR134, IR141, 6/4, IR150, IR157, IR171, IR184 and 6/5, IR203.
9 ATIS enemy publications, AWM 55, 5/1, EP-05, 5/6, EP-70. ATIS interrogation reports, AWM 55, 6/3, IR127, IR134.
10 ATIS interrogation reports, AWM 55, 6/3, IR128, 6/4, IR165.
11 Ibid., 6/2, IR074.
12 Ibid., 6/2, IR068. 6/3, IR090, IR132. 6/5, IR198.
13 ATIS interrogation reports, AWM 55, 6/3, IR119, IR129. 6/4, IR158.
14 Ibid., 6/2, IR060. 6/4, IR151. ATIS enemy publications, AWM 55, 5/1, EP-05.
15 ATIS enemy publications, AWM 55, 5/1, EP-05. Advanced HQ Intel Section WD, AWM 52, 1/2/2/007, scan 115.
16 Gillison, *RAAF 1939–1942*, p. 690. Advanced HQ Intel Section WD, AWM 52, 1/2/2/005, scans 116 & 137.
17 Drea, *MacArthur's Ultra*, p. 68. Ultra was the code-name for this intelligence.
18 Blamey to Mackay, 27 February 1943, Mackay papers, AWM 3DRL 6850, item 148.
19 AAF Historical Office, AAFRH-13, pp. 5–6.
20 Ibid., p. 9.
21 Ibid., pp. 6–7.
22 Ibid., p. 7.
23 Ibid., pp. 7–8.
24 Ibid., pp. 59–60.
25 Drea, *MacArthur's Ultra*, p. 69.

26 Hemery, 'Target – Harbour shipping', NAA SP300/3, 399.
27 Claringbould, *Forty of the Fifth*, pp. 63–4. AAF Historical Office, AAFRH-13, p. 84. Kenney, *General Kenney Reports*, p. 201.
28 Gillison, *RAAF 1939–1942*, p. 572.
29 Ibid., p. 692. Bill Garing, Murdoch Sound Archive, S00586, p. 96.
30 Garing, Murdoch Sound Archive, S00586, pp. 94–5.
31 ATIS enemy publications, AWM 55, 5/6, EP-70. 6/2, IR074. US post-war interrogations, Lt Cdr Handa, AWM 54, 643/6/8. All timings are as per Allied time; Japanese time was two hours behind.
32 Gillison, *RAAF 1939–1942*, p. 691. Travis, 'The Battle of the Bismarck Sea', *Mensa Bulletin*, March 1993. ATIS enemy publications, AWM 55, 5/6, EP-70.
33 RAAF No. 22 Sqn WD, NAA A9186/45.
34 AAF Historical Office, AAFRH-13, pp. 88–9. McAulay, *Battle of the Bismarck Sea*, pp. 47–9.
35 ATIS enemy publications, AWM 55, 5/6, EP-70. ATIS interrogation reports, AWM 55, 6/3, IR130 and IR141. ATIS translations, AWM 55, 3/7, 078 and 3/8, 082.
36 McAulay, *Battle of the Bismarck Sea*, p. 50. Gillison, *RAAF 1939–1942*, p. 696.
37 Gillison, *RAAF 1939–1942*, p. 691. ATIS enemy publications, AWM 55, 5/6, EP-70 and ATIS interrogation reports, AWM 55, 6/3, IR126, 6/4, IR147. AAF Historical Office, AAFRH-13, p. 90.
38 Gillison, *RAAF 1939–1942*, p. 691. ATIS enemy publications, AWM 55, 6/3, IR141.
39 Minty, *Black Cats*, pp. 65–7. McAulay, *Battle of the Bismarck Sea*, pp. 56–8. Watson memoirs pp. 46–7. Timings and positions from No. 11 Sqn Operations Diary, NAA A9186/30.
40 Ibid.
41 Henebry, *The Grim Reapers*, pp. 59–60.
42 Gillison, *RAAF 1939–1942*, p. 392. No. 100 Sqn WD, NAA A9186/123. Hall was awarded a DFC.
43 No. 22 Sqn WD, NAA A9186/45.
44 Rice, *22 Squadron RAAF*.
45 Graham, *None Shall Survive*, pp. 58–9.
46 Ibid., pp. 60–1.
47 Claringbould, *Forty of the Fifth*, pp. 114–15.
48 'Bismarck Sea Battle', *RAAF Log*, p. 50. George Drury, RAAF No. 30 Sqn, interview.
49 'Bismarck Sea Battle', *RAAF Log*, p. 50.
50 McAulay, *Battle of the Bismarck Sea*, p. 79.
51 Leggett, 'Calling the Beaufighters', NAA SP300/3, 544.
52 George Drury, RAAF No. 30 Sqn, interview.
53 Ibid. Drury, *Memoirs of George Drury*, p. 83.
54 Fred Anderson, RAAF No. 30 Sqn, logbook entry, 3 March 1943 and interview. Bob Brazenor, RAAF No. 30 Sqn, interview.

55 'Bismarck Sea Battle', *RAAF Log*, p. 50. Accident report, NAA A9845/13, scans 043–4.
56 Graham, *None Shall Survive*, p. 68.
57 Dusting, *The 1942–1943 Diary of a Corporal Fitter*, p. 82.
58 Henebry, *The Grim Reapers*, pp. 60–3. McAulay, *Battle of the Bismarck Sea*, pp. 74–6. Craven & Cate, *The Army Air Forces in WWII*, vol. 4, p. 144.
59 AAF Historical Office, AAFRH-13, pp. 92–3.
60 ATIS interrogation reports, AWM 55, 6/4, IR158.
61 Lt-Col Handa's account, in Gillison, *RAAF 1939–1942*, p. 697. US post-war interrogations from Bismarck Sea Battle, AWM 54, 643/6/8. Masuda Reiji, in Cook & Cook, *Japan at War*, pp. 301–2.
62 ATIS interrogation reports, AWM 55, 6/3, IR116.
63 Yoshihara, *Southern Cross*, chapter 9.
64 Ibid., 6/3, IR103, IR119, IR123, IR129. US post-war interrogations, AWM 54, 643/6/8.
65 Graham, *None Shall Survive*, p. 76.
66 ATIS interrogation reports, AWM 55, 6/2, IR075 and IR079. 6/3, IR084, IR094 and IR118. 6/3, IR127. 6/4, IR147.
67 ATIS interrogation reports, AWM 55, 6/2, IR059. 6/3, IR091, IR098, IR117, IR126, IR134, IR141 and IR145. 6/4, IR157 and IR176. 6/5, IR203. Advanced HQ Intel Section WD, AWM 52, 1/2/2/009, scan 103.
68 US Army Japan, *Japanese Monograph 37–18th Army Ops*, vol. 1, p. 122.
69 ATIS interrogation reports, AWM 55, 6/3, IR090, IR122 and IR132.
70 Ibid., 6/2, IR074.
71 ATIS enemy publications, AWM 55, 5/6, EP-70. ATIS interrogation reports, AWM 55, 6/2, IR053. 6/3, IR115, IR127, IR130.
72 ATIS interrogation reports, AWM 55, 6/2, IR060, 6/4, IR184, 6/5, IR209A, IR218.
73 US post-war interrogations from Bismarck Sea battle, AWM 54, 643/6/8.
74 Travis, 'The Battle of the Bismarck Sea', *Mensa Bulletin*, March 1993.
75 Rice, *22 Squadron RAAF*.
76 RAAF No. 22 Sqn WD, NAA A9186/45. US post-war interrogations, AWM 54, 643/6/8.
77 Long records, AWM 67, 10/12.
78 Gillison, *RAAF 1939–1942*, p. 697. US post-war interrogations, AWM 54, 643/6/8. Yoshihara, *Southern Cross*, chapter 9. Craven & Cate, *The Army Air Forces in WWII*, vol. 4, p. 149. Long records, AWM 67, 10/12.
79 US post-war interrogations, AWM 54, 643/6/8. Orita & Harrington, *I-Boat Captain*, p. 141.
80 Drury, *Memoirs of George Drury*, p. 92.
81 NGF HQ WD, AWM 52, 1/5/51/030, scan 099.
82 Advanced HQ Intel Section WD, AWM 52, 1/2/2/007, scan 107.
83 ATIS interrogation reports, AWM 55, 6/3, IR141, IR145. 6/4, IR153, IR155.
84 Ibid., 6/3, IR125, IR126 and IR140.

85 Ibid., 6/3, IR122. 6/5, IR203. Report by Lt-Col H Tasker, AWM 93, 50/2/23/584.
86 McWatters to Long, AWM 93 50/2/23/584. Dexter, *The New Guinea Offensives*, pp. 10–11.
87 Travis, 'The Battle of the Bismarck Sea', *Mensa Bulletin*, March 1993. Lewis Wood, 'Bismarck Sea epic', *New York Times*, March 1943.
88 Bismarck Sea actions and DW cablegrams, AWM 123/431.
89 Craven & Cate, *The Army Air Forces in WWII*, vol. 4, pp. 147–8.
90 Kenney, *General Kenney Reports*, p. 205.
91 Parer Diary, SLNSW, ML MSS 1097/1.
92 US post-war interrogations, AWM 54, 643/6/8.
93 Advanced HQ Intel Section WD, AWM 52, 1/2/2/006, scan 009.
94 Craven & Cate, *The Army Air Forces in WWII*, vol. 4, pp. 145–6.
95 US Army Japan, *Japanese Monograph 37–18th Army Ops*, vol. 1, p. 112.
96 Sinton (ed.), *The Menace from Moresby*, Commendatory Messages.
97 Kitamoto, *A Record of Marathon Adventures in the New Guinea War*, p. 1.
98 Yoshihara, *Southern Cross*, chapter 10.

2 Opposing forces

1 3rd Division War Diary, AWM 52, 1/5/4/019, scan 059.
2 Mackay papers, AWM 3DRL 6850, item 150. NGF HQ WD, AWM 52, 1/5/51/030, scan 027.
3 Bob Hancock, 2/3rd Ind Coy, letter, 6 April 1943.
4 Drea, *In the Service of the Emperor*, pp. 91–109.
5 Bullard & Tamura (eds), *From a Hostile Shore*, p. 102.
6 ATIS interrogation reports, AWM 55, 6/3, IR141.
7 Kitamoto, *A Record of Marathon Adventures in the New Guinea War*, p. 50.
8 US War Department, *Handbook on Japanese Military Forces*, pp. 28–34.
9 Ibid., pp. 34–5. ATIS interrogation reports, AWM 55, 6/4, IR177 and IR192.
10 ATIS interrogation reports, AWM 55, 6/4, IR167 and 6/5, IR223.
11 US War Department, *Handbook on Japanese Military Forces*, pp. 76–7.
12 McCarthy, *South-West Pacific Area: First Year*, p. 349. Boechi, *Senshi Sosho*, chapter 5.
13 ATIS interrogation reports, AWM 55, 6/4, IR193.
14 Ibid. and 6/5, IR212.
15 McCarthy, *South-West Pacific Area: First Year*, p. 575.
16 Advanced HQ Intel Section WD, AWM 52, 1/2/2/007, scan 114.
17 ATIS interrogation reports, AWM 55, 6/5, IR207.
18 Savige, interview with Long, AWM 67, 2/40.
19 ATIS interrogation reports, AWM 55, 6/4, IR166, IR173, 6/5, IR220.
20 Bradley, *On Shaggy Ridge*, pp. 159–60.
21 Ed Drea, email, 5 August 2003.
22 Miller, *Cartwheel: The Reduction of Rabaul*, pp. 11–16, p. 19.
23 Herring comments on Official History, AWM 67, 3/167.

24 NGF HQ WD, AWM 52, 1/5/51/030, scan 099. ATIS enemy publications, AWM 55, 5/1, EP-05.
25 Tanaka, *Operations of Imperial Japanese Armed Forces*, p. 156.
26 Dexter to Long, AWM 93, 50/2//23/99.
27 3rd Div WD, AWM 52, 1/5/4/023, scan 050.
28 NGF HQ WD, AWM 52, 1/5/51/031, scans 148–9. The Wau area flights operated in groups of nine aircraft, six to Wau and three to Bulolo. A second flight would follow the first, timed for landing after the first group had finished unloading and taken off again.
29 NGF HQ WD, AWM 52, 1/5/51/031, scans 148–9.
30 Ibid.
31 Ibid., scan 099.
32 AAF Historical Office, AAFRH-13, p. 6.
33 Mackay papers, AWM 3DRL 6850, item 151. Moten to Long, AWM 93, 50/2/23/387.
34 Palazzo, *Defenders of Australia*, pp. 108–13.
35 Keating, 'Savige, Sir Stanley George (1890–1954)', *Australian Dictionary of Biography*, pp. 179–80.
36 Savige records, 3DRL 2529, item 126.
37 Savige, interview with Dexter, AWM 172/7.
38 Herring comments on Official History, AWM 67, 3/167.
39 Savige records, 3DRL 2529, item 126.
40 Long diaries, AWM 67, 2/27, pp. 42–3.
41 Refshauge interview with Long, AWM 67, 2/99.
42 Herring comments on Official History, AWM 67, 3/167.
43 Damien Parer diary, SLNSW, ML MSS 1097/1.
44 NGF HQ WD, AWM 52, 1/5/51/032, scans 061 & 192–3.
45 Mackay papers, AWM 3DRL 6850, item 150.
46 3rd Div WD, AWM 52, 1/5/4/023, scan 050.
47 Horner, *Strategic Command*, p. 90.
48 Savige, records, AWM 3DRL 2529, item 126.
49 Ibid.
50 Herring comments on Official History, AWM 67, 3/167.
51 Savige, interview with Dexter, AWM 172/7.
52 Moten to Long, AWM 93, 50/2/23/387.
53 Herring, interview with Dexter, AWM 172/6.
54 Herring comments on Official History, AWM 67, 3/167.
55 Blamey report on Salamaua operations, AWM 54, 519/6/58.
56 Berryman diary, AWM PR 84/370, item 3. Horner, *General Vasey's War*, pp. 202–3.
57 Savige records, AWM 3DRL 2529, item 126. Herring interview with Dexter, AWM 172/6. Savige interview with Dexter, AWM 172/7.
58 Moten to Long, AWM 93, 50/2/23/387. Herring interview with Dexter, AWM 172/6.
59 Mackay papers, AWM 3DRL 6850, item 148.
60 Horner, *Strategic Command*, pp. 94–5.
61 Gillison, *RAAF 1939–1942*, pp. 698–9.

62 Bill Murray, 2/3rd Ind Coy, memoirs, p. 118.
63 RAAF No. 22 Sqn WD, NAA A9186/85, scan 184.
64 ATIS enemy publications, AWM 55, 5/4, EP-44, 51st Div Intel Report 13, 24 March 1943. Also Weate, *Bill Newton VC*, pp. 65–7.

3 Warfe's tigers
 1 17th Bde WD, AWM 52, 8/2/17/079, scan 002.
 2 NGF HQ WD, AWM 52, 1/5/51/029, scan 021.
 3 Smith to Brill, AWM 93, 50/2/23/495. Bob Hancock, 2/3rd Ind Coy, letter, 26 March 1943. James Matheson, 58/59th Bn, interview.
 4 Moten to Long, AWM 93, 50/2/23/387. 15th Bde WD, AWM 52, 8/2/15/017, scan 039. Savige comments on official history, AWM 3DRL 2529, item 126.
 5 Peter Pinney, 2/3rd Ind Coy, diary transcript, Freyer Library, University of Queensland, Brisbane, UQFL288. Pinney later wrote a book based on his diary, *The Barbarians*.
 6 2/3rd Ind Coy WD, AWM 52, 25/3/3.
 7 Keith Myers, 2/3rd Ind Coy, interview.
 8 Norm Bear, 2/3rd Ind Coy, interview.
 9 Bill Murray, 2/3rd Ind Coy, memoirs, pp. 112–3.
10 Brian Walpole, 2/3rd Ind Coy, interview.
11 17th Bde WD, AWM 52, 8/2/17/083, scan 002.
12 Pinney, diary transcript.
13 17th Bde WD, AWM 52, 8/2/17/079, scans 007, 009 & 010. 2/3rd Ind Coy WD, AWM 52, 25/3/3.
14 2/3rd Ind Coy WD, AWM 52, 25/3/3. NGF HQ WD, AWM 52, 1/5/51/030, scan 031.
15 ATIS enemy pubs, AWM 55, 5/4, EP-44, 51st Div Intel Report 23, 3 April 1943. The Japanese report refers to the soldiers at the observation post as Americans.
16 17th Bde WD, AWM 52, 8/2/17/083, scan 006. 2/3rd Ind Coy WD, AWM 52, 25/3/3.
17 Yoshihara, *Southern Cross*, chapter 10.
18 2/3rd Ind Coy WD, AWM 52, 25/3/3.
19 3rd Division GS branch, AWM 52 1/5/4/065, scan 188. 2/3rd Ind Coy WD, AWM 52, 25/3/3 Appendices. *Bui* means water in the local dialect.
20 Garland, *Nothing is Forever*, p. 107. 2/3rd Ind Coy WD, AWM 52, 25/3/3, appendices.
21 ATIS enemy pubs, AWM 55, 5/4, EP-44, 51st Div Intel Reports 11 & 26, 23–24 April 1943. Arai's men were from the 102nd Regiment, Gunji's from the 115th.
22 ATIS enemy pubs, AWM 55, 5/4, EP-44, 51st Div Intel Report 13, 29 April 1943.
23 Garland, *Nothing is Forever*, pp. 109–10. 2/3rd Ind Coy WD, AWM 52, 25/3/3, appendices. Joe Taylor's death was initially misreported as that of Fred Taylor.
24 2/3rd Ind Coy WD, AWM 52, 25/3/3, appendices.

25 ATIS enemy pubs, AWM 55, 5/4, EP-44, 51st Div Intel Reports 27, 26 April 1943 and 29, 1 May 1943.
26 2/3rd Ind Coy WD, AWM 52, 25/3/3, appendices. Garland, *Nothing is Forever*, p. 110.
27 Warfe to Dexter, AWM 93, 50/2/23/489. Garland, *Nothing is Forever*, pp. 110–1. 2/3rd Ind Coy WD, AWM 52, 25/3/3. ATIS enemy pubs, AWM 55, 5/4, EP-44, 51st Division Intel Report 29, 1 May 1943.
28 Savige comments on official history, AWM 3DRL 2529, item 126.
29 Christensen, *That's the Way It Was*, pp. 39–51. 24th Bn WD, AWM 52, 8/3/62/20, scan 012. 'Snarler' is derived from the term 'Services No Longer Required'.
30 Savige records, AWM 3DRL 2529, item 126.
31 Smith to Brill, AWM 93, 50/2/23/495.
32 ATIS enemy pubs, AWM 55, 5/6, EP-71, 51st Div Operational Orders, 26 April 1943.
33 Ibid., 5/5, EP-53, 51st Div Tactical plan, 22 April 1943.
34 3rd Div GS branch, AWM 52 1/5/4/065, scans 268–9.
35 Savige records, AWM 3DRL 2529, item 126.
36 ATIS enemy pubs, AWM 55, 5/4, EP-44, 51st Div Intel Report 27, 26 April 1943.
37 Pinney, diary transcript.
38 Ibid.
39 Warfe to Dexter, AWM 93, 50/2/23/489.
40 Pinney, diary transcript.
41 Ibid.
42 Warfe to Dexter, AWM 93, 50/2/23/489.
43 Pinney, diary transcript. Warfe to Dexter, AWM 93, 50/2/23/489.
44 Pinney, diary transcript.
45 Dexter, *The New Guinea Offensives*, p. 35. Warfe to Dexter, AWM 93, 50/2/23/489.
46 2/3rd Ind Coy WD, AWM 52, 25/3/3. Warfe to Dexter, AWM 93, 50/2/23/489.
47 Pinney, diary transcript.
48 Bob Hancock, 2/3rd Ind Coy, letter, 10 May 1943.
49 2/3rd Ind Coy WD, AWM 52, 25/3/3, 12 May 1943. Keith Myers, 2/3rd Ind Coy, interview.
50 Brian Walpole, 2/3rd Ind Coy, interview.
51 ATIS enemy pubs, AWM 55, 5/6, EP-71, 51st Div Operational Orders, 9 May 1943.
52 2/3rd Ind Coy WD, AWM 52, 25/3/3.
53 Bob Hancock, 2/3rd Ind Coy, letter, 10 May 1943.
54 Savige records, AWM 3DRL 2529, item 126.
55 Pinney, diary transcript. Dexter, *The New Guinea Offensives*, p. 44.
56 Warfe to Dexter, AWM 93, 50/2/23/489. Brian Walpole, 2/3rd Ind Coy, interview.
57 ATIS enemy pubs, AWM 55, 5/6, EP-72, 9 Coy III/115th Regt Orders, 11 May 1943.

58 Ibid., 5/6, EP-71, 51st Division Orders, 12 May 1943.
59 2/3rd Ind Coy WD, AWM 52, 25/3/3.
60 ATIS enemy pubs, AWM 55, 5/6, EP-72, 9 Coy III/115th Regt Orders, 11 & 13 May 1943. Japanese POW notes, AWM 54, 779/3/119, p. 16. Also Yoshihara, *Southern Cross*, chapter 10.
61 Warfe to Dexter, AWM 93, 50/2/23/489.
62 Ibid.
63 Ibid. 2/3rd Ind Coy WD, AWM 52, 25/3/3.
64 Barney Barron, from Garland, *Nothing is Forever*, p. 127.
65 Keith Myers, 2/3rd Ind Coy, interview. Pinney, diary transcript.
66 Vin Maguire, 2/3 Ind Coy, interview. ATIS enemy pubs, AWM 55, 5/4, EP-44, Intel report 17, 18 May 1943 and 5/6, EP-71, 51st Div Orders, 27 May 1943 and EP-72, 9 Coy III/115th Regt Orders, 14 & 17 May 1943. General Murotani is also referred to as General Muroya.
67 3rd Div GS branch, AWM 52 1/5/4/064, scan 16. Savige records, AWM 3DRL 2529, item 126.
68 ATIS enemy pubs, AWM 55, 5/4, EP-44, 51st Div Intel Report 04, 22 May 1943 and 5/6, EP-72, 9 Coy 3/115 Regt Operational Orders, 17–24 May 1943.
69 Ibid., 5/4, EP-44, 51st Div Intel Report 17, 18 May 1943. Pinney, diary transcript. Bob Hancock, 2/3rd Ind Coy, letter, 20 May 1943.
70 Dexter interview with Savige, AWM 172, item 7. Dexter, *The New Guinea Offensives*, p. 46. 3rd Div GS branch, AWM 52 1/5/4/064, scan 015.
71 Warfe to Dexter, AWM 93, 50/2/23/489.
72 3rd Div GS branch, AWM 52 1/5/4/064, scan 015.
73 Looker diary, AWM 93, 50/2/23/620. Smith notes, AWM 93, 50/2/23/495.
74 ATIS enemy pubs, AWM 55, 5/4, EP-44, 51st Div Intel Report 01, 18 May 1943.
75 Christensen, *That's the Way It Was*, pp. 72–3. 3rd Div GS branch, AWM 52 1/5/4/039, scan 085.
76 Savige records, AWM 3DRL 2529, item 126.
77 Christensen, *That's the Way It Was*, pp. 73–4.
78 Smith to Brill, AWM 93, 50/2/23/495.
79 Christensen, *That's the Way It Was*, pp. 74–5. Garland, *Nothing is Forever*, p. 140.
80 Looker diary, AWM 93, 50/2/23/620.
81 Pinney, diary transcript. Ormond 'Screamer' Hetherington was awarded an MM but died of his wounds on 30 May. 'Chocko' is a derogatory reference to a militia soldier. It is taken from the playwright George Bernard Shaw's *Arms and the Man*, which refers to a man carrying chocolates in his pack instead of ammunition.
82 Savige records, AWM 3DRL 2529, item 126.

4 Supply lines

1 NGF HQ WD, AWM 52, 1/5/51/030, scan 084.
2 Yoshihara, *Southern Cross*, chapter 10.
3 Advanced HQ Intel Section WD, AWM 52, 1/2/2/007, scan 009.

4   ATIS interrogation reports, AWM 55, 6/5, IR226.
5   ATIS enemy publications, AWM 55, 5/5, EP-51, 66th Regt shipping details.
6   Ibid.
7   Shinoda, *The 66th Inf Regt at Salamaua*.
8   ATIS interrogation reports, AWM 55, 6/4, IR182, IR191.
9   Ibid., IR180 and 6/5, IR200.
10 Richard Dunn, Tuluvu's Air War, chapter 4, 'Most successful attack', www.j-aircraft.com/research/rdunn/tuluvu/tuluvu_5.htm; viewed 31 December 2009.
11 ATIS interrogation reports, AWM 55, 6/5, IR231.
12 Ibid., 6/4, IR180 and 6/5, IR200, IR209A, IR228.
13 Yoshihara, *Southern Cross*, chapter 10.
14 ATIS interrogation reports, AWM 55, 6/4, IR192 and 6/5, IR223 and IR230. ATIS enemy publications, AWM 55, 5/4, EP-44, 51st Div Intel Report 01, 18 May 1943. Captured documents, AWM 54, 423/4/71.
15 Shinoda, *The 66th Inf Regt at Salamaua*.
16 ATIS interrogation reports, AWM 55, 6/4, IR182, 6/5, IR228.
17 Ibid., IR180, 6/5, IR200, IR209A.
18 ATIS enemy publications, AWM 55, 5/4, EP-44, 51st Div Intel 2, 35, 38 and 39.
19 Ibid., 51st Div Intel 6, 25 May 1943. NGF HQ WD, AWM 52, 1/5/51/035, scan 023.
20 ATIS interrogation reports, AWM 55, 6/4, IR173, IR175 and 6/5, IR205. Tanaka, *Ops of IJAF*, p. 50. Boechi, *Senshi Sosho*, vol. 3, pp. 330–1.
21 ATIS interrogation reports, AWM 55, 6/5, IR221.
22 Tanaka, *Ops of IJAF*, p. 60. ATIS interrogation reports, AWM 55, 6/4, IR166, 6/5, IR209.
23 ATIS interrogation reports, AWM 55, 6/5, IR207, IR216, IR217. 5th Div WD, AWM 52, 1/5/10/031, scan 004.
24 ATIS interrogation reports, AWM 55, 6/5, IR209, IR220, IR229, IR234.
25 NGF HQ WD, AWM 52, 1/5/51/032, scan 145.
26 Feldt, *The Coastwatchers*, pp. 220–2. NGF HQ WD, AWM 52, 1/5/51/032, scans 118 & 161.
27 Feldt, *The Coastwatchers*, pp. 222–7. Hall was awarded a DCM.
28 Yoshihara, *Southern Cross*, chapter 10. Miller, *Cartwheel: The Reduction of Rabaul*, pp. 194–5.
29 ATIS interrogation reports, AWM 55, 6/5, IR212.
30 Wada, *The Lae Naval Guard Unit*.
31 Captured documents and translations, AWM 54, 423/4/78. ATIS interrogation reports, AWM 55, 6/5, IR202 and IR212. Shinoda, *The 66th Inf Regt at Salamaua*. Miller, *Cartwheel: The Reduction of Rabaul*, p. 194.
32 Orita & Harrington, *I-Boat Captain*, pp. 138–9.
33 ATIS interrogation reports, AWM 55, 6/5, IR218, 6/4, IR193.
34 ATIS enemy publications, AWM 55, 5/6, EP-71, 51st Div order 142, 26 April 1943. ATIS interrogation reports, AWM 55, 6/4, IR194, 6/5, IR226.

35 Perrin, *The Private War of the Spotters*, pp. 152–4.
36 Orita & Harrington, *I-Boat Captain*, pp. 143–7. Mochitsura & Colegrave, *Sunk*, pp. 74–85.
37 NGF HQ WD, AWM 52, 1/5/51/ 035, scans 004 & 006. Henebry, *The Grim Reapers*, pp. 78–81.
38 Orita & Harrington, *I-Boat Captain*, p. 138.
39 NGF HQ WD, AWM 52, 1/5/51/032, scan 159. ATIS interrogation reports, AWM 55, 6/5, IR212 & IR223.
40 Shinoda, *The 66th Inf Regt at Salamaua*.
41 ATIS enemy publications, AWM 55, 5/4, EP-44, 51st Div Intel 23. 17th Bde WD, AWM 52, 8–2-17/083, scan 007.
42 ATIS interrogation reports, AWM 55, 6/4, IR191. Shinoda, *The 66th Inf Regt at Salamaua*.
43 NGF HQ WD, AWM 52, 1/5/51/030, scan 025.
44 Advanced HQ Intel Section WD, AWM 52, 1/2/2/007, scan 101. Gill, *Royal Australian Navy 1942–1945*, pp. 279–83.
45 3rd Div Operations Report, AWM 54, 587/2/28.
46 Reinhold, *The Bulldog–Wau Road*, pp. 3–4.
47 Ibid., p. 10.
48 NGF HQ WD, AWM 52, 1/5/51/025, scan 027.
49 Reinhold, *The Bulldog–Wau Road*, pp. 15–6.
50 Ibid., pp. 17 & 24. NGF HQ WD, AWM 52, 1/5/51/030, scans 71–2.
51 Reinhold, *The Bulldog–Wau Road*, pp. 43–4.
52 Ibid.
53 Ibid., pp. 44–8 & 52.
54 Ibid., pp. 37 & 53.
55 3rd Div Operations Diary, AWM 52, 1/5/4/064, scan 006.
56 Reinhold, *The Bulldog–Wau Road*, pp. 40–1.
57 ATIS enemy publications, AWM 55, 5/4, EP-44, 51st Div Intel Report 12, 27 April, Report 28, 28 April, Report 19, 28 May, Report 20, 15 June 1943. Reinhold, *The Bulldog–Wau Road*, pp. 30–1.
58 Mackay to Blamey letter, March 1943, Mackay papers, AWM 3DRL 6850, item 150.
59 3rd Div Operations Report, AWM 54, 587/2/28. 17th Bde WD, AWM 52, 8/2/17/094, scans 068–70.
60 15th Bde WD, AWM 52, 8/2/15/017, scan 039, 8/2/15/067, scans 143–4.
61 15th Bde WD, AWM 52, 8/2/15/067, scans 22–4. Report on Wau operations, AWM 54, 583/7/10.
62 3rd Div Operations Report, AWM 54, 587/2/28.
63 15th Bde WD, AWM 52, 8/2/15/067, scans 22–4.
64 Dickson, *Flying for the Army*, pp. 17–18. 15th Bde WD, AWM 52, 8/2/15/067, scan 022.
65 15th Bde WD, AWM 52, 8/2/15/067, scans 19–20.
66 2/3rd Ind Coy WD, AWM 52, 25/3/3, 16 April 1943. Hammer to Long, AWM 93, 50/2/23/440.
67 Savige records, AWM 3DRL 2529, item 126.

5 Mubo stalemate

1   2/5th Bn WD, AWM 52, 8/3/5/012, scans 057, 062 & 065. ATIS enemy publications, AWM 55, 5/4, EP-44, 51st Div Intel Report 1, 1 March 1943.
2   17th Bde WD, AWM 52, 8/2/17/079, scans 002-3.
3   17th Bde WD, AWM 52, 8/2/17/075, scan 059.
4   Berryman diary, AWM PR 84/370, item 3.
5   O'Hare to Brill, AWM 93, 50/2/23/585.
6   Ibid. Salamaua Operations – Artillery, AWM 54, 587/6/9. 3rd Div WD, AWM 52, 1/5/4/065, scan 211.
7   John Tyree, 2/7th Ind Coy, letter.
8   1st Mountain Battery WD, AWM 52, 4/9/1.
9   Allan & Cutts, *As It Seemed to Us*, p. 95. 1st Mtn Bty WD, AWM 52, 4/9/1. 17th Bde WD, AWM 52, 8/2/17/083, scan 004.
10 17th Bde WD, AWM 52, 8/2/17/079, scan 005. Davidson, *With Courage High*, pp. 118–19.
11 Pinney, diary transcript.
12 17th Bde WD, AWM 52, 8/2/17/079, scans 005–6.
13 Clive Jarman, 2/7th Ind Coy, interview. Kelly, *Allied Air Transport Ops SWPA in WWII*, vol. 2, p. 71. The aircraft serial number was 41-18642.
14 NGF HQ WD, AWM 52, 1/5/51/030, scan 088. Davidson, *With Courage High*, pp. 120–9.
15 NGF HQ WD, AWM 52, 1/5/51/030, scans 040 & 084, 1/5/51/031, scan 100. Mackay papers, AWM 3DRL 6850, item 151.
16 2/5th Bn WD, AWM 52, 8/3/5/012, scan 069. John Tyree, 2/7th Ind Coy, interview.
17 17th Bde WD, AWM 52, 8/2/17/079, scan 012. Moten, interview with Dexter, AWM 172/9.
18 17th Bde WD, AWM 52, 8/2/17/079, scan 012. Conroy service record, NAA, B883.
19 Savige records, AWM 3DRL 2529, item 126. Mackay papers, AWM 3DRL 6850, item 151. Bennett, *Rough Infantry*, p. 169.
20 Williams diary, AWM PR00057.
21 AWM 52, 8/3/5/012, scan 137. Also Trigellis-Smith, *All the King's Enemies*, p. 218.
22 ATIS enemy publications, AWM 55, 5/4, EP-44, 51st Div Intel Report 24, 9 April 1943. This report confirms that Private Feeley was killed in action.
23 NGF HQ WD, AWM 52, 1/5/51/033, scan 010. Also Trigellis-Smith, *All the King's Enemies*, p. 218.
24 NGF HQ WD, AWM 52, 1/5/51/032, scan 093.
25 Savige records, AWM 3DRL 2529, item 126.
26 Williams diary, AWM, PR00057.
27 Bruce Peterson, 2/7th Bn, interview. Olsen, 'Death lurks on the jungle track', *Argus*, 1943.
28 Shinoda, *The 66th Inf Regt at Salamaua*.
29 17th Bde WD, AWM 52, 8/2/17/083, scan 010. 17th Bde Ops Report, AWM 3DRL 5043, item 108.
30 Williams diary, AWM, PR00057. Jack Mitchell, 2/7th Bn, diary.

31 Report on Ops in the Mubo area, AWM 54, 587/6/2. ATIS interrogation reports, AWM 55, 6/5, IR223.

32 2/7th Bn WD, AWM 52, 8/3/7/030, scans 073–4.

33 Williams diary, AWM, PR00057. 2/7th Bn WD, AWM 52, 8/3/7/030, scan 015.

34 3rd Div WD, AWM 52, 1/5/4/065, scan 230.

35 2/7th Bn WD, AWM 52, 8/3/7/030, scan 016. Williams diary, AWM, PR00057.

36 ATIS enemy pubs, AWM 55, 5/4, EP-44, 51st Div Intel Report 29, 1 May 1943.

37 17th Bde WD, AWM 52, 8/2/17/083, scans 012–13. NGF HQ WD, AWM 52, 1/5/51/032, scan 200. Report on Operations in the Mubo area, AWM 54, 587/6/2.

38 Allan & Cutts, *As It Seemed to Us*, pp. 93–4. For his 'coolness and devotion to duty' Colless was awarded a Military Cross.

39 Bruce Peterson, 2/7th Bn, interview and diary notes.

40 Dexter interview with Guinn, AWM 93, 50/2/23/453. Russell was awarded an MM.

41 Bruce Peterson, 2/7th Bn, interview.

42 Reg Saunders, 2/7th Bn, Murdoch Sound Archive, S00520, p. 107.

43 Ibid., p. 110. 2/7th Bn WD, AWM 52, 8/3/7/030, scan 005. Clyde Stiff, 2/7th Bn, interview.

44 Analysis of Ops, report on Doublet, AWM 54, 587/6/2.

45 2/7th Bn WD, AWM 52, 8/3/7/031, scans 002–3. AWM 55, 5/4, EP-44, 51st Div Intel Report 31, 5 May 1943. *Battle of the Ridges*, pp. 19–20. 17th Bde WD, AWM 52, 8/2/17/093, scan 018.

46 Baird to Long, AWM 93, 50/2/23/598. Savige records, AWM 3DRL 2529, item 126. 3rd Div WD, AWM 52, 1/5/4/064, scan 012.

47 2/7th Bn WD, AWM 52, 8/3/7/031, scans 006–7. 3rd Div WD, AWM 52, 1/5/4/064, scan 012.

6 *On Lababia Ridge*

1 'The Seventeenth Australian Infantry Brigade', p. 108. 2/7th Bn WD, AWM 52, 8/3/7/031, scan 009. Analysis of Operations, report on Doublet, AWM 54, 587/6/2.

2 Allan & Cutts, *As It Seemed to Us*, p. 95. Analysis of Operations, report on Doublet, AWM 54, 587/6/2.

3 Charles Germaine, 2/7th Bn, quoted by anon., 'Wau–Mubo – Land of Ambush', *Thirtyniner*, March 1962, p. 40.

4 2/7th Bn citation records, AWM 119 /26. Also *Battle of the Ridges*, p. 22. Waters and Bowen were both awarded the MM. Joe Howard, 2/7th Bn, memoirs.

5 'Bren guns cut Japs to ribbons', *Daily Mirror*, 29 May 1943. Bruce Peterson, 2/7th Bn, interview.

6 Vin Tatterson, in *Battle of the Ridges*, p. 21. 'Bren guns cut Japs to ribbons', *Daily Mirror*, 29 May 1943. 2/7th Bn WD, AWM 52, 8/3/7/031, scan 012.

7   2/7th Bn WD, AWM 52, 8/3/7/031, scan 010. O'Hare to Long, AWM 93, 50/2/23/585.
8   2/7th Bn WD, AWM 52, 8/3/7/031, scan 010. Bruce Peterson, 2/7th Bn, interview.
9   Allan & Cutts, *As It Seemed to Us*, pp. 95–6.
10 3rd Div WD, AWM 52, 1/5/4/039, scan 054 and 1/5/4/064, scan 013. Guinn to Long, AWM 93, 50/2/23/453. ATIS enemy pubs, AWM 55, 5/4, EP-44, 51st Div Intel Report 17, 18 May 1943.
11 Tanaka, *Ops of IJAF*, p. 59.
12 ATIS enemy pubs, AWM 55, 5/4, EP-44, 51st Div Intel Report 31 and 17, 5 & 18 May 1943.
13 3rd Div WD, AWM 52 1/5/4/064, scan 013. Bolger & Littlewood, *The Fiery Phoenix*, pp. 396 & 402.
14 Dexter, *The New Guinea Offensives*, p. 52. Kasper and Mitchell, 2/7th Bn, interviews.
15 3rd Div WD, AWM 52 1/5/4/064, scan 013. 17th Bde WD, AWM 52 8/2/17/086, scan 009.
16 17th Bde Operation Report, AWM 3DRL 5043 item 108.
17 3rd Div WD, AWM 52, 1/5/4/039, scan 047. Dexter to Long, AWM 93, 50/2/23/99. Walter 'Bill' Dexter was the brother of David Dexter, who wrote *The New Guinea Offensives*.
18 Gullett, *Not as a Duty Only*, pp. 121–2.
19 Ibid.
20 Gibbons record, NAA B3856, 145/4/26. Dexter, *The New Guinea Offensives*, pp. 64–5. Gullett, *Not as a Duty Only*, p. 123.
21 NAA B3856, 145/4/26. ATIS translations, AWM 55, 3/10, 089. Dexter, *The New Guinea Offensives*, pp. 64–5.
22 ATIS captured docs, AWM 54, 422/7/8. ATIS enemy pubs, AWM 55, 5/3, EP-43, Operation order 88, 8 June 1943.
23 17th Bde WD, AWM 52, 8/2/17/094, scans 028–30.
24 Shinoda, *The 66th Inf Regt at Salamaua*. ATIS enemy pubs, AWM 55, 5/4, EP-44, 51st Div Intel Report 01, 18 May 1943. Captured documents, AWM 54, 423/4/71.
25 Advanced HQ Intel Section WD, AWM 52, 1/2/2/009, scans 093–4, 098–9, 107 & 117.
26 Shinoda, *The 66th Inf Regt at Salamaua*.
27 Ibid. Intelligence file reports, AWM 54, 587/7/5.
28 Company commander's report – Lababia, AWM 54, 587/7/31.
29 Noel Bisset, 2/6th Bn, in Hay, *Nothing Over Us*, p. 313.
30 Ibid., p. 314. Arnold Watt was awarded an MM. According to Captain Dexter and Colonel Wood, Watt had been recommended for a Victoria Cross (AWM 93, 50/2/23/99 & 50/2/23/469). Dexter, *The New Guinea Offensives*, p. 77.
31 Dexter to Long, AWM 93, 50/2//23/99. Bill Dexter, 2/6th Bn, in Hay, *Nothing Over Us*, p. 303. Jim Kerr, 2/6th Bn, interview.
32 Jim Kerr, 2/6th Bn, interview. Bill Dexter, 'The battalion my home', AWM PR01182/4. Laurie Roach, 2/6th Bn, in Hay, *Nothing Over Us*, p. 315. 17th Bde Ops Report, AWM 3DRL 5043, item 108.

33 Jim Kerr, 2/6th Bn, interview. Company commander's report – Lababia, AWM 54, 587/7/31.
34 Ray Mathers, 2/6th Bn, letter. Company commander's report – Lababia, AWM 54, 587/7/31.
35 Ray Mathers, 2/6th Bn, letter.
36 Ray Mathers, 2/6th Bn, interview. Laurie Roach, 2/6th Bn, in Hay, *Nothing Over Us*, pp. 317–18. Smith was awarded an MM.
37 Ray Mathers, 2/6th Bn, interview.
38 Jim Kerr, 2/6th Bn, interview.
39 Ibid.
40 Laurie Roach and John Hill, 2/6th Bn, in Hay, *Nothing Over Us*, pp. 317 & 319. Jim Kerr, 2/6th Bn, interview. Ray Mathers, 2/6th Bn, interview.
41 Bill Dexter, 'The battalion my home', AWM PR01182/4. 17th Bde Ops Report, AWM 3DRL 5043, item 108. Shinoda, *The 66th Inf Regt at Salamaua*.
42 Savige records, AWM 3DRL 2529, item 126. Bill Dexter, 'The battalion my home', AWM PR01182/4. 17th Bde Ops Report, AWM 3DRL 5043, item 108.
43 17th Bde WD, AWM 52, 8/2/17/094, scan 016. Company commander's report – Lababia, AWM 54, 587/7/31. John Hill, 2/6th Bn, in Hay, *Nothing Over Us*, p. 319. Shinoda, *The 66th Inf Regt at Salamaua*.
44 Company commander's report – Lababia, AWM 54, 587/7/31.
45 Gullett, *Not as a Duty Only*, pp. 118–19.
46 Savige records, AWM 3DRL 2529, item 126.

7 On Bobdubi Ridge

1 Dexter, *The New Guinea Offensives*, pp. 60–1. Travers and Newman to Long, AWM 93, 50/2/23/024 & 183.
2 Herring interview with Dexter, AWM 172/6.
3 Savige records, AWM 3DRL2529, item 126.
4 3rd Div War Diary, AWM 52, 1/5/4/055, scan 002. Herring interview with Dexter, AWM 172/6.
5 Hammer comments, AWM 93, 50/2/23/440. 58/59th Bn WD, AWM 52, 8/3/95/009, scans 005–8.
6 Savige records, AWM 3DRL 2529, item 126.
7 Ibid.
8 Harold Hibbert, 58/59th Bn, interview. Travers comments, AWM 93, 50/2/23/24. Parer Diary, SLNSW, ML MSS 1097/1.
9 2/3rd Ind Coy WD, AWM 52, 25/3/3.
10 2/3rd Ind Coy WD, AWM 52, 25/3/3, Appendices. Dexter, *The New Guinea Offensives*, p. 67. Travers comments, AWM 93, 50/2/23/024.
11 2/3rd Ind Coy WD, AWM 52, 25/3/3. ATIS documents, AWM 54, 423/4/71.
12 Dexter, *The New Guinea Offensives*, pp. 58–9. 15th Bde WD, AWM52, 8/2/015, scan 004.
13 Dexter, *The New Guinea Offensives*, p. 57. Boechi, *Senshi Sosho*, vol. 3, pp. 332–3.
14 58/59th Bn WD, AWM52, 8/3/95, May–June 1943, scan 131.

15 15th Bde Operations Report, AWM 3DRL 2529, item 130.
16 Savige records, AWM 3DRL 2529, item 126.
17 Guinn comments, AWM 93, 50/2/23/453. Dexter interviews with Berryman and Savige, AWM 172, items 10 & 7.
18 Berryman diary, AWM PR84/370, item 3. Dave Taylor, 58/59th Bn, interview. Guinn comments, AWM 93, 50/2/23/453. 58/59th Bn WD, AWM52, 8/3/95/009, scans 134–5.
19 15th Bde Ops Report, AWM 3DRL 2529, item 130. Starr to Dexter, AWM 172/53.
20 Mathews, *Militia Battalion at War*, p. 26.
21 58/59th Bn WD, AWM52, 8/3/95, May–June 1943, scan 132. Pinney, diary transcript.
22 Guinn to Dexter, AWM 93, 50/2/23/453. Jack Shewan and James Matheson, 58/59th Bn, interviews.
23 Pinney, diary transcript.
24 Harold Hibbert, 58/59th Bn, interview. Dave Taylor, 58/59th Bn, memoirs. Pinney, diary transcript.
25 Dave Taylor, 58/59th Bn, memoirs and interview.
26 58/59th Bn WD, AWM52, 8/3/95/9, scan 107. Pinney, diary transcript.
27 Mathews, *Militia Battalion at War*, p. 34.
28 Pinney, diary transcript. Griff comments, AWM 93, 50/2/23/608. 15th Bde Operations Report, AWM 3DRL 2529, item 130.
29 Dave Taylor, 58/59th Bn, memoirs.
30 Ibid. and interview.
31 Pinney, diary transcript.
32 Jack Shewan, 58/59th Bn, interview.
33 Pinney, diary transcript.
34 Dexter, *The New Guinea Offensives*, p. 110. Griff to Dexter, AWM 93, 50/2/23/608.
35 Mathews, *Militia Battalion at War*, pp. 30–1.
36 Ibid., pp. 31–2. Griff to Dexter, AWM 93, 50/2/23/608.
37 Pinney, diary transcript.
38 Ibid. 58/59th Bn WD, AWM 52, 8/3/95/9, scans 107–8. Mathews, *Militia Battalion at War*, p. 33.
39 'Attack and defence of Old Vickers position', 15th Bde report, AWM 52, 8/2/15/066, scans 120–4. 15th Bde Operations Report, AWM 3DRL 2529, item 130. ATIS translations, AWM 55, 3/7, 075 & 3/8, 082.
40 15th Bde WD, AWM 52, 8/2/15/017, scan 020.
41 Ibid., scans 020–1. Harold Hibbert, 58/59th Bn, interview. Recommendations for awards 58/59th Bn, AWM 54, 391/11/89. Duncanson was awarded an MM. Kevin Crimmins was killed six weeks later and is buried alongside his brother in Lae War Cemetery.
42 15th Bde WD, AWM 52, 8/2/15/016, scan 005.
43 15th Bde Operations Report, AWM 3DRL 2529, item 130. 15th Bde WD, AWM 52, 8/2/15/017, scan 021. 3rd Div WD, AWM 52, 1/5/4/055, scan 004.
44 Travers comments, AWM 93, 50/2/23/024.
45 15th Bde Operations Report, AWM 3DRL 2529, item 130.

46 58/59th Bn WD, AWM52, 8/3/95/9, scans 107–8. 15th Bde Operations
    Report, AWM 3DRL 2529, item 130.
47 15th Bde WD, AWM 52, 8/2/15/017, scan 016.
48 Ibid., scan 022.
49 Wilton diary, AWM 93, 50/2/23/444.
50 Matheson, 58/59th Bn, interview. Griff comments, AWM 93, 50/2/23/608.
51 AWM 55, 5/4, EP-44, 51st Div Intel reports, Intel 031. Tanaka, *Ops of
    IJAF*, p. 160. Yoshihara, *Southern Cross*, chapter 10, also mentions Hongo.
52 Griff comments, AWM 93, 50/2/23/608.
53 Maughan, *Tobruk and El Alamein*, pp. 558–9. Farquhar, *Derrick VC*, p. 85.
54 Travers comments, AWM 93, 50/2/23/024.
55 15th Bde WD, AWM 52, 8/2/15/016, scans 011–14.
56 Boechi, *Senshi Sosho*, vol. 3, pp. 328–30. Tanaka, *Ops of IJAF*, pp. 159–60.
57 5th Div WD, AWM 52, 1/5/10/031, scan 005. 29th Bde WD, AWM 52,
    8/2/29/015, scan 075.
58 Boechi, *Senshi Sosho*, vol. 3, pp. 355–7.
59 58/59th Bn WD, AWM52, 8/3/95/10, scan 004.
60 ATIS enemy pubs, AWM 55, 5/4, EP-44, Intel 031, 6 July 1943. Tanaka,
    Ops of IJAF, p. 160.
61 15th Bde Ops Report, AWM 3DRL 2529, item 130.
62 15th Bde WD, AWM 52, 8/2/15/016, scan 015. Dexter, *The New Guinea
    Offensives*, p. 128.
63 RAAF No. 22 Squadron WD, NAA A9186–85, scan 218.
64 15th Bde WD, AWM 52, 8/2/15/016, scans 015–16.
65 58/59th Bn WD, AWM52, 8/3/95/10, scan 006.
66 Dave Taylor, 58/59th Bn, memoirs. Mathews, *Militia Battalion at War*,
    p. 38. Jack Shewan, 58/59th Bn, interview. ATIS enemy pubs, AWM 55,
    EP-44, 51st Div Intel Report 031, 6 July 1943.
67 Mathews, *Militia Battalion at War*, pp. 38–9.
68 Hemery, 'Ambush on the Komiatum', NAA SP300/3, 414.
69 James Matheson, 58/59th Bn, interview. Mathews, *Militia Battalion at War*,
    p. 68.
70 Hemery, 'Ambush on the Komiatum', NAA SP300/3, 414. Mathews, *Militia
    Battalion at War*, pp. 69–70.
71 Mathews, *Militia Battalion at War*, pp. 71–3. 58/59th Bn WD, AWM52,
    8/3/95/10, scan 015.
72 Starr to Dexter, AWM 172/53. Harold Hibbert, 58/59th Bn, interview. 17th
    Bde WD, AWM 52, 8/2/17/094, scan 014. Parer diary, SLNSW, ML MSS
    1097/1.
73 15th Bde WD, AWM 52, 8/2/15/066, scans 120–4.
74 Wal Johnson, 58/59th Bn, in Dickins, *Ordinary Heroes*, pp. 220–1.
75 Damien Parer, 'Assault on Salamaua', *Salt*, 25 October 1943.
76 Mathews, *Militia Battalion at War*, p. 39.

8 Yanks
1 Blamey report on Salamaua operations, AWM 54, 519/6/58. Although the
   correct spelling is Nasau Bay, I have used Nassau Bay in conformity with
   reports of the time.

2   Morison, *History of United States Naval Operations in World War II: Breaking the Bismarcks Barrier*, p. 137.
3   Herring comments on Official History, AWM 67, 3/167.
4   McCartney, *The Jungleers*, p. 191. Savige records, AWM 3DRL 2529, item 126.
5   Alfred Smith, 532nd EB&S Regt, diary.
6   MacKechnie Force report, AWM 54, 587/7/32. Casey, *Amphibian Engineer Operations*, p. 65.
7   Morison, *Breaking the Bismarcks Barrier*, pp. 137–8.
8   ATIS interrogation reports, AWM 55, 6/4, IR192 & 6/5, IR211.
9   ATIS enemy publications, AWM 55, 5/3, EP-43, 29 June 1943.
10 Alfred Smith, 532nd EB&S Regt, diary.
11 Westerfield, 'Miracle landing at Nassau Bay', in *41st Infantry Division: Fighting Jungleers II*, pp. 412–13.
12 US Army, *History of the Second Engineer Special Brigade*, pp. 37–9.
13 Savige records, AWM 3DRL 2529, item 126.
14 Stephens, 17th Bde, *Khaki and Green*, pp. 149–50. Urquhart to Dexter, AWM 93, 50/2/23/457.
15 Stephens, 17th Bde, *Khaki and Green*, p. 151. Dexter, *The New Guinea Offensives*, p. 93.
16 Urquhart, Ellen and Burke to Dexter, AWM 93, 50/2/23/457, 607 and 808. As also noted in the Official History, Burke and Urquhart's accounts differed markedly on a number of points.
17 Alfred Smith, 532nd EB&S Regt, diary.
18 Jack Fleming, 741st Ordnance Coy, interview.
19 Stephens, 17th Bde, 'Rendezvous at Nassau Bay', *Khaki and Green*, pp. 149–52.
20 Hemery, 'The landing at Nassau Bay', NAA, SP300/3, 408.
21 Casey, *Amphibian Engineer Operations*, p. 67.
22 Hemery, 'The landing at Nassau Bay', NAA, SP300/3, 408.
23 MacKechnie Force report, AWM 54, 587/7/32. Westerfield, 'Miracle landing at Nassau Bay', in *41st Infantry Division: Fighting Jungleers II*, pp. 412–13.
24 Morison, *Breaking the Bismarcks Barrier*, p. 138.
25 ATIS interrogation reports, AWM 55, 6/5, IR211.
26 US Army, *History of the Second Engineer Special Brigade*, pp. 37–9. Alfred Smith, 532nd EB&S Regt, diary.
27 Westerfield and Devenney, 'Night in Green', in *41st Infantry Division*, pp. 63–64.
28 AWM 54, 391/11/22. Private Shadbolt was awarded the MM.
29 Tanaka, *Operations of IJAF*, p. 158. ATIS interrogation reports, AWM 55, 6/4, IR192.
30 Westerfield and Devenney, 'Night in Green', in *41st Infantry Division*, pp. 63–64. Bob Burns, 162nd Regt, interview.
31 US Army, *History of the Second Engineer Special Brigade*, pp. 37–9.
32 Dexter, *The New Guinea Offensives*, pp. 98–9. Dexter notes eighteen Americans killed and twenty-seven wounded.

33 Dickson, *Flying for the Army*, pp. 20–2.
34 Sinclair, *To Find a Path*, pp. 159–62.
35 Ibid., pp. 162–3. Simpson, 'From Nassau Bay to the Sepik', NAA SP300/3, 863.
36 Dexter, *The New Guinea Offensives*, p. 92.
37 Bill Dexter, 'The battalion my home', AWM PR01182/4.
38 Bill Dexter, 2/6th Bn, in Hay, *Nothing Over Us*, pp. 324–5.
39 Urquhart to Dexter, AWM 93, 50/2/23/457.
40 Shinoda, *The 66th Inf Regt at Salamaua*. Boechi, *Senshi Sosho*, vol. 3, pp. 328–30.
41 Morison, *Breaking the Bismarcks Barrier*, p. 138.
42 US Army, *History of the Second Engineer Special Brigade*, p. 214. Keele was awarded a DSC.
43 MacKechnie Force report, AWM 54, 587/7/32. Dickson, *Flying for the Army*, p. 22. 3rd Div WD AWM 52, 1/5/4/055, scan 012.
44 17th Bde Operation Report, AWM 3DRL 5043 item 108. Boechi, *Senshi Sosho*, vol. 3, p. 328.
45 Tanaka, *Operations of IJAF*, p. 159. ATIS interrogation reports, AWM 55, 6/4, IR192. Shinoda, *The 66th Inf Regt at Salamaua*.
46 17th Bde Operation Report, AWM 3DRL 5043 item 108. 17th Bde War Diary, AWM 52, 8/2/17/089, scan 008.
47 3rd Div WD, AWM 52, 1/5/4/064, scan 045.
48 Dickson, *Flying for the Army*, pp. 22–3.
49 Westerfield, Ricks, Reuter and Jones, 'Cannoneers up Bitoi River', *41st Infantry Division*, pp. 67–69.
50 3rd Div WD, AWM 52, 1/5/4/055, scan 016. Moten interview with Dexter, AWM 172/6.

9 Mubo falls

1 Blamey report on Salamaua operations, AWM 54, 519/6/58. Savige records, AWM 3DRL 2529, item 126.
2 17th Bde Ops Report, AWM 3DRL 5043 item 108.
3 Gullett, *Not as a Duty Only*, p. 124.
4 2/6th Bn WD, AWM 52, 8/3/6/023, scan 014.
5 17th Bde Ops Report, AWM 3DRL 5043, item 108. 2/6th Bn WD, AWM 52, 8/3/6/023, scan 014. 17th Bde WD, AWM 52, 8/2/17/089, scan 009.
6 Bruce Lang, 2/6th Bn, in Hay, *Nothing Over Us*, pp. 326–8. Perce Harris, 2/6th Bn, interview.
7 Jack Weeks, 2/6th Bn, in Hay, *Nothing Over Us*, p. 328.
8 Lou Nazzari, 2/5th Bn, interview. 17th Bde WD, AWM 52, 8/2/17/094, scan 040.
9 Hay, *Nothing Over Us*, p. 329. 17th Bde WD, AWM 52, 8/2/17/094, scan 040. Dexter to Long, AWM 93, 50/2/23/99.
10 Hay, *Nothing Over Us*, p. 330. Savige records, AWM 3DRL 2529, item 126.
11 Tanaka, *Ops of IJAF*, p. 161. Shinoda, *The 66th Inf Regt at Salamaua*.

12 Ron Moss, 2/6th Bn, in Hay, *Nothing Over Us*, p. 331. Moss was awarded a DCM for his 'coolness, sound judgement and courage' at Observation Hill.
13 Lou Nazzari, 2/5th Bn, interview. Pearson, *Brothers, Battlers and Bastards*, p. 112.
14 Pearson, *Brothers, Battlers and Bastards*, p. 112.
15 2/6th Bn WD, AWM 52, 8/3/6/023, scans 032-3. 17th Bde Ops Report, AWM 3DRL 5043 item 108. Weeks, 2/6th Bn, AWM PR85/241. Dexter to Long, AWM 93, 50/2/23/99.
16 Westerfield and Noble, 'Cutting the Komiatum Track', *41st Infantry Division*, pp. 305-307. 17th Bde Ops Report, AWM 3DRL 5043 item 108.
17 Shinoda, *The 66th Inf Regt at Salamaua*.
18 Ibid. 51st Div Intel, AWM 55, EP-44, Intel 35.
19 2/5th Bn WD, AWM 52, 8/3/5/013, scan 106. Cyril Miles, 2/5th Bn, interview.
20 Cyril Miles, 2/5th Bn, interview.
21 Westerfield et al., 'C Battery, 218 Field Artillery: Cannoneers up Bitoi River', *41st Infantry Division*, pp. 67-9. Dexter, *The New Guinea Offensives*, p. 127.
22 Westerfield, 'C Company 162 Infantry: Cless-Robson fight for Salamaua', *41st Infantry Division*, pp. 65-6.
23 Ibid.
24 3rd Div WD, AWM 52, 1/5/4/064, scan 042. 17th Bde WD, AWM 52, 8/2/17/089, scan 014.
25 Gullett, *Not as a Duty Only*, p. 120. Bill Quinn, 2/6th Bn, interview. After the war Gullett was elected to his father's former seat and held it for nine years.
26 Savige records, AWM 3DRL 2529, item 126. Dexter, *The New Guinea Offensives*, p. 137.
27 Blamey to Herring, AWM 54, 591/7/21.
28 Herring comments on Official History, AWM 67, 3/167.
29 Savige records, AWM 3DRL 2529, item 126.

10 'A bit of a stoush'

1 15th Bde Ops Report, AWM 3DRL 2529, item 130.
2 Ibid.
3 2/3rd Ind Coy WD, AWM 52, 25/3/3. Pinney, diary transcript.
4 Garland, *Nothing is Forever*, pp. 163-4.
5 ATIS Enemy Pubs, AWM 55, 5/4, EP-44, 51st Div Intel Report 33, 7 July 1943. 2/3rd Ind Coy WD, AWM 52, 25/3/3, appendices.
6 Pinney, diary transcript.
7 Garland, *Nothing is Forever*, pp. 165-6. Pinney, diary transcript.
8 15th Bde Ops Report, AWM 3DRL 2529, item 130.
9 Vin Maguire, 2/3rd Ind Coy, interview.
10 Warfe to Dexter, AWM 93, 50/2/23/489.
11 Ibid. 2/3rd Ind Coy WD. AWM 52, 25/3/3.
12 15th Bde WD, AWM 52, 8/2/15/017, scan 039.
13 Brian Walpole, 2/3rd Ind Coy, interview.
14 Ibid.

15 Pinney, diary transcript.
16 Norm Bear, 2/3rd Ind Coy, interview. Les Poulson, 2/3rd Ind Coy, in Garland, *Nothing is Forever*, p. 180. Taylor was awarded the Military Medal for his 'high courage and great skill'.
17 Robbie Roberts, 2/3rd Ind Coy, in Garland, *Nothing is Forever*, p. 179. Norm Bear, 2/3rd Ind Coy, interview.
18 Garland, *Nothing is Forever*, pp. 171–5. Pinney, diary transcript.
19 Pinney, diary transcript. 'Troppy' refers to George Tropman.
20 Ibid. 'Babe' probably refers to Harold Summerfield.
21 Dexter, *The New Guinea Offensives*, p. 132.
22 15th Bde WD, AWM 52, 8/2/15/064, scan 153.
23 2/3rd Ind Coy WD, AWM 52, 25/3/3. Pinney, diary transcript.
24 Pinney, diary transcript.
25 Norm Bear, 2/3rd Ind Coy, interview.
26 Dexter, *The New Guinea Offensives*, p. 134. 15th Bde WD, AWM 52, 8/2/15/067, scan 007.
27 Bob Hancock, 2/3rd Ind Coy, letter, 12 July 1943. 15th Bde WD, AWM 52, 8/2/15/067, scan 064.
28 Garland, *Nothing is Forever*, p. 183.
29 Keith Myers, 2/3rd Ind Coy, interview. McEvoy to Dexter, AWM 93, 50/2/23/638.
30 Ibid. Dexter, *The New Guinea Offensives*, p. 150. McEvoy was awarded a DCM, Wellings an MM.
31 Garland, *Nothing is Forever*, pp. 189–93.
32 Robbie Roberts, 2/3rd Ind Coy, in Garland, *Nothing is Forever*, pp. 193–4.
33 ATIS Enemy Pubs, AWM 55, 5/4, EP-44, 51st Div Intel Report 36, 19 July 1943. Tanaka, *Ops of the IJAF*, p. 163. Garland, *Nothing is Forever*, p. 198.
34 Pinney, diary transcript.
35 Garland, *Nothing is Forever*, p. 417. Neilsen was awarded the DCM for this and later actions.
36 Dexter, *The New Guinea Offensives*, p. 152.
37 Garland, *Nothing is Forever*, p. 205.
38 ATIS Enemy Pubs, AWM 55, 5/4, EP-44, 51st Div Intel Report 36, 19 July 1943.
39 Garland, *Nothing is Forever*, pp. 205–6.
40 Ibid., pp. 207–8.
41 Ibid., p. 209.
42 Ibid., p. 210.
43 Norm Bear, 2/3rd Ind Coy, interview.
44 Garland, *Nothing is Forever*, pp. 222–4.
45 Ibid., p. 220.
46 Brian Walpole, 2/3rd Ind Coy, interview.
47 Allan Oehlman, 2/3rd Ind Coy, letter, 20 August 1993, in Murray, *Memoirs*, attachment 4.
48 Norm Bear, 2/3rd Ind Coy, interview.
49 Allan Oehlman, 2/3rd Ind Coy, letter, 10 May 2002, in Murray, *Memoirs*, attachment 1.

50 Keith Myers, 2/3rd Ind Coy, interview.
51 17th Bde WD, 8/2/17/089, scan 019.
52 Keith Myers, 2/3rd Ind Coy, interview.
53 Travers, Wood and Price to Long, AWM 93, 50/2/23/024, 469 & 566.
54 Bruce Lang, 2/6th Bn, in Hay, *Nothing Over Us*, pp. 346–7.
55 Bruce Lang and Cliff Hirst, 2/6th Bn, in Hay, *Nothing Over Us*, pp. 347–9.
    Perce Harris, 2/6th Bn, interview and letter.
56 17th Bde WD, 8/2/17/089, scan 019. Garland, *Nothing is Forever*, pp.
    224–5. Dexter, *The New Guinea Offensives*, p. 155. 2/3rd Ind Coy WD.
    AWM 52, 25/3/3.
57 Garland, *Nothing is Forever*, pp. 227–8. 17th Bde WD, 8/2/17/089, scan
    020. 2/6th Bn WD, AWM 52, 8/3/6/023, scan 052. 15th Bde Ops Report,
    AWM 3DRL 2529, item 130.
58 2/6th Bn WD, AWM 52, 8/3/6/023, scans 054–5. Alan Henry, 2/6th Bn,
    interview. Lance Copland, 2/5th Bn, interview.
59 Price to Long, AWM 93, 50/2/23/566. Perce Harris, 2/6th Bn, letter.
60 Cliff Hirst, 2/6th Bn, in Hay, *Nothing Over Us*, pp. 351–2.
61 15th Bde WD, AWM 52, 8/2/15/067, scan 066. Garland, *Nothing is
    Forever*, p. 240. Doublet operations, AWM 54, 587/6/2.
62 Darren Robins, interview. Parer diary, SLNSW, ML MSS 1097/1.
63 Damien Parer, 'Assault on Salamaua', *Salt*, 25 October 1943.
64 Parer Diary, SLNSW, ML MSS 1097/1.
65 Parer, 'Assault on Salamaua'. 2/3rd Ind Coy WD, AWM 52, 25/3/3.
66 Parer Diary, SLNSW, ML MSS 1097/1. Parer, 'Assault on Salamaua'.

11 *The forbidden mountain*

 1 Caffin interview, AWM 54, 422/7/8. 17th Bde WD, 8/2/17/089, scan 017.
 2 Walters service record, NAA, B883.
 3 Arthur Carlsen, 2/5th Bn, letter. Mick Walters, 2/5th Bn, interview.
 4 Bennett, *Rough Infantry*, p. 166. Bryan Ryan, 2/5th Bn, interview,
    19 August 2007.
 5 51st Division Intel, AWM 55, EP-44, Intel 36.
 6 Mick Walters, 2/5th Bn, in *Salamaua Siege*, pp. 8–9. 17th Bde WD,
    8/2/17/089, scan 017.
 7 Arthur Carlsen, 2/5th Bn, interview and letter.
 8 Cameron to Dexter, AWM 93, 50/2/23/153. Bennett, *Rough Infantry*,
    p. 165. Ron Beaver, 2/5th Bn, interview.
 9 Cameron to Dexter, AWM 93, 50/2/23/153. Allan Jones, 'Japs tough, but
    AIF have their measure', *Sun*, 1943. 17th Bde WD, 8/2/17/089, scan 017.
10 Lieutenant Caffin, interview, AWM 54, 422/7/8. Walters notes, AWM 67,
    3/411.
11 Bryan Ryan, 2/5th Bn, interview.
12 Lance Copland, 'Ordeal by night' in Ross, *The Magazine of 17 Australian
    Infantry Brigade*, pp. 114–15.
13 Swan, 'Communications at Tambu', NAA SP300/3, 118. Trigellis-Smith, *All
    the King's Enemies*, p. 229.

14 3rd Div WD, AWM 52, 1/5/4/064, scan 052. 17th Bde WD, 8/2/17/089, scan 017.

15 The Official History uses a post-war sketch map drawn by Brigadier Moten upon which distances are based. Unfortunately that map has the distance between the southern edge of Mount Tambu and Tambu Knoll as approximately 200 metres when it is actually 1200 metres, six times the distance.

16 17th Bde WD, 8/2/17/089, scan 018. Walters notes, AWM 67, 3/411. Jackson was awarded a DCM.

17 Shinoda, *The 66th Inf Regt at Salamaua*. ATIS Enemy Pubs, AWM 55, 5/4, EP-44, 51st Div Intel 41, 18 July 1943.

18 Cyril Miles, 2/5th Bn, interview.

19 Ibid. Fred Allan, 2/5th Bn, letter.

20 Cyril Miles, 2/5th Bn, interview.

21 Ibid.

22 Shinoda, *The 66th Inf Regt at Salamaua*.

23 Percy Friend was awarded an MM and Bill Tiller a DCM, although he would not live to receive it.

24 Dexter, *The New Guinea Offensives*, p. 149. Mick Walters, 2/5th Bn, in *Salamaua Siege*, p. 11.

25 Trigellis-Smith, *All the King's Enemies*, p. 361. Beddome was awarded the MM.

26 Dexter, *The New Guinea Offensives*, p. 149. Ron Beaver, 2/5th Battalion, interview, 1 May 2004. Cameron to Dexter, AWM 93, 50/2/23/153. Mick Walters, 2/5th Bn, interview.

27 17th Bde WD, 8/2/17/089, scan 018.

28 Ibid., scans 018–19.

29 ATIS Enemy Pubs, AWM 55, 5/4, EP-44, 51st Division Intel Report 38, 23 July 1943.

30 ATIS interrogation reports, AWM 55, 6/4, IR191. Shinoda, *The 66th Inf Regt at Salamaua*.

31 Trigellis-Smith, *All the King's Enemies*, pp. 228–9. 17th Bde WD, 8/2/17/089, scan 123.

32 Allan Jones, 'Japs tough, but AIF have their measure', *Sun*, 1943. Dexter, *The New Guinea Offensives*, p. 198.

33 Cameron to Dexter, AWM 93, 50/2/23/153. 17th Bde WD, 8/2/17/089, scan 133.

34 Speed, *Esprit de Corps*, pp. 240–1. Cameron to Dexter, AWM 93, 50/2/23/153.

35 Cameron to Dexter, AWM 93, 50/2/23/153. Alvin Williams, 2/5th Bn, interview.

36 Cameron to Dexter, AWM 93, 50/2/23/153.

37 Ibid. Ron Beaver, 2/5th Bn, interview. Curtin papers, NAA, M1415, 329.

38 Caffin interview with Smith, AWM 54, 422/7/8.

39 ATIS Enemy Pubs, AWM 55, EP-44, 51st Div Intel 40, 27 July 1943. Shinoda, *The 66th Inf Regt at Salamaua*.

40 Savige records, AWM 3DRL 2529, item 126. Parer diary, SLNSW, ML MSS
    1097/1. Moten interview with Dexter, AWM 172/9.
41 Conroy to Brill, AWM 93, 50/2/23/174.
42 Westerfield and MacKechnie, '162d Infantry Assails Mount Tambu', *41st
    Infantry Division*, pp. 70–71.
43 Ron Beaver, 2/5th Bn, interview.
44 17th Bde Ops Report, AWM 3DRL 5043 item 108.
45 Westerfield and MacKechnie, '162d Infantry Assails Mount Tambu', *41st
    Infantry Division*, pp. 70–71.
46 Clyde Paton, in Warby, *The 25 Pounders*, p. 240.
47 Ron Beaver, 2/5th Bn, interview.
48 Westerfield and MacKechnie, '162d Infantry Assails Mount Tambu', *41st
    Infantry Division*, pp. 70–71. Clyde Paton, in Warby, *The 25 Pounders*,
    p. 240.
49 Westerfield and MacKechnie, '162d Infantry Assails Mount Tambu', *41st
    Infantry Division*, pp. 70–71.
50 Ibid. Ron Beaver, 2/5th Bn, interview.
51 Shinoda, *The 66th Inf Regt at Salamaua*.
52 Clyde Paton, in Warby, *The 25 Pounders*, pp. 240–1.
53 'Recock and refigure', *Wartime*, 46, p. 14. Lance Copland and Ron Beaver
    2/5th Bn, interviews.
54 Shinoda, *The 66th Inf Regt at Salamaua*.
55 Moten interview with Dexter, AWM 172/9. Savige records, AWM 3DRL
    2529, item 126.

12 Roosevelt Ridge

1   Dexter, *The New Guinea Offensives*, p. 138.
2   McCartney, *The Jungleers*, pp. 194–5.
3   3rd Div WD, AWM 52, 1/5/4/064, scan 046.
4   Dexter, *The New Guinea Offensives*, pp. 139–40. 3rd Div WD, AWM 52,
    1/5/4/055, scans 011–14.
5   17th Bde WD, AWM 52, 8/2/17/094, scan 019. Tanaka, *Ops of IJAF*,
    p. 162. Sinclair, *To Find a Path*, p. 164. Dexter, *The New Guinea
    Offensives*, p. 142.
6   Dexter, *The New Guinea Offensives*, pp. 142–3.
7   Hemery, 'Stocktaking', NAA SP300/3, 416. Tanaka, *Ops of IJAF*, p. 161.
8   Savige records, AWM 3DRL 2529, item 126. McCartney, *The Jungleers*,
    p. 61.
9   Dexter, *The New Guinea Offensives*, pp. 143–5.
10 Gomme, *A Gunner's Eye View*. Warby, *The 25 Pounders*, p. 238.
11 Salamaua Operations – Artillery, AWM 54, 587/6/9.
12 Westerfield and Helmer, 'Under the Japanese Cannon', *41st Infantry
    Division*, pp. 77–9.
13 Westerfield, Carlson and Dunkin, 'Roosevelt Ridge and Berger Hill', *41st
    Infantry Division*, pp. 272–3. Westerfield and Young, 'Roosevelt Ridge and
    C Ridge', *41st Infantry Division*, pp. 258–60.
14 AWM 55, 5/4, EP-44, 12 August 1943, 51 Div intel report 8.

15 Dexter, *The New Guinea Offensives*, pp. 179–80. Savige interview with Dexter, AWM 172, item 7. NGF WD, AWM 52, 1/5/51/040, scan 004.

16 42nd Bn WD, AWM 52, 8/3/81/014, scan 109.

17 Milford interview with Long, AWM 93, 50/2/23/445.

18 Milford comments, AWM 93, 50/2/23/445.

19 42nd Bn WD, AWM 52, 8/3/81/015, scan 090.

20 Benson, *The Story of the 42nd Battalion*, pp. 48–9. Davidson to Dexter, AWM 93, 50/2/23/486.

21 42nd Bn WD, AWM 52, 8/3/81, scan 111. The 2/5th Battalion men remained with the 42nd Battalion until 21 August.

22 Benson, *The Story of the 42nd Battalion*, pp. 53–4. 17th Bde Ops Report, AWM 3DRL 5043, item 108.

23 Iredale interview with Long, AWM 67, 2/28.

24 ATIS Enemy Pubs, AWM 55, 5/4, EP-44, 51st Div Intel Report 8, 12 August 1943.

25 29th Bde WD, AWM 52, 8/2/29/015, scans 73–6.

26 29th Bde WD, AWM 52, 8/2/29/015, scans 78–80. ATIS interrogation reports, AWM 55, 6/4, IR173 & IR175. Boechi, *Senshi Sosho*, vol. 3, pp. 353–5.

27 29th Bde WD, AWM 52, 8/2/29/015, scan 53.

28 Westerfield and Messec, 'Jungle Pursuit at Salamaua', *41st Infantry Division*, pp. 72–3. 29th Brigade reports have Messec's name recorded as Massey.

29 29th Bde WD, AWM 52, 8/2/29/015, scans 61 & 72. Westerfield and Messec, 'Jungle Pursuit at Salamaua', *41st Infantry Division*, pp. 72–3.

30 Westerfield and Camp, 'Sgt Camp's Patrol Against Oba's Raiders', *41st Infantry Division*, pp. 336–7. 29th Bde WD, AWM 52, 8/2/29/015, scan 061.

31 Westerfield and Messec, 'Jungle Pursuit at Salamaua', *41st Infantry Division*, pp. 72–3.

32 Dexter, *The New Guinea Offensives*, pp. 213–14.

33 Warby, *The 25 Pounders*, pp. 272–3. Marien, 'Japanese suicide patrol', NAA SP300/3, 647.

34 Marien, 'Japanese suicide patrol', NAA SP300/3, 647.

35 3rd Div WD, AWM 52, 1/5/4/023, scans 140–2. Wilton diary, AWM 93, 50/2/23/44. Boechi, *Senshi Sosho*, vol. 3, pp. 352–5.

36 41st Division artillery operations report, AWM 54, 687/6/9.

37 AWM 55, 5/4, EP-44, 51 Div intel reports 6 and 9, 10 & 14 August 1943. ATIS translations, AWM 55, 3/8, 082.

38 McCartney, *The Jungleers*, p. 63. Benson, *The Story of the 42nd Australian Infantry Battalion*, pp. 71–2. Jack Glynn, 15th Bn, AWM, PR 02039. Dexter, *The New Guinea Offensives*, p. 185.

39 Westerfield and Helmer, 'Under the Japanese Cannon', *41st Infantry Division*, pp. 77–9. Salamaua Operations – Artillery, AWM 54, 587/6/9.

40 Westerfield and Kelley, 'Epic Heroism On Scout Ridge', *41st Infantry Division*, pp. 88–90.

41 Westerfield, Lipke and Feele, 'K Co. 162 Infantry's Papuan Campaign', *41st Infantry Division*, pp. 417–18.
42 Westerfield, Pope and Kindt, 'Perimeter fighting on Scout Ridge', *41st Infantry Division*, pp. 91–2.
43 Westerfield and George, 'Battle on George Ridge', *41st Infantry Division*, pp. 82–3.
44 CMH, *US Army Campaigns of WWII: New Guinea*, p. 9.

13 Old Vickers

1 Starr to Dexter, AWM 172/53. Griff to Brill, AWM 93, 50/2/23/608.
2 Starr to Dexter, AWM 172/53. Proby to Dexter, AWM 93, 50/2/23/182.
3 Warfe to Dexter, Smith to Brill, Mathews to Brill, AWM 93, 50/2/23/178, 489 & 495.
4 Griff to Dexter, Proby to Dexter, AWM 93, 50/2/23/608 & 182.
5 Griff comments, AWM 93, 50/2/23/608. 17th Bde WD, AWM 52, 8/2/17/089, scan 154.
6 Proby to Dexter, AWM 93, 50/2/23/182. Griff comments, AWM 93, 50/2/23/608.
7 James Matheson, 58/59th Bn, interview. Award recommendations 58/59th Bn, AWM 54, 391/11/89.
8 2/3rd Ind Coy WD, AWM 52, 25/3/3, appendices.
9 15th Bde Ops Report, AWM 3DRL 2529, item 130. Mathews, *Militia Battalion at War*, pp. 45–6. 15th Bde WD, AWM 52, 8/2/15/064, scan 120.
10 15th Bde Ops Report, AWM 3DRL 2529, item 130.
11 Mathews, *Militia Battalion at War*, p. 44.
12 15th Bde WD, AWM 52, 8/2/15/017, scan 191.
13 Les Franklin, 58/59th Bn, in Mathews, *Militia Battalion at War*, p. 48.
14 Proby to Dexter, AWM 93, 50/2/23/182.
15 Parer diary, SLNSW, ML MSS 1097/1. Dave Taylor, 58/59th Bn, interview and memoirs.
16 Mathews, *Militia Battalion at War*, pp. 51–2.
17 Proby to Dexter, AWM 93, 50/2/23/182. Mathews, *Militia Battalion at War*, pp. 50–1.
18 Dave Taylor, 58/59th Bn, interview.
19 Griff comments, AWM 93, 50/2/23/608. Jack Shewan, 58/59th Bn, interview.
20 15th Bde Ops Report, AWM 3DRL 2529, item 130. 58/59th Bn WD, AWM 52, 8/3/95/10, scan 019.
21 Proby to Dexter, AWM 93, 50/2/23/182. 3rd Div WD, AWM 52, 1/5/4/026, scan 036.
22 Hammer comments on Official History, AWM 93, 50/2/23/440.
23 15th Bde WD, AWM 52, 8/2/015/017, scan 191.
24 Griff comments, AWM 93, 50/2/23/608. Parer diary, SLNSW, ML MSS 1097/1.
25 John Quirk, 58/59th Bn, in Mathews, *Militia Battalion at War*, pp. 58–9.
26 James Matheson, 58/59th Bn, interview.
27 Ted Griff, 58/59th Bn, in Mathews, *Militia Battalion at War*, p. 57.

28 Griff comments, AWM 93, 50/2/23/608. James Matheson, 58/59th Bn, interview.
29 James Matheson, 58/59th Bn, interview.
30 Ibid.
31 Griff comments, AWM 93, 50/2/23/608.
32 2/7th Bn WD, AWM 52, 8/3/7/35, scan 002. Dave Taylor, 58/59th Bn, notes on battalion history. ATIS Enemy Pubs, AWM 55, 5/4, EP-44, 51st Div Intel Report 1, 10 August 1943.
33 James Matheson, 58/59th Bn, interview. ATIS Enemy Pubs, AWM 55, 5/4, EP-44, 51st Div Intel Report 1, 10 August 1943.
34 2/7th Bn WD, AWM 52, 8/3/7/35, scan 002.
35 2/7th Bn citations, AWM 54, 391/11/23. Forst was awarded an MM.
36 Sym to Duell, AWM 93, 50/2/23/812.
37 Naismith service record, NAA B883/6. Sym to Duell, AWM 93, 50/2/23/812.
38 2/7th Bn WD, AWM 52, 8/3/7/35, scans 065–6. Bruce Peterson, 2/7th Bn, notes.
39 Win Howard, 2/7th Bn, memoirs.
40 Mathews, *Militia Battalion at War*, pp. 60–2.
41 ATIS Enemy Pubs, AWM 55, 5/4, EP-44, 51st Div Intel Report 1, 10 August 1943.
42 James Matheson, 58/59th Bn, interview.
43 15th Bde WD, AWM 52, 8/2/15/067, scan 051. 2/7th Bn WD, AWM 52, 8/3/7/36, scan 109.
44 15th Bde WD, AWM 52, 8/2/15/025, scans 002–3 & 8/2/15/024, scan 110.
45 2/7th Bn WD, AWM 52, 8/3/7/36, scans 014–16.
46 ATIS Enemy Pubs, AWM 55, 5/4, EP-44, 51st Div Intel Report 6, 10 August 1943.
47 Rooke to Long, AWM 93, 50/2/23/570. Jack Mitchell, 2/7th Bn, Diary.
48 2/7th Bn WD, AWM 52, 8/3/7/35, scans 011–13.
49 Olsen, 'Storming of the Coconuts', *Argus*. Jack Mitchell, 2/7th Bn, Diary. 15th Bde WD, AWM 52, 8/2/15/067, scan 112.
50 Olsen, 'Storming of the Coconuts', *Argus*. Tanaka, *Ops of IJAF*, p. 163. Jack Mitchell, 2/7th Bn, interview.
51 Rooke to Long, AWM 93, 50/2/23/570. Berry was awarded an MM for this action.
52 2/7th Bn WD, AWM 52, 8/3/7/36, scans 130–1. Peterson, 2/7th Bn, RAP diary.
53 Jack Mitchell, 2/7th Bn, interview.
54 Ibid.

14 *Komiatum Ridge*

1 Parer Diary, SLNSW, ML MSS 1097/1. Bennett, *Rough Infantry*, p. 172.
2 17th Bde Ops Report, AWM 3DRL 5043 item 108. 2/5th Bn WD, AWM 52, 8/3/5/13, scans 139–40.
3 Parer Diary, SLNSW, ML MSS 1097/1. Comber died of his wounds on 7 August.

4   Bryan Ryan, 2/5th Bn, interview.
5   Bill Hooper and Jim Gatt, 2/6th Bn, in Hay, *Nothing Over Us*, pp. 355–6. Jim Gatt, who was underage on enlistment, served as Jim Marshall.
6   Gordon Edgar, 2/6th Bn, in Hay, *Nothing Over Us*, p. 353.
7   Moten interview with Dexter, AWM 172/6. Hay, *Nothing Over Us*, p. 358.
8   Savige records, AWM 3DRL 2529, item 126.
9   Moten interview with Dexter, AWM 172/6.
10 Bennett, *Rough Infantry*, p. 172. 17 Bde WD, 8/2/17/089, scan 045. Bryan Ryan, 2/5th Bn, interview.
11 Hay, *Nothing Over Us*, p. 362.
12 Olsen, 'AIF triumph at Komiatum', *Argus*.
13 Davidson to Dexter, AWM 93, 50/2/23/486. Laver to Mrs Lamont, letter, 23 September 1943.
14 Benson, *The Story of the 42nd Battalion*, pp. 61–2.
15 Berryman diary, AWM PR 84/370, item 3. Wilton diary, AWM 93, 50/2/23/44.
16 42nd Bn WD, AWM 52, 8/3/81/14, scans 030–6.
17 Moten interview with Dexter, AWM 172/6. Berryman diary, AWM PR 84/370, item 3.
18 Bennett to Long, AWM 93, 50/2/23/605. Also Bennett, *Rough Infantry*, p. 173.
19 2/5th Bn WD, AWM 52, 8/3/5/13, scan 143. 17th Bde Ops Report, AWM 3DRL 5043 item 108.
20 Savige records, AWM 3DRL 2529, item 126.
21 3rd Div WD, AWM 52, 1/5/4/055, scans 018–19.
22 Moten interview with Dexter, AWM 172/6. Berryman mentioned this to Moten in 1951. To be given a bowler hat means being either kicked out of the army or (as in this case) promoted to a desk job, away from the action.
23 Berryman interview with Dexter, AWM 172/10.
24 Blamey report on Salamaua campaign, AWM 54, 519/6/58.
25 Milford interview with Long, AWM 93, 50/2/23/445.
26 Wilton diary, AWM 93, 50/2/23/44.
27 Berryman diary, AWM PR 84/370, item 3.
28 Savige interview with Dexter, AWM 172/7.
29 Brian Gomme, in Warby, *The 25 Pounders*, p. 281.
30 Tanaka, *Operations of the IJAF*, pp. 168–71. ATIS interrogation reports, AWM55, 6/4, IR180.
31 Boechi, *Senshi Sosho*, vol. 3, pp. 348–52.
32 Benson, *The Story of the 42nd Battalion*, pp. 75–7.
33 42nd Bn WD, AWM 52, 8/3/81/14, scan 046. Benson, *The Story of the 42nd Battalion*, pp. 78–9. Cole was awarded an MC, Gatton and Deal each an MM.
34 Benson, *The Story of the 42nd Battalion*, pp. 80–3. Joe Lee, 42nd Bn, interview.
35 58/59th Bn WD, AWM 52, 8/3/95/10, scan 125. Mathews, *Militia Battalion at War*, p. 89.

36 Win Howard, 2/7th Bn, memoirs.
37 2/7th Bn WD, AWM 52, 8/3/7/35, scans 025–7. Finn and Bayliss were both awarded the MM.
38 Harry Tebbutt and Sailor Pearce, 47th Bn, interviews. Warfe to Dexter, AWM 93, 50/2/23/489. 47th Bn WD, AWM 52, 8/3/86/9, scans 029–30. Citations, AWM 119–34. Domin was awarded a MM.
39 47th Bn WD, AWM 52, 8/3/86/9, scans 032–4. Citations, AWM 119–34. Barnett was awarded a MC.
40 Hammer to Long, AWM 93, 50/2/23/440.
41 47th Bn WD, AWM 52, 8/3/86/9, scan 037. Griffith, *World War II*, p. 157. 47th Bn WD, AWM 52, 8/3/86/9, scans 071–3. Lewis comments on official history, AWM 93, 50/2/23/603.
42 *Salamaua Siege*, p. 20. Benson, *The Story of the 42nd Battalion*, pp. 87–9.
43 Benson, *The Story of the 42nd Battalion*, pp. 90–1. ATIS interrogation reports, AWM55, 6/4, IR180.
44 *Salamaua Siege*, p. 20. 42nd Bn WD, AWM 52, 8/3/81/14, scans 072–4.
45 Benson, *The Story of the 42nd Battalion*, pp. 93–5. 42nd Bn WD, AWM 52, 8/3/81/14, scans 076–7.
46 42nd Bn WD, AWM 52, 8/3/81/14, scans 071, 074–5 & 081. Crosswell comments on Official History, AWM 93, 50/2/23/179.
47 42nd Bn WD, AWM 52, 8/3/81/15, scans 002–4 & 008. Dexter, *The New Guinea Offensives*, p. 309.
48 42nd Bn WD, AWM 52, 8/3/81/15, scans 014–15.
49 Ibid., scans 088–9. ATIS interrogation reports, AWM 55, 6/5, IR223 & IR226.
50 Benson, *The Story of the 42nd Battalion*, p. 107. 42nd Bn WD, AWM 52, 8/3/81/15, scans 021–3.
51 42nd Bn WD, AWM 52, 8/3/81/15, scans 029–30.
52 Joe Lee and Stu McKenzie, 42nd Bn, interviews.

15 *Across the Frisco*

1 Christensen, *That's the Way it Was*, pp. 98–9. ATIS Enemy Pubs, AWM 55, 5/4, EP-44, 51st Div Intel Report 14, 24 August 1943.
2 Savige records, 3DRL 2529, item 126.
3 Warfe to Dexter, AWM 93, 50/2/23/489. 58/59th Bn WD, AWM 52, 8/3/95/10, scan 112.
4 2/3rd Ind Coy WD, AWM 52, 25/3/3.
5 2/7th Bn WD, AWM 52, 8/3/7/35, scan 015.
6 2/3rd Ind Coy report, AWM 54, 587/6/2.
7 15th Bde WD, AWM 52, 8/2/15/024, scan 025.
8 Cyril Robb letter, 2 August 1943.
9 Bob Hancock, in Garland, *Nothing is Forever*, p. 267.
10 Norm Bear, 2/3 Ind Coy, interview. Cliff Crossley, in *Victorian Commando News*, July 1952.
11 Vin Maguire, 2/3rd Ind Coy, in Garland, *Nothing is Forever*, p. 260. Also interview.
12 Bill Cowie, 2/7th Bn, interview.

13 2/7th Bn WD, AWM 52, 8/3/7/35, scans 016–18. 2/3rd Ind Coy WD, AWM 52, 25/3/3.
14 Vin Maguire, 2/3rd Ind Coy, letter. Garland, *Nothing is Forever*, p. 260.
15 Garland, *Nothing is Forever*, pp. 264–7. 2/7th Bn WD, AWM 52, 8/3/7/35, scans 024–5.
16 15th Bde WD, AWM 52, 8/2/15/024, scans 032–3.
17 15th Bde WD, AWM 52, 8/2/15/024, scan 032.
18 Savige records, 3DRL 2529, item 126.
19 3rd Div WD, AWM 52, 1/5/4/019, scan 056. 2/7th Bn WD, AWM 52, 8/3/7/35, scan 021.
20 Dexter, *The New Guinea Offensives*, p. 287.
21 Hammer comments, AWM 93, 50/2/23/440.
22 Travers comments, AWM 93, 50/2/23/024.
23 58/59th Bn WD, AWM 52, 8/3/95/10, scan 132. 15th Bde WD, AWM 52, 8/2/15/025, scan 085.
24 Tanaka, *Ops of the IJAF*, p. 173. Boechi, *Senshi Sosho*, names the feature Mount Gourd.
25 58/59th Bn WD, AWM 52, 8/3/95/013, scan 190. Mathews, *Militia Battalion at War*, p. 94.
26 58/59th Battalion WD, AWM 52, 8/3/95/10, scan 133. Dexter, *The New Guinea Offensives*, p. 301. Sinclair was awarded an MM. 2/7th Bn WD, AWM 52, 8/3/7/35, scan 029.
27 58/59th Bn WD, AWM 52, 8/3/95/013, scan 190. Mathews, *Militia Battalion at War*, pp. 94–6.
28 58/59th Bn WD, AWM 52, 8/3/95/013, scans 135, 190–1. Mathews, *Militia Battalion at War*, p. 96.
29 15th Bde WD, AWM 52, 8/2/15/025, scan 103. Tanaka, *Ops of IJAF*, pp. 173–4.
30 15th Bde WD, AWM 52, 8/2/15/025, scan 103. Newman comments, AWM 93, 50/2/23/183. Bethune citation, AWM 119, 33.
31 Garland, *Nothing is Forever*, pp. 285–91.
32 Ibid., pp. 292–93.
33 Ibid., pp. 294–7. Also 2/3rd Ind Coy WD, AWM 52, 25/3/3.
34 2/7th Bn WD, AWM 52, 8/3/7, September–December 1943, scan 003. 58/59th Bn WD, AWM 52, 8/3/95/11, scans 007–9, 030. Mathews, *Militia Battalion at War*, p. 97. Griff comments, AWM 93, 50/2/23/608.
35 2/3rd Ind Coy WD, AWM 52, 25/3/3. 58/59th Bn WD, AWM 52, 8/3/95, September–November 1943, scans 016–19.
36 2/7th Bn WD, AWM 52, 8/3/7, September–December 1943, scans 006–7. Bolger & Littlewood, *The Fiery Phoenix*, pp. 283–4.

16 Salamaua falls

1 15th Bn WD, AWM 52, 8/3/54/013, scan 003.
2 Milford interview with Long, AWM 93, 50/2/23/445.
3 Dexter, *The New Guinea Offensives*, pp. 304–5. 15th Bn history of operations, AWM 345.

4 George Matthew, 15th Bn, interview. Doug Matthew was posthumously mentioned in dispatches.

5 Dexter, *The New Guinea Offensives*, p. 305. Citations records, AWM 391/11/31. Whitlam and Sallaway were awarded MMs.

6 15th Bn WD, AWM 52, 8/3/54/014, scans 039–40. 5th Div WD, AWM 52, 1/5/10/031, scan 004.

7 Milford interview with Long, AWM 93, 50/2/23/445.

8 Keith Ross, 2/6th Bn, interview. Dexter, *The New Guinea Offensives*, pp. 306–7.

9 15th Bn WD, AWM 52, 8/3/54/014, scan 010. Keith Ross, 2/6th Bn, interview and notes.

10 Sayers, *Ned Herring*, p. 263. Herring interview with Dexter, AWM 172/6.

11 15th Bn WD, AWM 52, 8/3/54/014, scan 057.

12 Keith Ross, 2/6th Bn, interview and notes.

13 Ibid. Troughton was awarded the MM.

14 15th Bn WD, AWM 52, 8/3/54/014, scan 061.

15 Milford interview with Long, AWM 93, 50/2/23/445.

16 Tanaka, *Ops of IJAF*, pp. 61 and 174. Boeichi, *Senshi Sosho*, vol. 3, pp. 367–70.

17 42nd Bn WD, AWM 52, 8/3/81/15, scans 042–4.

18 Griff comments, AWM 93, 50/2/23/608. Hemery, 'On Salamaua's doorstep', NAA SP300/3, 418. Jack Glynn, 15th Bn, AWM, PR 02039.

19 ATIS interrogation reports, AWM 55, 6/4, IR173, IR179 IR182 and IR183.

20 Mathews, *Militia Battalion at War*, p. 99. 58/59th Bn WD, AWM 52, 8/3/95, September–November 1943, scan 021. Newman comments, AWM 93, 50/2/23/183. Savige interview with Dexter, AWM 172/7.

21 2/7th Bn WD, AWM 52, 8/3/7, September 1943, scan 008. Joe Howard, 2/7th Bn, Memoirs. Bolger & Littlewood, *The Fiery Phoenix*, p. 280.

22 Hammer comments, AWM 93, 50/2/23/440.

23 ATIS interrogation reports, AWM 55, 6/4, IR 181. Tanaka, *Ops of IJAF*, pp. 174–5. Kitamoto, *A Record of Marathon Adventures in the New Guinea War*, p. 78.

24 Sayers, *Ned Herring*, p. 263.

25 Hemery, 'The flag flies again at Salamaua', NAA SP300/3, 426. The flag is now on display at the Australian War Memorial.

BIBLIOGRAPHY

INTERVIEWS AND PRIVATE COMMUNICATION

Agnew, Craig, 2/5th Battalion, interview, 1 February 2004

Allan, Fred, 2/5th Battalion, letter, 4 May 2005

Allen, Fred, 22nd Australian Cipher Section, interview, 9 October 2008

Anderson, Fred, RAAF No. 30 Squadron, interview, 28 March 2004, letter, 30 March 2004

Appleby, Walter, 3rd Division Headquarters, interviews, 10 & 14 October 2008

Arden, Jack, 2/3rd Independent Company, interview, 3 November 2004

Arkoff, Harold, US 162nd Regiment, email, 11 February 2005

Bear, Norm, 2/3rd Independent Company, interviews, 20 April, 4 May 2005, 6 January 2006

Beaver, Ron, 2/5th Battalion, interviews, 25 April, 1 May 2004

Beckett, John, 2/6th Battalion, interview, 28 September 2005

Benson, Albert, 47th Battalion, email, 18 February 2008

Blanch, Ivor, 2/32nd Transport Company, interview, 14 April 2006

Brazenor, Bob, RAAF No. 30 Squadron, interview, 27 March 2004

Bunker, Vic, 6th Division Signals, interview, 19 April 2005

Burge, Colin, 2/6th Battalion, interview, 22 February 2004, letter, 24 February 2004

Burns, Bob, US 162nd Regiment, letter, 12 March 2005

Byrne, Ted, 2/7th Independent Company, interviews, 6 January, 4 May 2005

Cameron, Wally, 2/6th Battalion, interview, 29 September 2004

Carlsen, Arthur 'Unk', 2/5th Battalion, interview, 28 June 2006, letters, 10 September 2007, 25 May 2008

Carroll, John, 2/5th Battalion, interviews, 22 July 2007, 30 October 2009

Chilcott, Don, 15th Brigade HQ, letter, 7 October 2008

Collins, Les, 58/59th Battalion, interview, 27 September 2007

Copland, Lance, 2/5 Battalion, interviews, 25 September 2005, 13 May 2008

Cowie, Bill, 2/7th Battalion, interview, 20 January 2009, letter, 14 January 2009

Davies, Ben, 2/7th Independent Company, interview, 25 January 2005

Drury, George, RAAF No. 30 Squadron, interviews, 1 & 6 April 2004, letter, 19 April 2004

Dunshea, Pat, 2/7th Independent Company, interviews, 29 November, 13 & 15 December 2004

Edwards, Owen, 2/7th Battalion, interview, 4 April 2004, letter, 10 February 2004

Evans, Neil, 2/7th Independent Company, interview, 12 November 2005

Fleming, Jack, US 741st Ordnance Company, interviews, 10 March 2005, 21 June 2008, letter, 5 March 2005

Hall, Frank, 2/7th Battalion, interview, 13 July 2004

Harris, Percy, 2/6th Battalion, interviews, 28 September 2005, 31 May 2008

Hay, David, 2/6th Battalion, interview, 17 February 2004, emails, 17 & 18 February, 31 March, 2 April 2004

Henry, Alan, 2/6th Battalion, interviews, 9 November 2004, 28 September 2005

Herman, Harold, 2/7th Battalion, interview, 24 September 2004

Hibbert, Harold, 58/59 Battalion, interview, 23 April 2009

Howard, June (wife of Joseph Howard, 2/7th Battalion), interview, 16 September 2005

Jarman, Clive, 2/7th Independent Company, interviews, 25 November 2004, 9 November 2005

Kasper, Roy, 2/7th Battalion, interview, 17 February 2007, email, 17 July 2009

Kerr, Jim, 2/6th Battalion, interview, 14 March 2004

King, Eric, 41st Landing Craft Company, interview, 5 May 2003

Kost, Robert, 6th Troop Carrier Squadron USAAF, emails, 1 & 4 March 2005

Lamont, John (son of George Lamont, 2/6th Battalion), interview, 26 February 2004

Lee, Joe, 42nd Battalion, interview, 22 June 2008

L'Estrange, Bruce, 2/7th Independent Company, interview, 19 January 2005

Littler, Arthur, 2/3rd Independent Company, interview, 28 June 2004

Lonergan, Charlie, 2/7th Independent Company, interviews, 4 July 2004, 30 January 2006

McGilvray, Jack, 2/5th Battalion, interview, 30 March 2006

McKenzie, Stuart, 42nd Battalion, interviews, 10 April, 20 June 2008, letter, 8 May 2008

Maguire, Vin, 2/3rd Independent Company, interview, 19 November 2007, letter, 2008

Malmstone, Bud, 6th Troop Carrier Squadron USAAF, emails, 3, 6 & 7 March 2005

Mathers, Ray, 2/6th Battalion, interviews, 2, 18 October, 7 November 2004 letter, 8 November 2004

Matheson, James, 58/59th Battalion, interview, 1 October 2007

Matthew, George, 15th Battalion, interview, 28 September 2005

Mears, Allan, 42nd Battalion, letter, 10 May 2008

Miles, Cyril, 2/5th Battalion, interviews, 29 February, 12 April 2004, 9 August 2007

Mitchell, Jack, 2/7th Battalion, interviews, 22 February 2005, 16 June 2008

Monson, Robert, 33rd Troop Carrier Squadron USAAF, email, 13 January 2005

Morcom, Stan, 3rd Division Headquarters, interview, 17 October 2008

Myers, Keith, 2/3rd Independent Company, interviews, 10 & 29 October, 2 December 2004, 19 July 2006, 21 May 2008

Nazzari, Lou, 2/5th Battalion, interview, 5 May 2004, letter, 30 May 2004

Pearce, Herb 'Sailor', 47th Battalion, interview, 11 March 2008

Peart, John, 2/5th Battalion, interview, 25 April 2004

Peter, Guadagasal villager, interview, 11 April 2005

Peterson, Bruce, 2/7th Battalion, interviews, 3 December 2004, 9 May 2005, letters, 24 November, 8 December 2004

Pinney, Sava (daughter of Peter Pinney, 2/3rd Independent Company), emails, May–July 2007

Pop, Alim (carrier number 355), Kaiapit villager, interview, 6 August 2006

Price, Ron, 2/6th Battalion, interview, 18 March 2004, letter, 7 March 2004

Quinn, Bill, 2/6th Battalion, interviews, 17 March, 10 April 2004

Regan, Robyn (daughter of Jim Regan, 2/5th Battalion), letter, 5 June 2004

Robins, Darren (grandson of Herbert Robins, 2/3rd Independent Company), interview, 15 August 2008

Ross, Keith, 2/6th Battalion, interviews, 14 April, 6 May 2004, letters, 16 April 2004, 26 May 2008, emails, 2004–09

Ryan, Bryan, 2/5th Battalion, interviews, 5 February 2004, 19 August 2007, letter, 5 April 2004

Ryan, Peter, ANGAU, interview, 5 January 2006

Shewan, Jack, 58/59th Battalion, interview, 25 September 2007

Smith, Richard, 39th Fighter Squadron USAAF, letters, 24 May 2004, 31 December 2005

Steeles, Phil, 2/55th Light Aid Detachment, interview, 8 March 2005

Stewart, Douglas (son of Wilton Stewart, 47th Battalion), email, 19 November 2008

Stiff, Clyde, 2/7th Battalion, interview, 10 November 2004

Taylor, Dave, 58/59th Battalion, interviews, 21 November 2007, 1 January, 20 April 2008

Tebbutt, Harry, 47th Battalion, interview, 9 March 2008

Turner, John, 6th Division Transport, interview, 28 September 2005

Tyree, John, 2/7th Independent Company, interviews, 26 November, 8 December 2004, letters, 15 December 2004, 25 January 2005

Walpole, Brian, 2/3rd Independent Company, interview, 18 September 2004

Walters, Mick, 2/5th Battalion, interview, 24 August 2000

Wamsley, Robert, 33rd Troop Carrier Squadron USAAF, letters, 10 March, 5 April 2005

Watson, Geoff, RAAF No. 11 Squadron, letter, 24 September 2008

Waugh, Dulcie (wife of Harry Waugh, 2/7th Battalion), interview, 9 October 2008

Williams, Alvin, 2/5th Battalion, interview, 22 August 2007

Wood, Bob, 2/3rd Independent Company, interview, 6 December 2005

PUBLISHED REFERENCES
Books

Allan, Jack & Cutts, Chris (eds), *As It Seemed to Us: The 1st Australian Mountain Battery, RAA, AIF*, Æbis Publishing, Brisbane, 1994

Australian Military Forces, *Khaki and Green*, Australian War Memorial, Canberra, 1943

Bennett, Cam, *Rough Infantry: Tales of World War II*, Warrnambool Institute Press, Warrnambool, Vic., 1985

Benson, Stanley, *The Story of the 42nd Australian Infantry Battalion in World War II*, Dymocks, Sydney, 1952

Bergerud, Eric, *Fire in the Sky*, Westview Press, Boulder, CO, 2000

Boeicho Boei Kenshujo Senshishitsu (ed.), *Senshi sosho (War history series: South Pacific area army operations (3) Munda–Salamaua campaigns)*, Asagumo Shinbunsha, Tokyo, 1970

Bolger, William & Littlewood, Jack, *The Fiery Phoenix: The Story of the 2/7th Australian Infantry Battalion 1939–1946*, 2/7th Battalion Association, Parkdale, Vic., 1983

Bradley, Phillip, *On Shaggy Ridge*, Oxford University Press, Melbourne, 2004

———*The Battle for Wau*, Cambridge University Press, Melbourne, 2008

Bullard, Steven & Tamura, Keiko (eds), *From a Hostile Shore: Australia and Japan at War in New Guinea*, Australian War Memorial, Canberra, 2004

Casey, Hugh J., *Engineers of the Southwest Pacific 1941–1945*, vol. 4: *Amphibian Engineer Operations*, United States Army, Washington DC, 1959

Christensen, George, *That's the Way It Was*, 24th Battalion (AIF) Association, 1982

Claringbould, Michael, *Forty of the Fifth*, Aerothentic Publications, Kingston, ACT, 1999

Collins, Lloyd, *New Guinea Narrative 1942–1943*, self-published, 2001

Cook, Haruko Tayo & Cook, Theodore F., *Japan at War: An Oral History*, New Press, New York, 1992

Craven, Wesley & Cate, James, *The Army Air Forces in World War II*, vol. 4, *The Pacific – Guadalcanal to Saipan, August 1942 to July 1944*, University of Chicago Press, Chicago, 1950

Davidson, Reginald, *With Courage High*, 2/8th Field Company RAE Association, Melbourne, 1964

Dennis, Peter, Grey, Jeffrey, Morris, Ewan, et al., *The Oxford Companion to Australian Military History*, 2nd edn, Oxford University Press, Melbourne, 2008

Department of Information, *Battle of the Ridges*, Government Printer, Sydney, 1944

———*Salamaua Siege*, Government Printer, Sydney, 1944

Dexter, David, *Australia in the War of 1939–1945*, series 1, vol. 6: *The New Guinea Offensives*, Australian War Memorial, Canberra, 1961

Dickins, Barry, *Ordinary Heroes*, Hardie Grant Books, South Yarra, Vic., 1999

Drea, Edward J., *MacArthur's ULTRA: Codebreaking and the War against Japan 1942–1945*, University Press of Kansas, Lawrence, 1992

———*In the Service of the Emperor*, University of Nebraska Press, 1998

Dusting, Louis, *The 1942–1943 Diary of a Corporal Fitter*, Adam Press, Glenbrook, 1995

Farquhar, Murray, *Derrick VC*, Rigby Publishers, Adelaide, SA, 1982

Feldt, Eric, *The Coast Watchers*, Currey O'Neill, Melbourne, 1975

Garland, Ron, *Nothing is Forever: The History of 2/3 Commandos*, Ron Garland, Sydney, 1997

Gill, G. Hermon, *Australia in the War of 1939–1945*, series 2, vol. 2: *Royal Australian Navy 1942–1945*, Australian War Memorial, Canberra, 1968

Gillison, Douglas, *Australia in the War of 1939–1945*, series 3, vol. 1: *Royal Australian Air Force 1939–1942*, Australian War Memorial, Canberra, 1962

Gomme, Brian, *A Gunner's Eye View*, Brian Gomme, Nambucca Heads, NSW, 1997

Graham, Burton, *None Shall Survive*, F.H. Johnston Publishing, Sydney, 1946

Griffith, Douglas, *World War II: Times–Places–Events and Reminiscences*, Brisbane, 1998

Gullett, Henry 'Jo', *Not as a Duty Only: An Infantryman's War*, Melbourne University Press, Melbourne, 1976

Hara, Tomeichi, Saito, Fred & Pineau, Roger, *Japanese Destroyer Captain*, Ballantine Books, New York, 1961

Hashimoto, Mochitsura & Colegrave, E., *Sunk*, Cassell & Company, London, 1954

Hata, Ikuhiko & Izawa, Yasuho, *Japanese Naval Aces and Fighter Units in World War II*, Naval Institute Press, Annapolis, MD, 1989

Hay, David, *Nothing Over Us: The Story of the 2/6th Australian Infantry Battalion*, Australian War Memorial, Canberra, 1984

Henebry, John, *The Grim Reapers: At Work in the Pacific Theatre*, Pictorial Histories Publishing Company, Montana, 2002

Horner, David, *High Command*, Allen & Unwin, Sydney, 1982

——*General Vasey's War*, Melbourne University Press, Melbourne, 1992

——*Blamey: The Commander-in-Chief*, Allen & Unwin, Sydney, 1998

——*Strategic Command*, Oxford University Press, Melbourne, 2005

Horner, David (ed.), *The Commanders*, Allen & Unwin, Sydney, 1984

Jacobsen, Richard S. (ed.), *Moresby to Manila via Troop Carrier*, Sydney, 1945

Kelly, Robert, *Allied Air Transport Operations: South West Pacific Area in WWII*, vol. 1, Harding Colour, Brisbane, 2003

——*Allied Air Transport Operations: South West Pacific Area in WWII*, vol. 2, Harding Colour, Brisbane, 2006

——*Allied Air Transport Operations: South West Pacific Area in WWII*, vol. 3, Harding Colour, Brisbane, 2008

Kenney, George C., *General Kenney Reports*, Duell, Sloan & Pearce, New York, 1949

Kitamoto, Masamichi, *A Record of Marathon Adventures in the New Guinea War*, Australian War Memorial, Canberra, 1968

Lindsay, Neville, *Equal to the Task*, vol. 1, Historia Productions, Kenmore, Qld, 1992

McAulay, Lex, *Battle of the Bismarck Sea*, St Martin's Press, New York, 1991

McCarthy, Dudley, *Australia in the War of 1939–1945*, series 1, vol. 5: *South-West Pacific Area – First Year*, Australian War Memorial, Canberra, 1959

McCartney, William F., *The Jungleers*, Battery Press, Nashville, TN, 1988

McNicoll, Ronald, *The Royal Australian Engineers, 1919 to 1945*, vol. 3: *Teeth & Tail*, Corps Committee of RAE, Canberra, 1982

Mathews, Russell, *Militia Battalion at War: The History of the 58/59th Australian Infantry Battalion in the Second World War*, 58/59th Battalion Association, Sydney, 1961

Maughan, Barton, *Australia in the War of 1939–1945*, series 1, vol. 3: *Tobruk and El Alamein*, Australian War Memorial, Canberra, 1966

Middlebrook, Garrett, *Air Combat at Twenty Feet*, Garrett Middlebrook, Fort Worth, TX, 1989

Miller, John, *Cartwheel: The Reduction of Rabaul*, Office of the Chief of Military History, Dept of the Army, Washington DC, 1990

Minty, Albert, *Black Cats*, RAAF Museum, Point Cook, Vic., 1994

Mochitsura, Hashimoto, & Colegrave, Edward, *Sunk*, Cassell & Company, London, 1954

Morison, Samuel, *History of United States Naval Operations in World War II*, vol. 3: *The Rising Sun in the Pacific*, Little, Brown & Co., Boston, 1953

Naval Analysis Division, *US Strategic Bombing Survey (Pacific): The Campaigns of the Pacific War*, US Government Printing Office, Washington, 1946

———*US Strategic Bombing Survey (Pacific) – Interrogations*, US Government Printing Office, Washington, 1946

Odgers, George, *Australia in the War of 1939–1945*, series 3, vol. 2: *Air War against Japan 1943–1945*, Australian War Memorial, Canberra, 1957

Orita, Zenji & Harrington, Joseph D, *I-Boat Captain*, Major Books, Canoga Park, CA, 1976

Palazzo, Albert, *Defenders of Australia: The 3rd Australian Division, 1916–1991*, Australian Military History Publications, Loftus, NSW, 2002

Pearson, Arthur, *Brothers, Battlers and Bastards*, Boolarong Press, Brisbane, 1995

Perrin, Alex, *The Private War of the Spotters*, NGAWW Publication Committee, Foster, Vic., 1990

Powell, Alan, *The Third Force: ANGAU's New Guinea War 1942–46*, Oxford University Press, Melbourne, 2003

RAAF Directorate of Public Relations, *RAAF Log*, Australian War Memorial, Canberra, 1943

Reinhold, William, *The Bulldog–Wau Road*, University of Queensland, Brisbane, 1945

Rice, Bert, *22 Squadron RAAF*, 22 Squadron Association of Victoria, Mount Waverley, Vic., 1987

Robins, Darren, *Proud to be Third*, Darren Robins, Sunshine Coast, Qld, 2007

Robinson, Neville, *Villagers at War: Some Papua New Guinean Experiences in World War II*, Australian National University, Canberra, 1981

Roscoe, Theodore, *United States Submarine Operations in World War II*, United States Naval Institute, Annapolis, MD, 1949

Ross, Alan (ed.), *The Magazine of 17 Australian Infantry Brigade 1939–1944*, 17 Brigade, Melbourne, 1944

Sayers, Stuart, *Ned Herring: A Life of Sir Edmund Herring*, Hyland House, Melbourne, 1980

Semmler, Clement (ed.), *The War Diaries of Kenneth Slessor*, University of Queensland Press, St Lucia, 1985

Shinoda Masuo, *The 66th Infantry Regiment and the Defensive Battle in Salamaua*, Testaments of the Pacific War Series, Maru, supplement no. 2, Ushio Shobō, Tokyo, 1986

Sinclair, James, *To Find a Path*, vol. 1, Crawford House Press, Bathurst, NSW, 1990

Sinton, Russell (ed.), *The Menace from Moresby*, Battery Press, Nashville, TN, 1989

Speed, Frank, *Esprit de Corps: The History of the Victorian Scottish Regiment and the 5th Infantry Battalion*, Allen & Unwin, Sydney, 1988

Stanaway, John & Hickey, Lawrence, *Attack and Conquer: The 8th Fighter Group in World War II*, Schiffer Publishing, Atglen, PA, 1995

Tanaka, Kengoro, *Operations of the Imperial Japanese Armed Forces in the Papua New Guinea Theatre during World War II*, Japan Papua New Guinea Goodwill Society, Tokyo, 1980

Trigellis-Smith, Syd, *All the King's Enemies: A History of the 2/5th Australian Infantry Battalion*, 2/5 Battalion Association, Melbourne, 1988

Turner, Jim, *The RAAF at War*, Kangaroo Press, Sydney, 1999

United States Army, *History of the Second Engineer Special Brigade*, Telegraph Press, Harrisburg, PA, 1946

United States Army Japan, *Japanese Monograph 37–18th Army Operations*, vol. 1, Department of the Army, Washington DC, 1958

United States War Department, *Handbook on Japanese Military Forces*, Louisiana State University Press, Baton Rouge, 1995

Wada, Kiichi, *The Lae Naval Guard Unit that Crossed Saruwaged Range*, Testaments of the Pacific War Series, Maru, supplement no. 2, Ushio Shobō, Tokyo, 1986

Walker, Allan S., *Australia in the War of 1939–1945*, series 5, vol. 3: *The Island Campaigns*, Australian War Memorial, Canberra, 1957

Walpole, Brian, *My War*, Australian Broadcasting Corporation, Sydney, 2004

Warby, John, *The 25 Pounders – From Egypt to Borneo: Campaigns in Syria, Kumusi River, Salamaua, Lae, Finschhafen*, 2/6th Field Regiment Association, Pymble, NSW, 1995

Weate, Mark, *Bill Newton VC*, Australian Military History Publications, Loftus, NSW, 1999

Westerfield, Hargis, *41st Infantry Division: Fighting Jungleers II*, Turner Publishing, Paducah, KY, 1992

Yoshihara, Kane, *Southern Cross*, trans. Doris Heath, Australian War Memorial, Canberra, 1955

Newsletters

2/5th Battalion Association, newsletters, 2004–09

Commando Association, *Double Diamond*, December 1998

PNG War Museum, *Nius Leta*, June–July 1993

Queensland Commando News, July 2004
Victorian Commando News, July 1952

Newspaper, journal and magazine articles
Anon., 'Wau–Mubo – Land of ambush', *Thirtyniner*, March 1962
Australian Army Education Service, *Salt*, 25 October, 1943
'Bren guns cut Japs to ribbons', *Daily Mirror*, 29 May 1943
Jones, 'Japs tough, but AIF have their measure', *Sun*, 1943
Olsen, Axel, 'Death lurks on the jungle track', 'Storming of the Coconuts' & 'AIF
    Triumph at Komiatum', *Argus*, August 1943
Pedersen, Peter, 'Recock and reconfigure', *Wartime*, issue 46, 2009
Travis, William, 'The Battle of the Bismarck Sea', *Mensa Bulletin*, March 1993

Internet
Australian National University, www.adb.anu.edu.au
Australian War Memorial, www.awm.gov.au
National Archives of Australia, www.naa.gov.au
Pacific Wreck Database, www.pacificwrecks.com
Second Engineer Special Brigade, www.2esb.org
Tuluvu's air war, www.j-aircraft.com/research/rdunn/tuluvu
USAAF Records, www.usaaf.net
Veterans' Affairs, Department of, www.australiansatwarfilmarchive.gov.au
Veterans' Affairs, Department of, www.ww2roll.gov.au

UNPUBLISHED REFERENCES
Dickson, Ron, No. 4 Squadron RAAF, 'Flying for the Army', personal memoirs
Drury, George, No. 30 Squadron RAAF, personal memoirs
Hancock, Bob, 2/3rd Independent Company, letters (courtesy of Norm Bear)
Howard, Joseph 'Win', 2/7th Battalion, 'Win and Ernie's story', personal memoirs
Lamont, John (son of George Lamont, 2/6th Battalion), Captain Harold Laver
    letter
Matthew, Douglas, 15th Battalion, 'Poems'
Miller-Randle, Alec, No. 4 Squadron RAAF, 'Invictus Asbestos', personal mem-
    oirs
Mitchell, Jack, 2/7th Battalion, diary
Murray, Bill, 2/3rd Independent Company, personal memoirs (courtesy of Norm
    Bear)
Peterson, Bruce, 2/7th Battalion, notes and RAP diary
Robb, Cyril, 2/3rd Independent Company, letters
Ross, Keith, 2/6th Battalion, personal memoirs
Ryan, Bryan, 2/5th Battalion, 'From Bush to Battlefield', personal memoirs
Strike, Bill, 2/7th Independent Company, personal memoirs
Taylor, Dave, 58/59th Battalion, personal memoirs
Tyree, John, 2/7th Independent Company, photographs
Watson, Geoff, RAAF No. 11 Squadron, personal memoirs and photographs

UNPUBLISHED RECORDS
National Archives of Australia
A9186, RAAF Squadron Operational Records
A9845, RAAF Accident Records
B3856, 145/4/26, Gibbons record
B883, Second Australian Imperial Forces Personnel Dossiers, 1939–47
M1415, Personal papers of Prime Minister Curtin
SP300/3, ABC Radio Transcripts, 1939–45

Australian War Memorial, Canberra
Official records
AWM 52, Unit histories, 1939–45 War
AWM 54, Written records, 1939–45 War
AWM 55, ATIS records of POW Interrogations and Captured Documents
AWM 57, Records of the Allied Geographic Section, SWPA (South West Pacific
    Area)
AWM 64, RAAF formation and unit records
AWM 67, Gavin Long, papers of the Official Historian
AWM 93, 50/2/23, Official Historian correspondence
AWM 119, Office of Military Secretary, Army honours and awards: confidential
    working files
AWM 172, Official History, 1939–45 War, Series 1 (Army), vol. 6: Records of
    David Dexter
AWM 218, Card Index to interrogation reports of captured Japanese personnel
AWM 254, Written records, 1939–45 War, second series
AWM 345, Operations records

Murdoch Sound Archive
S00520, Reg Saunders, 2/7th Battalion
S00586, Bill Garing, RAAF

Private records
AWM 3DRL/2529, Papers of Stan Savige
AWM 3DRL/5043, Papers of Murray Moten
AWM 3DRL/6850, Papers of Iven Mackay
AWM PR00057, Owen Williams, 2/2nd Ambulance, diary
AWM PR01182, Bill Dexter, 2/6th Battalion, memoirs
AWM PR02039, Jack Glynn, 15th Battalion, letters
AWM PR84/370, Papers of Frank Berryman
AWM PR85/24, Frank Casey, 2/6th Battalion, memoirs
AWM PR85/25, Allan Smith, 2/6th Battalion, memoirs
AWM PR85/241, Jack Weeks, 2/6th Battalion, memoirs
AWM PR87/13, John May, 2/2nd Field Ambulance (attached), memoirs

Freyer Library, University of Queensland, Brisbane
UQFL28, Peter Pinney, 2/3rd Independent Company, diary transcript

State Library of NSW, Sydney
ML MSS 1097/1, Damien Parer diary

USAAF Records
39th Fighter Squadron War Diary
Army Air Forces Historical Office, The Fifth Air Force in the Huon Peninsula
    Campaign: January to October 1943 (AAFRH-13), 1946

INDEX